LOVE and WORK

Books by Reuben Fine

The Personality of the Asthmatic Child
The Development of Freud's Thought
The Psychology of the Chess Player
Psychoanalytic Psychology
The Development of Psychoanalytic Thought
The Intimate Hour
The Psychoanalytic Vision
The Healing of the Mind
The Logic of Psychology
The Meaning of Love in Human Experience
The Forgotten Man
Narcissism, the Self, and Society
The History of Psychoanalysis (New Expanded Edition)

REUBEN FINE

LOVE and WORK

The Value System of Psychoanalysis

CONTINUUM • NEW YORK

1990

The Continuum Publishing Company
370 Lexington Avenue, New York, NY 10017

Library of Congress Cataloging-in-Publication Data

Fine, Reuben, 1914–
    Love and work : the value system of psychoanalysis / Reuben Fine.
      p. cm.
    Includes bibliographical references.
    ISBN 0-8264-0482-0
    1. Love. 2. Psychoanalysis. 3. Work — Psychological aspects.
I. Title
BF575.L8F515 1990
150.19'5 — dc20   90-32642
                                           CIP

Contents

Preface

*P*SYCHOANALYSIS AND THE SOCIAL SCIENCES have undergone many changes in the course of the century. Usually books confine themselves to technical discussion, such as the problem of the borderline patient. My goal instead has been to cast some light on the underlying philosophy that has guided psychoanalysis from the very beginning.

Recent research has shown that Freud was drawn to philosophy from his early years at the university, particularly by the philosopher-priest Brentano. Freud managed to curb his philosophical interests until late in life, when he could bring to bear on them the imposing psychological edifice that he had built up in the meantime.

It is one thesis of this book that the numerous and apparently endless controversies in psychoanalysis go on because the philosophical roots of the field are overlooked. Psychoanalysis is not a branch of medicine, as Freud emphatically insisted over and over again, nor does it have much connection with academic psychology. But what is it? My reply here is that psychoanalysis is *a theory of happiness*, and I have tried to draw the implications of this point of view for psychology, psychiatry, psychotherapy, and society at large.

Most persons in the field are unaware of the tremendous changes that have occurred. For example, Fisher and Greenberg, in a recent work (1989), have for the first time carefully reviewed all the drugs used on the contemporary scene in psychiatry, and have come to the astonishing conclusion that there is no clear-cut evidence for the real effectiveness of *any of them*. They cautiously conclude (p. 309) that "statements about the results of somatic treatment approaches for 'psychiatric disorder' *should be viewed with caution and perhaps, even with a fair amount of skepticism*." More dramatically their reserve casts doubt on the entire range of psychiatric claims for drug treatment, while psychiatrists on the scene today boast of the explosion in neuroscience, and stress the importance of the "drug revolution."

If this is all myth, as Fisher and Greenberg show, then the claims of psychiatry are of dubious value, and the practice of drug therapy (now the most commonly used modality for all psychiatric disorders) may be largely malpractice, of no more value to the sick person today than bleeding was two hundred years ago.

A new model for viewing "mental health" is often called for, and this book offers such a model, based on the most significant findings of psychoanalysis and its related fields.

In the midst of an unexpected world revolution in which all existing ideologies have been put to the test and found wanting, we have also been going through a more quiet, but equally significant psychoanalytic revolution, in which the exaggerations, inconsistencies, and errors of the early psychoanalysts have been eliminated and the extraordinary truths about human nature brought to the fore by Freud and his co-workers have been put in intelligible form.

Although psychoanalysis has been "demolished" over and over again by so-called scientific criticism, it persists and expands, and is gradually spreading around the world. In this growth, the battle of the American psychologists against the reactionary medical environment, which ended in a total victory for the psychologists, has played a tremendous role. The term "lay analyst" no longer exists; a person is either an analyst or not. It has been made abundantly clear that medicine, as Freud insisted, is not at all central to psychoanalysis; in fact, medicine may be more of a handicap to the practitioner than assistance because the overemphasis on the physical can lead the practitioner into one blind alley after another.

The first chapter of this book is a historical introduction, in which the growth of psychoanalysis and psychoanalytic thought is traced — a growth process largely unknown to the average practitioner. The numerous splits and deviations in the fields can be attributed more to the terrible socioeconomic conditions that have ravaged the world than to any cool passion for truth. Freud remains the greatest creator of a new humanity, as Thomas Mann sagely observed as long ago as 1911.

Next I turn to *the analytic ideal*, or the value system of psychoanalysis. The question, what is psychoanalysis? posed by many theoreticians today, can readily be answered by reference to the analytical ideal. Psychoanalysis is a system of values that analysts believe is most likely to lead to happiness. The technical arguments about id, ego, superego, self, and the like are all secondary to the philosophy, as was the case with Freud.

The interminability of psychoanalysis, a frequent criticism leveled at it, is discussed in chapter 3. On the basis of case histories, I try to show that this interminability results from the effort to find the answer to eternal human problems, such as love, sexuality, happiness, the ideal family structure, and the like. The notion of a concrete end or a "quick fix" is a holdover of the antiquated notion that neurosis can be blown away by easy interpretation or that it will simply disappear of its own accord, like a bad cold. Good therapy is necessarily a difficult long-term process that requires extensive training; the most thorough training is still that provided by the psychoanalytic institutes.

Chapter 4 offers a view of the structure of psychoanalytic theory in terms of the analytic ideal, that is, the philosophy of psychoanalysis rather than its psychology or technical recommendations.

The next two chapters deal with *love*, the central value of psychoanalysis. I have discussed this question in detail in an earlier work, *The Meaning of Love in Human Experience* (Wiley, 1985) and the main arguments are summed up here. In 1914 Freud wrote that "we must begin to love in order not to fall ill, and we are bound to fall ill if, in consequence of frustration, we are unable to love."

Most people overidentify love with romantic love, which is more of an infatuation than a deep feeling, and which usually passes quickly, sometimes changing to intense hatred. More significant is the normal love that derives from growing up in a happy family with happy parents. This is the kind of love that has been so extensively explored in the analytic literature, over the past twenty or thirty years. It is this normal love that is so essential to a happy life.

Chapter 7 takes up work, and traces the development of the concept of job satisfaction, so crucial to the present-day marketplace and far from the slavery that was the basis of work throughout the ages. Particularly notable is the enthusiasm with which women have embraced the idea of work, an enthusiasm that never existed before.

The next topic discussed is sexuality. In 1898 Freud predicted that it would take humankind a hundred years to come to grips with its sexuality, and by now the sexual revolution that he initiated has reached its maturity. Few people look upon sexuality today as inherently bad, as was the rule in pre-Freudian times. Nevertheless the integration of sex and love is still a problem.

The loving family remains the core of the analytic philosophy. This value has been extended to the idea of family therapy, but the problem there is that everything depends on the kind of people in the family. Here philosophy is still more important than technique.

Finally, the last four chapters seek to draw out the implications

of the psychoanalytic view of happiness for the mental health professions and for the world at large.

In a recent paper, Joseph Montville, of the U.S. State Department,
argued that the "analytic ideal is also the goal of a global society whose
members, in the nuclear age, must strive to reach a level of balance
and integration which would finally inhibit the surge toward group
violence and war-making which have characterized human history."
Thus the basic philosophy of psychoanalysis has already penetrated
to the highest reaches of diplomacy and government. Psychoanalysts
themselves have been too busy squabbling about trivialities to pay
attention to the wider meaning of their findings, but that need not
be the case with others.

This book follows up on my work *The History of Psychoanalysis*
(Continuum, 1990). *History* deals with the past; this work suggests
ideas for the future. I hope that this work will engender fruitful discussion and help to resolve the terrible dilemma from which the world is
trying to escape. I wish to thank Michael Leach at Continuum for his
encouragement and Steno Service for their usual outstanding typing
assistance.

1

Historical Introduction

PSYCHOANALYSIS WAS BORN AS A MEDICAL DISCIPLINE. This origin however is misleading, since Freud branched out of medicine very quickly. It is not generally realized that Freud had developed an intense interest in philosophy during his university years, particularly around the philosopher Franz Brentano (McGrath, 1986). Freud repeatedly stated throughout his life that medicine was not his primary interest, and in his later works he said that he was coming back to philosophy, the love of his youth. To these statements too little attention has been paid.

As McGrath has shown, Freud was deeply influenced by Brentano. At one point he contemplated a dual major in philosophy (with Brentano) and zoology (Darwin was the Freud of Freud's day). Freud always had broad humanistic interests, which he was later to develop. In 1874 in a letter to his adolescent friend Silberstein he wrote:

> I'd gladly confess to you my need to be instructed even in what is developing in the other faculties and other branches of knowledge in order to avoid the danger of insensibility (e.g., typical Bohemian, typical M.D.), to which every individual working in his field is exposed.

Brentano has been underestimated as an influence on Freud because Freud got away from him so quickly. Nevertheless there are profound traces of Brentano's thought in Freud's later work. This has been overlooked because the correspondence with Silberstein, in

13

which this influence is described, was not available at the time that Jones wrote his extraordinary biography of Freud.

Brentano was a remarkable man with a most unusual background. A member of a prominent German family, he decided to become a Catholic priest and was ordained in the Dominican order. As a theologian, however, he opposed the doctrine of papal infallibility then under discussion, and when it was promulgated he resigned his university position and left the priesthood. Brentano was appointed professor at the University of Vienna in 1874, the year Freud first enrolled in his courses. He came as a controversial figure, since his appointment was opposed by both the emperor and the cardinal. Freud's letters to Silberstein show how much Brentano's courses had inspired a philosophical interest in him.

During his third year at the university (1875–76) Freud continued his two-track educational program in philosophy and zoology with a philosophy course from Brentano each semester, a broad range of science courses, and specialized work in zoology and physiology with Claus and Bruecke. His first research project came after his work with Claus. It involved the sexuality of the eel, a fact not lost on his biographers.

While Freud's philosophical studies have in general been overlooked or ignored, his shift to medicine because he had to make a living has not. Medicine was for him a strictly practical choice, while his heart belonged to philosophy.

This orientation explains the course of Freud's early work, in the period before 1914. From strictly medical work with hysterics and other neurotics, who were then totally misunderstood, Freud branched out very quickly into fields completely foreign to medicine: dreams, slips of everyday life, jokes, sexuality and sexual development, eventually even anthropology, law, and other intellectual disciplines. He embraced all that was human.

In the meantime most of his work was devoted to the medical questions of neurosis. Here his philosophical outlook stood him in good stead, and he resolved these questions by applying philosophical principles ordinarily not found in medicine. A simple instance is the fact that though Freud was a professor of neurology at the University of Vienna, then the most prestigious medical school in the world, after his early work he never again ventured to write a paper on neurology; his papers were always more philosophical than technical.

The patients whom Freud encountered in his early practice were deeply disturbed. Very quickly the question posed itself: what is the difference between the neurotic and the normal? This question still haunts psychoanalytic theory.

At first the answer was this: the neurotic person is one who cannot function in society; the normal person is one who can. Such an easy answer could not hold up for long.

While psychoanalysis before World War I dealt with deviant minorities, the field quickly expanded, especially after World War I and even more so after World War II. This is seen above all in the patient population. In his final essay on technique ("Analysis Terminable and Interminable," 1937), considering the question of normality, Freud wrote: "Every normal person, in fact, is only normal on the average. His ego approximates to that of the psychotic in some part or other and to a greater or lesser extent..."(p. 235).

It was in such an atmosphere of therapeutic advance that ego psychology was born, and the tripartite structure of id, ego, and superego became the cornerstone of psychoanalytic thought. It was soon clear that the difference between the normal and the neurotic (and psychotic) lay in the structure of the ego — the controls exercised over the impulses — and that the task of psychoanalysis lay in the strengthening of the ego.

While Freud had restricted psychoanalysis to the classical neuroses, i.e., hysteria and obsessive neurosis, feeling that psychotics were unamenable to treatment, others, especially between the two world wars, enlarged the scope of psychoanalysis to include many other kinds of patients and many modalities other than the classical five times a week on the couch. Aichhorn in Vienna (1925) showed that juvenile delinquents could be treated. Sullivan showed that schizophrenics could be helped and not have to waste their lives in dingy, cramped mental hospitals (Sullivan, 1931; Bleuler, 1978; Basaglia, 1977; Frosch, 1983); children could be analyzed with much the same effect as adults (Melanie Klein, 1948; Anna Freud, 1928, 1963); psychoanalysis could be conducted in groups as well as individually (Wolf, 1949, 1950). Since neurosis came from the family structure, families could be treated as well as individuals (Ackerman, 1958). Even primitive groups could be handled, and they showed much the same dynamic structure as advanced civilizations (Parin, Mergenthaler, and Matthey, 1980). In short, Freud's famous discovery that he had the whole world as his patient was verified many times over.

World War II, in a fashion parallel to the reversal of all previous knowledge of the human condition in World War I, brought home the devastating effects of psychotic leaders like Hitler, Stalin, and others. In the course of World War II psychiatry was dramatically transformed from a rigid, organically based science to a dynamically oriented series of disturbances that arose because of disturbed family conditions in early childhood. This continuum theory of mental disorder was fundamental to Freud's thought, but it was perhaps expressed most clearly in a famous definition by Ernest Jones in 1929. Jones gave full credit to the developments in America:

> So much impressed is the outside observer by [these developments] that it does not seem unmerited to say that America has actually created a new profession. In a very important sense one can almost say that the profession of psychiatry does not exist in any other country in the world. . . . I venture to predict that in a not far distant future psychopathology . . . will constitute the standard study of psychology, the basis from which the student will later proceed to the more obscure and difficult study of the so-called normal and moreover I should not be altogether surprised if America achieved this consummation before any other country. (pp. 365–68)

As in so many other matters Jones was making an astute observation; his prediction later materialized in the profession of clinical psychology, which grew up after World War II had made it obvious how widespread the need for psychological services was. Naturally this development, which meant the incorporation of psychoanalytic thought into psychiatry, psychology, and all the social sciences, was bitterly fought by all the older professions. Once clinical psychology was established, the competition for patients and money entered into the picture, which created more complications and tended to discolor the theoretical arguments or distort them beyond recognition. This will be discussed in more detail later.

A considerable gap was thus created between the usual approach to mental illness and the psychological approach. In the first large-scale statistical study of mental illness, Rennie and his collaborators (1962), and later Leighton and his collaborators (1963), produced findings that pointed to the frequency of emotional disturbances of all kinds, in all classes, in virtually all cultures studied. These findings, as well as others, led to such an enormous growth in the mental health professions that the initiative was taken out of the hands of the pure psychoanalysts who were, generally speaking, not competent to cope with the new state of affairs. The older naive notion, which dominated the thought of Freud's day, that there were three classes of people, normals, neurotics, and psychotics, had to be thrown out in total. A new conceptualization of mental health was needed, but though it was inherent in psychoanalytic thought, it was not forthcoming.

The numerous splits and controversies within the field of psychoanalysis are too well known to require more elaboration. Historically the earlier analysts, surprisingly, were more concerned with the broader philosophical questions, while the later analysts (after World War II) busied themselves more with acrimonious disputes relating to technique, e.g., what is analysis and what is not. Ernest Jones, one of the giants of psychoanalytic history, expresses profound thoughts couched in relatively simple language.

In a paper on the normal mind, published in 1931 in a book by Schmalhausen, *The Neurotic Age*, Jones begins by observing that the question of what a normal mind is has received little attention from psychoanalysts, who are more preoccupied with what is abnormal. In fact most psychoanalysts, as Trotter had already pointed out, assumed a kind of unthinking acceptance of the normality of the social environment. As noted, as time has gone on, this assumption seems more and more questionable. Jones goes on to enumerate what he considers three aspects of the ideally normal mind: (1) happiness, (2) efficiency in mental functioning, and (3) positive social feeling. Of these three the central question is that of happiness. As two of the main constituents of happiness he names freedom and self-control. Here too he affirms that happiness is rarely seen.

Although Freud is generally regarded as a pessimist, he did emphasize that human beings continually search for happiness and should be encouraged in this search. Thus in *Civilization and Its Discontents* (1930) he wrote:

The program of becoming happy, which the pleasure principle imposes on us, cannot be fulfilled; yet we must not — indeed, we cannot — give up our efforts to bring it nearer to fulfillment by some means or other. Very different paths may be taken in that direction, and we may give priority either to the positive aspect of the aim, that of gaining pleasure, or to its negative one, that of avoiding unpleasure. By none of these paths can we attain all that we desire. Happiness, in the reduced sense in which we recognize it as possible, is a problem of the economics of the individual's libido. There is no golden rule which applies to everyone: every man must find out for himself in what particular fashion he must be saved. (SE, XXI, p. 83)

One of the major principles of therapy that Freud had insisted upon was the principle of neutrality. Laplanche and Pontalis (1973) define it as follows:

> One of the defining characteristics is the attitude of the analyst during the treatment. The analyst must be neutral in respect of religion; he must not direct the treatment according to some ideal, and should refrain from counseling the patient. He must be neutral too as regards to the manifestations of the transference (this usually being expressed by the maxim "Do not play the patient's game"). Finally, he must be neutral towards the discourse of the patient; in other words he must not, a priori, lend a special ear to particular parts of this discourse, read particular meanings into it according to his theoretical preconceptions.

For this reason analysts have been, in general, reluctant to raise questions of value in psychoanalysis; to put it in a quite forthright manner: psychoanalysis is a technical procedure; it does not concern itself with values. Yet, as we have seen, Freud himself was in sharp disagreement with such a view.

Looked at more carefully, Freud expressed two different and contradictory positions, one focusing on technique, the other on goals. On the one hand he said that analysts should model themselves on the surgeon, who has one aim and one aim only: performing the operation as skillfully as possible. On the other hand he urged love as the goal, telling Blanton, for example (1971):

> The child's desire for attention is only a diminished desire for love. It is not attention that the child is seeking but love. Of course, a child must sometimes be thwarted. But if this thwarting occurs in a background of love, it will cause no harmful effects. The fundamental principle of psychoanalysis in education is the question of the economics of love. [Note: Blanton notes that when he asked Freud whether he had ever used this phrase in writing Freud replied no: "Training is a question of how to give the child the right amount of love."] (p. 40)

Because of the singular importance that Freud holds in the history of psychoanalysis and psychology, it is worthwhile examining his views in more detail. Persons within the profession have primarily been interested in technique, the ways of handling their patients; hence they have seen Freud as an impartial technician who was not concerned with values. Persons outside the profession have emphasized the values inherent in psychoanalysis or the values that should be inherent in psychoanalysis. Marcuse, for example, at one time a popular hero among the youth, held that the full development of Eros is the goal of analysis (1952). Marcuse argues for a "nonrepressive sublimation": the sexual impulses, without losing their erotic energy, transcend their immediate object and eroticize normally nonerotic and antierotic relationships between the individuals and between them and their environment. Sexuality spreads into formerly tabooed dimensions and relations.

For the first twenty-five years of analytic history the question of values was virtually untouched. Then the American neurologist James Jackson Putnam, whom Freud valued very highly, insisted that the neurotic patient suffered from moral weaknesses — a position that has disappeared today, but was popular enough then (1910) — and that analysis should undertake to correct these weaknesses. The exchange of letters between Putnam and Freud on these and related questions is found in a book by Putnam (1971).

Freud, while he relied for the therapy of his patients on the existence of an ethical order in the world, nevertheless had reservations: "But this is not a logical consequence of psychoanalysis, one may or may not graft religion into it; as a matter of principle I should not like to have psychoanalysis placed at the service of any specific doctrine."

Then he expressed two notions, first, that he had no need for a higher mental synthesis and, second, since the scientific structure of psychoanalysis was not yet complete to establish such a structure remained the most important imperative. In Letter 22 (August 15, 1910) he wrote:

I was grieved that you should believe that I possibly could consider your idealistic views as nonsense because they wish to make a law out of a deficiency in my own make-up. I feel no need for a higher moral synthesis in the same way I have no ear for music. But I do not consider myself a better man because of that. I console myself with this reflection: the idealistic trust which you are not willing to give up cannot be so certain if the basic principles of the science on which we agree are so difficult to determine.

The next year a change emerged. Moral and philosophical improvement was desirable, but could take place only after the repressions had been lifted psychoanalytically. In Letter 36 (May 4, 1911) he wrote:

> If we are not satisfied with saying "be moral and philosophical" it is because that is too cheap and has been said too often without being of any help. Our art consists in making it possible for people to be moral and to deal with their wishes philosophically. Sublimation, that is, striving towards higher goals, is of course one of the best means of overcoming the urgency of our drives. But one can consider doing this only after psychoanalytic work has lifted the repressions.

Several years later Freud again shifted his position. Now he argued that moral and ethical improvements are desirable, but are not the province of the analyst. In Letter 80 (March 3, 1914) he wrote:

> I comprehend very little of philosophy and with epistemology (but not before) my interest ceases to function. I quite agree with you that psychoanalytic treatment should find a place among the methods whose aim is to bring about the highest official and intellectual development of the individual. Our difference is of a purely practical nature. It is confined to the fact that I do not wish to entrust this further development to the psychoanalyst.

A little while later Freud took still another tack in response to Putnam's constant urging for a moral stance. His own moral conduct, he said, was beyond reproach. The world was evil; he knew it and deplored it. But the task of psychoanalysis remained that of seeking truth and certainty. Thus in Letter 92 he wrote:

> I consider myself a very moral human being, who can subscribe to the excellent maxim of Th. Vischer: what is moral is self-evident. I believe that in a sense of justice and consideration for one's feel of men ... in discomfort at making others suffer or take advantage of them, I can compete with the men I have known. I have never done anything shameful or malicious, nor do I find in myself the temptation to do so. I interpret morality, such as the peak of it here now, in the social rather than the sexual sense. Sexual morality as society — and at its most extreme, American society — defines it, seems very despicable to me. I stand for a much freer sexual life. However, I have made little use of such freedom, except insofar as I was convinced of what

was permissible for me in this area. The public emphasis on ethical demands often makes a painful impression on me. What I have seen, of religio-ethical conversion has not been inviting. Jung, e.g., I found inviting so long as he lived blindly, as I did. Then came his religio-ethical crisis, with higher morality, "re-birth" and at the very same time lies, brutality and anti-semitic condescension towards me. It has not been the first or the last experience to reinforce my disgust with saintly converts.

At the moment psychoanalysis can accommodate itself to any number of different Weltanschauungen, but has it really said its last word. For me an all-embracing synthesis has never been its last word. Certainty rather always has been worth the sacrifice of everything else.

This antiphilosophical and antisystematic stance was reaffirmed many times in the pre–World War II period. In *The History of the Psychoanalytic Movement* (1914) he took Adler to task for his attempt to create a complete human psychology. In 1914 he wrote:

Psychoanalysis has never claimed to provide a complete theory of human mentality in general, but only expected that what it offered should be applied to supplement and correct the knowl-edge acquired by other means. Adler's theory, however, goes far beyond this point; it seeks at one stroke to explain the behavior and character of human beings as well as their neurotic and psy-chotic illnesses. It is actually much more suited to another field than that of neurosis, although for reasons connected with the history of its development it still places this in the foreground. The Adlerian theory was from the very beginning a system which psychoanalysis was careful to avoid becoming....

The view of life which is reflected in the Adlerian system was founded exclusively on the aggressive instinct; there is no room in it for love. We might be surprised that such a cheerless Weltanschauung should have met with any attention at all, but we must not forget that human beings, weighed down by the burden of their sexual needs, are ready to accept anything, if only the "overcoming of sexuality" is offered to them as a bait. (SE, VI, pp. 50–58)

In his autobiography (1926) Freud makes two rather enigmatic remarks:

Neither at that time, nor indeed in my later life, did I feel any predilection for the career of a doctor. I was moved rather by a sort of curiosity which was, however, directed more towards human concerns than towards natural objects; nor had I grasped the importance of observation as one of the best means of gratifying it. (SE, XX, p. 8)

And some pages later he said:

In the works of my later years I have given free reign to the inclination, which I have kept down for so long, to speculation. (p. 576)

Some comments are in order about the significance of philosophy in the sciences. As a consequence of the vast changes that occurred in the nineteenth century, philosophy has diminished continuously until today it is scarcely regarded as having any relevance to science or human concerns; most college students experience it as a "snap" course that if required can be mastered in a few afternoons. The role of philosopher of science scarcely has any meaning, since scientists handle their own philosophical problems without outside help.

Further, philosophy remains more or less undefined, like all the social sciences (Fine, 1981). Hence would-be philosophers define their own terrain and discuss what they please (e.g., Foucault in our times). Without realizing it, Freud became such a philosopher, defining and expanding the field (psychology) to which he devoted his major efforts. Only it was to be a different kind of psychology, allied with philosophy, and entirely different from the statistical confusions into which it later descended. Freud, however, brought up in an atmosphere in which science reigned supreme, continued to the end of his life to insist on the scientific character of his pursuits, rather than admit to the broader humanistic interests that had fascinated him so much when he was a young man. It is for this reason that the value system of psychoanalysis, which seems to be beyond science, has been a relatively unexplored field, even for psychoanalysts.

Self-Analysis

As Sandler (1983) has emphasized, the growth of psychoanalytic thought never proceeded along a straight line. Freud tackled the topics that were of concern to him, leaving others to one side. Moreover, he soon began to have friends and enemies, each of whom picked on different aspects of his theoretical structure. Hence, as he once observed, whole decades could go by and obvious features of human existence could be overlooked. Thus, for example, in spite of Freud's emphasis on childhood the relationship between mother and child was not fully explored until after his death in 1939.

The first topic to which Freud turned, and which he pursued in great depth, was his self-analysis. Freud himself now wrote much about it: the few fragments in his official autobiography tell us little. But more recently the French analyst Didier Anzieu (1975) has put together all the information about himself contained in Freud's writings and summed it up in coherent form.

Self-analysis had been tried many times in history but Freud's was the first that was successful. It rested on his exploration of the unconscious and of childhood.

His self-analysis opened the road to entirely novel sources of information and human experiences. After a certain point, he once argued, only the psychic is real. In this way he opened the path to a new psychology, one that would explore the inner world rather than the outer. It was this that led to the development of a whole new science.

Through his self-analysis Freud also showed that the difference between the neurotic and the normal is one only of degree, thereby cutting the Gordian knot that had through the ages puzzled everyone about the meaning of psychosis and insanity. As Sullivan once put it, "We are all more simply human than otherwise."

In his correspondence with Putnam, Freud had taken the position that the ethical demands made on people should come after analysis and be imposed (or recommended) by someone other than the analyst. Thus personal analysis became the basis of all further progress. This is universally accepted today, so that anyone who wishes to go through psychoanalytic training must first (or at some point in the training) go through a personal analysis.

This requirement has come under bitter attack, but it has stood the test of time. Over and over it has been shown that people who have not been through a personal analysis simply do not grasp the concepts involved.

As far as the theory is concerned, Anzieu (1975) has shown that there were literally twice as many fundamental concepts present in Freud's writings after his self-analysis than before. Thus in many senses psychoanalysis came out of Freud's self-analysis.

In public Freud never discussed his self-analysis; he was a most private man and did not disclose his feelings easily. But it soon became known that he had been through a self-analysis, and by 1920, when the first psychoanalytic institute was set up in Berlin, personal analysis by a more experienced member of the group became an unchangeable requirement at the institute.

What was made public was his book on dreams in 1900. This is an epoch-making book, one that changed the whole course of history, but it took many years for his fellow professionals to appreciate what Freud had done, and even then only his immediate followers understood his accomplishment. Other members of the profession took more than fifty years to catch up with him.

This gap explains some of the resistance to Freud. Almost all social scientists in 1900 were behaviorists in one form or another, even though the strict adherence to the erroneous tenets of behaviorism was limited mainly to America.

The dream, and the fantasy, in Freud's theory represented the psychic fulfillment of a forbidden wish (or fear). This interpretation gave a coherence to the mental life that had never been there before. It also showed that the differences between normal, neurotic, and psychotic were all matters of degree (Fine, 1979) and that the dream was a universal phenomenon.

Devereux, a distinguished psychoanalytic anthropologist, listed the characteristics of the primitive attitude to dreams as follows:

(1) There is a tendency to define the manifest content of the dream as a genuine and partly extrapsychic event that occurs not merely on a supernatural plane but also on the level of objective reality.

(2) There is a tendency to feel morally and otherwise responsible for dreamed behavior. Dawson, for example, (in Kiev, 1964) relates that among the Temme a number of mothers who had lost their children dreamt that they had given their babies to be ritually eaten by the witch cult. This was called: "I dream a witch." The native doctor would elicit the dream and force the woman to confess, after which she was "cleansed" and could resume her activities.

(3) The form, style, and pattern of dreams are rather consistently influenced by cultural expectations and predilections.

(4) The manifest content of the dream is considered of primary importance.

These characteristics of dreams were all typical of the primitive psychiatry and psychology of Freud's day. He realized that the culture in which he had grown up was dominated by magical thinking, just like the primitive peoples whom the "civilized" persons in his day held in such contempt. This understanding was also one of the reasons for the widespread rejection of Freud.

The repressed wishes that dreams express are all sexual and/or aggressive (although for a while Freud limited himself to the sexual); this interpretation focuses the investigation on an individual's love life. Many thinkers in Freud's day had condemned the sexual code of that time as barbarous in the extreme, but only Freud was able to show that consistent sexual repression leads to illness — often of a physical nature (hysteria).

Freud's theories of sexuality created an enormous furor. In effect, he was condemning an entire civilization as neurotic. In the course of the twentieth century this position was confirmed by numerous studies, especially those of Kinsey and Masters and Johnson, but it took a long time for humankind to accept the disturbed nature of its sexual mores.

Here, virtually for the first time, the question of normality came to the fore. If the normal human being was sexually crippled, as Freud maintained, what was one to say about the civilization?

Gradually the furor about Freud's sexual theories died down and eventually disappeared. In the main Freud's ideas have won out: sexual pleasure is a normal accompaniment of human existence, and its denial is propagated only by "certain queer fanatics" and some scientists. But this included the majority of humankind up to that point.

Of course it must be understood as well that Freud's ideas were largely misunderstood. He showed that sexuality does not spring into existence full-blown at puberty, as the naive view holds, but that its roots go back deep into childhood.

On the issue of sexuality Freud first saw the sharp contradiction between his views of normality and the ordinary ones. In a paper in 1898 he wrote:

In matters of sexuality we are at present, every one of us, ill or well, nothing but hypocrites. . . . We see that it is positively a matter of public interest that *men should enter upon sexual relations with full potency.* [To have mentioned women here would have been too horrifying for that day: that came later.] In matters of prophylaxis, however, the individual is relatively helpless. The whole community must become interested in the matter and give their assent to the creation of generally acceptable regulations. At present we are still far removed from such a state of affairs which would promise relief, and it is for this reason that we may with justice regard civilization too as responsible for the spread of neurasthenia. (SE, III, pp. 266–78)

While the psychoanalytic views about sexuality were to undergo considerable changes in the course of time, they never really deviated from the goal of a freer and happier sex life. This goal is already in such sharp contrast to legal and moral prohibitions prominent in Western culture that fifty years later Kinsey could state that "if the laws were strictly enforced, 95 percent of our young people would end up in jail."

The ideal solution of the sex problem is a matter of dispute, even among analysts; but the ultimate goal is not.

It is noteworthy that Freud never identified sexual abstinence with morality, as most authorities had done up to that time. For him, steeped in the classical world of Greece and Rome more than in the contradictions and hatreds of his own day, sexuality was a positive good; in 1908 he even recommended setting up an Academy of Love in Vienna, such as had existed in ancient times.

Sexual conduct was part of life, and as such it had to be analyzed, like everything else. In his paper on "Wild Psychoanalysis" in 1910, he reported the case of a forty-seven-year-old woman in Austria who came to a physician with nervous problems. He told her that someone in Vienna had recently discovered a way out for her: she could either get married, or take a lover, or masturbate. Freud pointed out that the physician had omitted the one procedure that could have offered most help — psychoanalysis. Misunderstandings of this kind abounded through the years, and even today many persons do not realize that lack of sexual desire is a reason for psychoanalysis, not for condemnation or praise. Total sexual abstinence is as harmful as total deprivation of nutritious food.

The notion that sexual pleasure is not only acceptable but desirable has become the most popular view, and in a recent review of the lives of married couples (Schwartz and Blumstein, 1983) the researchers found many couples, both men and women, who accepted illicit sexual pleasures as essential to life if legal pleasures could not be obtained. A happy marriage is still the ideal solution, but is actually rare (Cuber and Harroff, 1965; Horney, 1928). On the other hand, whether a happy marriage is the ideal solution is doubted by some theoreticians (Horney, 1928).

Freud also opened up many areas that had hitherto been neglected by conventional theoreticians. In *The Psychopathology of Everyday Life* (1901) he directed attention to what are now called Freudian slips, unconscious errors that point to repressed or vulnerable areas of the personality. In his book on jokes (1905) he analyzed the subtleties of jokes and humor.

Meanwhile most of his time was spent doing therapy. He could establish readily enough that the same principles that operated in therapy, such as wish-fulfillment, repression of forbidden desires, and the like, operated in much more common experiences like Freudian slips and jokes.

With his two books on dreams (1900) and sexuality (1905) and the allied material, Freud laid the basis for a new psychology, dynamic and radically different from the more conventional approaches of the academicians of his day. In spite of much academic opposition, the essentials of this new psychology have been worked out by Freudian analysts in the twentieth century.

In the first decade of this century Freud continued, at first alone, then with some followers, to develop his new psychology. In *Religion and Obsessional Neurosis* (1907) he pointed to the similarities between the rituals of religion and the rituals of the obsessional neurotic. This led him to declare that religion was the universal obsessional neurosis.

In a world where religion still was so basic to millions of people, what could be said about the mental health of the religious person? At first slowly, then with increasing momentum, the various neurotic aspects of religion were uncovered. But this again meant a clash with the established order.

It was clear that the concepts of neurosis and psychosis required extensive alterations. Eventually it became apparent that neurosis was a universal phenomenon not limited to certain queer deviants, and that it was only through psychoanalytic concepts that mental illness could be understood. This understanding has defined the general course of mental health research in the twentieth century. (Other schools will be discussed later.)

But if mental health could be defined only through psychoanalytic concepts (the very term "mental health" comes from psychoanalysis) then a reexamination and redefinition of the whole value system was essential. This was what Freud began to tackle.

I have elsewhere suggested, as others have as well, that the terms "neurosis" and "psychosis" attached to psychiatric diagnosis tend to be misleading. Many people manage to come to grips with the demands of their society; these should be called "adjustment neurotics." The others, who are deviant, should be called "maladjustment neurotics." Ideal normality is rare, if it is ever found, even in analyzed people. But people can try to get closer to it. Ideal normality has to be defined in terms of inner equilibrium, not external adjustment.

And so Freud, still largely isolated from the main fellow professionals of his day (in 1926 he flatly declared that the "majority of quacks in the field are psychiatrists") went along his own way, bolstered by a growing number of supporters.

The history of psychoanalysis (Fine, 1990) is generally written in technical terms. But it would be more useful to view it in humanistic terms. The technical observations are essentially commentaries on the civilization of Freud's day.

New ideas, however, allow these technical observations to be more easily applied and understood. Thus in *Mourning and Melancholia* (1917) Freud drew the parallel between mourning, which involves an actual loss, and melancholia, which involves a psychic loss (what we call "object loss" today).

In the years during and after World War I Freud devoted his writings to a number of purely philosophical topics. These ideas were already present in the correspondence with Putnam cited above, but after 1918 Freud was able to put them into clearer form.

Technically much attention has been devoted to the structural theory of id, ego, and superego, and subsequently to the superego and ego psychology, with the id receding from the dominant position it had held until 1914. While human beings could not attain complete happiness, they had to strive for happiness, and in greater or lesser measure they could succeed. Psychoanalysis was not limited to the cure of the mentally ill; it was a generally applicable philosophical reorientation of life, relying on what Bellah and his colleagues (1986) called the "therapeutic revolution." In their survey of typical Americans and the changes they experienced between 1957 and 1976 Douvan, Kulka, and Veroff found that:

> In these characteristics — isolation, detachment, intellectual/ verbal analysis — psychoanalysis represents quintessential science. Its popularity marks the movement of the scientific revolution to the last frontier — the sphere of human behavior and the thickets of the human soul and represents above all, a remarkable faith in and optimism about the power of science. Its emergence as the model of human counsel marks modern sensibility and displaces a religious/moral model.

Thus the first century of psychoanalytic development (1886–1986) saw psychoanalysis move from a deviant sect that preached seemingly bizarre theories to a movement that, as Janet Malcolm (1981) remarked, "had improbably flowered into the vast system of thought about human nature — psychoanalysis — which has detonated throughout the intellectual, social, artistic and ordinary life of our century as no cultural force has (it may not be off the mark to say) since Christianity."

It is in this view of psychoanalysis as a wide-ranging system of thought which touches in greater or lesser degree every human concern that the value system of psychoanalysis must be sought.

The Therapist

Freud was technically a physician, and in the public mind psychoanalysis was associated with medicine, a view reinforced by the spectacular growth of neuroscience and the proliferation of mind-altering drugs after World War II. Yet psychoanalysis proper has been unaffected by these developments.

If psychoanalysis is a philosophical system, with essential values, how is it to be taught? In a unique way, through the process of psychoanalysis or therapy.

Psychoanalysis is not a branch of medicine, although it has its applications in medicine as well as other fields. On this point the sharpest conflicts arose, especially in the United States. The question of lay analysis (nonmedical psychoanalysis) was finally resolved by a lawsuit brought by a psychologist against the American Psychoanalytic Association and International Psychoanalytic Associations in 1985, resulting in a complete victory for the psychologists.

Freud himself was a great advocate of lay analysis. The Americans were the strongest proponents of the idea that analysis should be limited to physicians, and the strongest conflicts broke out in the United States, which came to dominate the world scene after World War II amid the havoc wrought by the war. As early as 1929 Freud had suggested a peaceful split between the American societies and the European; he thought the Americans would never accept the idea of lay analysis, while he would never condone its rejection. Freud even held that opposition to lay analysis was "the last mark of the resistance against psychoanalysis, and the most dangerous of all" (Jones, 1987, vol. 3, p. 298).

Why should the opposition to lay analysis be a mask of resistance to analysis? Because inevitably the physician will think medically and try to find medical reasons for every psychological disturbance (as has happened); the physician will be opposed in general to the use of psychotherapy, especially for severely disturbed individuals. Freud had foreseen the situation correctly, long before it flowered fully on American soil.

With the victory of the psychologists in 1985 Freud's dream came closer to reality. In 1926 he had written to the Swiss pastor-psychoanalyst Pfister (1926, p. 126):

I do not know if you have detected the secret link between the Lay Analysis and the Illusion. In the former I wish to protect analysis from the doctors and in the latter from the priests. I should like to hand it over to a profession which does not yet exist, a profession of lay curers of souls who need not be doctors and should not be priests.

The new profession that Freud envisaged has taken a long time to build, but with the growth of nonmedical analysis in the United States its eventual success is assured. It can be expected that eventually the older degrees of M.D., Ph.D., and M.S.W., which succeeded in securing various kinds of legal recognition, will disappear and be replaced by one uniform degree in psychoanalytic psychology, which will also in the long run obtain legal recognition. In this way we have come closer to his other dream, of 1926:

Our civilization imposes an almost intolerable pressure on us and it calls for a corrective. Is it too fantastic to expect that psychoanalysis may be destined to the task of preparing mankind for such a corrective? Perhaps once more an American may hit on the idea of spending a little money to get the "social workers" of his country trained analytically and to turn them into a band of helpers for combatting the neuroses of civilization?

For the therapist, the curriculum for a doctorate would be the present analytic curriculum, consisting of personal analysis, courses in psychoanalytic theory, and doing analysis under supervision. There have in the past been a number of schools that have come closer to such a course of study; in the future more will provide it, and psychology will move further along in a psychoanalytic direction.

The Analytic Ideal

In his correspondence with Putnam, Freud had insisted on the position of the detached scientist with regard to values. As he wrote later, psychoanalysis had no need of a Weltanschauung of its own; it participated in the Weltanschauung of science. This remained his position all through his life. Later (1932) he again took up specifically the question of whether psychoanalysis leads to a particular Weltanschauung, and if so to which, and answered it in the negative. Ever since, the model of the detached scientist who merely clarifies the client's problems but does not pass judgment on them, the cool surgeon who carries out the operation, has been the ideal of many analysts.

In his 1932 essay Freud defined Weltanschauung as an intellectual construction that solves all the problems of our existence uniformly on the basis of one overriding hypothesis; psychoanalysis has no such hypothesis available and does not lead to one. In this definition, however, Freud refers to the philosophies of the ages that still dominated philosophical thinking in the 1870s when he was thinking of making philosophy his career. Reliance on such an all-embracing explanation has since gone by the board. In fact, today no two philosophers would even agree on a definition of philosophy (Levi, 1976). What the philosopher can do, however, is to sift out values and to clarify them.

Later in the 1932 essay, Freud does say: "Our best hope for the future is that intellect — the scientific spirit — reason — may in process of time establish a dictatorship in the mental life of man" (p. 171). The language sounds a little peculiar, but it does express one of the basic values of psychoanalysis: to solve our problems by reason. Or, as he put it at another time, "The voice of the intellect is weak but it persists until it gets a hearing."

It is clear enough that Freud was speaking of values and Weltanschauung only in a special sense, and that if the broader meaning of these terms is considered, he was expressing values and building the basis for a philosophy of life in his work. Others took up some of his ideas and put them in more positive form. Thus Esman (1977) insisted that psychoanalysis has a value system of its own. Its essentials lie in the primacy of reason, the acceptance of delayed gratification in the service of future goals, the ideal of stable, monogamous heterosexual bonds, and a commitment to a lifelong career. These values are often briefly described by saying that the normal person is the one who can work and love; this is also known as integrative living.

Hartmann, who earlier had been critical of Freud's use of the word "Weltanschauung" (1929), in a later essay on psychoanalysis and moral values (1960) was in complete agreement with Freud's emphasis on the detached scientist. Still, even in this essay he said:

On the other hand it may also happen occasionally that contact with what analysis reveals about human motivation may

lead certain personality types to a devaluation of moral values.
Although this may occur in analysis, in a successful analysis it
tends to be a transitional phase only. (pp. 92–93)

Thus he too agrees that the basic psychoanalytic value is psychoanalysis itself — the use of reason to understand and resolve the
conflicts of human existence. The clearest formulation of this has
come from the noted writer Thomas Mann:

> I hold that we shall one day recognize in Freud's life-work the
> cornerstone for the building of a new...dwelling of a wiser and
> freer humanity.... Call this, if you choose, a poet's Utopia but it
> is not unthinkable that the resolution of our great fear and our
> great hate...may one day be due to the healing effect of this
> very science.

Most analysts agree that reason is the basis of a mature philosophy
of living. It is now time, in view of the political unification of the
field through the 1985 lawsuit, to tease out the essentials of how this
mature philosophy would look.

In a number of writings I have described the analytic resolution
as the analytic ideal. The nature of this ideal and its consequences
for science and therapy can be spelled out here in a little more detail.

Before proceeding to a description and discussion of the analytic
ideal I must make some theoretical-historical remarks.

The theme of the 1989 Rome Congress was "The Common
Ground in Psychoanalysis." Many people have been thinking of this
problem. In his presidential address at Montreal Wallerstein read
a paper entitled "One Psychoanalysis or Many?" (APS Newsletter,
vol. 22, no. 3, fall 1988). He sees a theoretical diversity in the field
and yet we're all psychoanalysts. What is there in common? This question was addressed in detail at Rome. My position is that we have in
common a set of values, which I call the analytic ideal — a vision of
what the mature human being can become, a vision that inspires us
in our daily analytic work and in our theoretical discussions.

Usually the common ground is sought in concepts or techniques —
the structural theory of id, ego, and superego, or classical psychoanalysis vs. supportive therapy. Here we have failed to learn sufficiently from our experience. The most extensive investigation of classical psychoanalysis was carried out by the American Psychoanalytic
Association from 1947 to 1967. The most important conclusions were
negative: analysts could not agree on a definition of psychoanalysis.

The outcome did little more than show the obvious, that those with strong egos do better in psychoanalysis than those with weak egos. To compound the fiasco, the committee lost some 70 percent of the original data. But even if they had the data the result would have meant little because the inquiry was conducted along psychiatric (diagnostic entities) rather than psychoanalytic lines (inner conflicts and inner changes).

In the Topeka study that Wallerstein finally completed and published (*Forty-two Lives in Treatment*, 1986) the results were surprising. Pure psychoanalysis and analytic psychotherapy could scarcely be distinguished from one another. With some patients for whom it could least be expected, analytic techniques were most successful; with others for whom the techniques seemed appropriate they did not work well. In few cases could pure psychoanalysis be maintained without supportive devices; and in few cases could supportive devices alone prove sufficient without analytic interpretation.

Resistances are universal, even in the most seemingly compliant of patients. Freud said in 1914 that whoever takes into account transference and resistances is working analytically, and he thus referred to a major part of the common ground that we are looking for.

But people are so diverse that theoretical concepts like ego repression do not cover the picture adequately. The patient must be approached in human terms. The diversity of patients can best be grasped in terms of their own lives as well as their own understanding of their problems and the world. We are only now beginning to come to this essential understanding.

By now psychoanalysis is close to a hundred years old. It has understandably been dominated by Freud, and the proper elucidation of his thought remains a problem. Many of the so-called deviant schools have, as I shall show later, simply restated Freud and called their formulations a new school. The present flirtation with Kohut, for example, obscures the fact that he represents for the most part a variation on the cultural schools, which in turn cover up their preference not to deal with instinctual drives (cf. Fine, 1979). The self-object that Kohutians make so much of is simply the mother, so that Kohut is saying that the experiences with the mother are more significant than the libidinal drives proper. With this most people would be in agreement. To call this neo-Freudian misses the fact that Freud himself neglected the first year of life, the theory of which came after his death (cf. Sandler's reworking of *The Ego and the Mechanism of Defense*). Change these terms around and it is hard to find something essentially new in Kohut (Rangell, 1982). But the Kohutians have become a fiery messianic group who insist that they are revolutionizing psychoanalytic theory.

Go back to an earlier time and you find to your surprise that Jungians insist that Jung elucidated the meaning of the dream, forgetting that Freud wrote *The Interpretation of Dreams* in 1900, years before Jung even started analysis.

The history of psychoanalysis is full of many blunders which analysts are reluctant to point out. If they do recourse is had to the schools rather than to the material. Rational discussions in psychoanalysis have become very difficult. Students can and must nod assent when they are in class, and then immediately forget what they have learned to go off on their own (Mercano, 1987).

In the light of this situation the effort to establish a philosophy basic to all psychoanalysts seems hazardous, yet it must be attempted. I offer this discussion of the analytic ideal as the best summary of current psychoanalysis information available. It is no longer a matter of pushing different schools; that is a regressive effort that gets nowhere because the same thing is said in a hundred different ways by various schools. The era of "schools" may be said to have passed; what we have now is an era of integration (Fine, 1981).

2

The Nature of Neurosis
and the Analytic Ideal

*T*HE MOST SERIOUS MENTAL DISTURBANCES, which we call psychoses, have been known from time immemorial and reappear in one form or another in all societies (Menninger, 1963). The minor disturbances, known as neuroses, were not even properly described until psychoanalysis came along, and their elucidation stems mainly from Freud. Thus the psychoanalytic theory of neurosis was grafted in a strange manner into psychiatry, with very confusing results.

When the DSM III, the *Diagnostic and Statistical Manual*, third edition, which is regarded as the official bible of psychiatry, was issued in 1980, the authors stated:

At the present time...there is no consensus in the field as to how to define "Neurosis." Some clinicians limit the term to its descriptive meaning whereas others also include the concept of a specific etiological process. To avoid ambiguity, the term *neurotic disorder* should be used only descriptively. This is consistent with the use of this term in ICD-9. The term *neurotic process* on the other hand should be used when the clinician wishes to indicate the concept of a specific etiological process involving the following sequence: unconscious conflicts between opposing wishes or between wishes and prohibitions, which cause unconscious perception of anticipated danger or dysphoria, which leads to use of defense mechanisms that result in either symptoms, personality disturbance, or both. (p. 9)

35

This mixture of descriptive and dynamic concepts is typical of the confusion that prevails in psychiatry. Laplanche and Pontalis, in their comprehensive work (1973), state:

> The task of trying to define neurosis, as revealed by clinical experience, in terms of the comprehension of the concept of neurosis, tends to become indistinguishable from the psychoanalytic theory itself, in that this theory was basically constituted as a theory of neurotic conflict and its modes.
>
> It is scarcely possible to claim that an effective distinction has yet been established between the structure of neurosis, psychosis and perversion. (p. 269)

This confusion about diagnosis has been deplored by many clinicians. Anna Freud (1965) noted that "the descriptive nature of many current diagnostic categories runs counter to the essence of psychoanalytic thinking." Menninger (1959) stated more emphatically: "Diagnosis in the sense in which we doctors have used it for many years is not only relatively useless in many cases; it is an inaccurate, misleading, philosophically false predication."

Because of the confusion about what diagnosis means, I have suggested elsewhere that neurosis and psychosis should be defined as the distance from the analytic ideal. This arises directly from the experiences of the clinical situation and can be linked most directly with the whole therapeutic process. Many examples of this linkage will be given later. Now it is necessary to define the analytic ideal more precisely. The analytic ideal is based on findings from clinical experiences that the human being is likely to achieve the greatest degree of happiness if he or she (1) loves; (2) has sexual pleasure; (3) has pleasure in general (rather than pain); (4) has feelings, yet (5) is guided by reason; (6) is part of a family; (7) is part of a social order; (8) enjoys work; (9) can communicate; (10) has creative outlets; (11) has a good self-image; and (12) is as free from psychiatric pathology as possible under the circumstances. Each of these requires some further discussion.

1. Love

Although Freud's total work should be looked upon as the greatest tract on love ever written, it took him quite a while to reach his conclusions. At first he emphasized sexuality in the physical sense, and even thought of love as the outgrowth of sexual satisfaction, while he thought that sexual frustration led to anxiety by some unknown biochemical process, a view he later abandoned.

In the first psychoanalytic paper (1895), by Josef Breuer, Freud's teacher and collaborator, Breuer mentioned that his patient Anna O. had never been in love. When Freud reported this case in his 1909 lectures at Clark University, he omitted this element of the history, concentrating instead on the more "scientific" elucidation of her bizarre symptoms. It was not until 1914 that Freud declared flatly "in the last resort we must begin to love in order not to fall ill, and we are bound to fall ill if, in consequence of frustration, we are unable to love" (SE, XIV, p. 95).

Later (1920) Freud was to modify this position somewhat by admitting the Nirvana principle, in which narcissistic bliss is the highest form of happiness. But in evaluating Freud we must consider the whole body of his work, not isolated fragments, as well as the work of those who have followed him.

Commentators on Freud have been misled by the early emphasis on instincts, which seemed to imply that the higher feelings like love were merely sublimations of the lower, and by the extensive material on the neurotic character of many of the love experiences that he encountered (particularly romantic love). The culturalists in their day made much of these arguments, but neglected to say that it was just a question of emphasis, not of really different views. Fenichel (1945) put it this way:

> Our insights make it plain that the insight into the formative powers of social forces upon individual minds does not require any change in Freud's concepts of instincts, as certain authors believe. The instinctual needs are the raw material formed by the social influences; and it is the task of a psychoanalytic sociology to study the details of this shaping. Different "biological constitutions" contain manifold possibilities; yet they are not realities but potentialities. It is experience, that is, the cultural conditions, that transforms potentialities into realities, that shapes the real mental structure of man by forcing his instinctual demands into certain directions, by favoring some of them and blocking others, and even by turning parts of them against the rest. (p. 588)

The situation as we see it today could be described theoretically as follows. While love is fundamental, instinctual drives can and do interfere with it and make its realization more difficult. Love develops through various stages, and through various interpersonal experiences, from mother to father to the outside world. When fully developed, and indeed at all ages, love is the happiest state that the human being can experience.

What is ordinarily called love, or romantic love, the love of man and woman, is a universal desire. In general, psychoanalysts have found that romantic love is a transference, a wish for the loving mother of childhood. It usually does not last and often leads to the most violent battles when the initial attraction has passed.

Critics of my book *The Meaning of Love in Human Experience* (1985) have objected that there is so little love in the world that it is useless to set up love as an ideal. They overlook, however, that the book, like psychoanalysis in general, is descriptive, not prescriptive. The fact of the matter is that love has been set up as an ideal by the vast majority of people in the world. Different cultures call for somewhat different emphases.

Much has been written on the proper definition of love (Hazo, 1957). The problem has been complicated by the overwhelming prevalence of hatred in Western cultures. A naive Tahitian informant, Manu, states: "Love is, I want her, I desire her. I am happy with her and when I am not with her I miss her." While more sophisticated definitions can be offered, this hits at the heart of the matter.

All psychoanalysts have placed strong emphasis on the way in which love develops. It is true that at the present time there is an enormous amount of violence in the family. This phenomenon is to be deplored, not set up as a norm. The historical record demonstrates extensive and lethal forms of violence by parents. The dictum "spare the rod and spoil the child" was stated and supported in the Bible. The Puritan laws threatening death to the unruly hung over children's heads, and parents supported their right to whip and punish with biblical quotations. The historical record continues though in somewhat attenuated form. Nevertheless, the statistics that emerge from the present scene are gory indeed. In 1968 it was estimated that more children under the age of five died from parentally inflicted injuries than from tuberculosis, whooping cough, polio, measles, diabetes, rheumatic fever, and appendicitis combined (Gelles et al., 1981, p. 9). De Mause (1974) has documented the nightmare-like nature of the way in which children were formerly brought up; yet historians in the main have simply ignored his detailed evidence.

Cases of battered women have also been frequent. The classic "rule of thumb" gave legal justification to common law that sanctioned a husband's striking his wife with a stick, provided the stick was no wider than the thumb. Wives in America have been raped; choked; stabbed; shot; beaten; struck with horsewhips, pokers, bats, and bicycle chains; and had their jaws and limbs broken. Yet wife abuse as a social problem did not receive national attention until the mid-1970s.

I have suggested (Fine, 1985) that cultures can be divided on the basis of the degree of love and hatred that they display. While some have doubted that love cultures exist, the evidence is clear that they do, even though they are in the minority. Furthermore, even within the worst hate cultures, some love is found. A culture that has nothing but hatred will soon destroy itself.

Western culture has been a hate culture from time immemorial (Fine, 1985). At the time of the Crusades Geoffrey Plantagenet put it very succinctly: "Do you not know that it is our inheritance from remote times that no one loves another, but always, brother against brother, and son against father, we try our utmost to injure one another?" The same could easily be said today.

The history of Western Europe reveals episodes of psychotic hatred released against innocent people which led to wholesale massacres — the Crusades (which one historian has called Operation Grave), the Inquisition, the witch hunts, the wars of religion. Even in our own century no one has yet calculated the enormous human toll taken by World War II — 100 million would be a low estimate. And even now the Soviets are for the first time admitting what the world knew all along — that the secret trials that led to the murder of several million Russians under Stalin were all frame-ups — and have pardoned the innocent people who went to their deaths.

How could love develop in such a hate-filled culture? Largely as a refuge from the surrounding turmoil. Human beings are preadapted to internalize the kind of care that we get from the surrounding environment; primarily this has been explored in terms of the mother-child relationship. Into this early love matrix elements of the hate culture sooner or later intervene to prevent the infant from developing in a healthy manner. Several generations of analysts and analytic researchers have provided voluminous evidence for how much can go wrong in the mother-infant love relationship. Mothers have been categorized as rejecting, possessive, schizophrenic, phallic, abusive, and the like. While many in the women's liberation movement in particular have rejected these as "male epithets," unfortunately they conform to clinical reality and to direct observation. Even the classical theory that the girl resents the penis that she longed for but could never get has much merit to it. The thesis is not that all women behave this way, but many do; how many is a matter for statistical research. But in the light of the widespread incidence of emotional disturbance it can realistically be assumed that a considerable percentage do.

For many, love, at every stage in the life span, becomes a refuge from the hatred experienced in the outside world. Because it is a refuge it often leads in the earliest love relationship, that between mother and child, to excessive possessiveness, jealousy, submissiveness, brutality, narcissistic grandiosity, and many other neurotic reactions. And in many cases it remains at that level.

In the analytic relationship the most common reaction of the patient is that he or she is unloved by the therapist, and the most common complaint is lack of love. The patient experiences this personally, but the experience is a reflection of the wider disturbance found in the culture at large.

Psychoanalysis thus appears as a corrective to the numerous interpersonal disturbances seen in the culture.

Ideally, love is an experience of mutual gratification. The analytic work aims to help the patient reach this definition of love, but the task is admittedly difficult; that is why true analysis takes such a long time.

The major schools of analysis recognize that love is the primary goal. Many, however, are confused by the whole diagnostic system and concentrate on symptoms rather than on the broader functioning of the patient. It is necessary to distinguish the analytic attitude from the nonanalytic and not to get lost in empty phrases like "a new point of view" or "a revisionist school." The therapist convinced that love is the real solution to human problems is an analyst; the therapist not so convinced has no real right to be called an analyst.

Patients will easily recognize the essential truths behind these remarks. They strive to get over anger, jealousies, resentments, paranoid distrust, and the like and move in a direction in which they can give and take love. The closer they come to this ideal, the more successful the analysis is.

2. Sexuality

Sexual malaise was the first large-scale disturbance that Freud pointed to in the 1890s. After 1900 he became aware that sexuality does not start at puberty, but goes back to the earliest experiences with the mother. In technical terms he discovered infantile sexuality.

It is surprising that even today, after a hundred years of therapizing, many people are so shocked by the notion of infantile sexuality. The clinical, anthropological, biological (animal behavior), sociological, and historical evidence is overwhelming. It is still true that, as

Freud once put it, only queer fanatics and certain scientists deny the fundamental importance of sexuality in human life. Indeed in all the higher mammals and throughout the evolutionary scale reproduction remains a fundamental function.

In the early days Freud confused sexuality with love, a confusion that persists with many people. If the nineteenth century epitomized sexless love (the "Victorian" era), the twentieth century has glorified loveless sex (the "zipless fuck" of Erica Jong). Neither one has grasped the role that love plays in the life of the individual who has to make his or her way in a hate culture.

In spite of all the publicity about it, in my experience sexual conflicts are still extremely widespread. It is hard to find a patient whose sex life is in perfect order. If it is, the person does not feel the need for help.

Sexual problems range from excessive promiscuity (the "Don Juan" syndrome) to excessive celibacy (withdrawal, lack of desire). Nevertheless, there are numerous social institutions in our culture that provide adequate instruction on how to have a more gratifying sex life, and how to overcome problems such as impotence, premature ejaculation, frigidity, and lack of desire.

Of course, the occurrence of sexually transmitted disease (STD, especially AIDS) has made people much more cautious about the partners with whom they engage in sex. But this is a practical problem which will no doubt be resolved in the course of time.

There has been a curious turn in the attitude of many toward homosexuality. Even some analysts have come to feel that homosexuality is a normal reaction (Marmor, Isay). This position represents a rejection of the obvious truth. Many people can be heard to make the bald statement that a hedonistic attitude toward life has proved bad. This is entirely untrue. Human beings are pleasure-seeking animals, like all animals, and what gives them pleasure can be considered desirable, while what gives them pain is undesirable.

3. Pleasure

Notwithstanding these truisms, the search for pain, what we call masochism, is a widespread disorder. Analysts have devoted many tomes to an unraveling of the preference for pain, and meaningful answers have been forthcoming. No one seeks pain without going through a series of prior experiences that have hurt badly. Masochism becomes a defense through which the hurts of childhood can be corrected.

The practical difficulties, of course, have to be overcome, but in the analytic ideal pleasure is a positive good.

Most often the problem revolves around seeking pleasures that in the long run prove harmful — such as excessive use of drugs or alcohol. And substance abuse is as a rule connected with the avoidance of anxiety. But instances of abuse do not alter the analytic emphasis on pleasure.

4. Feelings

A wide range of feelings is available to the happy person; a severe constriction of feeling is characteristic of the disturbed individual. The feeling life, however, must be guided by reason; otherwise an uninhibited display of affect without pattern or purpose results. It is this latter situation that G. Stanley Hall described when he wrote that "the intellect is a speck afloat on a sea of feeling."

5. Reason

Freud's call for a dictatorship of reason has much merit to it. Still, it is obvious enough that most people operate in many areas of life irrationally.

Rationalization is the process by which people attempt to justify their fixed prejudices on the basis of some pseudo-argument. The white prejudice against blacks in the United States is a case in point.

Bleuler in his work on schizophrenia (1978) estimated that people have schizophrenic episodes, and then recover. Thus the alternation of normal and psychotic states seems quite common. On this basis we could assume that such alternation has occurred throughout history.

The existence of large-scale psychotic manifestations in the general population can scarcely be doubted. The historian Heer in his work on the Middle Ages states that that period can only be understood on the assumption of mass psychoses. And of course in our own century, Hitler and Stalin must both be viewed as psychotic murderers who somehow managed to carry many of their followers along with them. The current revision of history by present-day governments is evidence that they agree with this evaluation, though they may be reluctant to say so.

6. The Family

The family is the quintessential human institution. Some animals do have family-like arrangements, but as a general rule only humans have real families, with all the physical and psychological consequences. All human societies ever investigated have been based on the family. According to Murdock (1947), the nuclear family (mother, father, child) is universal, though it may be embedded in other forms. There can be no doubt that a suitable family role is essential to human happiness.

Since children are an inherent part of every family, one of the major functions of the family is to oversee the proper development of the child. Here psychoanalysis has contributed a surprisingly simple formulation: neurosis represents a lack of development, or a fixation on certain periods of development (e.g., childhood). The task of the parents is to help the child grow up; when this fails, psychotherapy takes over the task of assisting the child (now often an adult) in growing up.

Many experiments have tried to vary the nuclear structure of the family: polygamy, polyandry (many husbands, much less common), artificial families (such as convents and monasteries), communal families (in which every man shares every woman with all other men). Many attitudes have been described in the way in which parents treat their children. De Mause (1974) has delineated six modes of child-rearing, identifying each with a specific period in history. His classification is as follows: (1) infanticidal mode (antiquity to fourth century); (2) abandonment mode (fourth to seventeenth centuries); (3) intrusive mode (eighteenth century); (4) socialization mode (nineteenth to twentieth centuries); (3) ambivalent mode (fourteenth to seventeenth centuries); (5) socialization mode (nineteenth to mid-twentieth centuries); (6) helping mode (begins mid-twentieth century). While historians have disagreed with the interpretation of the historical records, this is still a good way of understanding how parents deal with their children today.

The development of the child is a product of hereditary and socioeconomic factors. Today we would feel that in the majority of cases socioeconomic factors take precedence, so that neurosis is a product of parental hostility and misunderstanding. The analytic ideal takes as one of its goals the avoidance of pathological reactions in the child.

Without an intact family, the child feels severe conflict. Divorce presents an intense upheaval, even at best. Later, in adulthood the single person is at a severe handicap. "People who need people," as the song goes, are the happiest people in the world.

Psychoanalytic theory has gone on after Freud to stress the concept of object constancy — the ability to hold on to another person psychologically through all their various moods and emotional upheavals. Object loss, or the loss of an important person, is one of the most severe traumas in a person's life; among widows and widowers the incidence of death or severe illness is far higher than among married people. Object loss or interpersonal loss is one of the major motifs in contemporary psychoanalytic thinking.

From the very beginning Freud was oriented toward the family, although he tended to put it in different terms. The family, he argued at first, must socialize the youngster, which pits the family against the child's instinctual forces. This is still true, but the other function of the family, to provide security and safety (what has been called the "holding environment"), has become more important. In either case it is still true that emotional disorder results from family dysfunctioning. The happy person is the one who can find his or her way in a family.

7. The Social Order

The family is part of a larger social order, which may be viewed as a collection of families. In this social order the individual must find some kind of place. As with the family, at first the social order was seen to be in conflict with instinctual drives; later it came to be seen as a source of security and comfort. A disrupted social order produces a variety of neurotic problems.

Arguments about values have often centered on what kind of social order is best for humankind. To this question psychoanalysis as such cannot provide an answer, but in general psychoanalysis has flourished only in democratic climates, so that it can be assumed that happiness is most likely to occur in such democratic climates.

It is important that the individual find some place in the social order. The total rebel, the outlaw, may be glorified in saga or story, but is inherently an unhappy person. An exception can be made in a totally oppressive society, such as many that have appeared in the course of history; in such a society the rebel, the outlaw, may be happy in the effort to overthrow the oppressive society and to found a new society.

8. The Self: Sense of Identity

To be happy a person must have a high sense of self-esteem. This has been expressed as a good self-image (Freud), an adequate sense of selfhood (Jung), a cohesive self (Kohut), and in many other ways.

Although the concept of the self is ancient, it was not brought formally into psychoanalytic theory until Freud's 1914 paper on narcissism. This paper, however, was in many respects in serious error, and the errors have had to be corrected.

A major distinction not sufficiently emphasized by Freud is that between healthy and unhealthy narcissism. Likewise, the basic emotional split in the infant, between love and hate, while not given prominence by Freud, was stressed by a number of his followers. Narcissism, if it is to be healthy, must be based on self-love, which in turn derives from the love received in earliest infancy. Secondary narcissism, based at some level on hatred, is a defensive posture to be understood like any other defense mechanism.

Although the notion goes back to the beginnings of psychoanalysis, the concept of an introject, or introjected object, later the superego, is commonly traced to the 1914 paper. The introject becomes an important, if not vital, driving force within the individual.

Narcissism leads inevitably to the notion of the self. Here three strands can be traced: (1) the commonsense notion of the self, which was used freely by Freud and others in his immediate following; (2) the exploration of the social self, peculiarly the product of the American school of philosophers and psychologists; and (3) the self psychology introduced or described by Kohut in the 1970s, which totally disregarded the other two and has given rise to a school of self psychology on the current scene. Whether the Kohutian formulations have any real validity or are merely reformulations of concepts inherent in psychoanalysis from the beginnings remains a debatable point (*JAPA*, 1982).

Three states can be distinguished in the development of the self: (1) the early, preverbal self, in the infant up to about eighteen months of age; (2) the self-image of the growing child, which is intimately tied up with the family; and (3) the self-image of the mature individual, which continues to change and develop throughout the entire life cycle. This stage of the self is intimately tied up with the social order.

Identity, though different from self, was most thoroughly explored by Erik Erikson. "Identity" is used in a double sense, as the innermost individual aspects of a human being ("true identity") and as an index of the groups to which the human being belongs.

The implications of these concepts for psychoanalytic theory are many. The major new concept introduced after Freud is that of culture or the group. The human being functions intrapsychically in terms of instincts, drives, and defenses. The person also functions interpersonally in terms of the family and other human contacts. Finally, the person functions as a member of a larger community moving in life from one group to another. In all three of these aspects inner strength is the major feature of happy persons, that is, a lack of conflict about what they are and where they belong. Such conflicts have been common in modern society.

9. Work

The notion that work is a part of the happy life has been bitterly fought, especially in cultures where a life of leisure in which the gentleman did nothing but enjoy himself was idealized (cf. Veblen, 1900). In modern societies such a life where the man (or woman) does not earn his (or her) keep is no longer acceptable. The question then is only what kind of work for a man (or woman) is optimal for any individual.

In the past, the achievement motive (McClelland) and the Protestant ethic (Max Weber) have been stressed as part of the philosophy of work. In modern times scholars have moved in a different direction, toward the empirical improvement of the work situation, without much benefit from underlying theories. In this way work has become part of the analytic ideal.

A strong effort is now being made to make work more meaningful, not only for men but also for women, who as a rule are no longer satisfied with the traditional role of housewife.

With this in mind considerable experimentation has been going on for several decades to make work a pleasure rather than a chore. Flextime, profit-sharing, labor-management cooperation, educational incentives and provisions for education in industry, adjustment of the workers to their level of competence, whether up or down, and wide-scale support of psychotherapy for discontented workers are now accepted policies in many large companies. There are, for example, some 65,000 employee assistance programs (EAPs) in place. The Protestant ethic is being replaced by the analytic ideal (Fine, 1984).

10. Communication

One of Freud's great discoveries was that the classical symptoms of neurosis are unconscious forms of communication. In hysteria the patient speaks in symptom language. The typical scene of the Victorian lady who fainted in the drawing room and was promptly given smelling salts has disappeared today. The major disturbance confronting modern psychiatry has been schizophrenia, which can now be understood as a failure of communication.

Dreams are a form of communication. They are important for everybody, not just the psychotherapy patient.

Many neurotic symptoms, such as hysterical conversion and obsessional rituals, were "decoded" by Freud and his co-workers as symbolic ways of communicating with other people.

The process of psychoanalysis focuses in the most intimate detail on the ways in which two people communicate with each other, both verbally and nonverbally.

While truth and honesty are highly valued in all cultures, lying and dishonesty are more common. Even though lying is of fundamental importance, it has received almost no attention from psychologists, even analysts.

The extraordinary importance attached to propaganda in the totalitarian countries has emphasized more than any other single factor the distortions of communications that prevail in the everyday world. Hitler's notorious emphasis on "the big lie" has unfortunately been imitated all too often.

In everyday life, a primary distinction must be drawn between manipulative and expressive communication. Expressive communication is rational behavior, the main kind recognized by traditional psychology. More common, however, is manipulative communication, in which the intention, conscious or unconscious, is to manipulate another person to do something or feel a certain way. In disturbed conditions the communication is almost always manipulative. In the healthy person it is essentially expressive.

11. Creativity

That creativity is part of a happy life is another discovery of psychoanalysis. In the past the creative individual has been seen as a "genius" separated by a wide gulf from ordinary individuals. This is not true. Every person carries within a creative spark that can be lit with the proper handling.

Guilford (1950) viewed creativity as "divergent production" but did not try to explain why the creative individual should want to be divergent, or of what use it was to be so. Arieti (1974), although writing within a psychoanalytic framework, still clung to the old image of the artist as a genius. Creativity is a "magic synthesis." Baron (1972), studying art students at the San Francisco Art Institute, found his subjects to be notably independent and unconventional, vivid in gesture and expression, and rather complex psychodynamically, but with an emphasis on openness, spontaneity, and whimsicality rather than neurotic complicatedness. "They choose to do what they value most, and this itself sets them apart from many apparently better adjusted people who are doing what they would rather not." This view seems to be part of the glorification of the artist as genius; in psychoanalytic theory Otto Rank had stressed this view above all other features. As a general proposition, however, it is contradicted by the observation that so many artists are seriously miserable and disturbed, to such an extent that psychosis and depression are often regarded as everyday occurrences among them.

The uncreative individual tends to be passive, bored, and envious, which does not make for a happy life.

12. Freedom from Psychiatric Symptomatology

While a full-scale analysis of the nature of psychosis and mental illness would take us too far afield, it can be stated that the happy person is one who has no serious sign of mental illness. While it is probably true that some forms of mental illness are organically determined, these are exceptions rather than the rule. Most forms of mental illness, according to our best knowledge today, are forms of what Freedman and Redlich call "psychosocial disorders."

The "Schools" of Psychoanalysis

It is a truism that psychoanalysis has been characterized by a split into many different schools. But if these schools are examined carefully and compared with the original Freudian approach as elaborated and honed through the years, it can be seen either that (1) they stress one aspect of the analytic ideal to the exclusion of others or (2) they stress some point that others consider absurd or exaggerated. The schools that may properly be called analytic are those that help the patient pursue the analytic ideal in one form or another, and that view the analytic ideal as the heart of normality.

All the true analytic schools are those that adhere to the principles of the analytic ideal described here. There are differences in terminology, but not in ideas. The psychoanalytic theory of, for example, the Sullivanian school is a reformulation of the original psychoanalytic framework. Interpersonal relations, later dubbed object relations, are as much a matter of Freudian theory as of Sullivanian. In *The Three Essays* (1905), for example, Freud wrote: "Let us call the person from whom the sexual attraction proceeds the sexual object [italics in the original] and the act toward which the instinct tends the *sexual aim*" (VII, pp. 135–36). In Freudian theory interpersonal relations were treated in terms of object-choice, object relations, and the like. The term "object" came naturally to Freud, with his background in German philosophy, which since Hegel had distinguished sharply between the subject and the object, but the terms "object relations" and "interpersonal relations" have an identical meaning. "Interpersonal" flows more smoothly in English, and it is unfortunate that many wish to take Freud too literally and read "object" out of the book. But that is typical of the many useless controversies in psychoanalysis.

In the long list of "schools" that claim to be different from Freud, there are some that are different and in fact should not be called analytic. Jung's various emphases are really outside the framework of analysis: he ignored the importance of transference, he gave a slightly different twist to the interpretation of dreams, and his obvious hatred of Freud and flirtation with Nazism in the period of 1930–40 understandably did not endear him to his former colleagues.

Adler's work comes closer to the analytic ideal, but he omitted any consideration of the libido and the unconscious. Sullivan fully agreed with Freud and said so; his views were magnified into a school only after he died. Rank — with his will therapy, full-hour sessions, and nine-month therapy to duplicate the birth process — remains outside psychoanalysis. Wilhelm Reich, with his overemphasis on sexuality and peculiar emphasis on "abdominal stasis," which literally cost him his life, also remains outside analysis. Melanie Klein differed from Freud only in her theories of what happens to the infant in the first few years, theories which at first were rejected (Kernberg, 1969), then incorporated into analytic theory. Lacan remains virtually alien to anyone who disagrees with him or is critical of him; he is more a polemicist than an analyst.

In therapy all clinicians agree that theoretical diagnosis has little or no relationship to treatment (e.g., Wallerstein, 1986), so why continue to place so much emphasis on it? With the use of the analytic ideal at least some further light is shed on the areas in which the patient has to change.

Goals vs. Techniques

The arguments about schools generally revolve more around tec niques than anything else. We know that Freud laid down the basic technique of free association, and it is assumed that his theories came out of that. My thesis here is the reverse. Freud, as a student of philosophy under Brentano, already had visualized his theory, based on observation of the human condition and extending to all fields of human endeavor, a program that, as I have shown, he carried out in the course of time. Originally, in the 1890s, his technique was very simple: get rid of the symptom, or symptom analysis. While this worked in some, it did not in others, so he sought to refine his technique. How he hit upon the idea of free association we do not know; we only know that it happened around 1896 (Jones, vol. 1). In the hypnotic or cathartic technique the patient could be silent, or unresponsive, but in free association, Freud argued, a response always had to be forthcoming. Hence the transition from the narrow focus on symptoms of the 1890s to the broad focus on the total personality from 1900 on could be said to be the transition from symptom analysis to character analysis, the universal approach today. In the meantime Freud had also embarked on his self-analysis (Anzieu, 1975), which, as we have already seen, is the major source of psychoanalytic ideas. While he did not say so, it follows that Freud's self-analysis led to a deepening and broadening of the whole analytic process. The total personality could be analyzed only via free association, or a total examination of the patient's functioning.

Hence, it was not the technique that produced the theory, but the theory that produced the technique. The analytic ideal per se is not particularly novel; it is part of the thinking of the French Enlightenment and of democracy in general. But it cannot be taught via simple indoctrination. The French Revolution "ate its own children" as the saying went, and other revolutions also degenerated into massacres and dictatorships. Only recently the Soviets have admitted the truth of all the allegations about Stalin, which they had previously denied, and now the feeling is expressed more and more openly that the whole Marxist system is fallacious. Russia and China are surprisingly moving in a capitalist direction.

What is novel in Freud is the technique of psychoanalysis as a means of teaching the person the good life, or how to be happy. This comes out most clearly in the innovation of training analysis, a unique analytic experience.

Freud had already hinted at the need for training analysis in various ways, for example, in the letters to Putnam cited above. When the analytic institutes were formally established in 1920 in Berlin, the need for formal training analysis was felt most keenly; the analyst can only go as far as the analyst's own complexes permit. The students at Berlin were for the most part the intellectual cream of the crop — doctors, lawyers, professors, highly educated men. Yet they all felt problems in themselves that could be resolved only by personal analysis.

So personal analysis became the sine qua non of analytic competence, and has remained that ever since. At first Freud thought that persons could be analyzed by analyzing their own dreams, as he had done. But while at first he thought that anybody could do this, eventually it appeared that nobody could.

The intensity of the training analysis has varied. While originally it was six hours a week, eventually it was reduced to four a week, and now three (the IPA is willing to recognize three sessions a week under certain circumstances). Knight complained in 1953 that psychoanalysis had attracted too many "normal" characters who just wanted to get through the program without probing themselves too deeply; this is still the case.

It has repeatedly been emphasized by psychoanalytic writers that the most important ingredient in the make-up of a psychoanalyst is a certain aptitude for the task, which depends very strongly on the capacity to penetrate the inner life. Usually, however, this aptitude has been ignored in favor of academic and other credentials. Numbers can be counted; aptitude has to be evaluated. Thus the field has gradually gone over to the professionals with degrees in spite of all wishes of the training authorities to the contrary. With the new regulations of the IPA, it is to be hoped that we will be able to reemphasize talent and aptitude.

In general, it is difficult to specify techniques with absolute precision because of the variability of the patients. In fact, it could be said that the prime weakness in most treatises on technique is that they tend to ignore the special assets and liabilities of the patients involved.

Psychoanalysis and Psychology

The relationship between psychoanalysis and psychology has been a stormy one. Until recently academic psychology ruled out psychoanalysis as "anecdotal" or "unscientific." This assessment was for the most part based on a lack of understanding. It is noteworthy that in a book issued by the APA, *Psychoanalysis as Seen by Psychoanalyzed Psychologists* (1939), almost all the psychologists reacted favorably to their experience, but this did not prevent the academic community from continuing to ostracize psychoanalysis.

In considerable measure, this attitude has been fostered by the misconception of scientific method that is ordinarily taught to psychologists in undergraduate and graduate school (the same criticism applies to all the social sciences). As Nagel put it in his criticism of the "parochial" character of psychological training, science offers responsible explanations of phenomena. Academic psychology, rather than offer such explanations (e.g., of dreams or other phenomena dealt with by psychoanalysis), has preferred to leave the phenomena in question out of the picture. This has limited the field of psychology considerably. It is only with the advent of clinical psychology after World War II that psychoanalysis met with a more receptive audience among psychologists. Actually, many psychologists paid only lip service to the scientific credo of the academic community, as political events in the APA show. Psychologists voted with their feet against the distorted image of science that they were forced to swallow to get their degrees.

There have of course always been exceptions. John Dewey in his presidential address to the APA in 1899 said:

> The psychologist, in his most remote and technical occupation with mechanism, is contributing his bit to that ordered knowledge which alone enables mankind to secure a larger and to direct a more equal flow of values in life.

And the remark of William James to Ernest Jones on the occasion of Freud's visit to America in 1909 has become well known: "Yours is the psychology of the future."

James's remark was indeed prophetic. What Freud built up with the notion of the analytic ideal, and the techniques needed to teach it, was a system of psychology, based, not on flimsy experiments but on direct observation of the human being. For while some psychologists (mostly in the academic community) have embraced the experiment as the cornerstone of all scientific thinking, Wittgenstein, not a psychologist but a good theoretician of science, could say that in experimental psychology problem and method pass one another by.

Thus two psychologies have developed side by side: one experimental, the other psychoanalytic. It is clear that the psychoanalytic is gaining more and more recognition and that it is just as scientific as the experimental. Nevertheless, philosophers of science, who play no clear role in the hierarchy of the sciences, continue to attack psychoanalysis, primarily because they do not understand it. The success of the 1985 lawsuit, it is hoped, will help to change this state of affairs as well (Fine, 1983).

Psychoanalysis and Psychiatry

The psychiatric approach, which is all too often confused with the psychoanalytic, pursues Griesinger's aphorism that "mind disease is brain disease." But in spite of all the advances in neuroscience, the leap from body to mind is still quite mysterious.

If the thesis of the analytic ideal is accepted, it is clear that psychoanalysis is more a branch of philosophy than of medicine, as Freud repeatedly argued. Its central concern is with how people can find happiness, whereas the central concern of psychiatry is with the structure and functioning of the brain. Harold Searles (1965) once wrote:

If the psychoanalytic movement takes refuge in what he would regard essentially as a phenothiazine and genetics flight... then the long dark night of the human soul will have been ushered in, not only for... vast numbers of schizophrenic patients... but also for the profession of psychoanalysis generally and for the patients... whom psychoanalysis treats.

It is commonly but erroneously believed that schizophrenia can be treated only by drug therapy, not by psychotherapy. Many analysts, however, have urged far more psychotherapy for schizophrenia, and practiced it with good results. While we cannot discuss this question in detail, it is worth quoting recognized authorities. Kolb and Brodie in their *Modern Clinical Psychiatry* (1982) write:

Roughly, about one third of those patients who are hospitalized during the first year of their illness make a fairly complete recovery; one third improve and become able to return to outside life but remain damaged personalities and may have to return to the hospital from time to time. The remaining third will require indefinite care and of these perhaps 10 percent need protected institutional care. The introduction of the modern pharmaceutical therapies has not brought about a reduction in the number of schizophrenic patients requiring hospital care whose illness pursues chronic course.

Thus the extensive propaganda in praise of the "drug revolution" appears to be just that — propaganda. In view of the heavy financial investment in these drugs both by the profession and by the patients such propagandistic tactics seem all the more deplorable. (p. 388)

Because psychology bifurcated around 1900, one direction experimental (academic psychology), the other clinical (psychoanalysis), the fundamental significance of Freudian thought has largely been lost on psychologists. The only way in which physicians could incorporate psychoanalysis into their thinking was by being trained analytically. Now that psychologists are also free to undergo psychoanalytic training, it is hoped that this will liberate them from overemphasis on experimentation. Gardner Murphy, author of a standard history of psychology (1960), wrote:

The danger to science today lies not in making too much use of Freud, but in failing to use him as we use Darwin. Freud did build a systematic theory of human behavior, but what stands most in the way of appreciating adherence is his followers' too literal adherence to his verbal formulations. To integrate the theory properly, we have to have a more generous glory-sharing conception of human research in which all the human sciences contribute, one to another. (p. 149)

Here Murphy continues a thought expressed by Freud in 1910: "I am becoming more and more convinced of the cultural value of psychoanalysis and I long for the lucid mind that will draw from it the justified inherences for philosophy and sociology." Even then Freud was clearly hoping for the expansion of psychoanalysis to become a unified science of humankind.

I have indicated my conviction that this expansion takes place best through the concept of the analytic ideal.

Lawsuits can have their value. The destruction of the myth that psychoanalysis is a branch of medicine, a myth opposed by Freud but propagandized by the American psychoanalytic associations is of immense importance (to this day the Academy of Psychoanalysis will not admit non-M.D.'s, although their theoretical views are completely cultural and have no relationships to organic medicine at all). How it will be followed up is a task for the psychologists of the future.

Summary

The major thesis of this book is that there is a value system built into psychoanalysis. Psychoanalysis should be looked upon as a philosophical approach to happiness, rather than as a set of specific techniques. The techniques were developed by Freud as a method of teaching the philosophy, rather than the reverse, which is so often thought to be the case. The implications of this position for the general problems of diagnosis, therapy, and theory are drawn. It is the analytic ideal that represents the true common core of all the approaches that may properly be called psychoanalytic. It is, however, a mistake to try to include everything in the psychoanalytic frame of reference; there are many "schools" that represent obvious absurdities, and psychoanalysis should not be afraid to say so. In this way psychoanalysis comes closer to Freud's hope for a new profession of lay curers of souls, who need not be doctors and should not be priests.

3

The Interminability of Psychoanalysis

*I*T IS NO SECRET THAT PSYCHOANALYSIS TAKES A LONG TIME and the time seems to be growing longer rather than shorter. In 1937 Freud startled the analytic world with his paper "Analysis Terminable and Interminable," in which he made several important points:

(1) Analysis is an essentially interminable process.

(2) To use it to best advantage, the person should go back to analysis every five years or so. This applies to analysts as well as their patients.

(3) It is only in traumatic cases that the analysis can be resolved in a short time. In character analysis, which had already become the mode, it cannot.

(4) The interminability of analysis stems from the structure of the ego, which can never be permanently modified, but reacts to various anxiety-producing events in life, or simply to the course of life, as it is referred to nowadays.

(5) The bedrock that psychoanalysis cannot pierce is passivity in men and penis envy in women.

Since 1937 Freud's views have been discussed in innumerable panels and papers. As far as interminability is concerned, most analysts agree with Freud. As far as the bedrock is concerned, there is considerable divergence, especially since penis envy is no longer seen as the core of women's neurotic difficulties.

Analyses may take a long time, but not a lifetime. Freud laid down the principle that even though in theory analysis may be interminable, in practice termination is a matter dictated by various concrete contingencies. He wrote in this paper:

56

Our object will be not to rub off all the corners of the human character so as to produce "normality" according to schedule, nor yet to demand that the person who has been "thoroughly analyzed" shall never again feel the stirring of passions in himself or become involved in any internal conflicts. The business of analysis is to secure the best possible psychological conditions for the functioning of the ego; when this has been done, analysis has accomplished its task." (SE, XXIII, p 250)

In order to evaluate this position in the light of our present-day knowledge, it is helpful to examine published cases to see what has been done with them. Here, however, an unexpected difficulty arises. In his lifetime Freud published five case histories, of which only one (the Rat Man) was a completed analysis; it involved a man who was killed in World War I, so that no follow-up was possible. Many analysts have not published a single case, so that their writings on the topic of termination have a curious armchair flavor, as though they had never experienced what they are talking about.

In order to clarify the question it is necessary to examine the published cases in the literature. Perhaps in awe of Freud's monumental work, perhaps in fear of criticism, analysts are reluctant to present a whole case; they present case vignettes to illustrate some particular point of theory. But this leaves open the question of what really happened in the total analysis.

Freud's Wolf Man

We can begin with Freud's own most classic case, the Wolf Man. The patient, whose real name, Sergei Pankejeff, was not revealed until after his death, was a wealthy Russian who was in analysis with Freud from 1910 to 1914. He was a helpless young man of twenty-three, accompanied by a private doctor and valet and unable even to dress himself or face any aspect of life. He went through four separate analyses, two with Freud, and two later with Ruth Mack Brunswick. He initiated the first hour of treatment with the offer to have rectal intercourse with Freud and then to defecate on his head (Jones, vol. 2, p. 274). When I tell this to students they immediately respond that he must have been schizophrenic. This is a defect in the training system, which attaches labels rather than seeks humanistic understanding. In point of fact, through his numerous analyses the Wolf Man never really became psychotic. An interesting and unexpected feature of the case is that a Viennese journalist, Karin Obholzer, was in contact with him toward the end of his life, so that we have an unusual follow-up of fifty to sixty years.

Since there is no need to maintain the mystery about his name, I shall refer to him as Pankejeff or Sergei. Sergei lapsed into a stalemate of several years during his analysis with Freud. Then Freud used a new technique and told him that he had resolved to break off the treatment in whatever state the patient was in within a few months, which he did. The end-setting technique, as it has been called, did produce some new memories and the patient went back to Russia in a state of mental health he had never before known.

The patient remained free of any serious neurosis for twelve years after Freud's first treatment and then developed one of an entirely different kind, a paranoid psychosis (Jones, p. 275). In modern terminology he had peculiar paranoid ideas about his nose, which yielded to treatment quickly, so that he would not be considered psychotic today. Ruth Mack Brunswick treated him for four months in 1926–27 and several years later. The American analyst Muriel Gardner was in touch with him all through his life and reported that in 1940 he was still in excellent health.

Obholzer saw him for about five years before his death (although the secrecy persisted, since in her book she does not specify the exact dates when she did see him; one has to read between the lines).

Although Pankejeff denied to Obholzer that he had ever had anything really wrong with him, Jones tells us more details, including the fact that he was in regular correspondence with Pankejeff. The patient, says Jones, suffered from an extremely severe neurosis that rendered him totally incapable of dealing with even the simplest matters in life. He had undergone various treatments, e.g., hydrotherapy and electricity, and had visited sanatoria, all in vain.

He then consulted Prof. Ziehen in Berlin and Prof. Kraepelin in Munich. When he found that they could do nothing for him, he returned to his home in Odessa in despair. Fortunately there he came across a Dr. Drosnes, an enthusiastic believer in psychotherapy, whose optimism raised his hopes again. Drosnes treated him for a while, but realizing how severe the case was, asked him to go to Dubois in Berne and offered to accompany him on the journey. On the way they rested in Vienna for two weeks, and there it was suggested that he give Freud a trial. Freud at once made a deep impression on the patient, but Freud had no vacant hour at that moment. He said, however, that if the patient went to the Cottage Sanatorium for awhile he could see him there. After some hesitation because of his great dislike of sanatoria, the patient agreed and the analysis started. Later

he told Gardner that what impressed him most about Freud was that
Freud assured him that he could relate to women, whereas the others
viewed him as incurably ill and told him to stay away from women.
Later he married a woman, Therese, who had nursed him at one of
the sanatoria.

The patient was preoccupied with money and women. It is revealing that although he lived through three cataclysmic events, the
Russian Revolution, World War I, and World War II the patient never
mentioned them. Once settled in Vienna after World War I, he finished his legal studies and became a lawyer for the government. In
1940, with the outbreak of World War II, he retired on a state pension, and after the suicide of his wife (unexplained since she was a
native German in no danger) he lived to paint and to fornicate. When
Obholzer saw him, at eighty-six, he was in money troubles and trying
to escape from a woman, Louise, who had designs on him. Evidently
he felt constrained to give her money in order to have sex, continuing
his lifelong addiction to prostitutes. In earlier years he had become a
painter contrary to Freud's direct advice. An exhibition of his paint-
ings has been promised but has never materialized, so far as I can
tell.

Since no one else has described encounters with Freud in such
detail, Pankejeff's recollections are worth repeating here. He states in
the book by Muriel Gardner:

I first met Freud in the year 1910. At that time psychoanalysis
and the name of its founder were practically unknown beyond
the borders of Austria. Before I report on how I came into analysis with Freud, however, I should like to recall to you the
desolate situation in which a neurotic found himself at that period before psychoanalysis. A sufferer from neurosis is trying to
find his way back into normal life, as he has come into conflict with his environment and then lost contact with it. His
emotional life has become "inadequate," inappropriate to outer
reality. His goal is not a real known object, but rather some other
object, hidden in his unconscious, unknown to himself. His affect by-passes the real object, accessible to his consciousness.
As long as nothing was known of this state of affairs, only two
explanations were possible: one, that of the layman, concerned
itself with the increase in intensity of affect, which was out of
proportion to the real situation, it was said that the neurotic
exaggerated everything. The other explanation, that of the neurologist or psychiatrist, derived the mental and emotional from

the physical, and sought to persuade the patient that his trouble was due to a functional disorder of the nervous system. The neurotic went to a physician with the wish to pour out his heart to him, and was bitterly disappointed when the physician would scarcely listen to the problems which so troubled him, much less try to understand them.... After the first few hours with Freud I felt that I had at last found what I had so long been seeking.

It was a revelation to me to hear the fundamental concepts of a completely new science of the human psyche from the mouth of its founder. This new concept of psychic processes had nothing to do with the school psychology which I knew from books and which left me cold. I perceived at once that Freud had succeeded in discovering an unexplored region of the human soul, and that if I could follow him along this path a new world would open to me.... The error of classical psychiatry had been that, ignorant of the existence and laws of the unconscious, it derived everything from the physical, from the somatic. A further consequence of this error was a too sharp distinction between healthy and sick.... For Freud the "Breakthrough" to the woman could under certain circumstances be considered the neurotic's greatest achievement, a sign of his will to live, an active attempt to recover.... Although Freud certainly did not underestimate the neurotic in his patients, he attempted always to support and strengthen the kernel of health, separated from the chaff of neurosis.

"This feeling of working together" was increased by Freud's recognition of my understanding of psychoanalysis, so that he even once said it would be good if all his pupils could grasp the nature of analysis as soundly as I.... Freud told me once for example how the "psychoanalytic situation" came about.... Freud told me that originally he had sat at the opposite end of the couch, so that analyst and analysand could look at each other. One female patient, exploiting this situation, made all possible — or rather impossible attempts to seduce him. To rule out anything similar, once and for all, Freud moved from his earlier position to the opposite end of the couch....

In the weeks before the end of my analysis, we often spoke of the danger of the patient's feeling too close a tie to the therapist. If the patient remains "stuck" in the transference, the success of the treatment is not a lasting one, as it soon becomes evident that the original neurosis has been replaced by another. In this connection Freud was of the opinion that at the end of treatment a gift from the patient could contribute, as a symbolic act, to lessening his feeling of gratitude and his consequent dependence on the physician. So we agreed that I would give Freud something as a remembrance. As I knew of his love for archeology, the gift I chose for him was a female Egyptian figure, with a mitershaped headdress. Freud placed it on his desk. Twenty years later, looking through a magazine it was still there. (p. 135ff.)

The Wolf Man's history can be summed up this way, from all the sources available. Born to a wealthy Russian family in which his father, one uncle, and his sister were all mentally unstable (all died of suicide), Sergei was neurotic from an early age. Gonorrhea in his adolescence made his situation much worse. He dropped out of law school and wandered around Europe, looking for a psychiatrist to help him. Finally he got to Freud, for whom he developed an immediate positive transference.

Freud saw him for four years, working through the patient's childhood conflicts, as a result of which he was much improved. He settled down, married Therese, became a lawyer in Vienna, and painted as a hobby. In the period between the two wars he was relatively calm, though he did develop one neurotic symptom about a spot on his nose. This passed too.

At the outbreak of World War II his wife, Therese, committed suicide. He then became an indefatigable chaser of women, largely prostitutes. He lived out his life on his state pension. Toward the end of his life when Karin Obholzer approached him, he developed a transference to her too. In the meantime he had taken up with Louise, who was milking him of his money; evidently he was helpless in her hands. Shortly before the end of his life he was in a mental hospital for awhile. No explanation is given to this episode. He was seen by a number of analysts in the last few years of his life; he became the showpiece of psychoanalysis.

Was this case successful or not? He did get over the infantile neurosis for which he came to Freud, but then after his wife's suicide he regressed again. He was always a solitary man (nowhere does he speak of any friends) whose sexual life was, after his wife's death, largely with prostitutes.

There it all is, for better or worse. As Freud once commented, the only true control to test analysis is for the patient to live out his life all over again and see what happens.

Freud left an analyzed patient, a magnificent theory, and many questions. Should the patient have been terminated when he was?

How are we to evaluate the ultimate outcome? No good answers are available.

In any case it is clear that Freud introduced a humanistic element into his therapy that was totally absent from that of the other psychiatrists of that day. He spoke to him of love, of work, of sexuality, and the other components of the analytic ideal. Freud short-circuited the process by encouraging the patient to get married, a decision he later regretted. But the times were so chaotic (World War I had just ended, Austrian inflation was raging, the world was entering the turmoil that led to World War II) that it is understandable that Freud wanted a successful result to show the world.

After Freud left the scene two questions became particularly prominent: (1) What does psychoanalysis do? and (2) Can analysis be shortened? In his 1937 paper he attempted to answer these questions.

The unity, such as it was, of the early psychoanalytic movement was shattered when it moved to America. There psychoanalysis was confronted by psychiatry, with its organic claims, by psychology, with superficial therapy of the Rogerian variety, and by social work, with its Lady Bountiful tradition. Conflict, confusion, and controversy have marked the course of psychoanalysis ever since.

In 1947 a Committee on the Evaluation of Psychoanalytic Therapy was set up within the American Psychoanalytic Association (Rangell, 1954). In the years of its work since then, this committee was never able to pass beyond the initial and vexatious point of trying to arrive at some modicum of agreement as to exactly what constitutes psychoanalysis, psychoanalytic psychotherapy, and possible transitional forms. In its last report in 1982 the committee not only failed to arrive at any acceptable formulation in this regard but was forced to conclude, incredibly enough, "that a strong resistance to any investigation of this problem existed among the members of the American Psychoanalytic Association" (Rangell, 1954, p. 735).

The rules of the American Psychoanalytic Association on what is good psychoanalysis are arbitrary statements not buttressed by any survey data or objective findings. The same holds true for the rules of the International Psychoanalytical Association. There is certainly room for discussion and research here, but it is not likely to come from official circles, which discourage any honest soul searching or objective experimentation. The sharp distinction between psychoanalysis and psychotherapy drawn by the official bodies, for example, has repeatedly been questioned. One of the member institutes of the Committee on Evaluation of Psychoanalytic Therapy stated: "There is unanimous opinion in our group that no sharp demarcation can be drawn between psychoanalysis and psychoanalytic therapy" (Rangell, 1954, p. 736).

The same conclusion was reached by Wallerstein in his survey (1986) of forty-two patients treated at the Menninger Clinic. Yet the sharp split between psychoanalysis and psychoanalytic therapy is upheld by the official bodies.

Subsequent developments have not cleared up the early uncertainties. The Committee on Evaluation of Psychoanalytic Therapy gave up its task and was turned into a fact-finding committee. After the establishment of two more committees, a third committee was appointed, which issued a report in 1987 (Hamburg et al., 1967). In the meantime a large percentage of the original data had been lost. Under these circumstances the whole enterprise can only be labelled a total fiasco; we remain in the dark about what psychoanalysis really is and what its effects are.

In its report in 1967, the committee stated:

> Since specifying the diagnostic category had proven, over the years, to be most frustrating to the participating analysts, and probably quite unreliable as well (and the reliability not subject to check) we decided to eliminate the original diagnostic categories from further use.

The diagnoses were eliminated but replaced by other psychiatric categories, not humanistic ones, thus negating the whole thrust of Freudian theory. There was no doubt that medical psychoanalysis was eager to move closer to psychiatry, which is where these dubious diagnoses originated. However, in the *Diagnostic and Statistical Manual*, third edition, these diagnoses still stand, in one form or another, while most of the case histories cited come from Kraepelin, who, one might think, could have been eliminated from the picture by now. The whole question of diagnosis and the outcome of analysis has entered the political arena, from which it is difficult to disentangle it.

Politics means money, and not surprisingly in the lawsuit between the American Psychoanalytic Association and the psychologists (GAPP), one outstanding member of the American after another testified that the only reason for excluding lay analysts from the American was financial (lawsuit protocol). The minutes of a 1981 meeting of American members bluntly stated: "There was never any question during the discussion about the feasibility of nonmedical training." And in 1983 Dr. Robert S. Wallerstein stated to the executive council of the IPA:

Now that it [the issue of training non-M.D.'s] is coming to a vote, the climate has shifted back the other way, and very strongly. For two reasons — one is economic; there are less patients and people will say quite openly, "We've got to keep this patient population for ourselves, the M.D.'s, but also the reimbursement through the national insurance systems, and if we've got any chance of getting in on that, we have got to cut ourselves off from non-M.D.'s." *The economic pressure is very strong.* But there is another reason: "We want to maintain our position with Medicine, and within Psychiatry, again by distancing ourselves from our nonmedical colleagues." (lawsuit protocol, p. 66)

An impartial observer would say, as Freud did in 1929, that truth is being sacrificed to economic interests (Fine, 1982).

Inasmuch as psychoanalysis still has had no official recognition, the American Psychoanalytic Association applied to the Federal Office of Education a number of times, the last in 1975, to be the official certifying board for psychoanalysis. This request was rejected, after which the group turned to internal certification. All members were invited to take an examination to be certified. In this process, about one third were turned down, even though they were graduates of component societies of the American and in practice a long time (lawsuit; personal communication from Clifford Stromberg).

These political developments and the failure of the committees to define psychoanalysis have led to much uncertainty and confusion. It can only be said that the field is wide open for new suggestions. It is in this spirit that I have proposed the analytic ideal as the basis for diagnosis therapy and education (cf. paper by Montville, *JAPA*, 1989, #2).

We can return now to our examination of completed cases in the literature.

Wallerstein's Phobic Woman

In 1986 Wallerstein published his book *Forty-two Lives in Treatment*, which described the results of an eight-year study at the Menninger Foundation. Of twenty-two patients started in analysis, of whom sixteen were maintained formally in analysis throughout their entire treatment, eight had very good, clear-cut treatment outcomes. Of these he reports two cases in considerable detail.

One he calls the phobic woman. The patient's overt illness (according to Wallerstein) had started at age four: she cried and howled, terrified, when her mother was supposed to leave her on her first day at kindergarten. This separation crying typically occurred whenever the parents tried to leave her with a baby-sitter, so that the family took her everywhere if at all feasible (she was an only child). At fifteen, an embarrassing episode with her schoolmates (she was censured for openly kissing several boys at a party) precipitated a phobic reaction to returning to school and a referral for psychotherapy. She suffered a widening fear of being left alone, and soon had to be accompanied everywhere by one of her parents or a close friend. When she was taken into the Menninger study, she was twenty-three years old and had been in therapy since she was fifteen.

The patient was in analysis four years and nine months (1,012 hours). Though the treatment was avowedly classical analysis, the analyst also played a directly guiding and encouraging role in getting the patient to confront her phobic situation and, as the treatment proceeded, to enter into a more active sexual life, expand her social life, have a child, and go on with her education.

Through the analysis two life events stood out as of signal intrapsychic importance. The first the birth of her first child. The patient was actively encouraged in this by the analyst; it was clear to her that he "looked on it with favor." The second was a gift of $75,000 from her father, which had a dual and contradictory meaning. It provided a perpetual gratification of the patient's dependency strivings.

A follow-up is available twenty years after treatment termination. The patient and her husband now live in another state. Both of them are mental health professionals; they practice together as "sex counselors" (in the follow-up study, there was an evasiveness about discussing her own sexual life and hints that she was still beset by inhibitions). They have four children, all presumably doing well. The patient has had no further therapy; she seems to have no troubling phobic constraints.

Although the results seem good, Wallerstein himself has some reservations. He regards it as a "transference cure" in which she made progress for the sake of the beloved analyst, but did not fully work out her transference to him. Transference, of course, is a debatable point in the literature: many analysts feel that the transference can never be fully resolved, while others feel that it can.

While she is called a phobic woman, her clinging dependency is even more noticeable than her phobia, and this too was apparently never resolved.

In any case, we have here an excellent example of dramatic change through the analytic process — the formerly shy, frightened, clinging little girl became a mature "sex counselor" and mother, able to function independently in the mature world.

Her case could very well be described in terms of the analytic ideal. It is notable how Wallerstein avoids all psychiatric jargon, except for the title "phobic woman," and discusses her problems and her progress in human terms.

Kohut's Mr. Z

Kohut's case of Mr. Z, "The Two Analyses of Mr. Z," has historical importance in that Kohut used it to bolster his new theory of the self and the system of self psychology. His analysis took place in two series of sessions, each conducted five times a week and lasting about four years; the series were separated by an interval of about five and one-half years. The second series occurred when Kohut was writing *The Analysis of the Self*, which coincided with the period in which he was testing a new frame of reference, "a new viewpoint which allowed me to perceive meanings or the significance of meanings which I had formerly not consciously perceived" (p. 3).

The patient was a graduate student in his midtwenties who lived with his widowed mother in very comfortable financial circumstances; the father, who had died about four years earlier, had not only been a highly successful business executive but had himself inherited a considerable fortune. Mr. Z was an only child.

The complaints were initially quite vague. He complained of a number of somatic symptoms, extrasystole, sweaty palms, feelings of fullness in the stomach, and periods of either constipation or diarrhea. He felt socially isolated because he was unable to form any relationship with girls.

When he was about three and a half, his father became seriously ill and was hospitalized for several months. During this hospitalization, his father fell in love with a nurse who was taking care of him, and he went to live with her. He stayed with her for about a year and a half, then broke off with her and returned home.

The theme that was most conspicuous during the first year of the analysis was that of a regressive mother transference. In the course of the early analytic material he revealed that when he was about eleven he had been involved in a homosexual relationship, lasting about two years, with a thirty-year-old high school teacher. The patient evidently had no feelings of guilt or remorse about this affair, nor did Kohut see its relevance to his later difficulties with girls.

In the first part of the analysis Mr. Z's masochistic preoccupations disappeared and at the end were almost nonexistent. He moved from his mother's house to an apartment of his own, and finally he not only began to date but also had several sexually active, brief relationships with women of approximately his own age, cultural background, and educational level.

About six months before termination he had a dream that related to the time when his father rejoined the family; he was in a house at the inner side of a door that was a crack open. Outside was his father, loaded with gift-wrapped packages, wanting to enter. The patient was immediately frightened and attempted to close the door in order to keep his father out.

In spite of the apparently good result, Kohut felt that it had come about as the direct result of the mobilization and the working through of nuclear conflicts. Yet there was something wrong: "What was wrong at that time is much harder to describe than what seemed to be right."

At about four and one-half years after termination, Mr. Z let Kohut know that he was again having difficulties.

In the second analysis the most important new material was the overt psychosis of his mother. Kohut now focused on the pathological personality of his mother and his enmeshment with her. She had always been an odd person and had involved him in many bizarre rituals, such as the inspection of his feces and the inspection and removal of his blackheads. The second analysis focused on the depression and hopelessness that the mother's attitude evoked in him. But Kohut frankly admits that he had overlooked the pathology of the mother relationship in the first analysis. He says:

> We are again confronted by the puzzling question why this crucial material had not appeared during Mr. Z's first analysis. To be sure it had appeared but — what is even more incomprehensible — it had failed to claim our attention. I believe that we come closest to the solution of this puzzle when we say that a crucial aspect of the transference had remained unrecognized in the first analysis. Put concisely: my theoretical convictions, the convictions of a classical analyst who saw the material that the patient presented in terms of infantile drives and of conflicts about them, and of agencies of a mental apparatus either clashing or cooperating with each other had become for the patient a replica of the mother's hidden psychosis, of a distorted outlook on the world to which he had adjusted as reality....(p. 15)

In the second analysis Kohut concentrated on what happened to the self-image of the little boy. But as he himself frankly admits, the pathological material and the sick aspects of the transference had simply been overlooked. At this point Kohut switched to a new paradigm — self psychology. There is nothing in classical analysis that prevents one from talking about the self (Rangell, 1982) or from relating the patient's difficulties to his mother's psychosis. Later Kohut was able to trace the boy's move from mother to father — again reinterpreting it in terms of self psychology.

Self psychology has been considered in many places. It is essentially a cult phenomenon, separate from the mainstream of psychoanalytic development. In this case it becomes clear that it arose from a transference error on Kohut's part. Its main ideas have been considered in great detail and found wanting by most analysts (*JAPA*, 1982).

In this case Kohut in the second analysis took up the pathological relationship with the mother, and the shift from mother to father, which he had omitted in the first analysis. He blames this omission on classical analysis rather than his own blindness.

Self analysis will be discussed in more detail below. Suffice it to say here that the self has been an essential part of psychoanalytic theory, but since it was not discussed in detail by Freud, it has been omitted from theoretical discussions (Brenner, 1982). In the most extreme Freudian theories, people were entirely omitted. This was only partially true of Freud himself. In the case of the Wolf Man, for example, the psychosis and suicide of his father were not taken up seriously. But as Sandler has commented (1983) psychoanalytic theory has not moved forward in a straight line, but irregularly. The inclusion of interpersonal relationships in various ways is one of the moves that must be integrated into a full psychology.

The main question in this chapter is termination. What does this case contribute to termination theory? When Kohut began to bring in the relationships with the parents, the case moved along more swiftly and smoothly, and the patient was able to terminate. Regardless of the terminology, his termination was based on a satisfactory resolution of his interpersonal difficulties, again a humanistic rather than a psychiatric accomplishment.

Sandler's "Body as Phallus"

In 1959 Sandler published a case history with the title "The Body as Phallus." It was the digest of a two-year analysis of an airline navigator, South American in origin. The presenting symptoms were that he would lose his erection whenever he got into bed with a woman, even though he had no difficulty getting women to go to bed with him.

In the analysis it appeared that he had shared a bed with his mother for the first sixteen years of his life. When the interpretation was first offered that he wanted to have sex with mother, he denied it vehemently; eventually he came to see its pertinence.

His mother was an extraordinary woman. From the early years of her marriage she had several lovers, and during periods of crisis she managed to sustain the family through donations from "friends." His father had once been wealthy, but he had lost his business. His mother continually reproached his father for being impotent, and it seemed certain that he must have known of her frequent infidelities. She had transferred to the patient, her only child, many of the feelings that she might otherwise have lavished on her husband. His mother treated his father with disdain and contempt.

His mother was seductive in the extreme. The patient would be entertained each morning by his mother doing physical exercises in front of him in the nude. She would also ask him to scratch her when in bed, and he believed that he had occasionally scratched her pubic hairs. She would sleep on her side with her back toward him.

His mother's nudism was not confined to the bedroom, for she would bathe at a special part of the seaside reserved for nudists, and would take her son with her, even when he was an adolescent. She introduced him to her female acquaintances (also in the nude) as her brother or her "friend." This continued until the patient left home in his late teens. As he recalled this in the session, he experienced great embarrassment, blushing fiercely, saying that he had a feeling as if his leg were cut off. The analyst now showed him that being with his mother must very naturally have excited him sexually and that his sexual excitement must have led him to have erections — which frightened him terribly; he would then wish that his penis would be cut off so that it would not give him away. If he had shown his mother by his erection that he was sexually excited, then he would surely not have been allowed to remain with her in bed. This process was repeated whenever a woman undressed, which led to his loss of erection As analysis progressed, he became more and more excited and more and more afraid of showing his thoughts and his excitement to the analyst; as a result he felt impotent in the analysis. He described another symptom, blushing, as a feeling that his whole body was swelling up, that his body was being filled with blood and felt as if it were going to burst. It was pointed out that when he blushed he reacted as if his whole body were a penis and that the blushing was a substitute for erection. When he had blushed in the analytic session, it revealed his underlying wishes toward the analyst and in this the analyst represented his mother.

Thereafter it became clear that the fear of erection pervaded his whole existence. At school he would first show promise and then fail. At the university when he enrolled for a course in chemistry, he liked the professor but failed to attend for his final examination. Later he had trained as a pilot and had done very well until the final examination, when he failed. Specifically he was persistently unable to place the undercarriage of the aircraft properly when landing; as a consequence he was made a navigator. He excelled at one subject, astro-navigation, and when this was linked with his sexual fantasies at night, he revealed that his mother's name was Estrella (star).

Apart from his identification with his impotent father, it gradually emerged that the patient defended himself against sensations from his penis by a psychical dissociation of the penis from the rest of the body.

In telling the analyst of his relationship with his mother, he referred to himself as "Dodo" and told the analyst that it was Dodo who wanted to screw his mother. However, Dodo and he were not the same person. He said that he felt a splitting of himself into two whenever he was with a woman, and also in certain situations with men.

With the working through of his defenses against erection, he found himself increasingly capable of intercourse with his wife. His financial situation also improved, because he could now allow himself to win at poker.

The patient's symptoms cleared up rather dramatically, and in the course of the analysis he had insight into his homosexual wishes, castration fear and castration wishes, fantasies of being castrated as a defense against sexual excitement, inhibition of feelings, the dissociation of body and penis, strong guilt feelings toward the father, and a negative Oedipus complex. All of these and related feelings could be expanded to illuminate his entire life.

While the analyst in this case could focus most strongly on the sexual feelings, which were easy to analyze because his mother's seductiveness was so much out in the open, sooner or later all the components of the analytic ideal could be brought up. Eventually his fear of becoming a father was overcome; he was able to get his wife pregnant and enjoy the whole family feeling.

Winnicott's Schizoid Physician

The British analyst Donald Winnicott made many contributions to psychoanalytic theory and practice. Perhaps the most important is his concept of the "holding environment." What the analyst does, according to this theory, is to provide a holding environment in which the patient can develop. It is similar to the mother-child situation, in which the mother provides the social support that allows the child to pursue its own growth. In 1986 Winnicott's heirs, particularly his widow, published a fragment of an analysis by Winnicott that illustrated this principle.

Winnicott states that this fragment is given as an illustration of the depressive position as it can appear in the course of an analysis. The patient was a man of thirty, married, with two children. He had a period of analysis with Winnicott during World War II, which had to be broken off because of war conditions as soon as he became clinically well enough to work. In the first phase he came in a state of depression with a strong homosexual coloring but without manifest homosexuality. He was in a bemused state and rather unrealistic. He developed little insight although he improved clinically so that he could do war work. His very good mind enabled him to juggle with concepts and to philosophize, and in serious conversations he was generally thought of as an interesting man with ideas.

He qualified for his father's profession, but this did not satisfy him and he soon became a medical student, probably (unconsciously) retaining Winnicott as a father figure displacing his real father, who had died.

He married and in so doing offered a woman who needed it a chance for therapy through dependence. He hoped (unconsciously) that in this marriage he was laying down a basis for a therapy through dependence for himself but, as so often happens, when he in turn claimed special tolerance from his wife he failed to get it. She fortunately refused to be his therapist, and it was partly his recognition of this that led him to a new phase of illness. He broke down at work (as a doctor in a hospital) and was admitted to an institution himself, suffering form unreality feelings and a general inability to cope with work and with life.

He was not aware at that time that he was seeking out his former analyst and was quite incapable even of asking for analysis; this is precisely what he was doing and nothing else would have been of value. After about a month of the new analysis he was able to resume work as a hospital officer. He was by this time a schizoid case. His sister had had a schizophrenic illness treated with considerable success by psychoanalysis. He came to analysis saying that he could not talk freely, that he had no small talk or play capacity, and that he could not make spontaneous gestures or get excited.

At first his speech was deliberate and rhetorical. Gradually it became clear that he was listening to conversations that were going on within and reporting any parts of these conversations that he thought might interest the analyst. In time he talked about himself as a mother or father might bring a child to an analyst and talk about the child. In these early phases, lasting six months, Winnicott felt he had no chance of direct conversation with the child, i.e., himself. By a very special route the analysis changed in quality, so that the analyst became able to deal directly with the child, who was the patient.

There was a definite end to this phase, and the patient said that he now came himself for treatment and for the first time felt hopeful. He was more than ever conscious of being unexcitable and lacking spontaneity. He could scarcely blame his wife for finding him a dull companion, unalive except in serious discussion of a topic set by someone else. Actual potency was not disturbed, but he had difficulty making love and he could not generally get excited about sex. He had one child, and has since had a second one.

In this new phase the material gradually led to a transference neurosis of a classical type. There came a short phase leading obviously to excitement, oral in quality. The excitement led to the work described in detail in the case notes (Winnicott gives a long recital of case notes taken during or immediately after the sessions). The case notes refer to the work done between the excitement that arrived in the transference but which was not felt, and the experience of the excitement.

The first sign of the new development was reported as a feeling, quite new, of love for his daughter. He felt this on the way home from a cinema where he had actually cried. He had cried tears twice in that week, and this seemed to him to be a good omen, as he had been unable either to cry or to laugh, just as he had been unable to love.

By force of circumstances he could come only three times a week, but Winnicott allowed that. The patient was most inarticulate for a long time, even falling asleep in some sessions. In a typical session he associated as follows:

> If I do not start I have a definite fear that I won't be able to begin. Each second provides a mounting difficulty and I also talk because I can't bear the time wasted, though of course trivial-

ities may be a waste too. This applies in my relationship with other people. I have a need to find something to say, though I probably feel like saying nothing for hours. I would like a relationship in which it was not necessary to talk or there could be a jumble of words and phrases and that would be no use. This happens with my wife. I try to say what comes, try to be natural, but there is nothing but a jumble of ideas. This seems artificial, glib. I am talkative, trying to be light hearted, but the result is confusion. This is why people lose interest in me. At times that could happen here and you would not be able to take in what I was saying because it would be too confused. That is why I edit everything. (p. 135)

After about two years of the second analysis, the patient received an appointment to a hospital some distance from London and could no longer come to treatment. His last communication, some nine months after termination, was as follows:

Dear Dr. Winnicott,
I feel that I owe you an apology for not writing before. When I last got in touch with you I decided to stop at least until Easter while I was working at ... and then let you know.
On the whole it has proved very satisfactory and my plans, so far, are to continue as at present until my appointment expires next August.
I am not at all sure what I will be doing after that. It is not yet possible for me to plan that far ahead. I am tempted at times to abandon analysis as I now feel so well. On the other hand, I realize that the process is incomplete and I may then decide to resume with you, or should that no longer be possible, to start with someone else. It seems to me to be a great step forward that I can accept that idea fairly easily.
Should we not resume later on, I would like to use this opportunity to express my gratitude for all that you have done....

In this case, a depressed physician with a poor capacity for communication did his best to tell Winnicott everything that was on his mind; Winnicott was acting as the good mother or the holding environment. This tactic worked out well, and the patient experienced considerable improvement, as well as insights into the various aspects of the analytic ideal. Had circumstances been right, he would have continued with Winnicott. But fate would have it otherwise. It is noteworthy that the patient himself recognized that the process of freeing him from his inhibitions was virtually interminable. Here too the case is best understood in the light of the analytic ideal.

In 1989 the Stolorows (*International Journal of Psychoanalysis*, 70, pp. 315ff.) published a case of what they called a delusional merger. Jessica, an attractive yet somewhat masculine-looking actress, entered psychoanalysis therapy at the age of twenty-six. The difficulties she initially described pertained to painful feelings of jealousy, which created arguments with her boyfriend and a "not-so-good" feeling about herself.

While this was the presenting symptom, it soon became clear that her disruptive affect states were often experienced somatically as episodic spells of dizziness, fainting, vomiting, and other gastrointestinal symptoms. Within a few sessions it became apparent that Jessica had been suffering from serious chronic depression punctuated by states of emptiness and suicidal thoughts and behavior. She felt that because of her psychosomatic ailments, particularly insomnia and nightmares, people would see her as strange and not quite right. One of her initial fears in the transference was that the therapist would see how "bad" she was and would realize that she should not be alive. Thus Jessica craved reassurance that the therapist both wanted her to live and would take a strong stand to this effect on her behalf.

Jessica's fears became more understandable as aspects of her inner world unfolded. When the anniversary of an older brother's death approached, for example, she became overtly suicidal. She was afraid both that she would die and that the therapist's life was in danger. Soon it became evident that her brother, Justin, who had died some twelve years prior to the beginning of treatment, had literally taken over her life in a most profound and fundamental way: Justin had become "part" of her. Not only did he live within her; she was convinced that she had become he. She felt she had no distinct entity — Jessica did not really exist.

In spite of her intense anxiety, she could not even imagine the reliable presence of a calming, benign parental figure. The closest she had ever come to such an experience was with her now-deceased brother, Justin, who during his short life gave her a sense of being loved and cared for.

The background for these feelings was brought out in the therapy. When Jessica was twelve years old, Justin was diagnosed as having a rare and usually fatal disease and for two painful years went through a seemingly endless barrage of treatments. During those years she experienced a sudden loss of Justin, who now had to spend many hours with the doctors, and also of her mother, who threw herself into the ultimately fruitless search for a cure. From the time the disease was discovered until her brother's death Jessica saw very little of either of them. Her mother would at times reassure her that Justin was really fine and there was no reason to worry, but of course this was contrary to what Jessica perceived. Even the night before Justin's death her mother was still swearing that he'd be okay.

The family never talked openly about what was happening to Justin or to the family. As Justin's health worsened and death became imminent, Jessica's parents seemed to picture Justin in ever more idealized, even godlike terms. At the same time they began to "see" more and more qualities that Jessica and Justin shared in common. Both parents felt that the two children looked more alike than ever before, and even Jessica, who since Justin's illness had been very frightened of being like him, started to become convinced that she really did bear a strong mental and physical resemblance to her older brother.

Jessica's father, who had been quite involved with the family, had a particularly difficult time with Justin's illness. During these years, and for many following Justin's death, the father could not look at Jessica because he perceived such a strong resemblance between her and Justin. Her father thereby showed his inability to experience Jessica as a separate person, distinct from his son. Like the experience of being shunned by her schoolmates, this too contributed to Jessica's delusion that she was Justin. "If your father can't even look at you, there must be a good reason. I reminded him too much of Justin."

Jessica's parents continued to fuel the delusion that their son had been transported into the body and mind of his younger sister. Jessica was, in effect, sacrificed to maintain the denial of their son's death. After Justin's death, all pictures of Jessica were removed from the house, except those in which Jessica showed a striking resemblance to Justin. Additionally, her parents would deny that Jessica had any likes or dislikes that were inconsistent with what Justin had liked or disliked. She felt required to take on all of Justin's qualities, feelings, and thoughts — his favorite food, sport, and even the clothes he liked to wear. Jessica's father refused to see her for many years following the death, which meant to her that he did not see her as a separate person and could not face the fact that he had lost a son. By incorporating and becoming Justin, Jessica protected her parents from the loss they could not tolerate.

The authors theorized that the case of Jessica provides a particularly clear example of the derailment of the developmental process of self-differentiation — the evolving sense of being a distinct center of affective experience and personal agency, with individualized aims and goals. From the material presented, however, the case permits of a more parsimonious explanation, more in line with the conceptualization of the analytic ideal. The parents, for whatever reason, were killing Jessica. The mother had experienced attending to Jessica's emotional state and needs as an odious burden, particularly when Jessica was very small and her father was virtually unavailable as an alternative source of care-giving functions. As with the marasmus cases uncovered by Spitz (1965), a child who is emotionally deprived of the parents' love tends to die. In this case Jessica experienced the death of herself as a separate entity. The case is almost reminiscent of the Japanese suicide of the followers of the Rev. Jim Jones in Guyana in 1978. One of the kamikazes wrote: "Insignificant little pebbles that we are, the degree of our devotion does not falter, as for our country we move toward our final rest" (Hoyt, 1983).

In the case of Jessica, the destruction of her soul took place at the behest of her parents, who must have had an extraordinary hatred of her. The Stolorows do not discuss the parents in the case of Jessica; they merely discuss the way in which they freed her to have a self of her own.

Here too love is the central issue. The parents loved Justin, but not Jessica (why is not made clear). The result was a soul murder, similar to that which Schreber experienced at the hand of his sadistic father (Freud, 1911).

This case may also be generalized to explain the development of various personality structures. The child unconsciously behaves in ways that gain the approval of the parents, viewing such behavior as "natural and normal" and eventually as coming from within. Again here the analytic ideal provides the best theoretical explanation of the events.

Firestein's Bisexual Actress

In 1978 Firestein of the New York Psychoanalytic Institute published his book *Termination in Psychoanalysis*, which reviewed the cases of eight analysts in training at the Institute. His work related directly to the problem under consideration here.

The main questions that Firestein investigated were what happens during termination, and why? The cases had to be terminated according to some logic inherent in the psychoanalytic process. Four such cases were identified. In all, the importance of countertransference factors in the termination phase stood out.

The study method was then revised to focus upon cases entering the termination phase under supervision. Successive canvasses of the Institute faculty yielded eight cases that were expected to be suitably terminated within approximately two years.

The method involved recorded interviews with the treating analysts at intervals of some weeks, depending upon the rhythm of developments in the case. These data were supplemented by (1) Firestein's summary of the pretermination analysis; (2) metapsychological summary by the treating analyst of the early portion of the analysis and its termination phase; (3) follow-up interview of the patient, when possible, a year or more subsequent to the date of termination; (4) interview of the faculty supervisor, who was offered a preliminary opportunity to review all the material of the investigator's case summary; (5) summary of the interview with the supervisor. One case may be examined in more detail, to evaluate the results obtained.

Marian W. (pp. 112ff.), an actress, sought analysis during her twenties primarily because of persistent depression and to a lesser degree possibly to break a conflicted homosexual pattern. The depression that spurred treatment had been initiated by the ending of a year-long homosexual affair with another, older performing artist. The latter had eventually precipitated the rupture by treating the patient cruelly. Yet in her subsequent loneliness the patient had felt even worse, and had thought of killing herself.

Little detailed information about Marian's childhood is given. She was the younger of two sisters. Her father revealed his disappointment that the patient was not a boy. The patient's mother was a mild-mannered, self-denying person, completely focused upon housewifely activities. She was prone to elicit sympathy by presenting a pathetic, implicitly reproachful appearance. Marian reported some shared parental preoccupation with conversation about sex, as well as maternal structures against any manipulation of anus or genitals.

Under the influence of her father's teaching, the patient became a tomboy, proficient in sports and mechanical skills. Her father simultaneously encouraged independence and yet tried to keep the patient in a close relationship with himself. For example, he gave her an automobile, yet was miffed when she did not ask him to chauffeur her around. He tried to influence her training, but she rebelled, and never acquired certain important skills upon which he insisted.

Late in childhood, Marian was strongly influenced by her sister, with whom she shared a room. In her earliest years, the patient had been so often rejected when she tried to cuddle with her sister that she took a variety of transitional objects to bed with her instead. Marian found herself in a conflict of loyalties between father and sister. He took her along to the sister's acting studio. When her sister changed teachers, she refused to have Marian accompany her any longer, which meant the temporary end of the patient's acting lessons. Marian decided to pursue a career in the theater with the thought of performing with her sister. This decision was confirmed during high school years when her sister had already demonstrated acting talent.

In elementary school Marian had difficulty using the school toilets if observed by other children. As a consequence she had occasional bowel and bladder accidents. Her problem with using the toilet persisted through high school. During the analysis Marian revealed that at about the age of six she developed a pattern of anal stimulation through relaxation of her anal sphincter and almost having a bowel movement. She also recollected exploring her anus and genitals with her finger during childhood. She attempted to give her doll an enema. Actual genital masturbation was attempted once, during adolescence, but promptly ceased because of feelings of guilt, not to be resumed until ten years later when she was in analysis. Marian had a vague recollection of some sexual play with her sister, when she crawled into bed with her during the earliest years. In childhood, she guiltily stole from stores, once taking a cylindrical toy, which she placed in her pants, pretending it was a penis.

When she dated during adolescence, Marian went to some lengths to avoid the possibility of being rejected by boys. She avoided group situations because of their emphasis on open rivalry with other girls, but sometimes she did date other girls' special boy friends.

Although she developed normally, menarche did not occur until midadolescence, a little late. Marian regarded menstruation as dirty and disgusting. She was paradoxically ignorant of sexual matters, such as the nature of menstruation, until some time during her analysis.

In high school and acting school, the patient had crushes on several teachers, yearning for and fantasizing sexual intimacy with some. Significantly, these infatuations cropped up when there was some normal separation from her sister. During this time, and later on, the patient had important relationships with a number of men, among them several teachers. These were characterized by marked ambivalence, oscillating between great admiration and resentful nit-picking.

Prior to and at the outset of the analysis, the patient's sex life had assumed a pattern in which a sexual interest in a man was followed by withdrawal in anger, which was succeeded by wishes, and perhaps action, aimed at impossibly idealized relations with a woman, both sexual and loving. The same sequence unfolded early in the analytic transference and was maintained for some time. Certain content would lead to expression of erotic feelings toward the analyst, followed by tears and then silence. The next day there would be reserve and frequently anger at the analyst, coupled with fantasies or actions directed toward sexual intimacy with women.

The first dream reported after a month of analysis had a homosexual manifest content. She behaved in the analytic hours on many occasions as though she were a man, wearing pants and affecting a gruff voice. In her lovemaking with her roommate she pretended to be a man who could do for her partner what no man had been able to do. Gradually a pattern emerged in which the patient experienced loving or sexual feelings for the analyst, struggled to evade verbalizing them, and then expressed a more masculine mode of feeling and behavior.

Just before the end of the first year of analysis Marian had a strong urge to depart from the analyst. At the same time she abandoned her soon-to-depart roommate by sexual involvement with a different woman partner.

During this final prerecess month, Marian also began an affair with a man. From then on she alternated sexual activity with male and female partners.

When she failed to reestablish the sexual tie with her roommate, she took up with another woman with whom the sexual relationship persisted for two years. In this relationship she fantasized being a man. This affair also marked the waning and ending of her homosexuality.

During the second year of treatment, the choice of passive men was prominent. She would manipulate the situation so that the man would give her some important gift, and then she would break off with him. At one time Marian asserted that in fact for a long time she believed that she had a penis.

Early in the third year of treatment she acquired a new boyfriend, and the relationship became sexual. Difficulty in orgasm led to a dream, the manifest content of which was that she and the analyst were about to make love, but considerations related to his wife and daughter interfered.

Marian now began to masturbate, as a sequel to a dream of masturbating in her room in her parents' home. She could regularly achieve orgasm with masturbation, while in coitus this was a rare experience. Subsequently she alternated between close relationships with men and with women.

In numerous sessions Marian expressed anger at the analyst, sometimes by lateness that was interpreted as an effort to control and dominate him. These expressions were succeeded by increased sexual activity with her boyfriend and her first orgasm with any man — albeit by direct clitoral stimulation. Her next reported dream was of the analyst handing her a bomb.

Frequent wishes to be a star emerged, coupled with strong yearnings for the analyst, which also involved much anger at him. Then she presented a number of dreams with manifest content focused on toilets, dirtiness, and menstruation. Eventually she did reach orgasm in coitus, which made her very anxious.

In the summer she looked for a job in the company of a number of older homosexual performers of both sexes. Although she had satisfactory heterosexual experiences by now, she still initiated a new homosexual affair. At this point the analyst informed her that this would be the last year of treatment, since he was planning to relocate the following summer.

This pattern of forced termination had been tried with mixed results in many of the cases that Firestein describes. Marian responded to the announcement that he was going to terminate the analysis by seeking out another therapist, this time with "an alleged therapy group" which the analyst interpreted as resistance. Marian's rage at the analyst had largely to do with the frustration of a most intensely invested wish — that he furnish her with a penis or with the ability to become a real boy.

At this time Marian revealed that she did not view the homosexual way of life as attractive; she wished to be married. At the same time she expressed the wish to become an analyst, a wish that appeared in a number of the analyses in the book. She became more feminine in her dress and manner and tried to work through the feelings of abandonment by the analyst. She began to date two men at the same time.

She moved to another city. After the termination of the analysis he heard from Marian through monthly letters. Their content reflected her continued inner ferment. He saw her dilemma as follows: being feminine led to abandonment by her father (the analyst). Being masculine (homosexual) was not a feasible solution. The prospect of termination elicited a number of regressive phenomena. She had various liaisons with men and women, but without resolution. During the first few weeks after termination Marian became more aware consciously that she was going to feel painful longing for the analyst after termination. The analyst felt discouraged for some time, but then became optimistic about the patient's prospects.

There was no new objective follow-up, and we are left wondering how she fared. There is certainly little or no evidence that her inner conflicts were satisfactorily resolved.

Summary

In all these cases with highly qualified analysts, the analysis was terminated, but how satisfactory was the termination?

In Freud's case of the Wolf Man, the patient actually continued in analysis throughout his life; toward the end he was in a mental hospital, but that could have been the consequence of his extreme age. However, he never satisfactorily resolved his conflicts with women.

Wallerstein's description of the phobic woman leaves little doubt that she could have used more analysis; he even questions the inner dynamics of her improvement, ascribing it more to a transference cure than a real inner realignment.

In Sandler's case of the body as phallus, the patient did overcome the worst of his sexual conflicts, but there are many indications that the preoedipal conflicts remained at some level. Indeed with so much overt sexual stimulation from the mother, it stands to reason that much more work was still needed to fully liberate himself from her.

Winnicott's schizoid physician certainly could have used more analysis. Winnicott himself says that it was broken off prematurely and the patient in his final communication states that he wanted more treatment.

In the case described by the Stolorows the girl did get over the worst of her loss of identity, but there still remains the question of how she could develop herself after the early rejection by the parents.

Finally Firestein's case admittedly remained unfinished. Bisexual from beginning to end, Marian waffled between homosexuality and heterosexuality and never completely resolved her gender identity.

Thus an examination of these cases reaffirms Freud's central position: character analysis is essentially an interminable undertaking, while the termination of analysis is a practical affair. In his 1937 essay Freud views analysis as interminable because of the time and effort required to modify the ego. Today we would see the interminability of analysis as due more to the fact that when a person undertakes a character reconstruction, which is what psychoanalysis is, the problems encountered are those that all human beings encounter and admit of no easy answer.

I am arguing that it would be more profitable for analysts to state these problems in more human terms, as is done in the actual analytic work, rather than in terms of abstract entities, even entities as useful as ego and superego. How much anxiety can a human being tolerate without resorting to unfruitful defense measures? What is a satisfactory sex life? This is an especially difficult question for young people to answer in the light of today's AIDS epidemic. Traditionally it was answered by saying, Experiment until you find the right persons. Such a solution is no longer feasible. At the same time even married couples seek to vary partners with greater frequency (Schwartz and Blumstein, 1983); homosexuality seems to be more frequent, or at least more open. "Alternative life-styles" are so common that new communes are established regularly in the United States, even though communal living, which involves a denial of individualistic needs, sooner or later fails.

Are we to conclude that psychoanalysis fails at the deepest level? After all, a medical treatment that usually fails of its ultimate purpose would be considered a failure.

The answer lies in a reconceptualization. Neurosis is not a medical entity. Indeed, the authors of the *Diagnostic and Statistical Manual*, third edition (DSM III), although unaware of all the issues, were right in refusing to define "neurosis" or to include it as such in their list of diagnoses (it was inserted only at the last minute at the insistence of the analysts).

In the next chapter I argue that psychoanalysis has remained undefined because it is essentially a theory of happiness, and happiness in the abstract has always eluded precise definition.

This by no means implies that psychotherapy is a waste of time. After all, perfect health is also somewhat of an illusion, but good health is not. The person in therapy improves: all the cases described showed improvement, some of it quite remarkable. On the whole, even crude statistical research (Lambert, Christensen, and De Julio, 1963) could conclude with an optimistic feeling about the value of psychotherapy, and Smith, Glass, and McGaw, using a somewhat dubious statistical technique (Meta-analysis of correlations, many of them inherently weak) also reached a positive conclusion.

But the problem lies with definitions. Most theoreticians still view neurosis and psychosis as fixed entities that point to psychopathology; all the research of the past fifty years shows that this is far from being the truth.

Human beings can be troubled by many conflicts, outer and inner; indeed in this day and age, which has been called the Age of Anxiety, to find a truly untroubled human being is something of a miracle.

But the troubles have to be assessed from the viewpoint of the analytic ideal, not from the viewpoint of traditional psychiatry. It is a sufficient negative judgment on the DSM III (and reported subsequent editions) that most of the case history material comes from Kraepelin, not Freud. And Kraepelin did not have the slightest notion of what we today would call psychodynamics.

Neurosis and psychosis, in the largest sense, are thus philosophical problems, which cannot be resolved by any mechanical, statistical legerdemain. Indeed, it was not so long ago that Kant, revered as the greatest name in Western philosophy, held that physicians should not be permitted to treat the mentally ill; since the mental is the province of the philosopher, the study of the mentally ill belongs to philosophy.

It is no accident that Freud studied philosophy very seriously, with Brentano, and that Brentano's two most famous students were Husserl and Freud. The term "mental illness" is misleading; what we are dealing with are patterns of living that lead to stress and unhappiness. Stress (what Engel called the biopsychosocial model) has become the key concept in the modern approach to mental health, and indeed even in the approach to physical health.

These points of view require more elaboration, which the following chapters will provide.

4

The Structure of
Psychoanalytic Theory

THERE IS NO UNANIMITY on the nature and content of psychoanalytic theory, though there are large areas of agreement. This is one reason for the underestimation of values in standard analytic theory of any kind.

In the wake of the 1985 lawsuit, the *Psychoanalytic Quarterly*, beginning in 1988, commissioned a series of articles on the future of psychoanalysis by some of the leading persons in the field. The articles can be examined profitably to see how these authorities visualize psychoanalytic theory.

Arlow and Brenner (no. 1, 1988) raise the question of whether there will be a future for psychoanalysis at all. This is in response to the claim of many that psychoanalysis will disappear as a body of theory and as a form of treatment. They feel unequivocally that psychoanalysis has a definite future. In the light of current trends, it seems most likely that analysts will continue to be drawn increasingly from the ranks of those without a medical degree.

They do not discuss theory in any detail, except to deplore archaic hangovers found in present-day training, such as excessive reliance on the dream. They feel that the setting of standards for training and practice in psychoanalysis may be removed from the authority of the practitioners and vested more and more in economic and political agencies. Viewing the notion that Freud had to persist in the face of inflexible opposition as a myth, they deplore the fact that psychoanalysis has been mired in this myth. This, of course, is a debatable point, since the contributions of Freud remain over-whelming.

Michels (no. 2) argues that psychoanalysis is alive and vigorous. It also has important unsolved problems, is beset by conflict, and is facing major decisions. The future may bring about a reorganization of its professional institute structure, a strengthening of its scientific base and research tradition, and a shift toward recognizing and in-tegrating the public responsibilities of an organized profession with its traditional primary concern for the individual analyst-patient rela-tionship. He concludes: "There has probably never been a profession whose knowledge and understanding provided a better basis for rec-ognizing and coping with its problems. If it pays attention to its own discoveries, the future is bright indeed" (p. 184).

Reiser's paper (no. 2, 1989) begins with what he calls "bad news." (It is not surprising that what he calls "bad news" is viewed as good news by Arlow and Brenner). Psychoanalysis is in trouble in United States medical schools. With few exceptions, the role of psychoana-lysts as educators and the central position that psychoanalytic con-cepts formerly enjoyed in departments of psychiatry have steadily diminished. "The number of bright and caring graduates of psy-chiatric residencies applying to our institutes has been declining" (p. 185).

For various reasons psychiatry has been engaged in a process of "remedicalization." The impetus for this has received reinforcement from a variety of pressures, such as new pattern of reimbursements, cost-effectiveness "criteria," and blurred professional boundaries in the field of mental health care and psychiatric practice, in both public and private sectors. He states that the requirement of a certification procedure for full membership after graduation from an accredited institute has not been easily accepted. (He does not mention that one-third of the candidates for certification failed in their first try nor the implications of this for traditional psychoanalytic education.) Reiser concludes with the hackneyed cry for more research.

Vann Spruiell (no. 1, 1989) is quite optimistic. He argues that the psychoanalytic revolution, begun by a lonely and brave conquistador, became a group activity transcending the man and the myths about the man. At its best, psychoanalysis offers the only reliable opportu-nities for human beings to change themselves on the level of deep structure. It is invaluable for those who engage in it, and within a free society there will always be people like Freud — conquistadors of inner space. In a free society, therapeutic psychoanalysts, if they are well trained, will survive.

And there will always be a place for psychoanalytic theory. It has influenced every educated person in our culture, whether a given individual knows it or not. It will continue to influence the culture in terms of all that is best in humans. The reason? It relies upon rationality, which includes the limits of rationality and the functions of imagination. And it allows us to apprehend pseudo-rationality in terms of the recognition of conflicts, of self-deceptions, of perversions of thought. That is why the psychoanalytic movement became a discipline, a proto-science, an early form of science. And that is the reason it will survive in some ways that are known, in others that are quite predictable.

The most extensive discussion of the question came from Wallerstein and Weinshel (no. 3, 1989). They discuss it from five perspectives: (1) the nature of psychoanalysis as a science; (2) its nature as a discipline; (3) psychoanalytic education and its relationship to the wider world for which Freud always yearned; (4) the nature of psychoanalytic research; and (5) the institutional expression of psychoanalysis in the International Psychoanalytic Association and its component organizations.

Briefly, they state the following:

(1) Psychoanalysis as science: They opt for a natural science model, and their allegiance, by training and practice, is to the ego-psychological, now the post–ego-psychological paradigm.

(2) Psychoanalysis as a discipline: Here the issue of lay analysis has created a fundamental change, particularly in America. As a result of the lawsuit, the institutes of the American Psychoanalytic Association will be training increasing numbers of nonphysicians and their percentage within the ranks of trained analysts within the American Psychoanalytic Association will rise significantly. Parallel developments in South America are also leading to increasing democratization. The full implication of this (when finally achieved) will be a fundamental shift in the conception of the nature of psychoanalysis as a discipline.

(3) Training for psychoanalysis: Two basic models have taken hold in America. One is that of the institute, developed by Eitingon at Berlin in 1920. The second, arising in the wake of World War II, is that of the creation of new psychoanalytic institutes within medical school departments of psychiatry.

(4) Research in psychoanalysis: Research in our discipline began with Freud's clinical case study method, and that is still the source of most of what we know in psychoanalysis. Unfortunately the supply of research workers in this area is drying up, and the new cry of

"remedicalization" in psychiatry is making it even more difficult to find properly trained researchers.

(5) Psychoanalysis as a profession: The profession is having a hard time, partly because of the decreasing number of patients and partly because of the increased number of practitioners. Insurance has provided more patients but has also hurt the psychoanalytic identity and psychoanalytic work. The demarcations between psychoanalysis and psychoanalytic psychotherapy are much less clear-cut today than they used to be. Thus the uncertainty persists about how to define clinical psychoanalysis.

The authors do not discuss in detail the last point — the institutional expression in the International Psychoanalytic Association. This evidently is reserved for a later paper.

Freud as Philosopher

It is clear from his early writings, some of which were never published during his lifetime, that Freud viewed himself as a philosopher who offered a philosophy based on a proper psychology. In a letter to Fliess of April 2, 1896 (*History*, p. 22) Freud wrote:

> When I was young, the only thing I ever longed for was philosophical knowledge, and now that I am going over from medicine to psychology I am in the process of attaining it. I have become a therapist against my will. I am convinced that granted certain conditions in the person I can definitely cure hysteria and obsessional neurosis.

On July 11, 1873, he wrote to his friend Silberstein:

> About the first year in the University, I can tell you that I shall spend it entirely in studying humanistic subjects which have nothing at all to do with my future profession but which will not be useless to me. (McGrath, p. 96)

The larger question of the applicability of psychoanalysis to the general cultural body of knowledge was not touched upon in any detail in the commentaries cited above, but obviously deserved more extended discussion, especially in clarifying what psychoanalysis is and what psychoanalysis might become.

Freud's trajectory, as well as that of most later analysts, can be traced as follows:

(1) From the medical to the psychological: The first step was to realize that the answer to neurotic and psychotic illness lay in psychology. As Jones comments, the idea of *defense* elaborated in his first paper on the topic in 1894, on the neuropsychoses of defense, remains fundamental to all subsequent thought. It can be broken down into two parts: (a) what is defended against and (b) how does the defense operate?

Other psychiatrists of his day were still operating largely in the framework of Griesinger's famous aphorism: mind disease is brain disease. With the explosive developments in neuroscience of the past few decades many are arguing that this is still the fundamental formula; most psychologists however would reject the total reduction of psychology to physiology that is implied. Such a reduction is not confirmed by our present-day results. What we can say is rather that the physiological basis of psychological functioning has been clarified to some extent, but the mysterious leap from the body to the mind still remains puzzling. Wilder Penfield, one of the most profound researchers in this field, who spent his life as a neurosurgeon actively observing the brain and the mind, finally concluded: "There is no good evidence in spite of new methods... that the brain alone can carry out the work that the mind does" (*The Mystery of the Mind*, p. 114). He suggested that the brain should be viewed as a computer, of which the mind is the programmer (p. 86).

(2) From the psychological to the cultural: Freud's psychological discoveries led him, as he had hoped they would in his earliest student days, to a philosophical understanding of human nature. This development has been overlooked because Freud created a new kind of philosophy, one that the academic schools could not grasp at that time, much as academic psychology could not grasp his more dynamic psychology.

To the extent that they have examined Freud and his writings, which is not much, philosophers have found him wanting in two respects: precision of definition and ideas of causality. These are, it is true, valid objections, but they ignore the main thrust of Freud's work, which is to clarify the nature of happiness for each individual (Wollheim and Hopkins, 1982). The same criticisms have long been offered by academic psychology and with the same negative results.

In modern textbooks of philosophy Freud is virtually ignored (Ayer, 1984; Russell, 1927). If cited, he is treated in a very abstract way, without actual reference to the problems that he is examining, the procedures that he is using, or the difficulties of the field in which he is working.

Freud pursued philosophy in an entirely new key. The traditional philosophical problems of the relationship to the external world, the body-mind problem, how we know what we know — all these are ignored by Freud. His is a philosophy of the human being in action, in that sense like existentialism, yet going far beyond existentialism with his profound system of psychology. In this way Freud also gives a new twist to the meaning of the term "philosophy," offering philosophers a chance to break loose from centuries of arguments about insoluble questions and participate in the fullness of everyday life. Unfortunately philosophers are not equipped to do this, unless, like Merleau-Ponty, they study psychoanalysis independently, at which point their philosophical background becomes irrelevant.

From an early date Freud carried out his plan to extend psychoanalytic insight to fields other than the purely medical ones with which he was concerned. The central notion that the key to the medical problem lay in psychology soon gave way to a more cultural approach and finally to the tackling of a number of philosophical problems, chiefly that of happiness. While this formulation may seem a bit strange, it conforms to the historical development and is the route that others have followed since. Many get stuck along the way; some see the problems as purely medical, others as cultural, still others as purely philosophical — that is, to be handled by armchair speculation as in the past. But a full psychoanalytic approach involves a full consideration of all the points of view.

In 1873, when Freud entered the university, the faculty of philosophy embraced all of what today we would call the social sciences. It was therefore natural enough for Freud to examine all these social sciences and develop psychoanalytic insights into them. In fact, it is only in recent years that the social sciences have completely emancipated themselves from philosophy, and even today in some countries they still have not. Thus growth is still highly uneven; it is only since the end of World War II that is has become uniform, after the example of the American universities. A continuous clarification of theory in all fields must be given due weight in evaluating the different points of view that are prevalent.

Freud's intellectual growth proceeded from the medical to the psychological to the cultural to the philosophical. It is only when all of these have been examined that the problem of termination can again be reconsidered.

Medicine

In order to apply the insights that he dimly sensed would come in the future and that did come in the course of the next century, Freud needed a base from which to operate, and the most convenient base was medicine.

As we know, Freud has been roundly criticized (and the criticism continues) for his lack of method. In reality, his method of direct interrogation, allowing free association and revelation of all that would make a person ordinarily feel ashamed, embarrassed, or humiliated, was one of his greatest contributions.

It is well known that all the social sciences broke away from philosophy in the years shortly before and after 1900. Freud did too, but he also created a new kind of philosophy that penetrated people's lives more directly.

Since he had to make a living, which he could do only if he had something to offer his patients, Freud soon learned to combine psychological observations with medical ones, as we see in the *Studies in Hysteria* case histories published in 1895. But the medical phase was elaborate and always preceded the psychological.

In the oldest case, that of Anna O. (pp. 21ff.) the patient's private theater (systematic daydreaming) passed over into illness, understood here as physical. She soon developed various symptoms, described as follows: left-sided occipital headache; convergent squint (diplopia), markedly increased by excitement; complaints that the walls of the room seemed to be falling over (affliction of the obliques); disturbances of vision hard to analyze; paresis of the muscles of the front of the neck, so that the patient finally could move her head only by pressing it backwards between her raised shoulders and moving her whole back; contracture and anesthesia of the right upper and, after a time, of the right lower extremity, etc. (p. 23). Today it would suffice to say that she had various somatic symptoms that could not be explained by standard physiological observations.

Once these physical symptoms were dealt with, the psychological could be approached. Actually the most significant observation that Breuer made here was that she had never been in love, an observation that Freud failed to repeat when he described the case in his lectures. Thus he was still bogged down in the idea of the greater importance of the physical; actually Freud reached the position of the supreme importance of the psychical only with *The Interpretation of Dreams*, which should therefore be regarded as the real beginning of psychoanalysis.

In the case of Frau Emmy von N., treated in 1889, Freud still began with an extended physical description:

> This lady, when I first saw her, was lying on a sofa with her head resting on a leather cushion. She still looked young and had finely cut features, full of character. Her face bore a strained and painful expression, her eyelids were drawn together and her eyes cast-down; there was a heavy frown on her forehead and the naso-labial folds were deep. She spoke in a low voice as though with difficulty and her speech was from time to time subject to spastic interruptions amounting to a stammer. She kept her fingers, which exhibited a ceaseless agitation resembling athetosis, tightly clasped together. There were frequent convulsive tic-like movements of her face and muscles of her neck, during which some of them, especially the muscles of the right sterno-cleido-mastoid, stood out prominently. Furthermore she frequently interrupted her remarks by producing a curious "clackin" sound from her mouth which defies imitation. (p. 48)

In other cases in the book Freud continues to make extensive remarks about physical symptoms. In the case of Lucy R., "as regards hysterical symptoms she showed a fairly definite analgesia" (p. 106). Lucy's symptoms were explained as due to her being in love with her employer, though perhaps without being aware of it, and to her secret hope of taking his wife's place (Lucy was the governess of the children).

Katharina's symptom, which she brought to the doctor on vacation, was that she got out of breath and sometimes it caught her so that she thought she would suffocate.

Fraulein Elizabeth von R. was referred by a physician because of recurrent pains in her legs and difficulties in walking for the past two years. Freud soon ascertained that

> a fairly large ill-defined area of the anterior surface of the right thigh was indicated as the focus of the pains, from where they most often radiated and where they reached their greatest intensity. In this area the skin and muscles were also particularly sensitive to pressure and pinching (though the prick of a needle was if anything met with a certain amount of unconcern). This hyperalgesia of the skin and muscle was not restricted to the area but could be observed more or less over the whole of

both legs.... If one pressed or pinched the hyperalgesic skin and muscles of her legs, her face assumed a peculiar expression.

To press or pinch the muscles of a woman's legs can be highly stimulating erotically, so that no analyst today would engage in such behavior, but this occurred in the early 1890s before Freud had made his major discoveries. The case was quickly reduced to that of a proud girl with a longing for love that could not be satisfied. Freud says that she "had formed an association between her painful mental impressions and bodily pains which she happened to be experiencing at the same time and that now, in her life of memories, she was using her physical feelings as a symbol of her mental ones.... These, incidentally, were not the kind of questions that physicians were in the habit of raising" (p. 144). Freud uncovered a feeling of disappointment in her first love. Eventually it appeared that she was in love with her sister's husband and that she avoided this awareness by having physical pains in her legs.

In the discussion to this case Freud states:

...it still strikes me as strange that the case histories I write should read like short stories and that, as one might say, they lack the serious stamp of science.... The fact is that local diagnosis and electrical reactions lead nowhere in the study of hysteria, whereas a detailed description of mental processes such as we are accustomed to finding in the works of imaginative writers enables me, with the use of a few psychological formulas, to obtain at least some insight into the course of that affection. (pp. 160–61)

In this way, and on the basis of numerous other case histories, Freud discovered that the etiology of neurosis is to be sought in sexual factors. Later he enlarged this sexual dimension to include love, but at that earlier time he was more specific, since even the sexual factors had in his mind some physiological component, to which he gave the name "actual neurosis," a term that has virtually disappeared. The idea is that sexual frustration leads by some unknown pathway through physiological changes into the affect of anxiety.

Thus the medical element remained strong in Freud's thinking until he had a more complete psychological system, which was presented in *The Interpretation of Dreams* in 1900. But the path from the medical to the psychological is clearly traced in *Studies in Hysteria*.

Two major changes have affected this relationship between the physical and the psyche. First, it is no longer permissible for psychotherapists to examine their patients physically; they are required to refer their patients to another physician to perform a complete physical examination. Second, the progress of medicine has made it impossible for any one physician to reach a conclusion without elaborate studies, including microscopic examinations that are not readily available nor easily carried out. A further consideration is that in psychosomatic conditions (a term that today replaces the older term "hysteria") not infrequently by accident or design new curative devices are utilized that will relieve the physical symptoms without probing the psychic state.

Nevertheless, in many parts of the world, there is still so little progress that serious errors are common. Here is a simple example:

A young man of thirty had a hypertensive syndrome, which did not yield to any of the usual medications. His physician said you need analysis but your condition is so mild that I can handle it. I will give you psychotherapy. The physician had no training in psychotherapy. He applied a kind of common sense approach. But occasionally the patient's anxieties and blood pressure would rise. On these occasions the physician would perform a physical examination of the patient and assure him that everything was all right — his blood pressure was of psychological origin. This procedure produced, as expected, a vicious circle. The patient eventually could only emerge from this by going to a trained therapist who would not examine him physically.

It is difficult for the physician to get over this reliance on his medical knowledge. At one time I was teaching a group of middle-aged physicians how to do psychotherapy. All were greatly concerned how they could get patients. All agreed that they would start with their own patients, completely ignoring the likelihood of transference impasses such as those described above.

Psychology

The next step, historically, as well as on the current scene, is the recognition that many problems are psychological in origin. Such a step requires a fair amount of sophistication; it is important to see how it came about. After the 1890s, when Freud was still not far from the other psychiatrists of his day, he made three fundamental discoveries: the unconscious, the significance of sexuality, and the central role of transference and resistance in the therapeutic process. Through the exploration of these ideas it will become clearer how we get to the conceptualization of the analytic ideal.

At first Freud limited himself to the classical neuroses: hysteria and obsessional neurosis. Hysteria, of course, was a common diagnosis, but obsessional neurosis was clarified by Freud virtually single-handedly. Throughout his investigations the question was always present: what is the difference between the neurotic and the normal? While at first he concerned himself with the classical symptoms, eventually he saw that there could be people who had all the character traits of the neurotic but were symptom free. For example, men who are punctilious, well ordered, extremely careful about handling their assets, and fearful of even the smallest spot of dirt on their clothes have major obsessional traits, but may have none of the symptoms such as excessive fear of stepping on cracks or of having their rigid patterns upset, or continuous obsessions about one thing or another.

In one essay he compared religion with obsessional neurosis and found that religion was the universal obsessional neurosis.

Thus from neurotic symptoms he moved on to neurotic character structures without symptoms. Why one person should have symptoms and another not remained a difficult question. Generally he would attribute it to the failure of repression; later (after 1923) he ascribed it to the relative strengths of the id and the ego. The normal person, in other words, struggles with the same problems as the neurotic but has learned to handle them better.

The fundamental observations still centered around his earliest observation (1894) that neurosis involved a defense against unbearable ideas. Logically, the further explorations of this conflict involved, first, the study of defenses and, second, the study of what is defended against. For various reasons, the second came first historically. In the beginning the great threat was sexuality, and Freud wasted no words in stigmatizing the neurotic as sexually immature. But he was referring to sexuality in the sense of the total sex life, i.e., from infantile sexuality on, not just sexuality as it begins at puberty. Sexuality in turn was intimately bound up with love and could not be properly understood without a clarification of love. Initially he saw love as the union of tender and sexual feelings toward a person of the opposite sex and as the overcoming of the Oedipus complex. Later, when the full life course of the individual could be traced, love could be seen as arising from the loving attention and care of the mother.

As Freud and other analysts proceeded along these lines they gradually ascertained that the average person did not live up to the analytic notion of normality. Sexual conflicts were widespread, love was more often than not conspicuous by its absence (as one critic of my book on love put it, the title might better have been *The Absence of Love in Human Experience*), people tended to suffer rather than enjoy life, and so on. Wherever one turned conflict and neurotic suffering were the rule rather than the exception.

Pressed to state what was "normality" Freud made only one statement, in 1917, in *Introductory Lectures on Psychoanalysis*, where he said:

> The distinction between nervous health and neurosis is thus reduced to a practical question and is decided by the outcome — by whether the subject is left with a sufficient amount of capacity for enjoyment and of efficiency.... I need not tell you that this discovery is the theoretical justification for our conviction that neuroses are in principle curable in spite of their being based on constitutional disposition. (XVI, p. 457)

Following World War I two main changes occurred: first, Freud in theory now posited two instincts, sexuality and aggression, and, second, there was a noticeable shift away from the classical symptom neuroses of hysteria and obsessional neurosis to broader categories of character neurosis with a variety of symptoms. Analysts at that time generally believed that the majority of the population was more or less seriously disturbed and could benefit from analysis. This conviction, however, was not shared by the majority of professionals or the majority of the population.

Another momentous shift occurred before and during the period of World War II. Hitler based his theories on an absurd belief in the "Aryan race," a concept devoid of scientific justification. And Stalin indulged in horrible atrocities, such as the destruction of the kulaks in the Ukraine and his wholesale purges that reeked of paranoid fantasies. In the democracies, under the universal draft, the incidence of rejection for psychological disturbance was incredibly high — sometimes amounting to almost 40 percent of possible inductees. Verily the world seemed to be mad.

Once peace was restored, severe neurotic disturbances seemed to be present everywhere. In the first large-scale survey of the average population, Rennie and his colleagues (1962) studied every person within a circumscribed area of New York City. They surprised the psychological world with their finding that some 80 percent of the population suffered from neurotic disturbances, 25 percent so serious that they could scarcely function or had to be hospitalized. Their study was replicated by many others, with varying results. Obviously it depended on what criteria were used to measure "disturbance." If analytic criteria were used, the incidence of neurosis was much higher than if conventional psychiatric criteria were used. Illness of such a magnitude could no longer be ignored, and the profession of mental health, in all its branches, burgeoned. Two new professions came into being: clinical psychology and psychiatric social work. Eventually it was estimated by Morton Hunt, a well-trained investigator of the mental health scene, that one person in three in the United States was in psychotherapy.

The term "shrink" became so popular that it even crept into children's comics.

Some rationale had to be found for this enormous shift to psychotherapy. Bellah and his colleagues, competent sociologists, tried to clarify it in *Habits of the Heart* (1986) but could not explain in sociological terms why so many people felt so disturbed. Kadushin, a social psychologist, could not understand it in psychological terms, and he fell back on the notion of "friends of psychotherapy," positing that somehow certain people were drawn to psychotherapy, and they expanded the circle to include more and more of their friends. The notion of widespread emotional disturbance, elementary to psychoanalysts, could not be explained in sociological terminology.

What had happened was a continual expansion of the concept of disturbance. Obsessional neurosis was expanded to the obsessional character, which in turn was expanded to include the many rigidities that people build up in their lives. They could function in society at a price that could only be ascertained by careful individual examination. One after another of the components of the analytic ideal were studied and found to be absent in many "normal" people. The whole concept of "normality" required extensive reevaluation in accordance with analytic criteria.

Startling revelations came with the Kinsey reports in 1948–53. Kinsey and his staff found that actual sexual behavior deviated markedly from the prescribed "normal" sexual behavior. They showed that if the laws were strictly enforced 95 percent of the population would go to jail. Furthermore, sexual incapacity, such as premature ejaculation, impotence, homosexuality, even sex with animals, were all rampant. Kinsey confirmed the psychoanalytic observations about widespread sexual disturbance in the population, but he did not appreciate what he was discovering.

Having ascertained that the average American male ejaculates very quickly (within ten seconds or so) Kinsey went on to a bizarre (mis?)interpretation of his findings. He wrote:

> The idea that the male who responds quickly in a sexual relation is neurotic or otherwise pathologically involved is, in most cases, not justified scientifically.... Far from being abnormal, the human male who is quick in his sexual response is quite normal among the mammals and usual in his own species. It is curious that the term "impotence" should have ever been applied to such rapid response. It would be difficult to find another situation in which an individual who was quick and intense in his responses was labelled anything but superior, and that in most instances is exactly what the rapidly ejaculating male probably is, however inconvenient and unfortunate his qualities may be from the standpoint of the wife in the relationship. (p. 580)

Such views are all the more ludicrous coming from a trained biologist. If, for example, the heart accelerates from a normal seventy-two beats per minute to one hundred fifty per minute, we call it "tachycardia" and regard the person as ill, not superior. All physiological measures move between two extremes — too slow and too fast. Kinsey was giving voice to the prejudices of his era, and the prevalent antianalytic attitude, not to any scientifically based opinion.

Similarly with the female orgasm. He called it a "biological impossibility" and derided the whole analytic theory of the transition from clitoral orgasms to vaginal (vol. 2, 1953). He wrote:

> It is difficult however in the light of our present understanding of the anatomy and physiology of sexual response, to understand what can be meant by a "vaginal orgasm."... Those females who have extensive spasms throughout their bodies when they reach orgasm are the ones who are likely to have vaginal convulsion at the same time.... There is no evidence that the vagina responds in orgasm as a separate organ and apart from the total body. Whether a female or male derives more or less intense sensory or psychological satisfaction when the vaginal spasms are more or less extreme is a matter which it would be very difficult to analyze....

Some of the psychoanalysts, ignoring the anatomic data minimize the importance of the clitoris while insisting on the importance of the vagina in female sexual response. (pp. 582–83)

This denial of vaginal orgasm was followed by the Masters-Johnson studies in the 1950s and 1960s, in which they not only confirmed the existence of a vaginal orgasm but even took pictures of it and measured its various aspects, such as speed and other physiological concomitants. Kinsey was merely verbalizing the antianalytic prejudices of his day.

Masters, a gynecologist, and Johnson, a psychologist, carried out a much more intensive study of human sexual response than Kinsey. They divided the male and female's cycles of sexual responses into four separate phases: (1) the excitement phase, (2) the plateau phase, (3) the orgasmic phase, and (4) the resolution phase. Then they said:

In brief, the division of the human male's or female's cycle of sexual response into four specific phases admittedly is inadequate for evaluation of finite psychogenic aspects of elevated sexual tension. However, the establishment of this purely arbitrary design provides anatomic structuring and assures inclusion and correct placement of specifics of physiological response within the sequential continuum of human response to effective sexual stimulation.

The basic physiological responses of the human body to sexual stimulation are twofold in character. The primary reaction to sexual stimuli is widespread vasocongestion and the secondary response is a generalized increase in muscle tension. (p. 7)

Masters and Johnson, however, were still ignoring the psychological aspects of sexual responsiveness (it is not clear what kind of a psychologist Johnson is; Masters is a gynecologist with no additional specialization). Without an understanding of psychology, such as that provided by psychoanalysis, the whole nature of sexuality cannot be properly apprehended. Since we know today to what extent psychological factors, or stress, as it is usually called, affect so many parts of the body, such as the heart, breathing, the skin, the digestive apparatus, and the eliminative apparatus, it is the more surprising that in sexuality, which is so preeminently related to psychological reactions, the psychological factors should be ignored. But the times were not yet ripe for a full acceptance of the psychoanalytic explorations of sexuality.

One aspect of the Masters-Johnson work has been widely misunderstood. They showed that the woman's physiological responses in intercourse and clitoral masturbation are identical. This was widely interpreted to mean that the analytic theory of the transition from clitoral to vaginal orgasm is incorrect. But the analytic theory is a developmental one: the little girl has clitoral pleasure and does not reach vaginal pleasure until she is mature. Masters and Johnson completely ignored the development process.

The psychological component was overlooked by Kinsey, Masters and Johnson, and others. Freud made the same mistake at first, but managed to overcome it.

In the creation of concepts that have both a psychological and asomatic meaning psychoanalysis made one of its most essential contributions. Thus Bergman and Spence (1941) say:

> Historically and psychologically, then, the creation of helpful concepts is a very essential part of a scientific achievement.... Actually much of what is usually called theorizing in empirical science consists... in the creation of these organizing empirical constructs.... (in Bakan, *On Method*, p. 57)

Bakan makes a number of points about psychoanalytic concepts. Among these are the following:

> Repression: This notion goes together with the conviction that through the turn inward, which is involved in overcoming repression, the person is brought to a point where he can cope better with the external. Freud discovered the paradox that the turn inward toward self-understanding entails greater outward effectiveness.
>
> Sexuality: Freud's emphasis on sexuality is essentially an emphasis on the deepest existential core of the personality, and an emphasis on the necessity of consciously apprehending this existential core.
>
> Metaphor: Freud recognized that man often expresses himself concerning his deeper existential problems in metaphor; and that, in order to modify himself, man must become alert to the meanings metaphorically carried by his own expressions.
>
> And finally development: Development at root involves the continuity of the individual with the rest of the world. In the break of this continuity is development arrested; and it is facil-

itated by the restoration of the conditions associated with this continuity. (pp. 137–38)

Bakan's interpretations may be open to question. What is not open to question is that what is most essential to psychoanalysis is its underlying conceptual apparatus, and it is this set of concepts that makes up the psychology we call psychoanalytic. Other psychologies have not been able to deal with these concepts properly, and hence in defense they have simply labelled psychoanalysis "unscientific." But Freud, as we have seen, had already stated that psychoanalysis is the name of a procedure for the investigation of mental processes that are almost inaccessible in any other way (1922). Yet it remains within the realm of science. As he stated a little later:

It must not be supposed that these very general ideas are presuppositions upon which the work of psychoanalysis depends. On the contrary, they are its latest conclusions and are "open to revision." Psychoanalysis is founded securely upon the observation of the facts of mental life; and for that very reason its theoretical superstructure is still incomplete and subject to constant alteration. Secondly, there is no reason for surprise that psychoanalysis, which was originally no more than an attempt at explaining pathological mental phenomena, should have developed into a psychology of normal mental life. The justification for this arose with the discovery that the dreams and mistakes...of normal men have the same mechanism as neurotic symptoms. (XX, 1926, p. 266)

Here Freud clarifies the shift to the psychological from the medical, a shift which has often been misunderstood. For it involves a *new* kind of psychology, the psychology of the unconscious, which cannot be expressed in simple stimulus-response formulas as many behavioral psychologists have tried to do. Just as Freud had invented a new kind of philosophy, he invented a new kind of psychology. It is still scientific because it is based solidly on direct observation of the functioning human being.

The social sciences have been essentially behavioristic since the turn of the century, although the extreme form as seen in Watson and Skinner has largely been limited to the United States. This behavioristic stance is in a sharp clash with Freudian psychology, which is based on inferences about the unconscious made from observable data. When we talk about a shift we mean mainly the shift to a Freudian psychology, not to a behavioristic one.

In Freudian psychology, the case study method is primary, rather than the experimental or the statistical method. Again the clash occurs because in other psychologies the experimental-statistical dimensions are primary; as a result the practitioner of these approaches simply cannot grasp what Freudian psychology means.

The change to a psychology of the unconscious can occur in the other social sciences as well, but is more difficult to carry out. Hence these other sciences, like sociology and history, limit themselves to behavioristically observable facts that can be replicated and tested by ordinary statistical-experimental means.

The French sociologist Daniel Bertaux (1981) has chronicled how he experienced a similar change of view in his sociological research when he started to collect life histories. He related how the British sociologist John Goldthorpe hit upon the idea of following his huge survey about social mobility in Britain ($N = 10,309$ men) with reinterviews of a subsample of several hundred men. These reinterviews took the form of professional life stories, following the career of interviewed men year after year (while in the survey itself only a few moments of the whole career had been reported, as is usual in large social mobility surveys). Thus he was able to compare the image of real careers given by the quantitative survey with the image yielded by the life histories. One of his conclusions was this:

> We may first note, as a matter of major methodological interest, how adopting a diachronic or biographical perspective on mobility produces a very different picture from that derived from the synchronic, cross-sectional view of a conventional mobility table....
>
> Why address this paper to a specific public? Because I am convinced that the development of that new approach will only take place with the help of (former) positivists. Because they believe in an ethic of scientific validity, because they are thoroughly honest, they are ready to change their methods and approaches whenever it is shown that new methods and new approaches "work better"; whereas pure theoreticians and especially philosophically trained sociologists, being spontaneous idealists, are lost forever to concrete sociology, especially if they have spent all their lives in academic circles and their universes of discourse. This is why I think it useless to try and convince them. (Bertaux, p. 31)

Bertaux is discussing the opposition of professional sociologists, following an abstract notion of science, to concrete sociology, i.e., how the individual actually lives and gets along. Such an opposition is similar to the opposition of scientifically oriented psychologists in the abstract tradition to concrete psychological investigations of the psychoanalytic variety. Psychoanalysts, from Freud on, have been aware of the difficulties inherent in their method, but have not been able to find anything better to replace it, certainly not the stimulus-response approach of classical or instrumental conditioning.

Culture

Once the psychology was established in the early 1900s, Freud turned attention to his next question: What is the difference between the civilized and the primitive? — a question much discussed in European intellectual circles in the nineteenth century. The answers remained highly speculative until, under the influence of Franz Boas, anthropologists began to go out into the field after World War I and examine primitive peoples directly. The first psychoanalyst-anthropologist to perform such a task was Geza Roheim, who went to Central Australia in the 1920s and wrote up his findings in 1932. Thereafter there followed a host of field-workers who have studied virtually all the primitive peoples on earth (Harris, 1968).

Many questions were approached in direct fieldwork. In terms of the main concerns of psychoanalysis, the same or similar mechanisms were uncovered by Freud in his book *Totem and Taboo* (1913). No facile generalizations could be offered, other than that the Oedipus complex was found in all cultures. What Freud had discovered was thus an essential part of human nature.

Perhaps most important was the revelation that all cultures are organized, though each in a different way. There are no cultures in which there is an unregulated release of primitive passions. This view of the "primitive" was effectually scotched by the field-workers. In fact, it turns out that in primitive communities the individuals are even more closely regulated than in civilized societies.

Neurosis, and psychosis, turns out to be relative to culture. Every culture has its own neuroses. Thus the neurotic manifestations that were studied so carefully by the early psychoanalysts (before World War I) were seen to be an essential part of Western culture.

The more advanced fieldwork carried out by anthropologists and stimulated by Franz Boas took place between the two wars. By this time Freud had already changed his theory of instincts to include two classes, sexuality and aggression. Neither, it appeared, was ever completely unregulated. In every culture children had to be socialized to permit their participation in the wider culture.

The anthropological data fit very neatly with the psychoanalytic. While anthropologists on paper disagreed with the psychoanalytic theories, which they so often failed to grasp properly, in practice they interacted well with one another. Faced with such a variety of strange customs and beliefs, anthropologists perforce had to apply psychoanalytic ideas; there was nothing else.

What impressed anthropologists more than anything else was the inevitable internalization of parental commands and prohibitions, i.e., the superego. Thus Fortes (1977) wrote that while the central role of parent-child relationships was well appreciated by anthropologists before Freud, they did not realize the crucial importance of parental authority in the structure of these relationships, i.e., the superego. No culture so far examined has been found to exist without a superego. Furthermore, the superego of one culture many be diametrically opposed to that of another, with regard to dress, religion, food, or other patterns. Yet the members of any culture find themselves bound willy-nilly by the superego that they take over from their parents, and efforts to break away from this superego are seriously disruptive, both personally and socially.

Thus here too another branch of investigation confirmed the basic framework of psychoanalysis: id, ego, and superego are universally applicable concepts.

Every culture has its own superego, or ethos, a set of goals and ideals that are held out as desirable to young and old. Education is directed toward the formation of this superego. To an insider the superego may not be desirable at all, but that is the rule rather than the exception. When dueling was the standard method of settling quarrels in Europe, the man who would not engage in duels was humiliated and branded a coward. Today we view the duelers and their whole society as disturbed.

Our own society has gradually freed itself from many of the shackles of the past. With the development of democracy and humanism, a set of values once held as desirable are now, when brought under analytic scrutiny, seen as a form of pathology. Therapy often seeks to correct these values and bring them more in line with reality. For example, the machismo of the male, in which he feels obligated to "make" every woman, regardless of her desirability or willingness, is gradually brought under ego control in analysis and the man does not have to pursue such self-defeating goals.

Out of the therapeutic experience and other observations of the culture, we derive a set of values that I have called the analytic ideal. It begins with love and work, and moves on to sexuality, pleasure, part in a family structure, and so on. This analytic ideal may not be at all desirable to other cultures, but it does have a strong hold on ours. My goal in this book is to bring out these values and to show how neurosis is simply the failure to live up to what a mature person would do or think. The element of conflict, highlighted by many, is less essential: some people are in conflict about their immaturities, others are not.

A Philosophy of Living

The final step in the evolution of psychoanalysis is the creation of a philosophy of living.

When asked whether psychoanalysis promoted any given set of values Freud always answered in the negative. At the same time he insisted that each person must find happiness in his or her own way. This contradiction can be resolved in terms of the times in which he lived. The main clash at that time, between the two world wars, was between democratic and communistic or socialistic values. The communist propaganda machine at that time was pushing the idea that psychoanalysis is the last resort of capitalism, bizarre though that may sound today. Wilhelm Reich, a staunch adherent of communism, was expelled from the International Psychoanalytical Association for advocating his beliefs. During the 1920s other analysts also flirted with the idea of communism, although the flirtation did not last long; the best-known champions were Otto Fenichel and Erich Fromm. In this clash Freud wished to stand to one side. After the war ended there were few communists left among the analysts, although the ideal of a better social order appealed to many.

Since then, however, the main political clash has been between authoritarians and democrats, with the socialist-communists on the side of the authoritarians (Stalinism). In the meantime, psychoanalysis developed, many believed (Esman, 1977), into a full-scale philosophy of living. It is this individualistic philosophy of living that I am trying to clarify in the present volume, not any systematic political philosophy. (It is, however, worthy of note that psychoanalysis exists only in democratic climates, although recently there have been some stirrings indicating a change of heart in the Soviet Union and other communist countries.) Today many workers in psychoanalysis are seeking to clarify the essence of such a philosophy of living (Post, 1972; Brierly, 1951).

As a philosophy, psychoanalysis takes an integrative position, willing to incorporate whatever seems valuable in any of the social sciences. It is thus not a separate discipline, as many proclaim, but an integrative approach to human existence, in which technical psychology works side by side with philosophical insights and attitudes to present a complete science, with a therapeutic method and educational devices that can lead to a rounded set of goals.

Psychoanalysis as an Integrative Discipline

Psychoanalysis has been derided, attacked as unscientific, called a variety of names, dismissed from all "official" sources for decades — *e pur si muove*, and still, like Galileo, its eternal truths are appreciated more and more. At an early date the distinguished German writer Thomas Mann said of it:

> I hold that we shall one day recognize in Freud's life work the corner-stone for the building of a new... dwelling of a wiser and freer humanity.... Call this, if you choose, a poet's Utopia but it is after all not unthinkable that the resolution of our great fear and our great hate... may one day be due to the healing effects of this very science. (*History*, p. 451)

Here Mann senses that psychoanalysis is above all a theory of happiness, and expresses the hope — and foresight — that some day it will be a philosophy of a future happier civilization.

In a paper in 1960 Gardner Murphy cautioned that the danger to science today lies not in making too much use of Freud, but in failing to use him as we use Darwin. He showed that Freud did build a systematic theory of human behavior but that what stands most in the way of appreciating his achievement is his followers' too literal adherence to his verbal formulations. To integrate the theory properly, he urges, we have to have a more generous glory-sharing conception to which all the human sciences contribute, one to another.

Murphy was speaking as a psychologist, and psychologists have attacked psychoanalysis more viciously than any others. It is an irony that the great breakthrough that opened American psychoanalytic institutes to lay persons, especially psychologists, was brought about by the enthusiastic efforts of the psychological profession.

I have refrained from repeating the well-known technical theories of psychoanalytic psychology — the concepts of the unconscious, instinct theory, transference-resistance in therapy, the id, the ego, the superego, the self, and all those concepts that belong more correctly to psychoanalysis as a psychology than to psychoanalysis as a philosophy. As a psychology, it has already made considerable headway, perhaps more so than any other psychology, but there are still too few, even among the psychoanalysts, who fail to recognize it for its major contribution, namely, a philosophy of living that if carried out, could bring an end to the tragic consequences of centuries of war, massacres, and superstition.

The Scientific Status of Psychoanalysis

Part of psychoanalysis is of course a scientific psychology. And science demands not merely a bald statement that such and such is the case, but also verification. Surprisingly, in spite of all the attacks on it, there is a great deal of verification of the psychoanalytic point of view. This had been obscured because the putative scientists have failed to grasp the nature of psychoanalysis, even in its technical form. They have also tended to operate on the basis of serious misconceptions of the scientific enterprise (Fine, 1983). Psychoanalysis operates more in the spirit of Einstein, who wrote in 1938:

> Our intention was rather to sketch in broad outline the attempts
> of the human mind to find a connection between the world of
> ideas and the world of phenomena. (*The Evolution of Physics*,
> p. xv)

What characterizes Einstein and the other physicists of the twentieth century is a broad vision of the physical world that finally created the most momentous changes ever seen and never before even imagined. Likewise Freud and his followers have created a vision of the human being, which, together with the therapy attached to it, seeks to put an end to the misery that has gripped humankind in every culture ever investigated. Psychoanalysis in its deepest meaning is an imaginative reconstruction of the world of human beings.

Evidence must naturally be sought that this imaginative reconstruction has some validity and is not merely the fanciful hope of some disappointed Utopian. The evidence includes:

(1) The introduction and development of a viable psychotherapy that can at times cure even the deepest psychosis into which humans can deteriorate.

(2) A viable psychotherapy for the average person that can counteract everyday human misery and create the "wiser and freer humanity" of which Thomas Mann spoke.

(3) An approach to all the human sciences that makes sense of divergent observations in many different fields.

Here it can be observed that the social sciences, which broke away from a stagnant philosophy around 1900 and attempted to move forward along behavioristic lines, have all been vitalized and reinvigorated by the ideas of psychoanalysis. Even if there is no psychoanalytic history (psychohistory), psychoanalytic anthropology, or psychoanalytic sociology as such, the shift from a plodding, stagnant way of looking at these fields to a dynamic approach to a whole host of questions vital to human welfare is a marked step forward.

Here the comment of an astute observer, Janet Malcolm in her popular book *Psychoanalysis: The Impossible Profession* (1981), is especially noteworthy. Psychoanalysis, she says, has

> improbably flowered into the vast system of thought about human nature... which has detonated throughout the intellectual, social and artistic and ordinary life of our century as no cultural force has (it may not be off the mark to say) since Christianity.... It was as if a lonely terrorist working in his cellar on a modest explosive device to blow up the local brewery had unaccountably found his way to the hydrogen bomb and blown up half the world. (p. 22)

More than one person has witnessed this potentially explosive contribution of psychoanalysis — and many have spoken of the psychoanalytic revolution, or psychoanalytic movement, as it was called at one time. Such a revolution cannot be tested in any simple way, by formulating hypotheses and their consequences à la Skinner but has to be carried out by thousands of practitioners in accordance with the vision of their founder.

A word may be said here about the "problem" of lay analysis, more correctly the illusion of medical analysis. Although Freud was the most vigorous proponent of the idea that psychoanalysis is not a branch of medicine and was critical of the American attempt to have medicine absorb psychoanalysis — even going so far as to recommend a split in the psychoanalytic movement in 1929 into two branches, one American, and other the European — he did not neglect the scientific development of his brain child. But he was not caught up in the idealization of medicine; writing to Pfister in 1926, he said that:

> I do not know if you have detected the secret link between the *Lay Analysis* and the *Illusion*. In the former I wish to protect analysis from the doctors and in the latter from the priests. I should like to hand it over to a profession of lay curers of souls who need not be doctors and should not be priests. (p. 126)

The evidence for psychoanalysis is voluminous, but as with any science mingled with philosophy, it is not conclusive. It has to be tried out, and its conclusions have to be evaluated in an objective way. Much of this has been done: the psychology of psychoanalysis is far advanced, and the principles of therapy, based primarily on the working through of transference and transference neurosis, have been elaborated by thousands of workers since Freud over the past century. In these senses psychoanalysis represents an inspirational body of knowledge the ability of which to transform the world has not yet been adequately tested.

The "Schools" of Psychoanalysis

The splits in psychoanalysis have been numerous and far-reaching. Yet they have not destroyed either the science or the therapy, and psychoanalysis moves on more triumphantly than ever before.

When looked at more closely, the notion of "schools" of psychoanalysis, I have argued, is another illusion, aping the innumerable armchair theories of the speculative philosophers through the ages. The difference is that psychoanalysts are practitioners and hence their theories are put to the test in the crucible of practice.

The dividing line is to be found in the concept of transference and the related concept of resistance, which Freud pointed out in his memorable 1914 paper, "The History of the Psychoanalytic Movement." Neither Adler nor Jung, who had direct contact with Freud, had a clear idea of the fundamental importance of transference. But all analysts who came after them were trained in Freudian theory and paid attention to transference to a greater or lesser degree.

Because of this agreement that transference is so basic, the claims of the various "schools" can be evaluated with considerable caution. Usually they take one or two aspects of the analytic ideal, and build them up into the whole theory.

Thus Wilhelm Reich idealized sexuality, seeing it as the answer to a maiden's prayer. While he did make many astute observations on human sex life, foreshadowing the Master-Johnson research by almost fifty years, he ignored everything else so that his theories became a one-side error. Today no analyst follows directly in his footsteps, although some of his ideas are usable.

Usually theoreticians who propagandize new theories prefer to ignore the past. Kohut, for example, the high priest of the latest cult to appear on the horizon, says explicitly that he is dropping the baggage of former theories. Thus the reader may not be aware that narcissism has a long history, and that Kohut's first paper, on narcissism (1966), is egregiously incorrect (Rangell, 1982). The self–object, of which he makes so much, is simply another word for mother, and the relationship to a self–object is a relationship of dependency. His limitation of transference in narcissistic characters to idealizing and mirror-imaging is woefully incomplete, since they can show the whole range of transference reactions. The self was defined a century before Kohut came on the scene, and his failure to define self, like his notion of the bipolar self, are both simply defects.

The culturalists in their day (primarily the 1930s) limited Freud to a pure instinct theory, leaving out the wealth of psychological data that Freudians had accumulated and are still accumulating. But now the notion that pure instinct theory can explain all higher mental functioning is scarcely common, even among convinced Freudians.

In other words, what is needed is an integrative view of psychoanalysis that will give due credit to all the ideas put forth since Freud, but will not attempt to demolish the fundamental nature of his theories. Such an integrative view is what I have attempted to provide in many of my writings, including the present book. For psychoanalysis in my opinion is characterized not so much by theories of technique as by concepts of human happiness and of what makes for human happiness.

In the main practitioners in the mental health field give the impression of being confused partly because of their doctrinaire training and partly because it takes such a long time to find maturity in the field. Kris once spoke of the "formative decade" but I would say the formative period is more like twenty-five years. This is one of the tasks that psychoanalysis should set itself: to teach the discipline correctly from the very beginning, instead of dividing it up into four-hundred different schools, each of which erroneously overemphasizes one point. There is still no place to learn analytic theory other than psychoanalytic institutes, and these invariably teach a set of partisan views (Kernberg, 1986; Mercano, 1987).

Because of their faulty education, practitioners in the fields of mental health almost invariably approach Freud with a negative transference; they come in with all kinds of wild ideas about what Freud actually said. Now that psychoanalysis is officially and legally part of psychology, it becomes more incumbent than ever to start teaching psychoanalysis earlier and more correctly in order to avoid the many misconceptions and downright errors with which students enter the field (Fine, 1984, 1985).

Nor should psychoanalysis hesitate to assert itself if its principles are distorted beyond recognition, if its valid claims are given no credence, and if the search for novelty, so strong in American life, involves sweeping away all the hard-won achievements on the past. Psychotherapy practitioners feel some curb on their theorizing powers because they have to deal with living patients, but others from literature, history, sociology, and the like feel no such constriction and frequently speculate and misinterpret wildly. Thus Gruenbaum, so widely hailed as "refuting" analysis, confuses analysis with the notion that everything has a childhood root. This is one aspect of analysis, but not the only one, and in fact misses the most essential contributions to knowledge that we owe to Freud.

As I shall try to show in subsequent chapters, it is the analytic ideal that lies at the basis of all valid therapeutic work. No other school offers such a broad range of conceptualizations of the human enterprise; indeed, some even insult the reader's intelligence. Skinner's book *Beyond Freedom and Dignity*, for example, is an affront to the basic principles of democracy, since he insists that both freedom and dignity are illusions. They may be illusions, like the patriotism of the Fourth of July orator, but inherently they are valuable ideas that play an important role in everyday living (Fine, 1975).

The clinical case history method, introduced and elaborated to its fullest extent by psychoanalysis, has turned out to be the most penetrating method ever devised to get at the peculiarities of the human mind. As Fenichel pointed out fifty years ago, it is not the psychoanalyst who is irrational in positing entities such as the "mother's penis," for such notions are presented by real human beings. To deal with irrational material requires an entirely different approach than to deal with rational material. Psychoanalysis was developed in recognition of this fact, while behaviorism simply sidestepped the whole problem, resulting only in a vast waste of effort and a destructive sense of futility about ever understanding people.

There has been much discussion about whether there is one psychoanalysis or many (Wallerstein, 1989). Wallerstein describes psychoanalysis since Freud's death as a science and a discipline characterized by an increasing pluralism — of theoretical perspectives, of linguistic and thought conventions, and of distinctive regional, cultural, and language emphases. His thesis is that what unites us is our shared focus on the clinical interactions in our consulting rooms. This question was made the topic of the meeting of the International Psychoanalytical Association at Rome in 1989.

My suggestion is that what unites psychoanalysis is a set of shared values that I have called the analytic ideal. So long as this ideal is kept in mind in the clinical interactions, the process may be called psychoanalytic; if it is lost sight of, as with Wilhelm Reich or Jacques Lacan, the process should not be called psychoanalysis. This approach places the emphasis squarely on the cultural conceptualizations of psychoanalysis, rather than on the technical recommendations that vary widely and that display the wide diversity that Wallerstein deplores.

Summary

We have undertaken to answer or at least discuss three question: (1) What is psychoanalytic theory? (2) What is neurosis? and (3) Is psychoanalysis interminable and if so, why?

(1) *Psychoanalytic theory:* Psychoanalysis represents a combination of philosophy and psychology. Most discussions focus on the psychology, or specific aspects of it, such as the id-ego-superego tripartite structure, omitting philosophical considerations as too abstract or unanswerable.

I have taken the position that such an approach is too parochial. Naturally psychoanalysis includes a system of psychology, largely discovered by Freud with minor emendations since. But it also embodies a philosophy of living, which is what has captured the imagination of so many thinkers, from Thomas Mann on. As a philosophy, psychoanalysis concerns itself with the theory of happiness. Freud approached this question by saying that while complete happiness is unattainable, every person strives for happiness in his or her own way. To this question of how each person can attain happiness, psychoanalysis makes an important contribution.

Indeed, psychoanalysis confronts the question of happiness from the very beginning. When a person comes for treatment he or she is saying in effect: this and this makes me unhappy; what should I do to overcome it and be happier? Technically we call this ego analysis or character analysis rather than id analysis, or overcoming a trauma, but with the careful scrutiny of character structure eventually some plan for happiness will crystallize in the patient's mind. It may not be what others think of as happiness, but it fits that person's life plans and life goals.

It is this approach to happiness, this restless search for a better life, that raises psychoanalysis above the level of a technical psychology and to a true philosophy.

It is not necessary that the answers given should be the same for all people. That was the mistake that philosophers made through the centuries: to describe one *summum bonum* that would apply to all. Freud paraphrased the famous saying of Frederick the Great ("In my kingdom everybody finds happiness in his own fashion"), arguing that each person can seek happiness in his or her own way. But in any full analysis, or what we ordinarily call character analysis, the question of happiness must be raised and must be answered in some manner consistent with the person's past.

(2) *The nature of neurosis:* Neurosis is a technical concept that is also used in everyday language. As a technical concept it has not received any really adequate definition. In fact, the question is so confused that in the DSM III of the American Psychiatric Association the term was left out until, at the insistence of the analysts, it was inserted.

Analysts, however, have no magic password to the nature of neurosis. One defines it as the conflict of ego vs. id, another as the sum total of psychoanalytic theory. Analysts are agreed only on the statement that neurosis may take many forms, and that it is in essence milder than psychosis.

In terms of the analytic ideal, which is posited as the most desirable set of goals for analysis, neurosis may be defined most simply as the distance from the ideal. The element of conflict, stressed by many theoreticians, is not essential because of the human being's capacity to deny and distort reality. For example, the psychotic will generally deny any inner conflict, as will the alcoholic, the drug addict, and many other types of personalities.

At an early state Freud adopted the continuum theory that there is a gradual transition from normal to neurotic to psychotic, and that all human beings, as Sullivan said, are more simply human than otherwise. This dispels once and for all the antiquated notion that neurosis has some peculiar organic basis (which Freud also assumed at the beginning of his career).

Furthermore, there is the indisputable fact that what one culture calls neurosis another calls normal and a third calls psychotic. In the June 1989 issue of *Culture, Medicine, and Psychiatry*, there is an extended discussion of neurasthenia in Asiatic cultures. It appears that the term is still very widely used there, while in the United States, the country of its origin, it has almost disappeared as a diagnostic category.

Since psychoanalytic theory becomes more important than technical diagnostic terms, it follows that the vagueness of the concept of neurosis renders virtually meaningless all the diagnostic systems that have ever been devised. Human beings must be seen in human terms, not in terms of dry labels.

(3) From Freud on (1927) it has been assumed that psychoanalysis is inherently an interminable process, with certain exceptions for traumatic neuroses. The reason that Freud gave was that psychoanalysis involves the alteration of the ego, such alterations being either hereditary or acquired. This view derived from his effort to force everything into the tripartite structure.

If, however, the problem of emotional disturbances is viewed from a more humanistic perspective, taking the analytic ideal as a guide, it becomes clear that we are dealing with aspects of living which admit of no simple or clear-cut answer; such questions as love, the ideal sex life, self-image, and the like have always been with us. They will be answered in different ways by different people in different cultures and require extended, virtually endless, discussion.

The reason for the interminability of analysis then lies with the extension of psychoanalysis to all areas of living, away from the simple traumatic causation erroneously assumed at first to be the case. In this way the philosophical nature of psychoanalysis is again emphasized because we are dealing with human problems that are too complex to be pinned down in a simple way.

Thus psychoanalysis, if it really tries to tackle the ultimate problems of living, does become an interminable process. It is only if it focuses on one small deviation, as in behavior therapy, that it can be brought to a speedy termination. Yet, even when that happens, the deeper underlying problems that all people face are merely swept under the rug.

5

Romantic Love

*A*FTER THESE PRELIMINARY DISCUSSIONS we can proceed to a more detailed discussion of the various components of the analytic ideal.

The first is love. Freud himself, who outlined a complete theory of love, perhaps the greatest treatise on love ever written, still took a long time to reach his main conclusions. Initially he stressed the sexual aspect, and even overlooked Breuer's comment about Anna O. that she had never been in love with anyone but her father. By 1914 however, he had rounded out his theory sufficiently to be able to say:

> ...in the last resort we must begin to love in order not to fall ill, and we are bound to fall ill if, in consequence of frustration, we are unable to love. (XIV, p. 85)

Two aspects of love must be considered separately. One is the heightened delights of romantic love, a momentary bliss that has no other parallel in life; the other is a calmer, more considerate attraction to the other person, and capacity to enjoy him or her.

Romantic love will be examined in this chapter, normal, or mature, love in the next.

Most people, when they think of love, are thinking of romantic love. "All the world loves a lover." "O mistress mine, where are you roaming? O stay and hear; your true love's coming, that can sing, both high and low; Trip no further, pretty sweeting, Journeys end in lovers' meeting. Every wise man's son doth know" (Shakespeare). "Only love, yes, only love is capable of granting you a happy life. O God, let me

114

find her at last, the woman who may strengthen me in virtue, who is permitted to be mine" (Beethoven). "A book of verses underneath the bough; a jug of wine; a loaf of bread and thou beside me singing in the wilderness — Ah wilderness were paradise enow" (Omar Khayyám). "It was many and many a year ago, in a kingdom by the sea; That a maiden there lived whom you may know by the name of Annabel Lee, And this maiden she lived with no other thought than to love and be loved by me" (Edgar Allan Poe). Then Poe describes Annabel Lee's untimely death and concludes: "For the moon never beams without bringing me dreams of the beautiful Annabel Lee; And the stars never rise, but I feel the bright eyes of the beautiful Annabel Lee; And so, all the night-time I lie down by the side of my darling, my darling, my life and my bride in the sepulchre there by the sea in her tomb by the sounding sea" (Poe). "My love is like a red rose; Like a red rose is she; And I would travel ten thousand miles just for her to see" (Robert Burns).

These passages highlight the characteristics of romantic love — idealization (or admiration) attachment; excitement; sexual desire; a state of bliss, sometimes followed by a state of despair; heightening the moment of pleasure; suffering; and, last but most surprising, love as a defiance of the established order.

The ancients did not have a concept of romantic love; theirs was a glorification of the instinct, not, as ours is, of the person (Freud). Historians have been able to trace the vogue of romantic love to the twelfth century, at the court of Eleanor of Aquitaine in southern France. There Andreas Capellanus, in 1180, wrote *The Art of Courtly Love*, a work which became a guide for all lovers. Capellanus wrote:

> Love is a certain inborn suffering derived from the sight of and excessive meditation upon the beauty of the opposite sex, which causes each one to wish above all things the embrace of the other and by common desire to carry out all love's precepts in the other's embrace. (1941, p. 2)

For centuries now lovers everywhere in the Western world have made this definition their own. They have sought the person who fit the prescription or longed indefinitely for "Mr. Right," or "Miss Right." Poets have continued to sing of love, for example, Metcalfe in 1953:

> You are my one and only and...My heart belongs to you....
> Because whenever you are near....The sky is always blue....

There is no rain to hide the sun.... Or any cloud of gray....
No matter what the world may see.... Or weathermen may say.
...You lift me up above the strain.... Of struggle and of strife.
...And you are all the happiness...For which I ever long....
You are the only one I want.... Wherever I may go.... Because
you are an angel...and...Because I love you so.

Thus Freud and psychoanalysis in general express two views of
love: on the one hand it is the most sublime and gratifying feeling
that human beings can have; on the other hand it brings despair and
misery in its train. To this should be added that only psychoanalysis
could discover that sexual difficulties are closely related to love as
well.

Freud dealt with sexual and love problems, particularly in several
papers in the second decade of this century.

In the first paper, in 1910, he examined the preconditions for loving shown by many men. The loved one should not be unattached
like a prostitute. The high value the man sets on the beloved, his
need for feeling jealousy, his fidelity and the urge to rescue her —
all these derive from a single source: the attachment to the mother.
Here he made his first clear-cut connection between sexual difficulties
and the Oedipus complex. The one the man desires (his mother) he
cannot have. The same considerations apply to the woman and her
father. The sexual difficulties for the man derive from the fact that the
beloved is a mother substitute with whom he is forbidden to have sex.

In his second paper, in 1912, he stressed the need of many men to
debase the sexual object. This again derives from the Oedipus complex — the mother who is not sexual, as compared with other women
who are. This is the classical split between the good girl and the whore,
which has played such an overwhelming role in modern civilization
(while incest is also taboo in primitive societies the regulations for
sexuality are often different).

Finally, in a third paper (1916) on the taboo of virginity he takes
up the psychology of women. Comparing the idea of virginity in
modern society to some peculiar customs of primitive tribes, such
as defloration by an elder (father figure), Freud argues that the first
sex act arouses hostility on the part of the woman and by deflecting
the act to a man other than her lover this hostility is avoided.

These considerations have played a tremendous role in the education of several generations, so that the psychology that Freud
describes has in many cases been overcome. But there are still men
and women who display the same neurotic conflicts about sex.

Arlene, a forty-five-year-old nurse, had never had sex in her life; she had dated only twice. She was the youngest of four children; the older three were male. Toward the end of his life, her father became ill, and Arlene took over his care in Florida. She did everything for him, including bathing him and washing his genitals. This had fixated her so strongly that she could not even bring herself to kiss a man. Although brought up in the 1940s, she was identical with many of the women in Freud's case histories (e.g., Anna O.) who were crippled by sick-nursing of the father. Therapy in her case could not overcome the fixation; the idea that sex was bad had taken too strong a hold on her.

Statistics in these cases are inadequate because every case is so different.

It should be noted that Arlene, like Anna O., had never been in love with any other man. The fixation on her father had crippled her for life.

Although modern psychoanalysis has gone on to other conceptualizations, especially ego psychology and the self, the sexual conflicts that Freud first described are by no means rare and are encountered in the practice of any psychoanalyst. He called the shift in attachment from the mother to some other woman in adulthood transference. Today transference and its proper analysis have become the cornerstone of any treatment procedure that calls itself psychoanalysis. In this sense, as Freud had already realized, he discovered something basic in human nature — the figures of childhood remain with the individual all through life. Whether transferences can ever really be resolved remains an open question among today's analysts. Transference in adult life can take many different forms. There are those who attach themselves to forbidden objects, like Philip in Somerset Maugham's famous novel *Of Human Bondage*, remaining miserable all their lives. Others attach themselves to a forbidden person. (*The Angel in the House* was the title of a famous Victorian novel that served as a model for that ascetic period.) Men felt obligated to see "good" girls as angels, and no one had yet written a book such as *Good Girls Can*, giving women permission to enjoy their bodies.

When the Oedipus complex is unresolved, it sometimes leads to terrible attachments or marriages, or to worshiping idealized persons from afar. In general, the outcome of romantic feelings can be grouped under three headings: (1) romantic bliss; (2) romantic agony; (3) romantic rage.

Romantic Bliss

It is odd yet revealing that so little attention has been paid to romantic bliss, in which two people fall in love in adolescence, marry, raise a family, and live happily ever after. Since it happens so rarely, it has been neglected. Yet it remains the ideal of many people in modern life. Rather than resort to the idealization of poetry, some examples from real life are worth examination.

Historically, Catholicism prescribed marriage for most people, but it also emphasized that a person's chief of devotion must be to God. It was one aspect of the Protestant Reformation that marriage was extolled as a source of great happiness; the modern image of a happy marriage was in essence crystallized in the seventeenth century, especially, paradoxically, by the Puritans. John Milton, who did not exemplify a happy marriage in his own life, wrote: "Hail wedded love, thy mysterious law, true Source of human offspring, sole propriety in Paradise of all things common else. By thee Adulterous lust was driven from men...."

Conventry Patmore (Hunt, 1959) not only experienced an ideal marriage, but made it his goal in life to write the definitive portrait of such a relationship. His book on marriage, *The Angel in the House*, was one of the best-sellers of the nineteenth century.

Patmore was born in 1823 and early decided on a career in poetry. He took a position as an assistant librarian in the British Museum and began diligently writing poetry in his spare time. He had little success until after meeting and marrying Emily Andress, for domestic love was to be his fate and his grand theme. Patmore and Emily were typecast as the ideal Victorian couple.

Emily played to perfection the unassuming but omnipresent role of Victorian wife; when Patmore's friends, who included Tennyson, Ruskin, Carlyle, and Browning, came to call, she was always the hospitable, charming housewife, listening appreciatively to male talk but unassumingly doing a bit of needlework the while. She herself had an urge to write, but appropriately produced only a book of child's verse, which she entitled *Nursery Rhymes by a Mrs. Motherly*. She reared her own children with skill and care, lavished admiration upon her creative husband, accepted without complaint his various moods of brusqueness, imperiousness, sensitivity, and dejection, and was the principal inspiration in his life. It is intriguing to see his personal estimate of her. He noted in a private diary that she was unshakably mild, that she had a "milkmaid-like absence of pretensions," but a certain degree of "severity of feature" that her heart saw the right moral answer to every question and that she could keep a house in a state of "gem-like neatness." His life with her, he wrote, was ideal and flawless, but with great honesty he confessed that it was easily forgettable, for after her death in 1862 (after fifteen years of marriage) he wrote:

> Remember above all the 5410 days she was my wife, and on each one of which though nothing happened to be remembered, she did her duty to me, her children, her neighbors, and to God, with a lovely, unnoticeable evenness and completeness.

Early during this marriage, while recuperating from an illness, Patmore was struck by an idea he felt to be of major importance. In a state of great excitement, he realized that while poets had written of love through the ages, they had overlooked or slighted the greatest theme of all — *married love*. He was dumbfounded to realize how universally they had failed to see this and proposed to make good the lack himself.

The first product of this revelation was a long poem that he wrote at blinding speed in six weeks, and that was published as a separate book in 1854 entitled *The Betrothal;* it told of the conversations, moods, and ordinary incidents in the routine courting of a dean's daughter, first by one suitor then by another. Two years later there appeared a second installment carrying the woman, Honoria, into marriage with her suitor, Felix; two more installments appeared in the next six years, painting in detail the unruffled tenor of marriage, the tragedy of her death, and the survival of love in the faithful husband. He gave the overall epic the title *The Angel in the House*, therewith epitomizing the Victorian concept of women and marriage, a concept that had a profound impression in years to come. Love, he argued, whether successful or not, "leaves the heart more generous, dignified and pure." The supreme function of woman is to reign as the angel of the household. Despite her divinity she meekly and sweetly acquiesces to her husband's wishes, and thus rules him by her very weakness. Conjugal sex relations are better than any others because "life is sweetest when it's clean."

This kind of literature, idealizing the woman, is seen by most people today as fanciful, corny, or, in any case, unrealistic. And yet idealization is one aspect of love often overlooked. When it occurs later in life, as in the famous case of Edward VIII and the Duchess of Windsor, where Edward renounced the throne of England to pursue his love undisturbed, it is seen by many as adolescent or foolish.

The paradox is that it has become incorporated into the modern idea of marriage as an essential part of the relationship, even though it is rarely realized. It is this way that ideals, though literally almost impossible, go on generation after generation, playing a profound if unconscious role.

In his second marriage, Patmore also expressed great happiness, but in his second marriage he sought out a sexual relationship with another woman, stating that "his feelings for her were too much for the balance, peace and purity of my religion" (p. 328). After she rejected him, he felt desolate and wretched.

What kind of sexual life Patmore had with Emily we do not know. But there are records of other marriages from the nineteenth century with similar feelings, in which sex was gratifying (see Peter Gay, *The Tender Passion*). The desire for sexual gratification is embedded in many moderns, together with the desire for an "ideal marriage" (incidentally, the title of a widely read marriage manual of the 1920s by the Dutch gynecologist Van de Velde).

A second instance may be taken from American history: John Adams and his wife, Abigail. John's political activities led him to numerous stays abroad, when travel was dangerous and lasted a long time. While he was away he and Abigail kept in touch with letters, most of which have been preserved, giving us a rare glimpse into the life of an American family in the eighteenth century and early nineteenth. Abigail's life has been described in a book by Lynne Swithey, *Dear Friend*, which was how Abigail and John addressed one another (1981).

John and Abigail were both offspring of good families in the prerevolutionary period. They first met when she was fifteen and he ten years older; five years later they were married.

In their courtship they sent many love letters to one another. Often addressing each other by their classical names, Diana and Lysander, they gave free reign to their feelings. In one John wrote: "I saw a Lady tripping over the hills, on Weymouth's shore, and spreading light and beauty and glory, all around her. At first I thought it was Aurora.... But I soon found it was Diana, a Lady infinitely dearer to me and more charming.... Should Diana make her appearance every morning instead of Aurora, I should not sleep as I do, but should be all awake and admiring by four, at latest." Abigail wrote back: "The Nest of Letters which you so undervalue, were to me a much more welcome present than a Nest of Baskets, tho every strand of those had been gold and silver."

After marriage they moved immediately to their new home in Braintree, Massachusetts, which remained theirs all their lives. With the birth of their first child, Abigail took a serious interest in the theories of child rearing then current, and eventually became one of the leaders of the feminist movement in America. Through war and revolution, they had six children, though two died in infancy. Both were devoted, hard-working people all their lives. John wrote once in the early days: "I sometimes think I must come to this — to be the Foreman upon my own Farm, and the School Master to my own Children.... I shall arouse myself ere long, I believe, and exert an Industry, a Frugality, a hard Labour, that will serve my country.... If I cannot serve my Children by the Laws, I will serve them by Agriculture, by Trade, by some Way, or other." This wish and need to serve remained with him always.

Even after marriage and several children the romantic feelings remained strong. After John's absence of more than two months, Abigail wrote:

> My much loved Friend... I dare not express to you at three hundred miles distance how ardently I long for your return.... The Idea plays about my Heart, unnerves my Hand while I write, awakens all the tender sentiments that years have increased and matured.... The whole collected stock of ten weeks absence knows not how to brook any longer restraint but will break forth and flow through my pen.

Abigail took a strong interest in the position of women. In one of her most famous letters she said:

> I desire you would Remember the Ladies, and be more generous and favorable to them than your ancestors. Do not put such unlimited power into the hands of the Husbands. Remember all men would be tyrants if they could. If particular care is not paid to the Ladies, we are determined to foment a Rebellion, and will not hold ourselves bound by any Laws in which we have no voice, or Representation.

The long separations (John was involved in politics all his life) occasionally brought on depression in Abigail, which did not last long. Her problem was to keep the family fed, clothed, and out of debt, which she did very well. John wrote in mock jealousy that the neighbors would think his affairs were conducted better when he was away than when he was home. She wanted to accompany John on some of his trips to Europe, but did not do so until the 1780s. What bothered her most is that in some of his letters John seldom expressed any affection for her. When he did come home after a long separation it was like a new honeymoon. Much of their correspondence revolved about their four children, who were in their way quite adventurous. John Quincy, who later became president, went to Russia when he was fourteen.

By the fall of 1782 she and John had been apart more than three years, and she was quite depressed. In this mood she resented his fame. "I recollect the untitled man to whom I gave my Heart," she wrote, "and in the agony of recollection when time and distance present themselves together — wish he had never been any other." When Gilbert Stuart painted her portrait he said that he wished that he could have painted her when she was young, for he "would have had a perfect Venus."

She learned to put up with many of the hardships of the times. When she embarked for Europe in 1784, she took along a cow (!) and several trunks packed with clothes, dishes, and books. In Europe she was critical of the old world's decadence, corruption, and luxury, especially in Paris. Ever Puritanical, when she first saw dancing in Paris, she "felt her delicacy wounded." When she returned to America she wrote: "Tis domestick happiness and Rural felicity in the Bosom of my native land that has charms for me. Yet I do not regret that I made this excursion since it has only more attached me to America."

At the same time she familiarized herself with the then radical writings on the position of women, and she was especially impressed with Mary Wollstonecraft's *A Vindication of the Rights of Woman.*

When John was elected president, she reacted with an anxiety dream that highlighted her ambivalence about power: "She was riding in her coach when suddenly she saw many black balls the size of twenty-four pound cannon shot coming straight at her. They burst and fell to the ground before they reached her."

In spite of the separations, the two went through life together apparently a happy couple. Nonetheless, worried about his son Charles, who was ill (and who in fact did die young), John wrote to Abigail that children were nothing but trouble. George Washington he thought was a happy man because he had no children to give him pain.

No doubt much is omitted from the letters and the historical records. But what shines through is the devotion of Abigail and John to one another and their relatively happy life. Both lived to an old age, she to seventy-four and he into his nineties.

The final example of romantic bliss I shall discuss is Sigmund Freud. This consideration of Freud will no doubt be surprising to the reader, since more common are pictures of Freud's sexual monomania, authoritarian coldness, and hatred of women. All these, like so much else written about Freud, are largely untrue.

I have been surprised that in their love lives Freud and John Adams show so many similarities. Martha was twenty when she met Sigmund, he was twenty-six, an age discrepancy not very different from that of John and Abigail Adams. Both were apparently sexually abstinent in their adolescence and stayed for the rest of their life with the woman they married. They both had six children, two of Adams's died, but all six of Freud's lived. Both used their marriages as a firm anchor around which they could build their life's work. So the old clichés — they fell in love, they married, and they lived happily ever after — have happened more than once. Or rather, this is a script that many have followed.

Much speculation has gone on about Freud's early love life, especially since he was so absolutely secretive about it. He did have a few days of infatuation with Gisela Fluss, a girl in his native Freiberg, when he went on a visit there.

Freud was a bookworm, and he devoted much of his time to reading classics and other material. He is not known to have had any other interests, only an occasional card game or game of chess. Unlike most Viennese he was not musical, nor did he have any great love for skiing or for any of the mountains around Vienna.

Freud had five sisters and one younger brother, as well as two older brothers by his father's first marriage. He was the favorite of the family; no one, e.g., was permitted to disturb him when he was reading. This was one reason why no one in the household pursued music.

There has been much speculation about Freud's love life, but no real knowledge. However, we do know a lot about adolescents in Vienna. Freud could have had sex with servants or lower-class girls, but as a physician he was acutely conscious of the danger of venereal disease, and he seems to have stayed away from female companionship until he met Martha. As he once put it, he held on to his youthful comrades more than most other men.

Once he met Martha, the engagement came fairly quickly, although she lived in Hamburg, he in Vienna. It was a passionate love on both sides. Like Adams, he was a prolific letter writer, and it was their custom to write daily. Nor were the letters brief; one ran to twenty-two pages. There was naturally a great deal of idealization of his beloved:

In your face it is the pure noble beauty of your brow and your
eyes that shows in almost every picture. Then as if nature wanted
to preserve you from the danger of being merely beautiful she
shaped your nose and mouth more characteristically than beau-
tifully, with an almost masculine expression, so unmaidenly in
its decisiveness.

The engagement period, which lasted some four years, was full of
storm and strife: at one point Freud was in a battle with his future
brother-in-law; at another he demanded that Martha break off with
her family, especially her mother, who seemed to be opposed to the
marriage. Still Freud looked forward to the life of bliss that he expected in marriage and that for the most part actually came true. In
1882 he wrote:

Society and the law cannot in my eyes bestow on our love more
gravity and benediction than it already possesses. . . . And when
you are my dear wife before all the world and bear my name
we will pass our life in calm happiness for ourselves and earnest
work for mankind until we have to close our eyes in eternal sleep
and leave to those near us a memory every one will be glad of.

At another point he wrote: "I know now how dear you are to me.
I have no other wish than to kiss you once more and then die with
you. After we have lived so long in happy intimacy I have a horror
of living alone even another day."

Freud took great pleasure in his marriage. The six children were
his pride and joy, especially Anna, whom he clung to in his old age.

The sequence goes from the beloved wife to the beloved children
to the beloved activity, just as with John Adams. Once he had started
on his analytic career and realized how momentous his discoveries
were for humankind, Freud's love centered on analysis. His wife, not
as capable as Abigail Adams, did not share his passion for analysis,
and it is here that she was left behind. None of the numerous persons who visited the Freud household ever had a word to say about
Martha. She was truly her husband's appendage, just as Anna was
later to become her father's daughter. This, however, by no means
indicates that Freud was an unhappy man. On the contrary, he led
a happier life than most. And for this his ten-year love affair with
Martha must be given full credit.

These three examples (many more could be cited) show that romantic love, even though often a source of conflict, can become the

basis for a happy life. Freud himself came to describe romantic love as a transference, which is how we analyze it today. It is a man's wish to repeat the happy moments with his mother, a woman's wish to repeat those moments with her father. Yet above and beyond this, as Ethel Pearson has recently shown, it may be a touch of inspiration that pushes people forward.

Romantic Agony

While romantic bliss is seen often enough, as a rule it is followed by a letdown in which feelings of rejection and depression predominate. This pattern of excitement followed by depression is one of the commonest of all syndromes that the analyst encounters. Catullus, the Roman who was the first poet of love, wrote more than two thousand years ago: "Lesbia loads me night and day with her curses; Catullus always on her lips, yet I know that she loves me. How? I equally spend myself night and day in assiduous execration — knowing too well my hopeless love."

Rejection and a hopeless love, these are two of the commonest manifestations of romantic love. Analysts have explained romantic love as transference, and naturally it appears in the analytic situation as well. As Freud pointed out, all human relationships are guided by transferences, repetitions in adult life of feelings that were powerful in childhood. Sylvia, a twenty-two-year-old recently discharged from a hospital, had made many suicide attempts of an exhibitionistic nature before coming to analysis. Once in treatment she fell madly in love with the therapist. She would write him love letters every day.

Suddenly, without explanation, she stopped treatment. Later she explained that she had been paying for one session while her mother had been paying for a second. Since she did not tell her mother that she stopped, she made a profit by pocketing the fee that her mother was contributing.

Here as in so many instances love turns into an agonizing experience. The patient knows that the analyst will not respond, since he is forbidden by ethics and law to do so. But there is always the hope that he will change. This pattern was first noted in women patients with male analysts, since Freud and most of the early analysts were men. But now that women are more common in the therapeutic profession, it occurs with men with women as well.

John, who had had a number of marriages, all of which had broken up, was seeing a woman analyst. One time he came in and just stared at her for the whole period, without speaking.

Sometimes the demand for love may persist in spite of innumerable rejections. Once a woman made the rounds of many clinics in New York, engaging in the following behavior. She would seek out a male therapist, lie down on the couch, and for awhile talk normally. Then suddenly she would lift up her dress and say to the analyst: "When do we fuck?" Even though she had been dropped by many analysts, she persisted in her search. A poem by Robert Graves goes: "Love is a universal migraine, a bright stain on the vision blotting out reason. Symptoms of true love are leanness, jealousy, laggard dawns... Take courage, lover, Can you endure such grief at any hand but hers?"

Romantic agony has two aspects. One is outright rejection, in which the lover is simply dropped. The other is an intense longing for an unattainable person, which almost never goes away. Both of these can be traced to the Oedipus complex, though now it is usually traced to the first separation from the mother and the intensity of the earliest mother-child relationship and is referred to as separation anxiety. Since it first appears clearly at about eight months, Spitz (1965) called it separation anxiety, or eight-month anxiety. Spitz described it as follows:

> A decisive change in the child's behavior to others occurs between the sixth and eighth month. No longer will the baby respond with a smile when a chance visitor steps to his cot smiling and nodding. By this age the capacity for diacritic perceptive differentiation is already well developed. The child now clearly distinguishes friend from stranger. If a stranger approaches him, this will release an unmistakable, characteristic and typical behavior in the child; he shows varying intensities of anxiety and rejects the stranger.... The common denominator is a refusal of contact and turning away, with shading, more or less pronounced on anxiety. May we assume that the differences in individual behavior are somehow connected with the affective climate in which the child was raised? (p. 150)

This tie to the mother was overlooked for a long time in psychoanalytic theorizing; Freud was fixated on sexual conflicts and neglected the mother-child dyad. Since his day, of course, an abundant literature has grown up on the topic (Bowlby, 1969). While Spitz emphasized the anxiety, others have stressed the longing. Margaret Ribble (1944) argued that there is in infants an innate need for contact with the mother, like that of hunger for food. Therese Benedek referred to the "emotional symbiosis" between mother and child.

Numerous other authorities could be quoted. It is sufficient to note that there is a strong tie between mother and child and that later love experiences go back to this tie. If the love is happy, it is a refinding of the good mother; if it is unhappy, it is a refinding of the bad mother. The good mother–bad mother dichotomy, which begins virtually at birth, is basic. Of course the infant cannot express the longing; more observable is the anxiety as well as the behavior indicating longing.

Since the earliest mother-infant tie is involved, the emotional reactions connected with love become intense in the extreme. Here are a few clinical examples.

Elaine was a forty-five-year-old woman when she first came to therapy. She had been married to a psychiatrist who had left her for another woman. A suicide attempt led to a brief hospitalization. When she was released, she had such overpowering reactions to the therapist that she could not tolerate the situation. After a session, she would write him letters, going over the sessions in her own mind and of course with her own distortions: You said this and I said that and I want you to know this and that. The letter writing would continue for months, but she could not bring herself to see the therapist again.

At one point revenge got the better of her. Her husband had moved to another state, where he began to teach a course in marital relations at the local university. She found out about it and slipped a story about him to a local newspaper, which printed it. He sued for compensation, which the court granted by withdrawing her alimony for a year.

At another time the longing got the upper hand. She made up an elaborate story that someone was picking through her mailbox to discover who was writing to her. She was sure it was her ex-husband. She went on and on about how he was still strongly attracted to her and how he could not stand his present wife.

Elaine never really got over the desertion. She remained dependent and angry all her life.

Another typical instance occurs with rejection. Susan was rejected by her husband of long standing. Her reaction seemed calm enough on the surface, and she began to date again. But one peculiarity remained; whenever the man broke off with her, her story was always that she had broken off with him or that she had indicated to him that his attentions were no longer welcome. Eventually she married a man who was very sadistic, and who once hit her so hard that he punctured her eardrum.

A classic poem by Robert Burns, perhaps the greatest love poet who ever lived, also brings out these emotions of longing, depression, and rejection.

> O my Luve's like a red, red, rose
> That's newly sprung in June,
> O my luve's like the melody
> That's sweetly played in tune.
>
> As fair art thou, my bonnie lass
> So deep in luve am I;
> And I will luve thee still, my Dear,
> Till a' the seas gang dry.
>
> Till a' the seas gang dry, my Dear,
> And the rocks melt wi' the Sun
> I will luve thee still, my Dear,
> While the sands of life shall run.
>
> And fare thee weel, my only Luve,
> And fare thee weel, a while,
> And I will come again, my Luve,
> Tho' it were ten thousand mile!

The longing for an unattainable person is regularly seen by every psychoanalyst. Sometimes the analyst becomes this unattainable object, sometimes not. If the analyst does, we call it a transference neurosis, but the longing is a transference, whether positive or negative.

The recognition that much of what is called love is a transference of infantile feelings can be a humiliating one, yet vitally important to both the therapeutic enterprise and the individual's welfare. Here are two contrasting examples.

Beatrice, a twenty-five-year-old secretary, had fallen in love with a surgeon, who neglected her terribly. His constant excuse was that he either had to prepare for surgery or that he was in the operating room. He would not marry her. Finally she came to analysis to resolve her dilemma. In analysis she went over her early life, as the older daughter of an older man married to a younger woman. There were terrible separation conflicts with both parents, but particularly the mother, with whom there was a lifelong battle. Working out the childhood conflict and the transference neurosis eventually led her to give up the fantasy about her surgeon-lover. Eventually she made a happy marriage on the basis of a more normal love and moved on to a much happier life.

Elaine was a twenty-five-year-old nurse who was going with a thirty-five-year-old surgeon. One day he broke off the relationship and without explanation said that he did not want to see her again. She came to therapy, but spent the hours cursing him and asking incessantly why he had left her, without really trying to understand. After five sessions she left the treatment, left the hospital, left her home, and went away, never to be heard from again.

In a third case, the resolution was found by the patient. Joan was a college student who had a "crush" on a dental student, who did not reciprocate. She would go to his dental school, standing outside for hours at a time, hoping to get a glimpse of him, which she occasionally did. In the meantime, in a psychology class she heard that people who daydreamed too much are schizophrenic and untreatable. Since she daydreamed so much about him she was alarmed at this bit of misinformation. (How was she to know? The instructor was a member of a prestigious faculty.) She went to therapy. When the therapist disabused her of the notion that she was schizophrenic ("You're not sick, you're in love") she was able to get over her crush.

Still another instance of persistent longing in the face of rejection is provided by Bernard, a thirty-year-old mathematician. He had a brief fling with a woman, who then gave him up. But in his travels to and from work, he had the choice of picking a route that passed her home and one that did not. For quite a while he would pass by her house, occasionally seeing her in the window. It was only after long analysis that he could give up this regressive habit.

Many adolescent girls ("bobby-soxers") develop strong crushes on prominent figures in the entertainment world. The dynamics of this kind of attachment are complex and worth examining. Elvis Presley was one such figure, who had an enormous following. In his own life, Presley (also known as Elvis the Pelvis) showed extreme forms of disturbance. He lived with his mother till a late age. When he was sixteen, he suffered through a series of nightmares. Night after night he imagined he was attacked by a mob of angry men. Presley had numerous other psychological problems; he died young (forty-one) after a life as a drug addict and fabulously popular singer.

In his love life he quickly became attached to teenage girls, and he loved to have them wearing white panties in bed with him. For a long time he would not have sex with them, whom he described as "jail bait."

Elvis was extraordinarily popular during his lifetime, and still has a following today, some thirteen years after his death. This attraction of teenage girls to this near-psychotic young man requires some explanation, which must be sought in the pathology that is so common in fourteen-year-old girls. They are neither girls nor women: they are old enough to marry or have sex (Juliet was fourteen when she met Romeo), yet too young to act in a mature fashion. By sleeping in the same bed with Elvis they were both teasing him and being teased by him. There must be some identification with his psychotic behavior, since fourteen is an age when the girls want to let themselves go in many different ways.

Again the explanation of neurotic love or attachment must be sought in the cultural circumstances. Once more love is not a simple emotion, but one with deep roots in childhood as well as extensive connections with other events in a person's life.

Romantic Rage

While romantic bliss and romantic agony are common enough and relatively easily clarified, romantic rage, the hatred that two lovers feel for one another after the initial passion has cooled off, is more mysterious.

The British poet William Congreve noticed this strange shift from love to hate several centuries ago: "Heav'n has no rage, like love to hatred turn'd, Nor Hell a fury, like a woman scorned." It is rejection that leads to hatred, yet many who are rejected feel depressed or in agony, while others react with rage and fury. What accounts for the difference? Here again we have to go back to the clinical material.

The case of Eric may be mentioned here. He was a physicist who fell in love and married. For the first time he had a sex life that he could enjoy. Then his wife left him, becoming a lesbian for awhile. Further, she demanded and obtained an alimony allowance for three years after the marriage. He was not only deserted but also deprived of his money (though the amount did not really hurt him). He would fantasize constantly that she would become poverty stricken, develop a cancer, and come to him for help. Then he would refuse her and she would be brokenhearted.

In analysis he remained indifferent to the process for a long time; all his libido was focused on getting revenge on the woman who had deserted him. He was an only child, the son of a doctor who had emigrated to the United States during the Holocaust period. His father could not make a very good living, although his mother came from a comfortable family. Eventually his father committed suicide and his mother became a chronic invalid. Eric remained emotionally attached to his mother, who upon her death left him a tidy inheritance.

Thus his rage was a reflection of the deep battle that had gone on between his parents. He remained in love with his mother, and continued to hate his father all his life.

Again we are brought back to the childhood roots of personality: a father who could never find happiness with his wife, and a mother who could never find any happiness with her son. Presumably rejected at an early age by his mother, he spent his life taking revenge on her. Once more the adult pattern can only be clarified by reference to the childhood trauma.

In the case of Charles, a peculiar conflict presented itself. Charles lived in the age of sexual freedom, and he had many sexual contacts. Sexual difficulties did not appear in the analysis, except for his fear of cunnilingus and the alarm that he might really be a homosexual (there was nothing in his background that indicated that). Yet after each date on which he had had sex, he would come to the sessions and let out his hostility. She must be a "tramp" to have sex so freely; a decent woman would not do a thing like that; he hated all women.

In particular, he harped on one woman, with whom he had had a brief affair that took them to Europe. By the time he was in analysis, they had broken up. But one day she told him that she was going to Las Vegas to have a rendezvous with an older man. Charles was furious when he heard this story. How dare she go off with another man to a strange city, where they were bound to have sex. (He completely disregarded the fact that he had traveled to Europe to her to have sex.)

Charles was a teacher by profession, work in which he found very little happiness. He longed to go on to something bigger and more important. He was the son of two Holocaust victims, whom had met in an internment camp in Europe right after the war. But even more important, in childhood he had been his mother's darling. An only child, he would frequently feign illness in order to get her to take his temperature rectally, which she did; there was never anything wrong with him. In the usual Oedipus quarrels, he hated his father, and when he was eighteen Charles had even punched his father in the face.

This case represents a curious mixture of the old and the new. In Freud's day he would have been sexually inactive, or active only with prostitutes. Probably he would have manifested more sexual pathology than he showed. But the sexual freedom of the culture had helped him overcome the worst of what might have been a sexual neurosis. What remained was almost the pure oedipal fantasy. He hated both his mother and his father, and one of his worst fears was that one of them would die (they were both quite old, and this was a real possibility).

When children enter the picture, the hatred is often channeled through them. In their book on divorce, Wallerstein and Blakeslee present numerous incidents of children who continue to hate their parents all through adulthood. Usually it is the mother who brings them up, and the father who is hated. With so high a percentage of divorce on the current scene, the marital battles can only be expected to increase, which augurs for more hatred in the future.

A typical case where the children suffered the consequences of the parental battles is the following:

After a brief courtship, Hannah and Keith were married, and two children followed shortly thereafter, a boy and a girl. When the girl was about four, Keith "fell in love" with another woman and left Hannah and the children, not to be heard from again for many years. Hannah, a poor immigrant with little family and few friends, had to go to work to support her children. Understandably Hannah grew very bitter, even refusing to acknowledge her husband by name; he was always referred to as "that bastard." The children were instructed to say that their mother was a widow, which meant psychologically that they were perpetually killing their father.

Under these circumstances both children grew up with numerous psychological problems. The girl was shy and clinging; the boy was a fighter, not in trouble, but always angry. The mother remained full of venom and vindictiveness, which she passed on to the children.

The family went to live with the mother's sister and her husband, so that they in effect had two mothers and two fathers. It was hard for them to halt this split. The sister's husband took a fancy to the girl, who was easy to handle, while he disliked the boy intensely. This animosity was accentuated when he brought the boy a violin when the boy was five; in retaliation the boy broke the violin on his knee and shouted: "Get out of here you bastard!"

Eventually the girl grew up with many crushes on father figures. She eventually married, had two children, and led a fairly normal life, but one in which she virtually abandoned all expressions of her own personality. She was her husband's servant.

The boy had the advantage of being smart in school. Books and learning were where he could shine, and he became an academic. But the hatred of his father and the overattachment to his mother continued. Unfortunately for him, in an early sexual encounter with a prostitute he acquired gonorrhea, which at that time was harder to treat than now. The treatment was difficult and painful. Though he eventually recovered, the fear of another bout with VD pursued him all his life.

The boy became a love bug. At an early age he fell in love with an inappropriate girl, whom he married very quickly. Immediately battles erupted between his wife and his mother. The strain was so great that the two eventually had to part.

In his subsequent life, the boy went through many loves, each followed by disappointment, disillusionment, and depression. Eventually he was helped by analysis, which showed him the familial origin of his perpetual love-disappointment patterns.

But the problem with his hatred continued. As soon as he had children, he felt the urge to leave his wife and go off with another woman, just as his father had done before him. As though by prearrangement, all the women with whom he became involved were as vindictive as his mother. He had to go through numerous court battles to assert his rights over his children. His wives' vindictiveness accentuated these quarrels; for example, several times he was literally beaten up when he went to pick up his children for a court-decreed visit.

His sexual problems were also considerable: premature ejaculation and frequent impotence. Eventually analysis straightened out these problems, and after many years of effort he managed to work out a decent human existence.

In spite of the difficulties, the boy was very devoted to his own children, trying to save them from the hardships that he had had to face in his own life. Because of this fatherly devotion, he managed to have some affectionate relationships with his own children, but when they grew up they turned against him, and there was little that he could do about it.

There is no easy way to avoid the hurt and bitterness that are aroused in children when the parents engage in bitter legal battles. The courts issue decrees, but human feelings cannot be altered by legal decisions.

Ralph Slovenko, a lawyer who has had extensive psychiatric training, has described the problems involved in custody disputes. Especially since Anna Freud's book *In the Best Interest of the Child*, the best interests of the child largely became the determining principle in marital disputes about the children. In an earlier day, when divorce was exceptional, the father possessed the paramount right to custody and control of his minor children. The rule of Blackstone was followed that said "a mother as such is entitled to no power buy only to reverence and respect." The mother's right to custody of her children was recognized only upon the death of the father, and unlike his right, was not considered a natural right.

These principles prevailed throughout much of the nineteenth century. In the twentieth, with the increasing emancipation of women, the principles shifted to give the mother exclusive power over the welfare of the child, with the father relegated to support from the background. Innumerable cases revealed how this unlimited power released the vindictive wishes of many mothers, who used their children to "get even" with the fathers, who were generally the ones who had broken up the family. In more recent years, the balance has been redressed to some extent, but the mother still rules most of the time. The unfortunate consequences of this matriarchal arrangement have been pointed out many times.

Slovenko points out that the phrase "best interests of the child" is magnanimous. But what criteria or evidence do the courts use in reaching such a decision? Cases in which courts spell out their reasoning are few in number, resulting in the old observation that the words may be fine, but no one can say precisely what they mean. The broken marriage remains one of the worst experiences for a child, resulting as a rule in a lifetime of misery and revenge for the wrongs done.

Children find their own way of getting out of the parental tangles. The following case is not untypical:

Sally and John had a bitter divorce. He was a powerful lawyer who preferred other women to his wife. There were two girls, aged thirteen and fourteen. With the help of detectives he found his ex-wife with her lover and assumed custody of the children. But the children would not go; they preferred their mother. The mother would dutifully bring the girls back to their father, which was her obligation, but the girls would not stay.

Eventually the courts decided that the girls were old enough to make up their minds, and the father allowed them to do so.

Most significant is what happened in their adult lives. One daughter married a man with a business abroad, and never saw either parent. The other moved only a short distance away, but she also would never see either parent. In this way the children resolved their problems: a plague on both your houses.

In view of the many dire consequences of romantic love, which have been brought to light by literature, sociological investigation, and psychoanalysis, it may be questioned whether romantic love deserves to be included in the analytic ideal at all. Yet when successful, as in some of the cases described of happy marriages, it leads to a degree of happiness within the family not offered by anything else.

As for the custody problem, the legal solutions are clearly un-workable. The only real way out is to induce all parties to enter therapy at an early stage to get rid of the terrible hostilities that mar their lives. These scars remain forever, unless removed by psycho-therapy.

6

Normal Love

*W*HILE SUCCESSFUL ROMANTIC LOVE depends on varying cultural conditions and does not seem to occur very often, by direct investigation of infants psychoanalysts and experimental psychologists after Freud have delineated a series of stages that are biologically determined and that the mother therefore should consider in the development of the love feelings in the child. For the first relationship is still that with the mother, and the vicissitudes of the mother-child relationship play a determining role in how the love life of the infant will develop later. It is therefore worth recapitulating what has been discovered after Freud about the developmental process, since in *The Three Essays* in 1905 Freud limited himself largely to the oral, anal, phallic sequence, together with the division of the love life before puberty into infantile sexuality, the oedipal state, and latency.

As we have mentioned before, Spitz was the first to probe more deeply into the phenomena of the first year of life, although others had speculated about it before him. "During the first year of life experiences and intentional actions are probably the most important single influence in the development of the various sectors of the infant's personality" (Spitz, p. 123).

Spitz distinguished three stages in the development toward the object: the precursor of the object, the establishment of the libidinal object (eight-month anxiety), and communication (yes and no), the third organizer of the psyche. In each of these stages different substages can be specified or described. If the mother pays adequate attention to the infant's needs in these stages, the infant will feel loved and the mother in turn will be pleased and will feel the love of the infant for her.

Many workers have contributed to the clarification of these stages of infancy, until today we have a whole elaborate timetable of development. Anna Freud (1965) contributed the concept of developmental lines. The basic developmental line is the sequence that leads from the newborn's utter dependence on maternal care to the young adult's emotional and material self-reliance — a sequence for which the successive stages of libido development (oral, anal, phallic) merely form the inborn maturational base. The steps on this way, well documented from many sources, she lists as follows:

(1) the biological unity between the mother-infant couple with the mother's narcissism extending to the child and the child including the mother in its internal "narcissistic milieu" (Hoffer, 1952); the whole period is further subdivided (Mahler, 1952) into the autistic, symbiotic, and separation-individuation phases with significant danger points for developmental disturbances lodged in each individual phase.

(2) the part object (Melanie Klein) or need-fulfilling symbiotic relationship, which is based on the child's body needs and drive derivatives and is intermittent and fluctuating, since object cathexis is sent out under the impact of imperative desires and withdrawn again when satisfaction has been reached.

(3) the stage of object constancy, which enables a positive inner image of the object to be maintained, irrespective of either satisfaction or dissatisfaction.

(4) the ambivalent relationship of the preoedipal, anal-sadistic stage, characterized by the ego attitudes of clinging, torturing, dominating, and controlling the love object.

(5) the completely object-centered phallic-oedipal phase, characterized by possessiveness of the parent of the opposite sex, jealousy of and rivalry with the parent of the same sex, protectiveness, curiosity, bids for admiration and exhibitionistic attitudes, and, in girls, a phallic-oedipal (masculine) relationship to the mother preceding the oedipal relationship to the father.

(6) the latency period, i.e., the postoedipal lessening of drive urgency and the transfer of libido from the parental figures to contemporaries, community groups, teachers, leaders, impersonal ideals, and aim-inhibited sublimated interests, with fantasy manifestations giving evidence of disillusionment with and denigration of the parents.

(7) preadolescent prelude to the adolescent revolt, i.e., a return

to early attitudes and behavior, especially of the part-object, need-fulfilling, and ambivalent type.

(8) the adolescent struggles around denying, reversing, loosening, and shielding the tie to the infantile objects, defending against pre-genitality, and finally establishing genital supremacy with libidinal cathexis transferred to objects of the opposite sex, outside the family.

While exception may be taken to individual elements of this scheme, in its main essentials it has been accepted by all workers in the field, and has become the solid basis for a modern psychoanalytic psychology. Genetic factors may be interpolated in various places if evidence accumulates that they occur, but should not be interpolated if there is no evidence.

Put another way, what happens to the child, and especially to the child's love life, is that it centers around the experiences with the mother. Put in a larger context, it may be said (Fine, 1975) that development proceeds from mother to father to the outside world. If the mother pays sufficient attention to the child's needs and offers him or her sufficient satisfactions, the child will develop normally (i.e., with no psychiatric impairment) and will grow up into a loving happy human being. If the mother-child unity is disturbed in any way, or later the father-child unity or other interpersonal unity, the child develops various neurotic disturbances, which will prevent it from attaining the analytic ideal. Again, the analytic ideal is the guide that leads to a happy life.

So much has been written on the alleged organic origins of schizophrenia that a word should be said about that problem here. As Bleuler (1978) has shown in the most careful and detailed investigation of schizophrenics in print, the person who becomes schizophrenic in later life has always had a "horrible" childhood, though each person has had the "horrible" experience in a different way.

This point of view undercuts all the different schools and theories, providing a unified conceptualization of the human enterprise, as well as a solid back-up for all clinical interventions and educational programs. Naturally much detail remains to be worked out, but the general outlines of a sound psychoanalytic psychology are by now well established. Fundamental in this psychology is a clarification of how the love impulse develops or does not develop in any individual.

Brazelton and Als (1979) used feedback and mutual interaction as the basic concepts for understanding the infant's development. This feedback model allows for flexibility and reorganization. Within its envelope of reciprocal interaction, one can conceive of a rich matrix of different modalities for communication, individualized for each pair and critically dependent on the contribution of each member of the dyad or triad. At each stage of development, the envelope will be different, we hope, richer.

The First Love Affair in Childhood

Love feelings arise in the infant virtually from birth on. The first manifestation, similar in many ways to the feelings of adulthood, occurs in the oedipal period, when the child is about five or six. I call this the first love affair in childhood, and it is worth more extended investigation.

Around the age of five or six the vast majority of children become involved in a love affair, of greater or lesser intensity, with an opposite-sexed child of their own age.

—1—

The observation itself is not new. In fact, in the landmark work *The Three Essays on Sexuality*, Freud quoted a study by an American psychologist, J. Sanford Bell, published in the *American Journal of Psychology* in 1902. In his Clark lectures on psychoanalysis in 1909, Freud wrote of Bell's work as follows:

> The emotion of sex-love...does not make its appearance for the first time at the period of adolescence, as had been thought. He carried out his work in what we in Europe would call the "American manner," collecting no fewer than 2500 positive observations in the course of fifteen years, among them eight hundred of his own. Concerning the signs by which these instances of falling in love are revealed he writes as follows: "The unprejudiced mind in observing these manifestations in hundreds of couples of children cannot escape referring them to sex origin. The most exacting mind is satisfied when to these observations are added the confessions of those who have, as children, experienced the emotion to a marked degree of intensity and whose memories of childhood are relatively distinct." But those of you who do not wish to believe in infantile sexuality will be most of all surprised to hear that not a few of these children who have fallen in love so early are of the tender age of three, four and five. (SE, XI, p. 42)

At that time Freud's interest lay primarily in demonstrating that infantile sexuality exists. This battle is so completely won that the question does not even come up any more. Yet the initial observations, still valid, have to be reinterpreted in the light of our present-day knowledge of ego psychology. What is the meaning of this first love affair, and how does it fit into the general psychic economy of the developing child?

—2—

To begin with, some clinical data.

Case I: John, a college freshman, came to analysis to "change his personality altogether." He was particularly dissatisfied with his inability to approach girls. His first love affair was a mad crush on a girl in the first grade, followed by crushes on many other girls. Before the oedipal stage, he had felt deeply rejected by his mother; his mother confirmed this rejection, stating that for the first four months of his life she did not know what was meant by mother love.

Case II: Mary, a twenty-five-year-old clerical worker, came to analysis because of what she called her "basic Jewish depression." Her first love affair was at age six, with a boy with whom she engaged in anal play. Mary had not been properly bowel trained until the age of seven. In adult life she had several unhappy relationships, in which the unhappiness was defended against by a high degree of infantile omnipotence (e.g., she was certain that when she walked into a room everyone would drop what they were doing and look at her).

Case III: Lemuel, a forty-year-old college professor had vivid memories of his first love, whom he called "Tootsie." He worshiped her from afar. Once when she was sick and could not play with him he stood at the window crying, which aroused the amusement of his family. Son of divorced parents, he was caught in a bitter battle between mother and father. He had many unhappy love affairs in later life.

Case IV: Sally, a ten-year-old girl with a phobia about a man with a gun, was the daughter of overly permissive parents. At six she had a romance with a boy lasting all summer in a summer resort; some sex play was attempted. Around this time she also went through an intense oedipal crush on her father; she would unexpectedly grab his penis or pull her pants down in his presence. The mother, openly accepting of everything, was in reality full of passive aggression under the surface.

Case V: Gordon, a thirty-year-old musician, had his first love affair with a next-door neighbor. She offered to seduce him, taking him into a room where she was going to undress; they were both about six at the time. Just as the girl began to undress, her older sister came in and stopped the proceedings. In later life Gordon was continually plagued with a conflict between two women, having one and wanting another. His mother was distant, suffering toward the end of her life from a kind of religious psychosis. His father was supportive but infantilizing.

Case VI: Suzy, a thirty-five-year-old clerk, had a crush on a boy in her first grade, whom she worshiped from afar. At the same time she engaged in play, including some sex play, with her next-door neighbor, for whom she had little feeling. Her mother was a severe hypochondriac, her father an absent businessman, who evidently reacted to his wife's illnesses by a series of infidelities. In later life Suzy was timid, excessively jealous, and full of sexual conflicts. The crush on a distant man persisted.

In all of the above cases, as in many of the others, the first love affair is looked back upon with enormous tenderness and nostalgia. All too often, almost as a rule, parents laugh at the incipient lovers as a pair of demented children; at best they regard the love affair as a kind of play-acting (as some theoreticians do incorrectly). Once the childhood period is passed, the first love object becomes thoroughly internalized, to such an extent that when encountered by chance in later life, the former love is a matter of almost total indifference, remaining only as a memory. In no case that I have seen does a childhood sweetheart romance eventually leading to marriage begin at this age; usually such a romance begins to occur at about age ten and upwards.

It is readily apparent that the first love affair is an integral part of the child's development, linking on the one hand with the relationship with the parents that preceded it, and on the other with later love experiences.

It is also important to note that the childhood romance, in my experience, never ends spontaneously, but is always brought to a halt by the parents, either wittingly or unwittingly. The parents object to sex play, or laugh at the love feelings expressed; they may move away to another neighborhood or prevent the children from seeing one another for some external reason, such as religion or arguments with the parents.

Thus the first love affair invariably ends in a deep feeling of disappointment, which in turn leaves its imprint on all later love affairs, though in varying degree.

Looking at childhood love from the point of view of the id, Freud reached a similar conclusion. In his paper on female sexuality (1931) he wrote:

Childhood love is boundless; it demands exclusive possession; it is not content with less than all. But it has a second characteristic: it has, in point of fact, no aim and is incapable of obtaining complete satisfaction; and principally for that reason is doomed to end in disappointment and to give place to a hostile attitude. (SE, XXI, p. 231)

As will be seen, the explanation from an ego-psychological point of view is different.

Although arguments rage about the frequency with which a latency period is still seen in our culture, there can be no doubt that it remains the rule rather than the exception. The latency period is ushered in by the disappointment experienced in the first love affair; it becomes a kind of sour grapes defense: If I can't have it, I won't want it. Thus the hostile attitude displayed by the two sexes toward one another throughout latency derives primarily from the hostile prohibition of any kind of love play by the parents or parent-substitutes. This in turn, as will be seen later, derives from the parents' hostility to one another.

A rather amusing instance of this occurred in the son of two well-analyzed persons. When their son reached the age of seven and began to play with the other boys, the boys tried to argue him into hating girls. He objected strenuously, saying that girls were just like his mother, whom he loved very much. He had great difficulties with the other children.

Fortunately we are now in possession of a wide body of anthropological knowledge that acts as a kind of control and sheds considerable light on this topic.

We know of many cultures in which the parental authorities do not impose such a strict taboo on childhood sexuality as they do in our own culture. According to Gebhard (1963), in permissive societies the percentage of children who engage in sex play approaches 100 percent. Even in such a restrictive society as that of the United States, over half of the males and nearly half of the females in the Kinsey sample recollected "prepubertal sociosexual play" (Kinsey, 1948).

Recent research with animals, notably Harlow's work with rhesus monkeys, offers rather conclusive proof that the rehearsal of part-functions of the copulatory act, notably mounting and being mounted, with pelvic thrusting, excluding intromission, in the juvenile play of both sexes, is essential to successful copulation and breeding in adulthood. Isolated monkey babies of either sex, deprived first of mothering and then of play with other infants, grow up unable to breed.

Henry and Henry (1944) reported on the Pilaga, a group of Indians in Argentina. The Pilaga unambivalently prepare their children for adult heterosexuality. Juvenile sex play up to the age of five years includes play between children of the same sex. Boys openly masturbate and play with each other sexually in public. Girls masturbate against one another in public. From age five on, heterosexual play is common. Girls lie down with little boys of their own age, and the two may go through some of the movements of coitus. Forms of heterosexual coital play, along with masturbation, continue until age twelve. Although the status of women in this society is described as in general inferior, the marriages are monogamous. There is no evidence of any sexual psychopathology.

Money and Ehrhardt (1972) conclude from their study of sex reassignment and cultural variations that many forms of sex play in early childhood are compatible with a self-sustaining predominantly heterosexual adult society, with less incidence of individual sexual pathology and disturbance of gender-identity differentiation than in our own culture. The existence of gender dimorphism of behavior (two sexes) is itself invariant; the options are not limitless. Children growing up in a culture differentiate a gender identity free from ambiguity if the adults of that culture, especially those closest to them, transmit clear and unambiguous signals with respect to the procreative nucleus of gender dimorphic behavior, no matter what the signals with respect to peripheral options may be. One of their most significant findings is that gender identity is fixed in the parents' minds as early as twelve to eighteen months.

Although psychological states are not nearly as easily observed as physiological behavior, it is generally agreed among anthropologists that in cultures where there is free sexual behavior in childhood and adolescence, the unhappy love experiences so characteristic of our society are much less frequent. In these cultures people do not suffer the torments of love seen in our society (e.g., Roheim's study of the Central Australians, in which he could find no latency period at all — Roheim, 1932).

—3—

The standard description of development after the oedipal stage involves the establishment of a superego and identification with the parent of the same sex, with the various deviations from this development leading to the different forms of psychopathology. If writers mention the first love affair at all, it is only as an addendum to the Oedipus complex (Sarnoff, 1976). Since it is obvious that it is much more than that, some deeper consideration of the psychic events at this period is required. In other words, how are we to explain the universality of the first love affair in terms of ego psychology?

—4—

Imitation seems to occur as soon as the infant has the capacity to imitate, which is shortly after birth. (In fact, it may be noted that more recent studies have shown that the infant is reactive in many measures from birth on, pointing to some ego functioning as soon as it comes into this world.) Smiling is usually considered the first social response. The older textbooks gave six weeks as the average age at which the infant could be seen to smile, ascribing the apparent earlier smiling to gas. But the rule of monkeys can be applied here: monkey see, monkey do. The human infant is certainly as imitative as the monkey, and it should be assumed that the human infant will imitate to whatever extent its ego development allows. Besides smiling, as Bowlby (1969) has shown, sucking, clinging, following, and crying also belong to early attachment behavior. Bowlby postulates that between the ages of nine and eighteen months these become incorporated into far more sophisticated goal-corrected systems.

Every activity on the part of the infant arouses a corresponding reaction on the part of the mother. This reaction is determined far more by the personality of the mother than by any mythical "maternal instinct," or average expectable competency. It is one of our disappointing findings in the education of mothers that those most in need of it are also most resistant to it; a parallel is found later on in psychotherapy.

As a result of the complex interactions between mother and child, to which are soon added the interactions with the father and other significant figures as well as autonomous physiological factors, the development of the child does not lend itself to any facile formulas. The best that can be done at the present state of knowledge is to provide guidelines with which to approach the clinical observations.

Imitation is a readily observable phenomenon, which goes on all the time. Incorporation and introjection are inferences from other data. All contribute to the growing sense of identification of the child. However, this sense of identity or identification takes years to crystallize, and in the process of crystallization undergoes numerous changes. In view of this complex development, concepts such as Freud's primary narcissism, primary masochism, or Kohut's independently developing narcissistic libido have to be rejected because they ignore the constant interplay between child and mother.

According to Money and Ehrhardt, some sense of identification with the sex of the parents becomes manifest at twelve months to the parents and by eighteen months to the infant. Without becoming too pedantic about exact numbers (Galenson and Roiphe, 1981), we may say that the identification process — in which the infant can say: I am like him (her), or I want to be like him (her) — is sufficiently clear by about two years of age.

Out of these identifications emerges the sense of self, which begins at around this time; expressions such as "me too," "me do," and sometimes "I" begin to be heard (Fine, 1985). The self-image, however, takes years to develop and goes through many vicissitudes before it reaches anything like a final form.

Another recent development of relevance here is the confluence of psychoanalysis and cognitive psychology; Piaget has been particularly influential. In fact, in an invited address to the American Psychoanalytic Association in 1970 Piaget (who was for many years a member of the Swiss Psychoanalytic Association and underwent a didactic analysis at one time) drew wide parallels between his system and that of psychoanalysis. In particular the development of object constancy seems to be roughly parallel in the cognitive and the affective realms. Piaget has investigated the constancy of an inanimate object in the child's mind, while psychoanalysis has investigated the constancy of a significant person (actually the Freudian term "object" is unfortunate and should be replaced by person). Both kinds of constancy are mediated by the development of internal representations, which derive from the growth of the autonomous ego. Both reach a height some time in the third year of life. Hence the cognitive factors in psychosexual development can no longer be ignored, any more than the affective factors in cognitive development.

The establishment of the self-image is followed after several years by a true introjection of the parents, resulting in a superego, around the age of six years. It is only then that the child becomes more consistently subject to internal influences than to external ones, although, as will be seen, external influences always continue to play a role; one of the weaknesses of classical Freudian theory is that it tends to ignore this role of the environment too much. Here too cognitive factors remain of considerable importance.

—5—

We can now return to the main thread of the discussion. The first love affair is clearly related to the Oedipus complex; what accounts for the development of each of these?

Anthropological evidence fairly conclusively shows that the Oedipus complex is universal, as is the nuclear family and the incest taboo (Murdock, 1949). That the objects of desire and hatred can be persons other than the biological mother and father was readily accepted by Freud when it was demonstrated by the research of the 1920s. (As a human aside, it may be noted that Malinowski, who is widely credited by textbooks with having "disproved" the Oedipus complex, explicitly stated that his results confirmed the universality of the complex, with the sole proviso that the persons involved were culturally rather than biologically determined.)

Freud argued that the Oedipus complex is "biological." But in the seventy years that have passed since the publication of *The Three Essays on Sexuality* (1905), the meaning of "biological" has taken on a subtle twist. Originally it meant to Freud something physiological; later it has come to mean phylogenetic, as distinct from physiological. Now, the Oedipus complex is certainly inherent in human existence, but *extensive research has never uncovered any physiological basis for it.* "Oedipus," means both "swollen foot" and "erection" (apparently a slang Greek meaning), but the boy has erections from birth on, so that the desire cannot be equated with a newly acquired capacity for erection, as can the sexual desire of adolescence be equated with the newly acquired capacity for ejaculation. What has changed is merely the strength of the ego, a cognitive change, not a physiological one as such. The child, now more able to verbalize his identifications with the parents, and his concept of a self, wishes to do what the parents do. Not even the most puritanical of cultures has been able to conceal the sexual activities of the parents; anyhow the close connection of the sex organs with the organs of excretion, plus the child's capacity to fantasize, makes some knowledge of sexual intercourse inevitable. In less taboo-ridden societies the direct imitation of parental coitus and sleeping habits by children from about five on is obvious and open.

If the positive side of the Oedipus complex results from identification, based on the strength of the growing ego, what accounts for the negative, the hatred of the parent of the same sex? Here our theoretical analysis yields an unexpected and quite important result. Jealousy, as we know, is not an unavoidable instinctual development; it is culturally determined, and there are many cultures where jealousy is at a minimum or even absent. *Hence oedipal hatred also arises from identification with the parents.*

Freud himself, who was overly focussed on his own development as a child, overlooked the role of parental hatreds in the genesis of the Oedipus complex, and because of his enormous authority, others have overlooked it as well. Yet even a cursory examination of the clinical data reveals its significance. In families where the parents love one another and are happy, the oedipal conflicts are relatively mild and negotiated with a minimum of friction. But in families where the parents live in a state of perpetual warfare, the oedipal conflicts are sharp, central, and persistent. In these families, each child becomes a protagonist in the eternal battle between the parents, forced to take one side or another, regardless of his or her own preferences. That serious psychopathology results in such situations need not surprise us. Ultimately, however, this pathology goes back to the parental hatreds much more than to the Oedipus complex as such.

—6—

In spite of the most pronounced parental pressures, a first love affair is experienced by the vast majority of children. What accounts for it?

As before, the most cogent reason is the identification with the parents: monkey see, monkey do. But by this time a wide variety of relationships can be found between children and parents.

If the mother is too possessive, the child will not be free to move to another child. More often the result is one of a fantasy love, which is quite common. If the mother is too rejecting, the child may well move on to another child, but the disappointment will interfere. If the mother tries to live vicariously through her children, she may permit a first love affair of some intimacy, out of identification on her part, but then it breaks up because she wishes to have her needs gratified rather than have the children gratify theirs.

As noted above, the first love affair is almost always heterosexual. Its vicissitudes vary from culture to culture and from family to family. Apart from the mother, the father may also be involved at this time. The numerous possibilities that exist parallel the numerous varieties of love affairs in adolescence.

That the love affair breaks through in all cases indicates that the sexual drive, or heterosexual affectional system, is still powerful enough at this stage to overcome serious obstacles. This too is an important theoretical yield.

—7—

The clinical facts cited call for a reexamination of the growth process. What accounts for psychological growth?

On this point Freud was both ambiguous and ambivalent. At times he wrote as if all growth could result only from frustration, since, he argued, the human being will not willingly abandon a libidinal position. At other times he described a sequence of maturational stages, as in psychosexual development, which are biologically determined, and to which education has to bend its efforts; if education violates the biologically determined growth process, serious damage results.

Subsequent experience has led to a clearer image of growth. First of all the human being, like all biological organisms, is subject to a series of biological clocks. Much about these is known, much is unknown. At any rate, the inherent physiological growth process is determined by these biological clocks.

Psychological clocks seem to parallel the biological ones. The autonomous ego will develop independently of the id; hence it is called autonomous. In general it is satisfaction that leads to the passage to a new stage in development, while frustration tends to fixate the individual. Naturally some middle ground must be reached; the dangers of pampering were exaggerated in Freud's day, while the dangers of rejection have been exaggerated in ours. To get a rounded theory of growth, however, the newer data on the pathology induced by understimulation must be added to the older data of Freud's day on the pathology induced by overstimulation.

In general, in childhood there seems to be an enormous momentum toward growth, which often carries through in spite of enormous obstacles. This explains why by and large disturbances in children are less severe than in adults; the growth process carries them along. The oedipal situation and the first love affair appear to be integral parts of the growth process, with sufficient momentum to carry the child through a variety of traumatic experiences.

—8—

The first love affair disappears and the latency period ensues. In spite of numerous changes in the cultural attitude toward sexuality, the latency period still appears to be the norm in our culture. But viewed as a sequel to the first love affair, latency appears in a different light. In latency boys and girls hate and avoid one another. At first enforced by parental vigilance, primarily to avoid sex play, later this separation becomes internalized in the child's superego.

But then, as the child experiences it, love has turned into hate.

The love affair is replaced by a hate affair. This hate affair dominates the emotional relationship of the sexes in latency. When the child reaches puberty, the hate affair again has to be shifted to a love affair. It is not surprising that these numerous shifts are reflected in serious psychopathology in large numbers of cases.

—9—

The first love affair is an external event; identification with the parents and the formation of a superego are internal. What is the relationship between internal representations and external events?

Here a dichotomy presents itself in the psychoanalytic literature. The more classical Freudians (Klein, Mahler, Kohut, Kernberg, etc.) tend to concentrate almost exclusively on the internal events, while in contrast such modern movements as family therapy concentrate almost exclusively on external ones.

There can be little doubt that in the earliest years internalization derives entirely from external experience. For example, some studies of fantasy in preoedipal children have shown that as much as 75 percent of their fantasy play is a direct reflection of what goes on in their homes; Anna Freud's description of the defense of identification with the aggressor is a good example.

As the child gets older, however, the external world comes to be reflected through the prism of existing internal structures; the subsequent internalization then has less direct relationship to the outside than might be thought. The precise time when there is a clear-cut shift from external to internal determination is hard to pin down. Freud placed it at the oedipal superego period; Hartmann, Kris, and Loewenstein (1946) allowed for many changes in latency. The success of psychoanalytic therapy shows that under certain circumstances even the most deeply entrenched internal structures can be altered by suitably arranged external events.

Inasmuch as internal structures always take a long time (at least several years) to crystallize, their formation during this period is constantly subject to external influences. These mold or guide the internal structure until eventually a new amalgam comes into being.

The first love affair comes at around the same time as the formation of the superego; it seems reasonable to suppose that it is related to that formation.

I would hypothesize that the love affair is in certain essential respects a testing of the superego prohibitions. That it breaks through in spite of them shows how strong the drive is; that it then disappears shows how strong the superego is. But its disappearance is reflected in a taboo against sexuality. It is in this way that in our culture the hatred between the sexes in internalized with its disastrous consequences for human happiness.

Precursors of the love affair may be found in the relationships with mother, father, siblings, and other significant figures at earlier levels. In all of these cases (as in Mahler's separation-individuation phase) an internal structure is laid down over a period of time based on a series of external events; hence the variability of these internal structures, and their dependency on the personalities of the parents.

—10—

The total absence of a first love affair is so rare that when it occurs it must be regarded as an ominous sign of future psychopathology. It is a manifestation of a harsh superego that will not let the child leave the parents to go on to a new partner.

Inasmuch as analysts and other theoreticians have not been alerted to the significance of the first love affair, they may easily overlook it in their case histories. In the case history of the Wolf Man, for example, where Freud produces an exhaustive description of the patient's childhood, he does not mention any play with a child of the same age, though he does mention the attraction to the buttocks of the maid, and the sex play with his sister. It is difficult to say whether the Wolf Man had an affair or not. In any case it was not prominent.

—11—

The data likewise suggest a rethinking of instinct theory. Apparently the sexual instinct is still strong enough at this age to override all social barriers. Harlow in his studies of monkeys states that love appears in monkeys at two months, fear at three months, aggression at six months. Our data are consistent with a similar theory for humans: love is basic, appearing at birth; later comes fear, most pronounced in the eight-month anxiety and still later rage, when the executive apparatus for it develops. Hostility should be looked upon as basically a reaction to frustration; Freud's first theory (1905) makes more sense than his second (1914). The growth process in humans could be seen as attachment (love), fear of breaking the attachment (anxiety), and then anger when the attachment is broken.

—12—

In his classical paper on transitional objects and transitional phenomena, Winnicott (1953) has established the significance of transitional objects in the development of the infant. These transitional objects are seen by him as substitutes for the mother, necessary in the gradual process of separation from the mother.

All human development is gradual, and all development involves long periods of transition. However, except for Winnicott's observation, everything else points to the gradual substitution of one person for another. Thus the first love affair represents the substitution of a childhood experience for the observed adult experience, arising from the child's ego strength and sense of maturity. Since Winnicott's formulation does not quite fit in with this broader proposition, some closer examination may be useful.

If we look at the objects that the infant uses for transitions, they fall into two categories: one is the blanket, diaper, and the like, clearly representing the mother, but the other is the furry animal, or woolly toy, closer to the hairy (woolly) father. Winnicott does not consider the role of the father in the transitional process; the times emphasized the mother, who had been overlooked up to then.

But it is clear that the father also plays a role in this process. I would hypothesize that the transitional object is part of the move from mother to father, which is so central at this age. Then this basic developmental formula can be laid down: growth involves mother to father to outside persons. All stages of development involve moves from one person to another. All involve long transitional periods making use of symbolically meaningful substances in varying degrees.

—13—

In sum, the first love affair is an essential aspect of human experience. Up to now theory has missed its great significance. Freud once observed that psychoanalytic research can go on for decades and miss the most obvious observations. That is the case with the first love affair. It was originally described to prove that children have sexual feelings, but once that point was made it was forgotten. The present discussion has attempted to integrate a variety of points of view to show that the careful consideration of the first love affair leads to a more meaningful view of many aspects of psychoanalytic theory.

Adolescent Love

The next stage, after the oedipal, where love becomes the predominant source of conflict, is in adolescence. Here a comparison of Freud's *Three Essays on Sexuality* may be made with the modern emphasis on preoedipal determinants and liberation from the parents, as exemplified in Blos (1979). Freud's treatment of adolescence offered a mix of ideas. He attributed his work to plain common sense and emphasized the blindness of the scientific world to the most obvious phenomena of sexuality. He wrote: "If mankind had been able to learn from a direct observation of children, these three essays could have remained unwritten" (p. 133).

In Part III Freud deals with the transformations of puberty. Here he makes certain fundamental contributions that have been incorporated into all psychological theory worth the mention, e.g., that a normal sexual life is assured only by an exact convergence of the affectionate current and the sexual current, both being directed toward the sexual object and the sexual aim. "The new sexual aim in men consists in the discharge of the sexual products." He could just as well have added here that the new sexual aim in women relates to the discharge of blood from the vagina (menstruation). Thus the two sexes run parallel: the great change in puberty is the breakthrough of instinctual drives over which the child literally has no voluntary control, e.g., nocturnal dreams (wet dreams) in the boy, with the discharge of semen, and disturbances of menstruation in the girl. One could add here the innumerable social measures adopted to deal with these two bodily reactions, so that puberty rituals become universal. The most striking feature of the pubertal changes somatically is the changes in the genitalia, which lead eventually to fore-pleasure and the primacy of the genital zone. Here love develops as well. "There are thus good reasons why a child sucking at his mother's breast has become the prototype of every relation of love. The finding of an object is in fact a refinding of it" (p. 222).

This theory of love makes very good sense. In modern contemporary theories such as Blos (1979), however, it is omitted in favor of pregenital considerations. This is an error that has been justly described as the desexualization of psychoanalysis. Blos, in fact, like many other modern writers, omits Freud's observation that the great change of adolescence (or puberty — the concept of adolescence had just been introduced by Stanley Hall) is the development of bodily products that are *nolens volens* extruded from the body, and that in this process of extrusion arouse both great pleasure and great guilt feelings.

In the latter part of this essay of 1905 he later added the section on the libido theory, taking it over almost bodily from the essay on narcissism in 1914. Since that essay was full of errors, the essential simplicity as well as profundity of the *Three Essays* was spoiled by the addition. But since Freud's authority has been so great, the chronology of the additions has not been properly noted and the weakness of the modern position in omitting the profound observations of the original essay has been overlooked.

The rise of love feelings in puberty, together with sexual feelings, is the most obvious change that occurs and the one that make the greatest impression on the growing child. It is only because the parents and their representatives interfere with the expression of the love impulse through sexual behavior that guilt, shame, and their consequences arise in the adolescent. Later Freud was to say:

> Sexual love is undoubtedly one of the chief things in life, and the union of mental and bodily satisfaction in the enjoyment of love is one of its culminating peaks. Apart from a few queer fanatics, all the world knows this and conducts its life accordingly; science alone is too delicate to admit it. (XII, pp. 169–70)

Freud could not foresee that some of his own followers would be among the scientists who denied the fundamental importance of sexual love. Thus Blos does not mention the word "love" in his index, nor does he discuss adolescent love in any depth, especially in its relationship to sexuality. His emphasis throughout is on what he calls the second individuation process, and he hardly, if at all, mentions the momentous physical changes that adolescents undergo and that have such enormous influence on them. Four centuries earlier John Donne had written: "Soul to soul doth speak, but 'tis the body that's the book." The whole thrust of Freud's first theory, involving the intermingling of somatic and psychic processes, seems almost to have been lost in his presentation. As in the famous Shakespearean play *Romeo and Juliet*, adolescent love ends in tragedy, but that is not the only possible ending, and the tragedy is brought about by the families of the two adolescents, not by anything inherent in their love.

Norman Kiell, in his compendium *The Universal Experience of Adolescence* (1964), has put together a fascinating collection of studies of adolescent development and their basically uniform character through the ages of Western civilization. His chapters include: sexual awakening; heterosexual play; adolescent crushes or first love; the homosexual component; masturbation and nocturnal emission; the sexual enlightenment of adolescents; contradictions, polarities, and defenses; the conflict of generations; sibling feelings; the peer culture; conformity and the peer culture; the friendship pattern; social relationships; socioeconomic consciousness and prejudice; dislike for schooling; intellectual ferment; argumentation and debating; the compulsion to read; the influence of teachers; the use of language; God;

father and the adolescent vocation and identification; morbidity and the suicidal impulse; juvenile delinquency; gambling, lying, cheating, and stealing; toward adulthood.

It would be illuminating to give examples from each of these but it would take us too far afield. Suffice it to say that adolescence represents both physical and psychological maturity, and that love is its main pleasure as well as its main stumbling block.

Later Life Stages

The love that flourishes in adolescence is of the same quality as the love that is awakened later in life, except for the parental love that arises when a person has children. In principle, however, no new dynamic element is introduced by the love of children; it is simply a new experience, heavily dependent on previous life events. It is of some interest that Harlow in his book *Learning to Love* (1974) enumerates five stages in monkeys, which include parental love as the last, but most rudimentary stage. Biologically the main characteristic of human beings is their capacity to form a family and love their children.

With these considerations the developmental line of love is completed. It still remains true that love is an ideal that is desirable as a component of the analytic ideal, indeed the most important component. Yet it is difficult to fulfill, and in practice causes as much grief as pleasure.

Still, even if love is only a dream or an ideal, it took psychoanalysis to teach the world how important dreams and ideals are in human existence.

In adult life the love impulse goes through the same stages as in childhood, only ego and superego considerations come into play. The developmental line may be traced as attachment, admiration (oedipal), companionship (latency), sexuality (puberty), intimacy (late adolescence), and finally caring (parental). Each of these stages in the adult encounters various hurdles and resistances, much as in childhood. The ideals of the surrounding culture play an especially important part, more so than in childhood.

Religious Love

The reader may have been surprised that up to now nothing has been said about religious images of love, especially those of Christianity, which is allegedly the religion of love. The reason is that we are living

in an irreligious age, in which all the old ideals have been questioned
and evidence demanded that they are actually operative. The expression "practice what you preach" refers to the religious failure to heal
the gap between promise and performance. Oskar Pfister, a Swiss minister who became an analyst and a friend of Freud's, was dismayed
by the horrors inflicted in the name of the religion of love through the
ages. In his major book *Christianity and Fear* (1944) Pfister undertook
a careful historical study of Christianity to understand why it has so
often appeared in such perverted form. The only road to a true Christianity, he finally concluded, lay through psychoanalysis of Christians.
Otherwise, religion degenerates into dogma and the religion of love
becomes a religion of fear. "The neurosis of individuals leads to a
neurotic malformation of their Christian faith, and in certain circumstances must do so inevitably; and when this process is applied
to the masses it necessarily affects entire churches, the Protestant as
well as the Catholic" (p. 193).

In any case most enlightened people have lived without religion
since the French Revolution. Religion is not an essential part of the
analytic ideal.

7

The Transformation
of the Twentieth Century:
From Slavery to Work Satisfaction

*T*HAT LOVE SHOULD BE PART OF THE ANALYTIC IDEAL is no
surprise; after all it is a value shared by most cultures, in one form or
another. But that work should have become part of the analytic ideal,
for both men and women, requires some explanation.

The significance of work in the good life was not part of the thinking of the ancients. Ordinarily human beings curse work, find it a
burden, try to get away from it whenever they can, dream of the days
when they can retire and go fishing.

For most of human history slavery has been the source of the work
force. In the United States it has been customary to refer to slavery as
that "peculiar institution," but in point of fact it has not been unusual;
it has been a most common form of human interaction. Slaves are
mentioned in the Bible, without any apparent criticism.

As Patterson (1982) points out in his comprehensive study, slavery
is a form of social death. Slavery was connected with warfare, in that
men captured in battle became slaves for the rest of their lives. But
even without warfare, slavery was firmly established in all the great
early centers of human civilization and, far from declining, actually
increased in significance with the growth of all the epochs and cultures
that modern Western people consider watersheds in their historical
development. Slaves constituted such a large proportion of the Flo-
rentine population during the fourteenth and fifteenth centuries that

they significantly transformed the appearance of the indigenous Tuscan population. The historian Eric Williams even argued that the rise of capitalism itself can be accounted for largely by the enormous profits generated by the slave system of the Americas. It is clear, at least, that New World slavery was a key factor in the rise of the Western European economies.

The social system based on slavery is necessarily based on force, for no society has ever maintained slavery on a voluntary basis. The whole structure of interpersonal relationships in slavery is so repugnant to members of a free society that it can scarcely be discussed without heated passions. For example, a North Carolina judge, Thomas Ruffin, declared in 1820 that the intentional wounding of a hired slave by his hirer did not constitute a crime. He declared that "with slavery...the end is the profit of the master" (Patterson, p. 3). "...The power of the master must be absolute, to render the submission of the slave perfect."

Officially slavery was destroyed in most parts of the world in the nineteenth century. This in itself is an extraordinary fact that should have engaged the historians more that it has, since the abolition of slavery deprived the ruling classes of vast sources of wealth. Evidently the democratic image of human rights, so prominent in the American and French revolutions, finally permeated the rest of the world, and slavery became no longer acceptable.

But slavery did persist in parts of the world other than America and Europe. And it returned in the Nazi and Soviet systems. Manchester has written of the Nazi slave camps:

> We were not slaves; our status was much lower. True, we were deprived of freedom and became a piece of property which our masters put to work. But here the similarity with any known form of slavery ends, for we were a completely expendable piece of property.... The equipment in the shop was well maintained. It was operated with care, oiled, greased and allowed to rest; its longevity was protected. We, on the other hand, were like a piece of sandpaper which, rubbed once or twice, becomes useless and is thrown away to be burned with the waste.

Slavery was condoned by the Catholic church, since in its ideology what counts is not happiness on earth but the quickest way to get to heaven, where eternal bliss awaits the believer.

The psychoanalyst concludes from a consideration of slavery that wholesale psychoses were more the rule than the exception in the past. The historian Friedrich Heer has agreed, stating that the history of the Middle Ages can be understood only in the light of mass psychoses. Nor is it any different with the troubled history of the twentieth century.

It was not until the Protestant Reformation of the sixteenth century that work came to be seen in a different light, which Max Weber described in his classic term "the Protestant ethic" (1904). While Weber found the Protestant ethic in the ideas of religion themselves, others disagreed; Tawney (1926) argued that the Protestant Reformation was an expression of the aspirations of the rising groups of merchants and craftsmen in the later period of medieval society. The idea that work was both ennobling and a path to salvation was congenial to the new citizens of the growing towns and cities. It seems obvious enough, however, that once the horrors of the murderous slave societies had been brought to an end, someone would have to do the work, so to ennoble it sounds like a useful rationalization. These developments also indicate that sooner or later humankind turns against a social system of unmitigated hatred and oppression.

The rise of the notion of a "calling" is usually attributed to Martin Luther. From his time on, people sooner or later had to find a calling for themselves, an ideal that has persisted into modern times, though in far more sophisticated form.

With the French and American revolutions, slavery as an acceptable ideology came to an end, and a new ideology had to be found to make work palatable. In the nineteenth century this ideology was still based to a large extent on the power system, where employers could maintain their power by inducing people to work in a variety of ways. In the beginning these ways were more degrading than ennobling, and the term "wage slave" was born. Wage earners, it was realized, were little better than slaves. This was the system that Marx took strong objection to, building up his own mythology to preach its extermination. But Marx made the mistake of blaming capitalism for wage slavery, instead of human beings' hatred of their fellow human beings and wish to dominate them. Once capitalism in the old form came to an end in the twentieth century, a new ideology again had to be found to make work acceptable. Had Marx not made the mistake of attributing wage slavery to the greed of capitalists and had he seen that it was an expression of a basic hatred in human beings themselves, the monstrosities of the twentieth century might have been avoided. But it was not to be. And the exploitation of the wage slaves by the totalitarian regimes turned out to be even more horrible than anything capitalists had ever devised.

The twentieth century has not yet come to an end, and its history has yet to be written. But it is already clear that it is a history of wars, revolutions, atrocities of the most unbelievable kind, even wholesale murder of certain races or of the reputed "enemies of the state." It is in short a history of hostility run loose.

In such a climate the notion and importance of work once more had to be reevaluated, and here modern psychology comes in. Work as a means of earning a living and getting along well with one's fellow human beings makes good sense, so that the shift in thinking from Marx to Freud began to dominate the ideological discussions. In fact, many theoreticians of work, as will be seen, directly attribute their thinking and ideas to Freud.

When there is no other way out, people have to work, and a leisure class is no longer permitted. The robber barons of the nineteenth century temporarily did set up such a leisure class, based on money rather than hereditary privileges; they were mercilessly lampooned in Thorstein Veblen's classic *The Theory of the Leisure Class* (1899).

The image of a leisure class that must behave in certain ways had existed with a religious basis, e.g., monks and priests. The priests developed a stranglehold on the population to maintain their own domination; every revolution in modern times, except perhaps the American where the priests were not so strong, has begun by attacking, even murdering, the priestly caste. (In the United States before the Civil War, many southern churches even separated from their northern counterparts on the basis of a religious justification of slavery, what one might call Mammon before God.)

In the intermediate stage of the late nineteenth century, between the abolition of slavery and the establishment of a rationale for work, the notion of the "gentleman" became prominent. The prime requisite for being a gentleman was not to sully one's hands with work, or even business. Evans (1949) traced the origins of the notion to chivalry and saw this evolution as the process whereby the barbaric knights of the Dark Ages were transmuted (at any rate in theory) into the courteous gentlemen of subsequent times. While the church was trying to curb the brutality of the masses, the knightly class was evolving its own culture, with its peculiar code of rules, customs, and ceremonials; thus chivalry emerged. It was a complete way of life whereby behavior could be regulated and a system of thought whereby the whole course of history could be explained.

Evans argued that the origin of the conception of the hero lies in the fact that it is he who rebels against the father and kills him, but, as Freud noted, "The hero of the tragedy had to suffer; this is still the essential content of a tragedy" (*Totem and Taboo*, p. 238; Evans, p. 27).

The regulative principle of the gentlemanly code became that of "playing the game." But the knightly exploits are part of an organized self-deception in which the heroism and the suffering are counterfeit. The importance of this game is that by means of it the players can pretend that they are heroes and are emancipated from childhood; at the same time it provides a magnificent means of denying the unpleasantness of reality. "It is an historical fact that Chivalry became played out because reality perpetually gave the lie to it. Nothing could hide its inherent falsity. 'The game,' said the Dutch historian Huizinga, 'ended by boring the players themselves'" (*The Waning of the Middle Ages*, 1937, p. 116).

If a gentleman is willing to play the game, we need not be surprised at the corollary: he is not concerned to work, at least not for a living, for work is concerned with the reality principle. Work, one can add, is also concerned with competence and achievement, and the gentleman has neither; he lives on his hereditary laurels (in England, his estates) like the knights of old.

The unwritten ideal of the Englishman was to attain the position where he need not work and so realize the culturally determined ideal of being a man of leisure. The gentleman is thus the man who exercises power and does not have to dirty his hands with work. The gentleman is never introspective and never concerned with his inner feelings, lest he tamper with the carefully devised defenses that the generations have provided for his protection. But since this ideal involved hereditary power, it too had to pass before the onslaught of democracy. All men have to work, and even in modern America Marshall Field, as a result of his analysis, started a liberal newspaper.

The statement that love and work represent the normal resolution of life has usually been attributed to Freud, but while he very well may have meant it he never actually said it. In the Introductory Lectures (1916–17) he stated:

> The distinction between nervous health and neurosis is thus reduced to a practical question and is decided by the outcome — by whether the subject is left with a sufficient amount of capacity for enjoyment and of efficiency.... I need not tell you that this discovery is the theoretical justification for our conviction that neuroses are in principle curable in spite of their being based on constitutional disposition. (XVI, p. 457)

This quote is a good example of how the analytic ideal gradually evolved in the minds of leading analysts. Psychoanalysis sees all human beings as equal; it deplores social arrangements where people rule by brute force, as in slavery, or by mythological rationalizations, as in religion. Rather all people have to work to support the useful endeavors of the society. Hence love and work become an attainable ideal, difficult to achieve, yet worth the achieving.

The history of the last two centuries demonstrates the constant efforts on the part of many to achieve dominance over others and the resentment of such dominance. Rich people are not popular, and it has been noted that in the entire United States there is not a single statue devoted to a rich man because he made much money. The average person agrees that "no one ever made a million dollars honestly." The recent trial of Leona Helmsley, arguably among the richest people in the United States (the Helmsley's real estate holdings are said to be worth five billion dollars), once more brings these dynamics to the fore: some try to dominate (now by money), while others resent it and eventually get even. On the other side, the Helmsleys clearly seem to be psychopathic creatures who could benefit from analysis, since with billions in assets they have to stoop to steal a few million and at an advanced age risk a jail sentence as well as social ostracism.

In spite of the importance of work, a comprehensive discussion of work is nowhere to be found in the psychoanalytic literature. The most clarifying discussions are those in the works of liberal economists, such as Galbraith, McClelland, Allardt (Sweden), and others. The discussion here is designed to lay the basis for such a theory.

Summarizing some of the previous comments, we can say that the idea that work can make people happy is a fairly novel one in human experience. Aristotle did not think so, nor did Christians for many centuries look upon work as anything but an interference with service to God. In keeping with this ideology, the classical economists argued that people work only because they have to make money.

It is paradoxical that although Marx idealized labor to the point where all values come from labor, he too had no coherent theory of work. His whole philosophy is based on the notion of alienated labor and the assumption that all labor prior to the achievement of communism is essentially alienated.

Weber's compelling thesis is that capitalistic human beings are dominated by the Protestant ethic. This ethic emphasizes the virtues of industry, sobriety, work, and the accumulation of wealth, all with religious sanction. The *summum bonum* of this ethic is the earning of more and more money, combined with the strict avoidance of all spontaneous enjoyment of life.

A subsidiary confirmation of Weber's position is the work by McClelland on the achievement motive (1961). McClelland emphasizes that basic to capitalism, as to any society that grows rapidly, is a frame of mind that stresses achievement, responsibility, enterprise, and growth. His thesis is that it is not profit per se that makes the businessman tick, but a strong desire for achievement in doing a good job.

Galbraith in various works offers a total revision of the psychological economic bases of the system under which we are living. He makes free use of the findings of modern psychology, especially psychoanalysis.

He holds that there are four major motives that lead people today to work: pecuniary compensation, compulsion, identification, and adaptation. These can motivate an individual either separately or in combination. The strength of any given motivation or of any motivating system will be measured by the effectiveness with which it aligns the individual with the goals of the organization.

Perhaps the best known and the most profound of the empirical aspects of work satisfaction is found in the writings of Frederick Herzberg (1959).

On the basis of questionnaires submitted to two hundred engineers and accountants, Herzberg found that five factors, which he calls motivators, stand out as strong determiners of job satisfaction: achievement, recognition, work itself, responsibility, and advancement. The major factors that stand out as dissatisfiers are company policy and administration, supervision, salary, interpersonal relations, and working conditions.

The motivators all seem to describe the relationship to what people do: job content, achievement on a test, recognition of task achievement, nature of the task, responsibility for the task, professional advancement, and long-term growth in task capability.

The central theme for the dissatisfiers is that they describe the relationship to the context or environment in which people do their jobs. Since these factors serve primarily to prevent job dissatisfaction while having little effect on positive job attitude, he calls them hygiene factors. This is an analogy to the medical term referring to preventive and environmental factors. Dissatisfying factors do not effectively motivate the individual to superior performance and effort. The principal result of the analysis was to suggest that the hygiene factors must lead to job dissatisfaction because of a need to avoid unpleasantness; the motivators lead to job satisfaction because of a need for growth or self-actualization.

Paradoxically, yet not unexpectedly, the demand that work should be gratifying has brought about a searching reevaluation of the meaning of work, especially as the hold of religion and the Protestant ethic lessens. The Protestant ethic in practice is being replaced by the analytic ideal (Fine, 1984). The most recent and most comprehensive examination of the American work experience is found in the report of a special task force to the Secretary of Health, Education and Welfare, published in book form as *Work in America* (1973). The most comprehensive examination of work in general is found in *Working Life* (1981) edited by B. Gardell and G. Johansson, with numerous contributions by Swedish and other authors. Sweden has, as is generally recognized, made the most enlightened changes in the conditions of working life for all classes. Both of these books will be cited in detail.

The major study in *Work in America* was based on a representative sample of 1533 American workers at all occupational levels. It was undertaken by the Survey Research Center of the University of Michigan, with support from the Department of Labor.

Although a superficial Gallup poll question asking, "Are you satisfied with your work?" evokes positive responses 80 to 90 percent of the time, any more sophisticated approach immediately reveals the deep dissatisfactions that affect American workers. These can be grouped as follows:

(1) *Blue-collar blues:* Work problems spill over from the factory into other activities of life; one frustrated assembly line worker will displace his job-generated aggression on family, neighbors, and strangers, while a fellow worker comes home so fatigued from the day's work that all he can do is collapse and watch TV.

An earlier study of work alienation among 1,150 employed men revealed that the best independent predictors of work alienation are (a) a work situation and hierarchical organization that provide little discretion in pace and schedule; (b) a career that has been blocked and chaotic; (c) a stage in the life cycle that puts the squeeze on the worker (many dependent children and low savings).

(2) *Worker mobility:* Many blue-collar workers do not believe that there is a great deal of opportunity to move up the ladder of success, and the lack of alternatives produces frustration. Further, manual work has become increasingly denigrated by the upper middle class.

(3) *White-collar woes:* There is increasing evidence of managerial discontent. One out of three middle managers indicates some will-

ingness to join a union, while a large percentage seeks a change in middle life.

(4) *The young worker challenging the work ethic:* A consistent attack on the Protestant ethic is found to be particularly strong among young people. Yankelovich found that in 1968, 69 percent expressed the belief that hard work will always pay off, while by 1971 this had fallen to 39 percent. Young managers reflect the passionate concern of youth in the 1980s for individuality, openness, humanism, concern, and change, and they are determined to be heard. In short, there is an ongoing transition from the Protestant ethic to the analytic ideal in all walks of life (Douvan, Kulka, and Veroff, 1981).

(5) *The minority workers:* Minority workers and their families are serious casualties of the work system in our society. Unemployment is always much higher among blacks and other minority groups than among the white middle classes. One out of three minority workers is unemployed, irregularly employed, or has given up looking for a job. Another third of minority workers do have full-time jobs, but these are mainly laboring jobs and jobs in the service trades, which often pay less than a living wage.

(6) *Women and work:* In addition to the fact that half of all women between eighteen and sixty-four are presently in the labor force, Department of Labor studies have shown that nine out of ten women will work outside the home at some time in their lives. (This shift in women's ideal from home to the workplace is one of the most significant revolutions of the twentieth century.) Because of the widespread dissatisfaction that women have had with the kinds of jobs that they have traditionally held, women can be expected to speak out even more forcefully on the quality of working life.

(7) *Older workers and retirement:* In 1900, two-thirds of American men who were sixty-five and older were working. By 1971, the figure had dropped to one-fourth, with a smaller proportion on a year-round, full-time basis. Most of the members of this age group who are working today are expected to retire. The problem that has arisen is the inadequacy of pension plans.

(8) *Work and health:* A surprisingly positive correlation exists between work satisfaction and physical and mental health. (Thus Herzberg's analysis is confirmed in empirical studies.) In one fifteen-year study of aging (Palmare, 1969), the strongest predictor of longevity was work satisfaction.

Work is only part of the good life, but a very important one. What comes out in all the empirical studies is that workers somehow want to have the feeling of achievement, that they have done something in the social system. They can no longer get this feeling by identifying with religion; they must get it in some more personal way. The collapse of communist ideology all over the world shows that they cannot get it by identifying with the alleged progress of communism (which now appears more as a regression and a release of destructive force); again even in totalitarian countries there must be more emphasis on personal satisfaction.

The shift to the analytic ideal has not been readily accepted by analysts, who are still bogged down in meaningless "schools of psychoanalysis," each of which flourishes mostly on its anti-Freudian philosophy (which includes a gross misunderstanding of Freud). It has however been grasped by many liberal thinkers in the social sciences. Gardell in *Working Life* (1981) states:

> Criteria of social and psychological well-being are less well established. There is some convergence nevertheless around the Freudian definition of well-being as the ability to work, love and play, around the idea of freedom from distressing symptoms (gastric discomfort, inability to sleep, etc.), around veridicality of perception, and around positive affect towards self and towards life. (p. 19)

And Douvan, Kulka, and Veroff in their work on mental health in America (1981) state:

> In these characteristics — isolation, intellectual/verbal analysis — psychoanalysis represent quintessential science. Its popularity marks the movement of the scientific revolution to the last frontier — the sphere of human behavior and the thickets of the human soul — and represents, above all, a remarkable faith in and optimism about the power of science. Its emergence as the model of human counsel marks modern sensibility and displaces a religious/moral model. (p. 7)

The actual application of the analytic ideal, however, has led to more pessimistic feelings. At another point these authors state:

> Times change. Between 1957 and 1976 we acquired a good deal of experience with the application of psychological knowledge, and we have been chastened by the experience.... We have come to recognize that "human engineering" is not so simple as the analogy with the physical sciences implies. (p. 267)

Thus work problems call for psychological remedies. I have elsewhere suggested (*Vision*, 1981, p. 253) that we can single out psychoeconomic disorders, in which inner psychological disturbances lead to economic symptoms. It is just as ineffectual to handle them economically as it is to handle the psychosomatic symptoms medically. Six kinds of psychoeconomic disorders can be distinguished: (1) total inability to work; (2) work incapacity; (3) work instability; (4) work dissatisfaction; (5) underachievement; and (6) paradoxical overachievement. Characteristically these problems are receiving increasing recognition from industry. One of the surprising developments in the past decade has been the vast increase in insurance for psychotherapy allocated by the large corporations, which thus move toward the recognition that the need to maintain worker satisfaction is as important a part of their enterprise as the need to show a profit.

In spite of the enormous amount of research trying to improve worker satisfaction on the job, generalizations are almost entirely absent. Each situation has to be treated in a different way.

What is emphasized more than anything else is that work satisfaction or dissatisfaction does not necessarily relate to the work as such, but is part of the larger scheme of life. The Dutch-American publisher Kluwer has for a number of years issued a journal called *Social Indicators Research*, in which they have tried to pin down the variables that are important to each individual. This is another way of saying that they are looking for the analytic ideal, and in many cases the two approaches overlap. Before going on to cases in psychotherapy that involve work difficulties, I shall summarize some of the significant studies contained in the book by Gardell and Johansson: *Working Life*. The best way to summarize these papers is to relate them to the analytic ideal. In their study of married couples Schwartz and Blumstein (1983) have an extensive discussion of the conflicts surrounding work, and this material can be drawn on as well.

In the nineteenth century the world of paid employment had traditionally been thought to be comprised of men, while the household and children were considered women's domain. Though much has changed, feelings about this traditional male/female separation of work has persisted, even though the patriarchal household has in many instances been replaced by the egalitarian two-paycheck couple.

Since the notion that women ought to work rather than stay home and take care of the children is a fairly recent one (especially marked since World War II when the war forced women into many occupations previously out of bounds, even the military) the role of work for women is more ambiguous than for men.

Rita Liklestrom reported on a study (1978) that concentrated on women in "male" industrial jobs. The first observation is that many couples have to be able to synchronize their lives to take care of the children. Spouses showed considerable flexibility and inventiveness in setting up the family schedule. Liklestrom usually found the most equally responsible parents in families where the parents relieve one another. In a number of cases, the working hours did not conform to the usual societal rhythm of seven A.M. to six P.M. In fact, 31 percent of the wage earners put in inconvenient working hours every work-day and up to 49 percent have inconvenient working hours during the workweek.

The scheduling entails a series of consequences for health, family life, and social life. The social consequences of inconvenience and irregular hours are often dubious. Parents' worktimes have a profound effect on the life rhythms of their children.

Much discussion goes on about what a possible cut in working hours means. In a 1972 poll an overwhelming percentage of persons said they would prefer shorter worktime to take the form of a longer unbroken block of time ("block leisure") around weekends or, alternatively, longer vacations, a lower retirement age, or sabbatical leave. Later investigations on a smaller scale (1978) indicate that public opinion has shifted somewhat in favor of a shorter workday. The free time per "workday" is called "piece leisure." It is the piece leisure that changes the daily round. Block leisure is by its very nature a drawing back, a way to disengage oneself from society, to devote oneself to private activities.

A six-hour workday had been described in Sweden as a reform for women, while men strongly favor a four-day week. After much discussion pro and con, the whole issue was shelved.

Many people are now going in for part-time employment, especially women. Nine out of ten part-time workers are women. Among the men it is chiefly the very young and the elderly who work part time.

The British social scientist Stanley Parker has devoted considerable thought to the work-leisure relationship, and contributes a paper on this topic to the book. Work, he argues, is a basic condition of the existence and continuation of human life. It is only for the last few decades that we have any reasonably objective documentation on the meaning of work for the mass of people.

From the Greek background that mechanical labor was a curse and the Hebrew view of work as a painful necessity emerged a number of other views. With the Renaissance came the view that creative work could be a joy in itself. The early Utopians looked forward to a society in which people would be joyful because each would have work suitable to his or her character and need do it for only a few hours a day. The nineteenth-century socialists held similar views, and Marx went along with them.

Leisure can be properly understood only in relation to work. Historically, as we have seen, the person of leisure was considered socially superior to the person who had to do all the work, especially the menial kind. Veblen went back to the barbarian stage of social development to find the origins of his theory of the leisure class. During the predatory culture labor comes to be associated in people's habits of thought with weakness and subjection to a master. It is therefore a mark of inferiority and comes to be accounted unworthy of persons in their best estate. By virtue of this tradition labor is felt to be debasing, and this tradition has never died out. To gain esteem it is not sufficient merely to possess wealth or power; it must be put in evidence (conspicuous consumption). This is partly achieved by conspicuous abstention from labor. The leisurely life of a ruling class is thus a means of their gaining the respect of others.

In preindustrial societies the majority of people had leisure only in the forms of rest from toil and of participation in ceremonies. This was not conscious leisure, or the result of an exercise of choice, but part of the regular pattern of living. The same applies to many nonindustrial societies today, as well as to all of history before the modern period when people had to work so hard to sustain themselves and their families that their lives were almost devoid of leisure and spontaneous activities. In the countries affected by the Hebrew tradition there is the Sabbath, but that is not so much a day of leisure as a day of ceremonial inactivity, a day of restraint.

In the modern world data is available on the relationship between work and leisure characteristic of a wide variety of occupational groups. Thus for the manual laborer the decreased strain of work has brought about a change in the function of leisure. In this sense leisure is a development of modern society.

George Friedman (1960) quotes a study of the leisure habits of employees at the Postal Cheque Center in Paris, whose jobs are completely routine. On leaving the office, these clerks are either more active or, in contrast, withdraw into themselves, in a sort of apathy. But a different pattern of work and leisure is shown by those nonmanual workers in the Center whose work demands more involvement and responsibility. Of professional engineers studied by Gerstl and Hutton (1966), 23 percent said they had hobbies connected with the field of engineering and as many as 73 percent claimed work-connected reading as one of their hobby interests. Heckscher and de Grazia concluded from their survey that the way of life of American business executives permits no clear-cut distinction between work and leisure. To counteract the encroachment of work on leisure time the executive's work is penetrated by qualities that we would ordinarily associate with leisure. On the other hand, David Riesman (1952) remarks that the professional or business person is apt to leave work with a good many tensions created by reactions to interpersonal situations, and so may have to satisfy leisure needs before being able to rise from the level of recreation to the level of creation. It is among these people (professionals and executives) that the image of the "workaholic" has arisen, those who prefer work above all else.

Parker states that there are two classes in modern industrial society, the privileged with respect to a unified and fulfilling work-leisure life and the underprivileged. For some men and women the problem of leisure does not arise. They obtain satisfaction from their work. They have some sphere of independent action, or they are presented with problems and difficulties that they must grapple with and solve. None of them are automata.... Because they find satisfaction in their work, they do not desire to flee from it as soon as the immediate job is completed. The impact of their profession or work is clearly discernible in all their activities. There is for them no sharp break. The method of earning their living determines for them their mode of living. And it does this in such a way that they obtain satisfaction. Hence they need not search for compensation in another direction; they do not require soporifics from the world of amusement. They tend to bring to such aspects of their lives the same attitude and qualities of mind as are required and developed by their work.

Parker classifies people under three categories with regard to work and leisure: extension, opposition, and neutrality. The quality of the work and leisure lives of the mass of people in any society becomes a problem when the confrontation between the work and leisure spheres reveals shortcomings in either or both or when a minority appears to have achieved conditions and satisfactions that give the majority a sense of relative deprivation. The view that there are two kinds of person with respect to seeking fulfillment in either work or leisure makes the problem narrower: how to adjust to seeking fulfillment within the present societal division of labor and leisure. But if we reject the view that there are two kinds of person, the problem becomes much wider: what kind of social structure is necessary to give all people opportunities for fulfillment in work and leisure, and how can various individual needs be reconciled with the "needs" of society itself? A large number of people today have work and leisure lives that are neither satisfying nor creative. Two broad solutions are possible: differentiation and integration.

Wilensky (1960) sees three solutions to the problem of "stultifying labor": (1) develop patterns of creative, challenging leisure to compensate for an inevitable spread in dehumanized labor; (2) offer vastly better compensation to those condemned to alienating work situations; (3) redesign the workplace and the technology to invest work with more meaning and hence enhance the quality of leisure.

Parker recommends the development of flexible life-styles to solve the problems of work and leisure. The idea of cyclical life patterns and flexible life-styles is ambitious and far reaching in its consequences for people and institutions. The achievement of flexible life-styles could bring us a new kind of leisure and a new kind of work and a range of activities that would partake of the nature of both work and leisure.

Schwartz and Blumstein (1983) offer an extended discussion of the two-paycheck family, which has virtually become the norm in our contemporary society. They conclude: "We do not think that a single utopian vision of family life is likely to emerge from the debate. In our study we show the many different ways our couples coordinate work and home life and what happens when they do."

From childhood on, the ideals of men embrace having a family, working, and taking care of a wife and children. By contrast, the role of work in a woman's life is much more varied. If she is poor, she may have to become part of the labor force to help support her family. She may come to like working and develop a commitment to it. Or she may dream of a man who earns a living that enables her to quit. A girl who grows up with more advantages may think of work as something she might enjoy. If she goes to college, she acquires training that prepares her for a career. She may plan to continue working even after she marries, taking time out to raise children. This woman considers her work something she has chosen, not something her husband expects. Only recently have some women begun to plan careers in the same way men traditionally have. But even these women expect to be able to devote themselves to their careers at their own pace, not to become the primary financial support of their families. To them, work is not their duty. Depending on their husband's attitude, it may not even be their right.

Even though married couples (and now live-ins as well) have grown up with traditional ideas about work roles, before marriage and after they do not know quite what to expect of each other. Does a job that profits the individual and does not improve the couple's welfare make it difficult to develop a feeling of togetherness? In the absence of tradition, does a man do what his father did and assume the role of the provider? Do women subordinate their career goals to their partners' as their mothers did, even though it may not be in their best interest?

There is great division of opinion about whether wives should work. Among couples who disagree, there are more wives who want to work than husbands who want to let them. Clearly our society is in a transitional stage, in which traditional, radically new, and mixed ideas mingle side by side. Even though a wife may be employed, it does not mean that her husband has wholeheartedly acknowledged her right to be so. One example that Schwartz and Blumstein give is that of Nelson and Muriel. Nelson, forty-three, is an insurance salesman. Muriel, forty-two, is a computer programmer. They have been married for eighteen years and have no children. Nelson told the interviewers:

> I have always worked and I guess we have a rather traditional marriage from the standpoint that I expect to work and I am very happy to see her stay at home and do what she wants to do. And if she wants to work, okay, but I would rather see her join a club or something and just have a good time. (p. 119)

Obviously such views may often lead to marital disagreement, sometimes of a serious kind. In fact, they did find that married couples who disagree about the wife's right to work have less happy relationships. Most working wives work with the accord of their husbands, and husbands and wives decide together whether the woman will work part time or full time. But when the couple fights about her working, the relationship becomes strained. Sometimes the couple fights about the husband's reaction to the effect that the wife's full-time work has on the household. He considers the household to be her responsibility and is angry about her absence. An example is Amelia and Wayne, who have been married four years. Amelia, thirty-one, sells sportswear, and Wayne manages a fast-food restaurant. The way the house is kept is one of their major sources of conflict; it often leads to a quarrel about Amelia's work.

When a wife works, the couple fights more about how the children are being raised. Conventional wisdom (following psychoanalytic theory about the mother-child bond) says that children grow up best by having their mothers at home, at least until the end of their school years. Some studies indicate that this may not be true, but clinical experience does bear this out. If a mother of young children is out in the labor force, as more than half are nowadays, she may bring feelings of guilt to the job. One wife, married for two years, works as a part-time teacher's assistant. She described how she feels being away from her baby:

> I feel bad when I have to leave her. Usually I will bend over backwards to try and spend as much time with her as I can, but I always feel that I'm not giving her enough time. She's old enough now so that she will cling to me sometimes when I have to leave and that about breaks my heart. (p. 135)

Georgette, a legal secretary in her midthirties, has been married for three years. She has three children from a former marriage. She too is troubled by spending a lot of time away from them:

> I call them during my lunch hour and make noises to them over the phone at the babysitter's. The people in the office think I'm crazy, making baby noises over the phone.... But I feel sad about not being with them and I want them to remember that I am thinking about them.... Then I'll bring them things, too, or do something special on the weekends.... I think I'm always making it up to them. (p. 135)

Another woman disclosed a feeling many employed mothers have, that no matter what else is happening at the job, the children are always vivid in her mind.

Because working wives bring money into the household, their work helps equalize the balance of power in their marriages. Their work also brings them greater respect from their husbands. Each partner's relative income helps determine the balance of power in a marriage. Married couples do not automatically assume that both partners will have jobs. This means that some wives either because they do not want to work or are not allowed to, do not have access to an important source of power that would give them a more equal say in the marriage. A wife who is not employed outside the home is at a disadvantage. But this is only partly because she earns no money. Men often respect paid employment outside the home more than they respect housework. Men's own self-respect is in part derived from their success in the world of work, and while they may say they have as much respect for a wife who stays at home, they often do not.

Even when they work, wives often bear all the responsibility for housework. This is the case even among couples who profess egalitarian social ideals, including equal sharing of all the housework. While these men do more housework than those who are in favor of a traditional division of labor between the sexes, they are still way behind their wives. In fact, when the situation was analyzed in more detail, it turned out that the idea of shared responsibility is a myth. Actually, when husbands do a lot of housework, married couples have greater conflict, which indicates that the influence of the traditional norms is still being felt.

For employed wives, the happier they are with their job, the happier they are with their marriage. All persons are happier in their relationships if their partners are successful in their jobs. Thus achievement remains a prized goal among all Americans. Paradoxically, a working wife makes her husband more ambitious.

Contrasting the relationship with work, the researchers found that women and men who are compassionate, understanding, and tender are more relationship-centered and less involved in work and other interests. Couples without a relationship-centered partner are less satisfied and less committed. Fighting about the intrusion of work into the relationship undermines a couple's satisfaction. Young men have less desire for their partner's companionship than do young women, but the tables turn as the couple ages. Women, on the other hand, want more time to themselves than men do.

In summary, they say the world of work is no longer the private world of men. Couples face the dilemma of adjusting to life in a two-worker relationship, when most grew up in situations where only the man worked. Not only are men unused to having partners with high incomes; they are not familiar with women in prestigious jobs. Men are used to having partners who expect them to be ambitious, and this fits in with their own inclinations. At the present time, many women are employed, but most of the former wifely roles are still in place. The same thing is true of Soviet women, in spite of the intense propaganda that the revolution had dinned into them for more than fifty years. Work also raises the question of how to find time to be together.

In today's world, work and home life are more separate than ever, with work demanding much or all of a person's energy. The relationship may easily become a secondary aspect of the individual's life. Work-centered people may not really want the relationship to deteriorate, but if no one is serving as its advocate, the things that made a couple's life together special may be lost.

What can we say about these empirical findings of liberal economists and sociologists? In the first place the findings are written largely
in behavioral terms; inner feelings are either omitted or given short
shrift. Yet the formula is "love and work." How work life fits into
love life is the all-important question.

With all the improvements that have been made in the workplace,
work is still an important issue with regard to the quality of life.
Without relating it with other aspects of living, only clichés and empty
formulas result.

It is highly significant that today all people, both men and women,
want to work, deriving a higher sense of self-esteem from their work
than from anything else. Yet how does this fit in with their love lives?
That is a question that each couple asks and answers in their own way.

Again, it has to be emphasized that we are in the midst of a social
revolution in which most traditional values have been overturned,
yet new ones have not yet fully found their way. Thus all that can
be offered is guidelines for managing the individual situations. The
major guideline that we have to offer now is the analytic ideal. Not
work, not play, but the management of the whole analytic ideal is
what is most essential for happiness.

8

The Sexual Revolution Today

*E*VERYBODY KNOWS THAT FREUD started a sexual revolution, but no one knows whether it is finished or all its consequences. This chapter will take up those questions, in order to clarify where sexuality and sexual pleasure stand in the analytic ideal.

The world that Freud found when he started practice in 1886 was one in which sexual disturbances were one of the most prominent of all phenomena. It was the Victorian age, and in spite of all efforts to make it sound romantic it was one in which sexual pleasure was taboo, and love, which was prevented from finding a normal outlet in sexuality, was conspicuous by its absence.

I have argued elsewhere (*Psychoanalytic Vision*, 1981; *The Meaning of Love in Human Experience*, 1985) that Freud's world as well as today's can best be described as a hate culture. A love culture is one in which friendly feelings for other people prevail, and people live together in peace and harmony. Though rare, a number of love cultures are found (Montagu, *Learning Non-aggression*, 1978). A hate culture is one in which feelings of hatred and rivalry toward other people predominate; people live in constant fear of their neighbors, and war and murder are everyday expectations.

Freud was not the only thinker of his day who deplored the extraordinary incidence of sexual inadequacy — impotent men and frigid women. His contribution was to show that these sexual conflicts led to real illness, particularly hysteria, which had been a mystery since the time of the Greeks (hysteria = a wandering uterus).

Further, he recognized that sexual inadequacy was a social as much as an individual issue. In 1898 he wrote:

175

It is positively a matter of public interest that men should enter
upon sexual relations with full potency. In matters of prophylaxis, however, the individual is relatively helpless. The whole
community must become interested in the matter and give their
assent to the creation of generally acceptable regulations. At
present we are still far removed from such a state of affairs which
would promise relief, and it is for this reason that we may with
justice regard civilization, too, as responsible for the spread of
neurasthenia. (SE, III, p. 278)

A few lines further down he commented:

Above all a place must be created in public opinion for the discussion of the problems of sexual life.... And so here too there
is enough work left to do for the next hundred years — in which
our civilization will have to learn to come to terms with our
sexuality.

At this time Freud was thinking of sexuality in the ordinary everyday meaning of the term — genital sexuality. Later, when he discovered infantile sexuality, his views became deeper and more elaborate.
Sexual gratification in the old sense might in many cases today be
looked upon as acting out, rather than real gratification.

Freud's early work was soon superseded by the total theory of
psychoanalysis (Fine, 1990) and presented in *The Interpretation of
Dreams* (1900) and the *Three Essays on Sexuality* (1905). For the
most part Freud's emphasis on sexuality was criticized, sometimes
even branded as "pornographic," but there was also many favorable
comments. For the most part his work was reviewed by people in
medicine; the vastly greater importance of his ideas for the course of
civilization was thus overlooked.

Rosa O. Mayreder reviewed the *Three Essays* for the *Wiener Kili-
nische Rundschau* in 1906. She wrote:

There are books which are destined to be intellectual adven-
tures for their readers. They vibrate with new ideas. They open
a new intellectual era because they urge new points of view,
new concepts, new ways of seeing the world, new perceptions
of humanity. To such splendid and exceptional books belongs
the slender volume which Prof. Freud has published under a
modest title. These are not just contributions to the problem
of sexuality, they are solid fundamentals of a novel theory. It

does not matter if Freud's facts are persuasive in every case. It is not so much his observations alone as his method of combining them into patterns which give the book its extraordinary significance. At the same time the material defies imitation; it is the tool of an ingenious intellect which lies beyond the reach of ordinary men. (Kiell, 1988, p. 305)

When the second edition appeared in 1910 Carl Kunn wrote another review for the same journal. He wrote:

A great number of wholehearted admirers and followers are lined up against a number of stubborn opponents. It is interesting and perhaps suggestive of things to come that many a Saul becomes a Paul in the process. After all, every great pioneer who marches ahead of his time is fated to be misunderstood and persecuted and only the next generation can look back at the lack of understanding with surprise. (p. 304)

Paul Naecke, from whom Freud took the term "narcissism," stated in his review of the book:

I know of no other work which deals with the most important problems of sexuality in such an ingenious and inventive way....Few books can repay their readers as richly as this one. (p. 308)

Adolf Meyer wrote in the *Psychological Bulletin* for 1906:

In a systematic presentation of his experience with the sexual life of patients, Freud has opened the eyes of the physician to an extension of human biology which differs very favorably from the sensational curiosity-shop of the literature of perversions, and is especially important on account of the pedagogically important study of the infantile period.

The above reviews are on the whole favorable, and so they fail to convey the sense of opposition and even horror with which Freud's name was greeted by physicians and the general public. As Jones shows in his *Life and Work of Freud* (1953–57), by and large Freud and his followers were regarded not only as sexual perverts but as either obsessional or paranoid psychopaths as well, and the combination was felt to be a real danger to the community. Hitler had not yet come along to burn Freud's books, but the feelings were already there. Freud's theories were interpreted as direct incitements to surrendering all restraint and reverting to a state of primitive license and savagery. No less than civilization itself was at stake. Jones adds: "As happens in such circumstances, the panic aroused led itself to the loss of that very restraint the opponents believed they were defending. All ideas of good manners, of tolerance and even a sense of decency — let alone any thought of objective discussion or investigation — simply went by the board" (p. 109). Some people urged police action, and one actually occurred in Boston in 1913, though it was halted at the last moment. One neurologist proposed that a boycott be established at any institution where Freud's views were tolerated. In Australia a minister had to leave his pulpit because of sympathy with Freud's work. In 1908 Jones was forced to resign a neurological appointment in London for making inquiries into the sexual life of patients. He was even jailed overnight for talking to children about sex, but he was immediately released. The stigma this cast on his name, however, forced him to leave England for Canada, where he made good use of his stay: he founded the American Psychoanalytic Association.

The general opposition to Freud was experienced by every analyst who trained in this century; only now it is beginning to diminish. Freud was so critical of the civilization of his time that it is understandable why he was attacked by representatives of the establishment. Worse, however was the general refusal to teach psychoanalysis properly and the later emphasis on all the alternatives, especially the somatic therapies (cf. Valenstein: *Great and Desperate Cure*, 1986). While psychoanalysis is widely regarded as the intellectual core of psychiatry, psychology, and all the social sciences, it has never achieved any official recognition in the form of university departments (with one exception: Sandler's appointment as professor of psychoanalysis at the Hebrew University in Jerusalem and in London); it is still subservient to the older professions. The recent legal victory by American psychologists against the International Psychoanalytic Association, which opened the American analytic institutes to psychologists and forced the IPA to accept some "lay" institutes, will eventually, I hope, lead to some change in this situation.

The opposition to the notion that there is a widespread sexual disturbance in people today melted only slowly, and of course large segments of the population never accepted it at all. Yet it is obvious to anyone that there has been a gradual change in the attitudes of people toward their bodies.

This change in the feelings about the body has to be traced

throughout the century. Perhaps the most important single factor in reorienting the average person has been the savage release of hostility and hatred in the two world wars. When whole nations are exterminated by brutal conquerors, the niceties of polite decorum, so conspicuous in Victorian times, lose their hold. Thus in the wake of World War I, women's skirts were raised above the knee, and a period of free love, in which everyone was willing to accept sexuality, broke out all over the world. The Second World War raised women's skirts even higher and saw the widespread introduction of nude beaches. When murder is the order of the day, why avoid sex?

Two mistakes were widespread in this ongoing sexual revolution. One was the notion that all a person had to do to avoid neurosis was to have sex freely. The other, paradoxically, was that sexuality is of no greater importance than any other drive. This view had been prominent since Freud proposed the dual theory of instincts in 1920.

There are in fact many analysts, perhaps especially in the United States, who have placed aggression side by side with sexuality. But there is an essential difference between the two: in sexuality there is an ascertainable physiological stimulus in the body, while in aggression there is not (Brenner, 1971). This emphasis on aggression has led many thinkers to speak of the desexualization of American psychoanalysis.

In the meantime, theory advanced to a fuller understanding of the human life cycle. Freud had shown that sexuality does not begin at puberty, but goes back to early infantile experiences of all kinds. The next step was to specify more precisely in what way the bodily experiences in infancy, the mother-child bond, were related to adolescent and adult sexuality. This latter was one step beyond Freud, so the history of psychoanalysis after Freud is characterized by a much more detailed examination of the child's tie to its mother (Bowlby, 1969–80). Separation anxiety, which goes back to the mother-child relationship, has become as crucial a concept as the oedipal relationship was to Freud and his contemporaries.

Progress seemed to continue uninterruptedly, especially with the advances in modern medicine, until about 1980. Then herpes became a prominent side effect of promiscuous sex, although at first its virulence was overrated. Even more ominous was the appearance of AIDS, a fatal disease with no known cure.

It is AIDS that has brought the attention of the world most markedly to the dangers inherent in promiscuous sexual activity, especially homosexuality, since at first AIDS seemed to be confined to the male homosexual population. More recently reports have indicated that it is also spreading into the heterosexual community. The facts are obscure, but the recognition that protection (the condom or, in the extreme, abstinence) is essential for everybody has made everyone more cautious about one-night stands and other forms of promiscuous sex.

At the same time people began to see that sex without love is an empty and even destructive experience, and the slogan became "have a relationship." Love gradually came to be more important in the minds of many than sexual intercourse as such.

Psychoanalytic theory in the past twenty years has focused so strongly on the first few years of life that in a sense the true sexual period of the oedipal state and puberty has tended to be ignored. Thus, paradoxically, a viable theory of normal sexuality is lacking in contemporary psychoanalysis. Such a theory is obtainable through the application of the concepts of the analytic ideal. Certainly sex is one of the great pleasures in life, but it must be seen in balance, with due weight given to love, communication, the family, the feelings of the two sex partners, and the like.

The normal sexual pattern is an outgrowth of the developmental line of love (see chapters 5–6). Love without sex, such as predominated in the nineteenth century, has been outlawed by the Freudian revolution. But sex without love is also highly unsatisfactory to most people.

I have already mentioned (see chapter 6) the Kinsey studies and the Masters-Johnson work. Both have deepened and widened our grasp of normal sexuality and its concomitant love, as well as the stages of life in which each may be expected to predominate.

The earlier emphasis on the orgasm has been replaced by an effort to reevaluate the whole erotic experience (see Comfort, *The Joy of Sex*). The setting, the feelings, the relationship are all significant; the whole erotic experience is important, not just sex as such or even love as such. In a hate culture such as ours, humankind is deprived of the pleasures of the erotic experience; anthropological research has shown many other cultures in which sex and eroticism are made more gratifying than in ours.

The psychoanalytic view of sexuality today has already been indicated in previous chapters. Physical contact remains a basic need of all human beings, but the form it takes differs at different ages. In infancy, the need is for the breast, for infant-mother compatibility. The Klaus-Kennel theory that right after birth the infant should be placed on the mother's stomach and allowed to lie there awhile, sucking in the love so to speak, has been largely rejected, as have similar theories that overestimate the importance of the body. The physical is the product of the mental, and unless the underlying feelings of the two parties are warm and loving, the physical experience in itself is not sufficient.

Two social movements have erupted within the past few decades that have had a strong impact on psychoanalysis: homosexuality and women's liberation.

Homosexuality

The first essay in Freud's *Three Essays* in 1905 was on homosexuality; here he had already laid down the psychological foundations for an understanding of this deviation, which have remained the same in all of psychoanalytic theory. During the 1960s, however, many homosexuals grouped together and vigorously attacked psychoanalytic theory. There is no evidence, they claimed, that homosexuality is in any way abnormal; it is merely one possible choice among life-styles, neither better nor worse than heterosexuality. Homosexuals are born, not made so by their environment; they cannot be changed and society should leave them alone. There followed many changes in the law leading to much greater tolerance of homosexuality. The three major mental health organizations — the American Psychiatric Association, the American Psychological Association, and the National Association of Social Workers — all came out in favor of the view that homosexuality is a normal variation, vigorously criticizing any therapist who tried to "change" homosexuals. A parade of literature followed, almost all inadequate by any ordinary standards, but accepted as the gospel truth by the homosexual community.

The standard psychoanalytic study of homosexuality was that by Irving Bieber and his associates, published in 1961, in which a group of analysts attached to the Society of Medical Psychoanalysts pooled their resources and findings, showing that a considerable percentage of homosexual men were helped to a heterosexual orientation by analytic psychotherapy. Specifically, of those who were exclusively homosexual 19 percent became heterosexual, while of those who were bisexual 50 percent became heterosexual (p. 276). The difference in outcome among those who were initially bisexual is significant at the .01 level.

This study and others like it were attacked because it relied on studies of homosexual men who were in treatment, the argument being that if they were in treatment they were more disturbed. This argument has been taken up before and found wanting. It relies on the old distinction between those who are in treatment, called "neurotic," and those who are "normal." This is a misconception of the degree of disturbance present in the normal individual (see Rennie studies, 1962). It overlooks the fact that many homosexuals can change their sexual orientation with the help of psychotherapy. In fact, in view of the high incidence of homosexual activity in childhood before puberty and the low incidence after puberty (Kinsey, 1948) it becomes clear that a large number of homosexuals cure themselves even without therapy.

The psychoanalytic explanation of overt homosexuality is simplicity itself, namely, fear of heterosexuality, which is induced in the child by the parents before puberty. As a result of this fear of heterosexuality, the individual turns to the first available substitute, a person of the same sex.

Advocates of the view that homosexuality is a normal deviation have deluged the professional public with various studies that this is so. In the main, these studies are scientifically seriously deficient. In the famous Hooker Study (1957), for example, Hooker had three judges compare the Rorschachs, TAT, and MAPS of two groups, one of heterosexuals, the other of homosexuals. She could find no difference.

In itself, this could imply that the psychological tests were not sharp enough to differentiate. But more than that is involved. When I was invited some twenty years ago to investigate Hooker's study, I was surprised to find that Hooker had (apparently deliberately) misrepresented her findings. In the Rorschach studies a weak pattern of homosexuality appeared in the homosexuals, which she interpreted arbitrarily as being too weak to be of any significance. In the TATs, homosexuality appeared on the surface (the homosexuals all talked about homosexuality, the heterosexuals did not). This she rejected because it was on the surface. Similar defects can be found in many other studies in the literature; the raw data have to be carefully reexamined.

In any case, psychoanalysts in general rely more heavily on clinical information than on tests. Homosexuality is not reached without a long struggle, in the course of which heterosexuality is first rejected. The dynamic factors involved in the relationship are often overlooked. Here is one rather surprising example:

> Joseph and Sally were first cousins, he fourteen, she fifteen years old.
> They began to have sex, and continued daily. Every day they would come home from school and go to bed for a while. What a

casual researcher would not discover, but what a psychoanalyst did, was that Sally, who had sex with a number of men, used to taunt Joseph: You're nothing compared to other men; you can't do it very well yet; you have to be older.

After two years of this Joseph became an overt homosexual and continued to be one until he came to therapy. He moved on to a heterosexual orientation again, but then got into a terrible fight with a fellow worker, punching him in the nose. As a consequence he was fired and, without money, could no longer afford therapy. He then went back to homosexuality.

The evidence is clear for the psychoanalytic point of view. This view is in accord with the commonsense notion that if a person confines his or her sexual activities exclusively to a person of the same sex there is something wrong, which is attributable to that person's early environment. For the rest, the weak studies that are used to bolster the homosexual position and the scandalous endorsements by the major professional organizations point to the serious emotional and moral crisis in which we live. Heterosexuality has always been the normal resolution and will continue to be so for a long time to come.

A word could be said here about the violence that has of recent years accompanied the homosexual position. Some years ago at a meeting of the Columbia University Psychoanalytic Center devoted to a consideration of the scientific aspects of homosexuality, at a prearranged signal one member of the audience blew a whistle, which started a riot; the police had to intervene and the meeting had to be discontinued. In a meeting organized by our own group where a prominent researcher was going to discuss his findings, the police refused to guarantee us protection and our meeting too had to be called off. Later it was rescheduled in a very careful manner, with written reservations and a small fee required of all those who attended. This went off satisfactorily, but when it was all over I received a letter from a homosexual woman who stated that if she had known of the meeting beforehand she would have organized a demonstration outside and (by implication) forced cancellation of the talk. When it comes to actions of this kind, we can no longer blink at the fact that certain members of the homosexual community are ready to resort to violence to protect their neuroses, in spite of the fact that AIDS is still wreaking havoc with overt homosexuals.

Women's Liberation

Another attack on psychoanalysis has come from the women's liberation movement, which has done so much good in many ways, yet is totally misinformed about the purpose and nature of psychoanalysis and psychotherapy.

The main thesis of the women's liberation movement has been that women have been persecuted and mistreated throughout history and that this maltreatment should come to an end. The parallel thesis in psychoanalysis is that all people have been psychologically persecuted and mistreated in the conventional family structure and that it is desirable to have this maltreatment come to an end. Conventional psychology is so poorly informed about psychoanalysis that it is surprised to hear this thesis and fails to recognize its force and veracity. The solution is not to give up the thesis but to educate the psychologists to the realities of human existence.

A paradoxical situation, as will be expounded in more detail later, is that the major professions in mental health fail to understand that a social revolution is going on in all of them. Social work is still identified with the Mother Bountiful tradition; psychology still insists on its confused and mistaken notion that true science can be found only through experimentation; psychiatry is still looking for the hidden lesion in the brain that will confirm Griesinger's famous dictum of a hundred years ago that mind disease is brain disease. As a result these professions do not take the trouble to find out what psychoanalysis is all about; they teach it incorrectly, if they teach it at all, and leave the student confused and bewildered.

Much change is taking place, and the situation is much better than in Freud's day when all that psychoanalysis got was derision and occasional threats of police action. Yet it is still deplorably bad, and a great amount of education is necessary. Much is going on, yet it is still too little and too subordinate to making a living. The medical psychoanalysts who kept "lay" people out of the training institutes until recently, frankly admitted in the court action that their motive was almost entirely economic.

The women's liberation movement goes back a long way; the usual date given for its beginning is Mary Wollstonecraft's book *A Vindication of the Rights of Woman* in 1792, a product of the enlightened thinking of the French Revolution. As we have mentioned before, Abigail Adams, wife of America's second president, was a leader in early American feminism.

Women pursued liberation from the shackles of homes where they were virtually slaves to their men and children and housework. This led to many changes in the status of women — with regard to custody of children, the vote, entrance into professions, including law and medicine.

The battles for women's rights waxed and waned. Then in 1963 Betty Friedan published her book *The Feminine Mystique,* and the discussion took a new turn. This time it was the psychoanalysts who allegedly were preaching a return to peaceful domesticity for women, and nothing could be worse for women's morale. Eventually Friedan changed her mind and in *The Second State* once more saw a happy home life as the greatest boon for womankind. But her book unleashed a whole flood of antianalytic literature.

Feminists began to object to every aspect of the psychoanalysis of women. Penis envy was a myth; castration anxiety likewise. Women loved men, and it was always the men who were at fault in marital quarrels. Even the language had to change: to call a woman a girl was an outrage.

Eventually a better equilibrium was reached, but the idea that psychoanalysis is opposed to women's independence is a myth that has lingered. Actually, quite the contrary is true. Freud's own daughter Anna never married and devoted herself to her profession of psychoanalysis; she was her father's daughter and identified with him throughout her life. In the field of psychoanalysis many women have reached the top ranks, including Anna Freud, Melanie Klein, Helene Deutsch, Karen Horney, Edith Jacobson, and many others. There is hardly any other field in which women have gained as much equality with men as psychoanalysis. The major reason for the misunderstanding of psychoanalytic theory by feminists is that they confuse descriptive statements with prescriptive ones. Thus penis envy is not inherent in womanhood; it is merely part of the culture, and if the culture is changed men and women will see one other another on an equal basis, and neither will depreciate their genital apparatus. At present, women do have penis envy, while the parallel in men is castration anxiety. Furthermore psychoanalysis is tied to a therapeutic method, and if a woman has excessive penis envy, the analyst or the analytic process will make every attempt to help her get over it. In the analytic ideal neither sex should have hatred or contempt for the opposite sex.

Many of the changes sought by feminists are of a behavioral kind, and do not touch inner dynamics. On the whole, women still have a great deal to be dissatisfied with. In her book *A Lesser Life* (1986) Sylvia Hewlett deplores the harsh reality of contemporary women's lives and destroys some favorite myths. The gap between male and female earnings is precisely the same as it was in 1939. Fifty percent of fathers never see or support their children in the wake of divorce. Over half of all female executives remain childless while more than 90 percent of male executives combine their careers with children. Men can routinely expect to find fulfillment in love and work and women cannot.

Compared to European women, who enjoy job-protected maternity leaves, subsidized child care, child allowances, lower divorce rates, and a narrowing wage gap, American women have only a precarious security as workers, wives, and mothers. Despite their legendary claim to power and privilege, women in the United States actually face a bad and deteriorating economic reality. To better understand this paradox Hewlett explores the "aberrant fifties," the cult of motherhood, radical feminism, the battle to ratify the ERA, and government policies toward women and children. She describes her own poignant struggle to bear and raise children in mid-career. Hewlett tries to redefine how women see themselves and how policymakers respond to their problems.

It is clear that the feminist movement, which has placed such heavy emphasis on economics, has failed to take the question of love into account.

In a series of articles in the *New York Times* in August 1989, an attempt was made to evaluate the gains and losses produced by the feminist revolution. In a poll taken by the *Times*, both men and women said they were unhappy about the toll on their family and personal lives. Women who worked outside the home reported that their children and their marriages were being shortchanged, and they lamented having too little time for themselves. In the *Times* poll of 1497 adults, conducted from June 20 through June 25, 83 percent of working mothers and 72 percent of working fathers said they were torn by the conflicting demands of their jobs and the desire to see more of their families. Forty-eight percent of all women respondents said women had to sacrifice too much for their gains. Respondents of both sexes cited children and family life as the primary casualties.

Nevertheless, women want to work. Women now make up to 45 percent of the work force, as compared with 38 percent in 1970. By the year 2000, women are expected to represent about half the labor force.

These figures and similar studies show once again that economic changes as such, no matter how desirable, leave people unsatisfied.

In sexuality, love, and other intimacies of people's lives, there is no substitute for the analytic ideal.

Sex and Love

At an early date (in the 1890s), Freud still thought that sexuality as such had a physiological component that had to be satisfied. He coined the term "actual neurosis" for the condition in which there is no sexual release and hypothesized that normal energy is directly transformed into anxiety by some biochemical process not yet understood. This view was later abandoned, but since Freud had a way of abandoning some of his earlier views without saying so, many did not realize that there was a new theory current. This theory was based not on genital sex as such, but on the whole course of psychosexual development. This development culminates in genital primacy, in which the union of sexual and tender feelings is the hallmark of love. Thus, sex without love becomes an empty exercise, while love without sex involves excessive inhibitions and repressions of all kinds. The psychoanalytic view today is that there is a developmental line of both sex and love, which reaches its mature stage in genital primacy and love.

Certainly there are still many sexual problems on the current scene, but enormous progress has been made. A great deal is known about the development of sexuality, as well as the development of the love impulse from infancy on through the relationships with the various other people in the child's life: mother, father, peers, siblings, lover, and eventually the sex love experience of adolescence.

There has been much talk of alternative life-styles and of different ways of gratifying the needs for sex and love. Otto (1972) summarizes many of these trends. As far as the radical feminists are concerned, many have turned radically against love and in that sense against psychoanalysis. Rosalind Loring, an adult educator, characterizes the radical feminists' reaction to love as one of anger, hostility, pain, hurt, and grief. "Anti-male," the women in this movement reject men's love because they believe that love has and inevitably will continue to cause their downfall. Second-class status, loss of identity, and lack of autonomy, she argues, all are due to love. Love has been used as a tool by both men and institutions of society to keep women in their place and historically that place has been defined by men. The result has kept women from achieving their potential, from gaining ego strength, and from being fully functioning human beings.

Because the consequences of love have caused women to feel

and to be powerless, those in the movement frequently express their views in economic and political terms. Kate Millett in her book *Sexual Politics* (1970) has one constant theme: the relationship between men and women throughout all societies has been a political relationship, which has reached into every area of life. Radical feminist women, searching for the causes of their depressed and denigrated state, have decided that the achievement of love has meant the loss of self. The anguish heard throughout all the rhetoric of the movement is the feeling of betrayal: "You have loved me into oblivion."

It is clear that all of this is empty rhetoric that has nothing to do with psychoanalysis. The achievement of love, in the analytic ideal, accompanies the attainment of a healthy self, not the loss of self. Once more we see the need for education of writers, publicists, psychologists, and others regarding what psychoanalysis is all about. Distorted love should not be confused with normal love. Typical of the absurd charges against love are the comments of Ti-Grace Atkinson (p. 76): "Marriage means rape and lifelong slavery. Love has to be destroyed. Friendship is reciprocal, love isn't." Germaine Greer in *The Female Eunuch* charges: "Men have reduced heterosexual contact to sado-masochistic patterns by exploiting love and fantasies of romance." Again she is talking of neurotic love, not of normal love. These are the complaints of disappointed lovers, not of mature thinkers.

Martin and Mariah, in their chapters on homosexuality in Otto's book on love, write:

> Psychoanalysts, having largely adopted the theological doctrine of sex for procreation only, have made the value judgment that homosexuality is "a repetitive, compulsive sexual behavior." They have concentrated on the sexual activity therefore and have denied the possibility of any love relationship. From this perspective, any individual, heterosexual or homosexual, who is incapable of love is bordering on neurosis or psychosis. To say that the homosexual by definition cannot love is the Big Lie, a gigantic hoax compounded for too many centuries. (p. 126)

These absurdities, typical of the irrational attacks on psychoanalysis, ignore the major source of information, namely, the clinical study of homosexuals, as well as the total theory of psychosexual and human development.

Alternative Life-styles

Much attention has ben paid in recent years to "alternative life-styles." These include communes, sexual promiscuity, homosexuality, "swinging," and the like. All these styles are seen in the usual office practice of psychotherapy and are known historically. All leave the participant thoroughly dissatisfied.

Roger was a member of two communes, one in New York city, the other upstate. He had lived in rebellion against his family, a stolid bourgeois family where the father worked from nine to six and had little to do with the children. For years Roger had knocked around, not knowing what to do with himself. The commune experience was part of his rebellion. At first he was quite excited about it, but when two people in the commune began to have sex right in front of him, he became so jealous that he ran away.

This example, taken at random, offers a good clue to what goes on in communes: the basic human feelings break through and tear the members apart.

Nevertheless, the drive to form a commune, different from the standard family, is a powerful one. According to Zablocki (1980), for three centuries there has not been a single year without at least one historically documented communitarian organization in the United States. However, no more than one person in a thousand has gone to live in a commune, and communitarianism has never succeeded in becoming even a small part of American life. It has always functioned as a deviant, radical, or otherworldly fringe, drawing off idealists, social malcontents, and dreamers rather than finding, as for instance in Israel, a place for itself within the structure of societal institutions.

As in Europe, American communes have appeared not at a constant rate, but rather in waves (very much like epidemics) occurring once every forty or fifty years for the past two hundred years.

Communes in America flourished neither on the frontier itself, where the intensity of the struggle for survival was its own antidote to alienation, nor along the settled coast, where the expanding institutions of a new society still seemed capable of providing a portion and place for almost everyone. Instead, they clustered in that zone that had been the frontier a generation earlier and that now offered too many choices and less than encompassing social controls. The so-called burned-over district of western New York State in the first half of the nineteenth century is an example of such a region.

Communes flourished in America particularly in the nineteenth century when at one time there were more than one hundred in existence. But while new ones are constantly forming, the old ones have been dying out. There are a few Shaker elders around, the remnants of what was once a thriving community.

The relationship to sexuality must also be considered. In some communes, such as the Shakers, all sex was forbidden; in others sex was quite free, as in the Oneida commune. When sex was free, the members had to defend themselves against the neighbors, who often found such behavior offensive.

In any case, history has rendered the verdict. There is no magic in an arbitrary reshuffling of sexual priorities, nor is there any magic in any special rearrangement that people choose. Essentially it is the inner dynamics that casts the deciding vote.

Communes are rarely purely violent. Violence does occur, but it is incidental to the major functions. Order is the main goal, and this order can be imposed in many different ways. Kern (1981) calls his book on communes *An Ordered Love*. It does not seem to matter what the order is, as long as there is order that can be explained to members and that they can obey.

One of the most gruesome episodes in the history of communes occurred some years ago in Guyana. The leader, Rev. Jim Jones, gathered almost one thousand followers and led them to Guyana, where he was obeyed by everyone in the group. Complaints came from parents of some of the children in the commune, claiming that they had been abducted illegally. A congressman went to investigate and was murdered. Jones felt pressed to the wall. He ordered his followers to drink a fatal poisonous concoction. The great majority obeyed him and died. The whole episode was sensational and received extended coverage from the press. Here the followers clearly had abandoned their selves in favor of the leader (Fine, 1985).

Kanter has delineated six commitment-building processes to be found in contemporary communes: (1) sacrifice; (2) investment; (3) renunciation; (4) communion; (5) mortification; and (6) transcendence. By transcendence she means the experience of a higher power and meaning residing in the group, the felt connection with forces and events outside of and beyond the life of a single person. While she mentions the charismatic figure, she fails to mention obedience to this figure as one of the essentials of every group. Usually a leader is referred to as either father or mother. One of Kanter's interesting comments is that communal movements achieve communion in part by having enemies (1976) just as they gain energy and purpose by facing dangers and challenges from unconverted multitudes.

Another significant point is that in all communal groups intimacy is both discouraged and encouraged — too little or too much. Both destroy the group. Survival of the group is the essential demand. This is why the intense love experience has been so often discouraged by society. Goode (1965) points out that love, far from being rare, is a universal concern of organized societies and is usually proscribed because the close experience may destroy the group. This was one of the themes in Aldous Huxley's startling novel *Brave New World* (1932).

Swinging

Another variation that became popular a few years ago is swinging, or the "swing," in which each member has indiscriminate sex with all other members. For example:

Marie and Henry decided to become swingers after a lifetime of repression. They joined various swing clubs and went to swings two or three times a week. They saw one another have sex with various partners, and consciously felt no disturbance about it. Then one day Henry decided to seek out therapy for the problems he felt in his way of life. Marie was furious. It is paradoxical that for open sex there was no jealousy, but when he decided to confide in a therapist she could not contain her rage.

Bartell (1971), a sociologist, made a careful study of this phenomenon and concluded, surprisingly, that swingers did not differ much in their values from other segments of the population. This seems unlikely and is perhaps best explained by the fact that Bartell did not probe into his subjects' emotions very deeply.

In any case, with the outbreak of AIDS and other venereal diseases, it is probable that the incidence of swinging will diminish, although of course no exact figures are available.

Summary

The sexual revolution that Freud called for almost one hundred years ago has come and changed the face of the country. Sex is now so open that it is taught in school, and condoms are advertised everywhere, with the slogan "safe sex." Dr. Ruth Westheimer has become one of our cultural heroines, with her extraordinarily popular program "Good Sex."

The various developmental stages in the road to mature sex and genital primacy have been thoroughly explored by now and are well understood. Sex and love are closely intertwined. The infant begins with a warm close relationship with the mother, which includes physical caresses and contact of all kinds. It then moves on to other people — father, peers, the first love affair, friendships in the latency period, adolescent love, eventually marriage, ideally with full pleasure and gratification at each stage.

While sex and genital primacy have come under considerable attack, many people are guided by the analytic ideal, even if they do not know the term. Much discussion has surrounded the alternative life-styles, each of which has strong advocates. However, they are generally a passing passion, which may obsess the person for a longer or shorter time, but which eventually pass and give way to the desire for a normal home and family life, based on sex and love.

9

The Family

*T*O BE A HAPPY MEMBER OF A HAPPY FAMILY is one of the major aspects of the analytic ideal. This component requires more extended discussion.

The family is the most basic unit of humankind. There is no known society without a family structure. The family has accordingly been studied from every conceivable point of view, and a considerable body of data exists that has to be sifted to get at the essentials. The higher primates have many forms of social organization; some have what seem like a family structure, but without the feelings that human beings attach to their families. In any case family structure, as seen in humans, is rare among primates.

Anthropology and related sciences contribute the description of the many varieties of family found in the world; psychoanalysis contributes a description of the psychodynamic conflicts and rewards within the family. Information from both sources must be combined in a full theory.

Murdock (1949) states that the nuclear family (father, mother, and children) is a universal social grouping. Either it is the sole prevailing form of the family in a culture, or it exists as a strongly functional group. It is found in every known society, suggesting that it corresponds to a strong biological urge. Lowie (1920) wrote:

> It does not matter whether marital relations are permanent or temporary, whether there is polygyny or polyandry or sexual licence; whether conditions are complicated by the additions of

193

members not included in *our* family circle; the one fact that
stands out beyond all others is that everywhere the husband,
wife and immature children constitute a unit apart from the
remainder of the community.

The relationship between father and mother in the nuclear family
is solidified by the sexual privilege that all societies accord to married
spouses. As a powerful impulse, often pressing individuals to behavior
disruptive of the cooperative relationships upon which human social
life rests, sex cannot safely be left without restraints. Everywhere in
the world there are a variety of regulations that govern the sex lives
of the members of the culture.

In theory the family should make people happy. But the obvious
fact is that it does not. In our own society divorce has already passed
the 50 percent mark, and the frequency with which people get divorced has led to a whole new profession, marital counseling, and to
a whole new form of therapy, family therapy.

Psychoanalysis always deals with a person's family conflicts. The
life course of all individuals comes out of one family unit and goes
into another. Both of these family units must be carefully examined.

The discovery of major conflicts within the family that are related to basic human urges, such as sex and aggression, is one of the
contributions of psychoanalysis. These conflicts have led to a broad
psychoanalytic theory, including the analytic ideal.

Whatever the form of the family may be, love and hate remain
the most important single dimension of its inner life. In this respect
psychoanalytic theory has undergone some major changes; in the beginning violation of the sexual taboos was seen as the major cause
of neurosis, while in recent years the high incidence of violence has
been a major concern.

Richard Gelles has been one of the leaders in the study of violence in the home (Straus, Gelles, and Steinmetz, *Behind Closed
Doors*). Many of the facts he reports are frightening and surprising.
Men strike women, and vice versa; parents hit their children, sometimes to the point of killing them; two million women and children
are battered and beaten by family members each year. For Americans
the greatest risk of assault, physical injury, and even murder occurs in
their own homes by members of their own families. And other countries are even worse. Colombia seems to be a country run by thieves
who live on drugs and murder, and are now threatening to export
their specialities to the United States.

In 1968 Richard Nixon, stirred by the assassinations of Martin

Luther King and Robert Kennedy, appointed a commission to study the causes and prevention of violence. The committee's report, issued in 1969, was edited by Ted Gurr, assistant professor of politics at Princeton University, and Hugh Graham, assistant professor of history at Johns Hopkins. It presents a dismaying picture of life as it was in the United States in the 1960s and all through our history, even though the incidence of violence in other countries has often been many times greater than in the United States. In a summary of the book Gurr wrote:

> Americans have always been given to a historical amnesia that marks much of their turbulent past. Probably all nations share this tendency to sweeten memories of their past through process of selective recollection, owing to our historic vision of ourselves as a latter-day chosen people, a new Jerusalem. (p. xiv)

The historical record demonstrates a use of extensive and often lethal forms of violence by parents. Those who have examined the history of child abuse document a history of violence and infanticide dating back to biblical times. As de Mause (1974) has said: "The history of childhood is a nightmare from which we are just beginning to awaken."

The Bible itself chronicles parental violence, beginning when Abraham nearly killed his son as a sacrifice. Jesus' birth coincides with Herod's "Slaughter of the Innocents." Infanticide, mutilation, and other forms of violence were legal parental prerogatives from ancient Rome to colonial America. Children were hit with birch rods, switches, and canes. They were whipped, castrated, and destroyed by parents, often with the consent of the ruling religious and political forces in the society.

The history of violence in America goes back to the Puritans. Laws threatening death to children were passed, and parents supported their right to whip and punish with biblical quotations.

It was in this atmosphere of hatred and violence that the lunacy of the Salem witch trials took place.

Religious ideology held that all children were born corrupted by original sin and required salvation by their parents. To "beat the devil" out of a child was not just a phrase for the Puritans. It was a mandate to provide salvation for their children through physical punishment.

Thus historically America has a tradition of physical and emotional cruelty to children. As a society we have justified this cruelty through religious dogma or by maintaining that it was in the child's best interests. The social mandate and tolerance of physical violence toward children may have been one factor that delayed the identification of child abuse as an important social problem.

The Society for the Prevention of Cruelty to Children was established a year after the Society for the Prevention of Cruelty to Animals. Child abuse may have been identified as a social problem by church workers, social workers, and private citizens in the nineteenth century, but it took almost one hundred years after the first case for violence toward children to be considered a major national social problem. In 1946 physicians began to notice patterns of healed fractures in young children that could have resulted only from repeated blows. But it was not until C. Henry Kempe and his associates published their classic work, "The Battered Child Syndrome," in the *Journal of the American Medical Association* in 1962 that battering and abuse became focal points of public attention.

In 1968 it was estimated that more children under the age of five died from parentally inflicted injuries than from tuberculosis, whooping cough, measles, diabetes, rheumatic fever, and appendicitis combined (*Newsweek*, vol. 71, June 3, 1968).

By the end of the 1960s all fifty states had passed and instituted laws, mandating the reporting of child abuse and neglect, and had begun to take steps to treat abused children and their families. In 1974 the federal government established the National Center on Child Abuse and Neglect and had begun to identify steps that could be taken to prevent and treat abuse.

In itself this is a disheartening story. Yet it is also heartening. Children have been beaten, neglected, and traumatized since the world began. But it is only in recent years that the government has stepped into the otherwise absolute privacy of the home to cut down this violence.

While exact statistics are not available, the incidence of wife abuse has also been high. Studies have shown that wives in America have been raped, choked, stabbed, shot, beaten, had their jaws and limbs broken, and have been struck with horsewhips, pokers, and bicycle chains.

Laws and legal precedents sanctioned the right of a husband to use violence on his wife. The classic "rule of thumb" gave legal justification to common law that sanctioned a husband's striking his wife with a switch, provided the stick was no wider than

his thumb. But again wife abuse as a social problem did not receive national attention until the mid-1970s. Since 1975 a number of
American women charged with murdering their husbands have been
acquitted in landmark decisions on grounds of self-defense or temporary insanity after claiming that they had been abused and battered
wives.

Recognition of wife and child abuse as a problematic aspect of
family behavior is one aspect of the growth of understanding the an
alytic ideal. For psychoanalysis has held that people's problems are
made, not born, and that they are made by parental cruelty, both
physical and psychological. It may be recalled that all of Bleuler's
schizophrenic patients (1978) were reported to have had "horrible"
childhoods, although each in a different way. The course of psychoanalysis usually gives patients the right for the first time in their lives
to speak of how they were brought up. Griesinger's motto that mind
disease is brain disease should be modified to read mind disease is
parental sadism disease.

If wives and children are abused, other family members are also
abused. Currently there is a feeling of being abandoned by their children among many older people. Even in Italy, traditionally a land
of solid, three-generation families, a recent picture in the *New York
Times* showed a woman in Rome all alone in the city because her
children would not take her along on their vacation.

In this respect again psychoanalysis has been seriously misunderstood because of concern with other, less relevant questions. When
Freud began, the only known cause of any emotional disturbance
was "heredity." Now that we know so much more about heredity and
can even identify and handle genes that are responsible for certain
illnesses, the importance of the environment becomes doubly significant. First, that which is truly hereditary is identified and can be
handled, or at last recognized; prenatal examinations can detect defects and steps can be taken to deal with them. And second, that
which is not truly hereditary can be identified and managed by psychosocial measures. In this way the analytic ideal leads to social as
well as individual progress.

I have elsewhere suggested that cultures can de divided into love
and hate cultures (Fine, 1985). Some cultures foster the experience
of love, while in others hatred and violence are strongly encouraged.
Naturally pure cultures of love or hate are not to be found. When
the relationship of one person to another are based predominantly
on love, I call that a love culture; when the relationships are based
on hatred, I call that a hate culture. It thus becomes a relative matter

whether the forces of hatred or the forces of love have the upper hand. The question can be answered only on the basis of an intimate study of the society involved.

There is no doubt that ours has to be labeled a hate culture, and that it has been one for thousands of years. In part this is due to the Christian abhorrence of sex, which created a widespread sexual neurosis for centuries. It took a thousand years of bitter fighting and massacres of innocents to establish priestly celibacy in the Catholic church. Hildebrand, the monk who made the most progress in this campaign to stamp out sex, was described by Lea (*History of Sacerdotal Celibacy*, 1866) as a man who left a legacy of "inextinguishable hate and unattained ambition." When sex is repressed to such a degree, violence is bound to follow.

What happens to the family in such a hate culture? The answer is obvious: everybody hates everyone else, and violent battles ensue. As with Hildebrand, we find inextinguishable hate and unattained ambition. The violence within the family has to be seen as an outgrowth of a perverted philosophy of living that affects everyone in the society. It is this philosophy of living that should be replaced by the analytic ideal.

Arguments about whether aggression is innate or acquired have surfaced repeatedly and are still unresolved. The foremost proponent of the idea that aggression is innate is the ethologist Konrad Lorenz. The researcher-anthropologist who has contributed most to the elucidation of love cultures is Ashley Montagu in his book *Learning Non-aggression* (1978). Montagu writes:

The long extended period of infant and childhood dependence necessitates females who as mothers are efficiently able to minister to the dependent needs of their young over a considerable number of years, and of males who, as fathers and husbands, are capable of the cooperative behavior necessary for the development of the nuclear family.... In the small population of prehistoric man, which means during more than ninety-nine percent of man's evolutionary history, love and cooperation were vitally necessary and indispensable forms of behavior between members of the band if that band was to survive. (pp. 8–9)

This point of view, that love and cooperation were as necessary to human survival as Darwin's more famous "survival of the fittest" is less popular than Darwin's theory, but has much to commend it. The human being is neither all good nor all bad; both love and hate are experienced in the course of evolutionary history.

The most cogent test of this theory, apart from clinical experience, is the work of the anthropologist Ronald Rohner (*The Warmth Dimension*, 1981). For Rohner, parental acceptance-rejection theory, or PAR theory, is a theory of socialization that attempts to explain and predict major antecedents, correlates, and consequences of parental acceptance and rejection the world over. The theory focuses on four classes of issues:

(1) One is the consequences of parental acceptance and rejection for behavioral, cognitive, and emotional development of children everywhere, as well as for the personality functioning of adults. Two principal questions are asked here: (a) Do children everywhere throughout our species — regardless of differences in culture, language, race, or other limiting conditions — respond in the same way to the perception of prenatal rejection? (b) To what extent do the affects of rejection in childhood extend into adulthood, and what personality dispositions are likely to be modified in the course of developing maturity?

(2) Why are some children better able than others to cope with the effects of parental rejection and emotional abuse? What gives some children the resilience to cope with the corrosive drizzle of day-to-day rejection without developing personality, social-cognitive, and emotional impairments to the same degree that most rejected children do?

(3) In addition, the theory attempts to predict major psychological, environmental, and maintenance systems antecedent to parental acceptance-rejection. That is, why are some parents warmer than others?

(4) Finally, the theory is concerned with a class of issues regarding the sociocultural and expressive correlates of parental acceptance-rejection. For example, are the religious beliefs or other expressive behaviors of people related reliably and significantly to their childhood experiences of warmth or rejection? Why do some people choose one kind of occupation, profession, or task and other people choose a different one?

In his book he focuses primarily on the warmth dimension of parenting.

One chapter takes up the basic question of parental acceptance and rejection in life-span perspective. This is divided into the major periods of life: infancy, childhood, adolescence, adulthood, and old age.

(1) *Infancy:* Children seem to experience, process cognitively, and respond to parental rejection in qualitatively different ways during the three major development epochs prior to adulthood: infancy, childhood, and adolescence.

Rohner feels that there is little evidence that there are long-term effects of parental rejection in infancy. Here is where the clinical material begins to diverge from the experimental or statistical. Clinically we are convinced that maternal deprivation in the first year of life has devastating effects, though they are more correctable than later deprivations. Shifting the infant to a warmer mother can help overcome the effects of maternal deprivation, but such a shift is usually not feasible.

(2) *Childhood:* Rohner defines childhood as the period from two to twelve years. It is during this time, he believes, that rejection is likely to have its most pronounced impact. Although complex cognitive, social, emotional, physical, and other forms of growth and development occur in children from two to twelve years, there do not appear to be significant differences in children's responses to perceived rejection, at least with respect to the personality dispositions of major concern to personality theory. Generally, however, six-year-olds seem to respond to rejection in the same way as twelve-year-olds, with the exception, of course, of individual differences within and across age groups. Some six-year-olds, for example, have a more clearly differentiated sense of self than other six-year-olds or even than some seven-, eight-, or nine-year-olds. A differentiated sense of self seems to be one of the social-cognitive factors that help children cope with perceived rejection.

What makes childhood, as distinguished from infancy and adolescence, the time when humans are most vulnerable to rejection? The analytic explanation is the weakness of the ego. Rohner states that no doubt it has to do with the fact that children, unlike infants, are capable of complex linguistic and neurolinguistic symbolizing. Young children are in the process of constructing a "self" and "nonself," but they still tend to be quite egocentric in that they do not yet seem able to see the world as others see it. That is, they cannot yet take the perspective of the other person. As Piaget has put it, they cannot assume points of view different from their own, so when their mothers or fathers snarl at them after getting disappointing news that an anticipated event has been canceled, young children often seem unable to understand that their parents are not really angry.

(3) *Adolescence:* What happens if the rejection process begins for the first time during adolescence? Rohner states: "I expect that the effects of rejection, beginning for the first time in adolescence, are

likely, in most cases, to have less severe long-term effects than the effects of rejection that begins in childhood." Again an analyst would point to the strength of the ego and the cohesiveness of the self. It is also highly unlikely that a rejection would occur for the first time during adolescence. As with the notion that sexuality begins at puberty, such a perception of rejection would require a good deal of denial on the patient's part.

> A ten-year-old boy reached the waiting room where his mother was expecting him, together with the therapist. He said to the therapist: Tell her [pointing to his mother] not to shout at me so much. She replied in a loud tone of voice: You know that I never shout at you.

(4) *Adulthood:* Rejection is not likely to be as painful in adulthood as it is for the younger child. Rejection extending from early childhood into adulthood is another matter. Here the outcome may be felt for a lifetime.

(5) *Old Age:* As you sow, so shall you reap. Rejection of the elderly is not uncommon in America. Particularly adult offspring who have been rejected as children tend worldwide to reject their own parents when the parents reach dependent old age.

Birmingham (1982) found a worldwide tendency for overall parental acceptance-rejection to be related significantly to respect for the elderly. Parental hostility was related even more strongly, but negatively, to respect for the elderly.

Rohner also examined certain subsidiary aspects of the relationship between parental acceptance-rejection and other factors in the personality of the child. He found that the more extensively the correlates of parental acceptance-rejection in the sociocultural field are examined, the more one discovers how widely the effects of parental acceptance and rejection permeate the entirety of sociocultural systems. These effects not only deal with maintenance systems and with personality dispositions of children and adults but bear on the total functioning of societies, including expressive domains such as occupational choices, religious beliefs, and artistic preferences.

He includes one study of Vietnam War resisters and Green Berets, comparing the two. The actual family experiences of the two groups contrasted dramatically. Green Berets tended to be strict, authoritarian, emotionally cold and isolated, unresponsive, mechanical, formal, rigid, and dominating (Mantell, 1974). As individuals, the parents themselves tended to be intolerant, nonintellectual, tense, and sometimes violent. Nonetheless these families were, outwardly at least, also stable, self-sufficient, and psychologically cohesive. Punishment took the form of threats, blows, and other forms of intimidation. Parents of Green Berets provided little opportunity for the expression of individual feelings or opinions. Usually, only one opinion was expressed, and that was voiced as an absolute edict by the dominant parent. The family life of the Green Berets was governed by demands for conformity; deviation from the rules often brought swift and severe disciplinary action. Emotional sensitivity and expressions of affection were regarded as unmanly and signs of weakness. The youths, especially in the eyes of their fathers, were supposed to be emotionally "tough." Even though the majority of the Green Berets did not feel their parents rejected them, or that their parents were actively hostile toward them, most of the men did report that one or both parents were almost always irritable. In addition, 80 percent claimed to have never experienced emotional closeness with either parent; only 40 percent reported any parental affection, but this came from both parents in only 12 percent of the cases.

As adolescents, Green Berets tended to be passive toward their parents and had little conflict with them. They also appear to have stayed away from home as much as possible. To all outward appearances adolescence seems to have been a reasonably happy, successful, and active period for Green Berets. This public behavior contrasted sharply, however, with the youths' deviate activities. As described by Mantell:

> Most of them were involved in petty acts of juvenile delinquency, led a sexual life which would not have met with public approval, engaged in daring and adventuresome actions for thrills, were exposed to violent death as the passive witnesses of suicides, drownings, traffic accidents and as active hunters and were also involved in numerous fights. Thus they led double lives. They were outward conformers who were able to break easily with the standards prevailing in their communities. At the same time, they remained sensitive to social and legal sanctions, and altered undesirable behavior once they were detected and punishment became a real threat. (p. 147)

These life experiences and the personality and behavior dispositions that resulted from them seem to have made involvements in the Special Forces an attractive choice for the Green Berets. For most of them, killing men and sometimes women and children became routine and caused no discomfort. Indeed, the most frequent response to killing unarmed persons (men, women, or children) was "no feeling at all." Most of these men were uninformed and uninterested in the social or political issues surrounding the Vietnam conflict. Mostly they were seeking adventure and excitement, and in one way or another all of them were running away from their previous lives.

Childhood and adolescence were markedly different for the war resisters, who were raised by parents of whom one, or more often both, tended to be warm, affectionate, nonaggressive, friendly, gentle, calm, easygoing, and relaxed. Parental control in most of these families was fairly permissive, nonauthoritarian, flexible, and rational. Physical violence or the threat of it occurred in about half the families, but it played a subordinate role. Parents of war resisters did not demand compliance from their sons as did parents of Green Berets. Rather, they attempted to justify their actions and views in a rational way. These parents praised, reasoned with, and rewarded their sons as ways of encouraging compliance; they seldom used physical punishment or its threat — though war resisters recalled vaguely having been spanked when they were small children.

Another area that Rohner has investigated is artistic expression. Barry, drawing from a world sample of seventy-five societies, related levels of artistic complexity to measures of "severity of socialization." He found a strong worldwide correlation between the severity of socialization experienced by children in the sample societies and complexity of artistic designs typically produced in these societies. Societies above the world median on complexity of design tended to be above average in severity of socialization. Drawing stimulus from Barry's work, Rohner found that artistic productions in societies where children are rejected tend to be more complex than in societies where they are accepted. Thus it appears that a stable worldwide relationship exists between stressful family experiences in childhood and institutionalized expressive (artistic) productions in childhood. These results are consistent with a large body of holocultural literature showing that different classes of expressive behavior are positively related to specific socialization experiences in childhood.

Thus PAR theory (parental acceptance-rejection) provides a test of psychoanalytic theory and of the analytic ideal. In general, the evidence seems to be positive that love and hate in childhood lead to different kinds of personalities. In particular feelings of hatred and violence in adulthood are strongly related to experiences of indifference or punishment by the parents in childhood.

Within our own culture, numerous studies have been conducted to clarify the relationship between children's personality and the type of care that they received from their parents. One of the best studies of this kind is the work by Brody and Axelrad (1978). Theirs was a longitudinal study that tried to clarify the relations between the forms of parental care and the psychological development of the child. The original aim of the Infant Development Research Project was to discover whether there were stable types of maternal behavior with infants during the infant's first year, and if so, to assess the varying influences of those types upon the infant's behavior and development. That phase of the work lent support to certain theoretical propositions that were spelled out regarding the beginning of ego development in the first months of life. The favorable outcome of the initial project and a natural excitement to learn about the subsequent history of the infants prompted them to resume the study of the same mothers and children and to include the fathers. The children were followed through age seven. In this search, they looked for systematic evidence of connections between the behavior and attitudes of parents and the character formation of their young children. They also sought to identify modes of child rearing from infancy on which, in their view, promote mental health and sound character building. Thus their project was very similar to Rohner's, only it was limited to our own culture.

They found that two-thirds of the mothers in their sample were inadequate in their maternal behavior during the infant's first year, and they appeared to remain so as long as they were studied. In summary they said:

It seems to us that in a world overflowing with suffering, violence, confused values and the chronic waste of human capacities, the finding that a majority of mothers are wanting in competence and enjoyment in child rearing is realistic. Parental burdens may well be increased by our culture's current emphasis on the need for self-expression and individuality. In contrast, much less emphasis is now made on the need for socialization. (p. 259)

Thus here too is a finding similar to Rohner's, a confirmation of the psychoanalytic position that warmth and love in the mother are an indispensable part of healthy child rearing. The correlation between maternal warmth and intellectual development was high, and the main problem was neglect. The authors said:

Were we to single out a cardinal contribution to unfavorable development in the child we should, with knowing simplification, name neglect. We mean neglect, intentional or not, that appears in seemingly benign forms in ignorance — in an inability to recognize uneasiness, or distress or age-inappropriate behavior in the child, in intolerance, in over-hasty judgments of the child's motives, leading to erratic or excessive expectations of behavior, which are incongruent with the child's expectation in disinterest, in a reluctance to respond or to act on behalf of the child's emotional states, curiosities and other age-adequate needs, in excessive indulgence — in a failure to nourish the child's capacity for delay or for frustration tolerance and in carelessness in a failure to protect the child from excessive stimulations, gratifications and deprivations, from aggressive acts or libidinal seductions, physical or psychic, or from threats of such experiences. (p. 552)

Again there is confirmation here of one basic proposition of psychoanalysis, that love, especially in childhood, makes people happy and that hatred makes them unhappy. The implications of this proposition for both education and therapy are obvious. Thus once more wherever we look love becomes the major emotional need of the human being — as powerful a drive as food.

Single Men

Happy children grow up to be happy adults, and sooner or later start families of their own, where they can overcome conflicts or problems similar to those of their own childhood by virtue of their strong, secure self-image, based on love and competence. Yet while most people do marry and form a family, a large percentage of the population chooses to remain single.

Typical of the confusion in this field is a request I recently received from a journalist. There are many women in their thirties and forties who finally decide that they would like to have children. Unmarried, they seek to find a man to father their child, with no strings attached. The journalist wanted to know what kind of man would do a thing like that.

The analytic answer to this and similar questions is that no typology can be worked out in the adult; it depends on the individual's life history, what children mean to him or her, and numerous other factors in the personality.

For several hundred years the family patterns of the American family remained on the whole stable. Then came World War II, and with it a new social revolution that is still going on.

While the divorce rate had actually been rising since the turn of the century, it had done so at such a slow and steady pace that few observers were alarmed. By the 1950s the United States had entered the most family-oriented period of the century, the generation of the Feminine Mystique and the Baby Boom and marriages at the youngest ages in recorded American history. During the 1950s, 96 percent of people in the childbearing years were married. Women's magazines, newspapers, movies, and television all extolled the perfect family life. No one realized then that the family was in transition and that couples would never again be the same.

By the early sixties, radical changes were becoming evident. The marriage rate began to fall and the divorce rate, which had been fairly level, accelerated its historical trend upward. In the late sixties and early seventies fertility began to decline. It has stayed low — sixteen live births per one thousand population in 1982 (Schwartz and Blumstein, 1983). In the early seventies the marriage rate for people under forty-five was as low as it had been at the end of the Depression. As of now, the divorce rate is still rising in many parts of the country, and disaffection with the family is rampant in American culture.

But the solutions sought offer no improvement over the traditional patterns. One of these solutions has been the rise of a "singles culture," sometimes called "swinging singles." The complaint is that the standard forms of marriage impose too many restrictions on both parties.

The unvarnished truth is that no one past a certain age finds much happiness in the single life. As Samuel Johnson once put it: marriage has many pains, but celibacy has no pleasures (*Oxford Book of Quotations*, p. 278). After a certain age, single people are never very happy.

The realization that marriage is part of the analytic ideal is again one of the discoveries of psychoanalysis. Human beings are not really made to live alone.

In sophisticated circles in large cities like New York, there is a general realization that people who remain single until relatively late — the thirties are given as the latest age for "settling down" — have been struggling with some problem about the opposite sex, often latent homosexuality. Older terms such as "bachelor" and "spinster" have tended to disappear in favor of the simpler word: single.

Single men have ordinarily struggled with their conflicts about women all their lives. Here is a typical example:

Oliver came to therapy when he was about thirty because he could no longer tolerate his lonely life without love. He was a scientist working at a highly abstract level, so even in his work he did not have much human contact.

His mother had died when he was born. His father, a transit worker, then hired a woman to help him raise the boy, which he felt unable to do on his own. She devoted herself wholeheartedly to Oliver. His father was so impressed by her devotion that he married her. The trouble was that both married for the sake of the boy, not because they had any great love for one another. The marriage was cold, what Cuber and Harroff would have called "devitalized."

As Oliver grew up, his stepmother wrapped her life around him completely. Once he reached puberty, she began to warn him about girls. She told him that many girls had syphilis (AIDS had not yet entered the picture, otherwise she might have brought that in too). Because she was a nurse by background Oliver believed her. His stepmother also told Oliver that girls were out to "hook" a man into marriage and that they cared for little except money and the children that marriage could bring (reflecting, perhaps, her own life history). Oliver believed that too.

Once an adult, Oliver began to experiment a little with women. He began a sexual relationship with one whom he found attractive. She was willing and responsive. But once when they were having sex, she said to him, "Wouldn't this be so much nicer if we were married?" Frightened by this fulfillment of his stepmother's warning, he immediately broke up with the woman.

Not long thereafter he consulted an analyst. The transference was almost immediately positive. Oliver had found the kind, understanding father whom he had never known. Encouraged by this father substitute he began to experiment with other women as well as to work out the pernicious effect of his stepmother's dire admonitions. His work went well and did not involve him in any romantic entanglements.

Toward the end of his therapy the father had a kind of nervous breakdown and had to be hospitalized. The chief symptoms were severe depression and suicidal impulses.

It took Oliver a long time to find a woman whom he could love and with whom he could find happiness. But eventually at the age of thirty-six he did. With their marriage the therapy could be ended. The marriage turned out to be a very happy one.

In many ways this life history is typical of the man who remains a bachelor until late in life. In childhood there is a strong attachment to the mother, who prefers him above all else, including her husband. The parents do not get along well; he cannot marry his mother and he cannot identify with his father, so a bitter battle ensues. As a result, he cannot find much purpose in living and moves from one interest to another or from one place to another.

One could see why the transference became and remained so positive in Oliver's case. There was a powerful identification with the analyst, whom he saw as an omnipotent father figure, quite unlike the beaten-down, meek suicidal father he had known in reality. This homosexual identification with the strong father is an essential element in the growing boy's heterosexuality. If there is not a strong father or if there is no father at all, the boy's heterosexuality will not be based on any positive identification and will accordingly be much weaker and less gratifying. Without such an identification figure, Oliver would have drifted around much longer. In this way, unless analysis steps in, one generation of weak men produces another generation of weak men.

It is generally believed that psychotherapy is limited to the more affluent, better-educated part of the population. No doubt this is true as a general proposition, but the basic common sense of therapy is rapidly filtering down into those less favored by fate or endowment. The following case is a good example.

Ted, a thirty-one-year-old postal worker, came to analysis at the suggestion of one of his friends who said that "psychiatry helps." He was the older of two brothers, his father was dead, and his mother had remarried. In the first session he revealed that he drank too much; the drinking, however, apparently did not interfere with his work. He drank when off duty, never while working.

Although he had left school at fifteen and could not grasp some of the psychoanalytical concepts, he turned out to be a good patient. A satisfactory working alliance was established fairly quickly. At an early stage it was agreed that one of the main goals of therapy was to help him get married; he admitted that he was afraid of women who were too pushy or wanted him too much.

His brother was five years younger, and Ted had vivid memories of the time of his birth. When his brother was one, Ted began to bully the baby and was stopped by his parents. He was fond of his father, who "took me places and did things with me."

When the brother was born, his Aunt Sally, his mother's oldest sister, came to live with them. She lived there from the time Tom was five until he was eight, and he slept in the same bed with her all through her stay. When he was eight, she married and moved out.

Evidently there was quite a bit of seduction; he remembered how he had danced with her once when she was wearing nothing but a slip.

Tom was overweight and had always liked to eat too much. He had one uncle who had a grocery store, where he had worked. On two different occasions the store had been held up at gunpoint. One of the robbers had held a gun to Tom's head, which left him terrified of ever working in such a store again. While he was dissatisfied with the post office, he was afraid to try anything else.

Tom had sex occasionally (one night stands were his mainstay) but there were frequent fantasies of orgies and watching women dress and undress. The analysis showed that drinking served as a defense against the sexual fantasies. He had many sexual fears too, such as that if a woman performed fellatio on him, she would "suck him dry."

He was a prolific dreamer and much of the therapy centered around his dreams. The split between sex and tenderness came out very soon. In one dream: "I was in love with this girl and we couldn't get together. I was shot and she was waiting for me to die." Here he felt acutely the hostility of the woman toward him.

Transference material was sparse, as is common with men from Tom's socioeconomic background. (The doctor is too awesome a figure to allow familiarity.) But in the twentieth session he produced a direct transference dream: the therapist came to his house for a visit and Tom offered him a pickle. The homosexual meaning of this dream was not lost on him.

There was other homosexual material as well. When he was given a rectal examination by a physician, he felt squeamish and wondered how the physician felt.

After verbalizing his fears of affectionate women and diminishing his drinking considerably, he was finally able to find a woman whom he could like and have sex with. After about three years he married and ended the therapy.

In this case the various defenses against getting too close to a woman were systematically brought to light and analyzed. It was helpful that Tom was a prolific dreamer and had reasonably clear memories of his childhood. Even though in the beginning he was totally unsophisticated analytically and even rather paranoid about the whole process ("It was like a racket"), he could produce the material and succeed at reflecting on what it meant. What came out was the sibling rivalry with his brother, the incestuous relationship with his aunt, the anger and sexual desire for mother, the homosexual play at puberty and the sharp split between the virgin and the whore from adolescence on, which created so much anxiety that he covered it over with his drinking. The therapy had to convince him that not all women were money-grubbers out to get him, and that an exchange of mutual affection with a warm woman could in the long run be more gratifying than the one-night stands with pick-ups and prostitutes that had been the mainstay of his life before treatment.

Thus the major dynamics of Tom's bachelorhood came to the fore, typical of many such men: a deeply felt sense of inadequacy about himself including castration anxiety, homosexual wishes, and hostility toward and distrust of women. These are the factors that plague many men who remain single, though the degree of childhood attachments causing the symptoms varies from one to another.

Sometimes the attachment to the mother is more intense, sometimes less so. The affectionate feelings for the father play a significant role in the degree to which the man can separate himself from his mother.

Single Women

With women the unmarried state produces more of a feeling of shame and anguish than with men. Nevertheless most women get married, and the dynamics run parallel to those of men: conflicts with the parents, overattachment or underattachment to the father, homosexual wishes for the mother, all of which have to be overcome for marriage to occur. Today there is less guilt about sexuality; many girls are beginning to have sex in their teens, with their parents' consent and sometimes assistance. If they are brought up in the old repressed tradition, as with some Catholics, the difficulties in getting married are proportionately greater. The following case is not untypical of many of the conflicts inhibiting marriage that come to our attention.

Helen was a twenty-five-year-old secretary who felt so rejected by her boyfriends that she asked for a special appointment on New Year's Day. (For a fuller discussion of this interesting case see my book *The Intimate Hour*, chapter 5.)

Helen had fallen in love with a physician-surgeon who was apparently seeing her for his own amusement rather than with any serious intentions. He was also using his position as a surgeon to two-time her; often when she called him, he would say that he was in surgery, so that she could not reach him. On this occasion when she called for help, he had been unavailable for several days.

Helen's parents were in bitter conflict. Her father, a European businessman who could not make much of a living in this country, was much older than her mother, who was his second wife. He was her first husband, but she constantly made fun of him, intimating rather boldly and almost openly that he was impotent, too cold to satisfy a woman with her passions. She tried to teach her daughter that men were to be exploited by giving them sex or withholding it and then demanding favors in return. The oedipal conflict was intense: Helen was in love with her father and could not stand her mother. The sister did not play much of a role.

Because of her intense conflicts, Helen could not finish school properly and soon gravitated to New York from the midwestern city where she had been brought up.

Her father in turn, though fond of his older daughter, also made exorbitant demands on her, as though she were his wife. She was to obey him, and if she did not, he had the right to beat her. Physical punishment was administered all through her childhood. Still she loved him and put up with everything. In spite of her own financial hardships, she even managed to send him a little money from time to time.

Thus in the oedipal conflict the stage was set for both a rejection by a man and an acceptance by a man.

Once out of school, Helen began a long series of affairs, of which the current one, with the surgeon, was merely the latest version. She was madly in love with Stewart (the boyfriend's name) and felt terribly frustrated when she could not see him and deliriously happy when she did.

Helen remembered her childhood as an unmitigated horror. One of her earliest memories was of going to the roof alone, where she would daydream of a nice quiet house in the country, away from all the fighting and screaming of her mother. In reality her major outlet became school, where at first she did well. Later this became the source of constant conflict, but eventually of brilliant success. As in the ambivalent relationship with her father, school both nourished her and disappointed her. Helen cried a lot about her fate when she was a child; the crying continued throughout the entire analysis; tears came easily to her.

One of the few pleasant memories of her childhood represented a typical combination of gratification and punishment. Sunday mornings, when there was no work, she would manage to steal fifty cents from her father and sneak out to go horseback riding. The parents did not know where she was and would send out panicky alarms. When she came back after a few hours she was invariably beaten for her disobedience. Her father did not want her to ride a horse because she might "hurt herself." The sexual allusion was not lost on her.

There were boys in her life throughout her childhood, in spite of the severe restrictions placed on her. Her earliest experience was at the age of seven when a boy had anal intercourse with her. In the analysis she first thought of this as traumatic; later she recognized the pleasure she got out of it.

When she was twelve, the fights with her mother reached such a fever pitch that she was sent away to New York, where her father's brother lived (the same brother who later supported him). Here she enjoyed school, but felt herself to be an outsider in her aunt's house.

When she returned home, the situation was no better. But since she was now an adolescent, the fights were no longer so terrifying. Further, since her father's business was carried on at home, she began to help him with some of the minor manufacturing operations. Much of her free time away from school she spent in her father's shop assisting him. It was at this time that she also learned to cook for her father, which her mother refused to do, so that for several years she took her mother's place in many respects.

Her first love in adolescence was with a boy who left her very quickly — the abandoning father, an experience that set the tone for her relationship with Stewart and later disappointing love affairs. When her mother finally left her father, she was alone with her father for about a year, finishing school and taking care of him. In this period she was completely devoted to him, scarcely paying attention to her life outside.

Her full sexual life began in adolescence, with a variety of unsuitable men (the unattainable father). One would not ejaculate. Another father-figure, in his forties when she was eighteen, was a perfect oedipal figure. Thus Stewart was a continuation of the unhappy love affairs she had all her life. He became even more attractive by rejecting her (father again refusing her longings).

After about a year of analysis she was able to reveal two fantasies that were repetitive. In one she is sitting in the subway, spots a handsome man, gives him a sign that she is willing, and they go off to have sex together. In the other she is sitting in the movies. A man comes and sits down beside her; he begins to fondle her. She offers no resistance. Gradually he reaches her clitoris and fingers her to orgasm. She is ecstatic but says nothing.

This confession was followed by a waiting room affair, which revealed the core of her transference. Another patient approached her and they had a brief fling lasting about two weeks. When he dropped her, she let out a great deal of anger at the analyst, even accusing him of telling the man not to bother with her. Obviously the analyst here was another version of father, and as she worked out this oedipal projection, she was able to get over her infantile longing for love. Eventually she met and married a suitable man, had three children, and lived a very happy life. Some ten years after she finished, the analyst received a card from her telling him of her pleasure in her new life and her new hobby — mental health and psychotherapy. She had become attached to a clinic where she worked as a helper with the patients.

In this case what kept Helen from marrying was an excessively strong attachment to her father, which analysis helped her to overcome.

In the case of Susan the patient was a clinging vine, worshiping men who did not reciprocate. She was the youngest of three children, with two older siblings. Very much attached to both her mother and her father, she was also badly spoiled by them. In her childhood her mother had literally spoon-fed her for a long time, especially when she was ill with a respiratory infection. By some "accident" she had lots of respiratory infections.

There were two sides to her neurotic love problem. One was getting a "crush" on some older man who was never available for a serious relationship but would have sex with her. The other was to seek out a number of men who were superior to her in status and wealth; she would offer herself sexually to them in the hope that this would entice them to pay more attention to her, which never happened.

Because of the rapidity with which she got crushes, she never found a man who would take the time to get to know her better until very late in analysis. Although she didn't marry until late in life, that was due to peculiar circumstances over which she had no control. She had a love relationship that was the equivalent of marriage.

Summary

Human beings are born into families, outgrow them, and form other families. This involves detachment from one's family of origin and forming a new relationship with another family of one's own.

The basic conflict is that between love and hatred, which leads to the conceptualization of two types of culture, love cultures and hate cultures. Ours is definitely a hate culture, in which the predominant feeling of many people toward others is one of hatred. This explains the wars, persecutions, and massacres that have been the essence of our history for several thousand years.

Within this framework people still have to find some kind of love, and frequently do. But such love is limited by the intensity of the oedipal conflicts that are never resolved without analytic or therapeutic help.

Various studies have been cited to show that the way children are brought up exercises a definite influence on all their later activities. To the extent that such general propositions can be confirmed, there is ample evidence for the validity of the significance of the analytic ideal.

10

Implications for Psychotherapy

*A*LTHOUGH THE ANALYTIC IDEAL arose in the context of therapy, it is by no means confined to that. But it will be helpful to draw the implications for therapy of the conceptualizations presented in this book.

Psychotherapy itself is as old as the hills, and is known in every society ever investigated. But scientific psychotherapy of the analytic variety was discovered by Freud, and in effect all the alleged 136 varieties of psychotherapy take off from Freud. When Freud began his work in 1886, psychiatrists were completely in the dark. They were still working with mild faradic shocks (not the shock therapy that came later), suggestion, or labeling, but there was no understanding of the illness and no understanding of the methodology of intervention. Psychiatrists were at the bottom of the medical ladder, second only to the "ship's doctor." The only known etiological agent, if it can be called that, was heredity, with a bow to Beard's neurasthenia, which allegedly was due to the hectic pace of modern life after the American Civil War.

Generally people nowadays approach Freud with a negative transference, as a result of which they are unable to appreciate the enormous revolution that he brought about. Psychiatrists have opposed him from the very beginning and still do, stressing instead their own desire for power (Robitscher, 1980). In his book on Freud Ernest Jones had already warned readers not to trust anything written about Freud, since almost all of it was garbled and distorted.

It is with this background that we have to set the record straight on what has happened in psychotherapy. Freud formulated the first dynamic description of the nature of the illness, moved on to develop a technique for dealing with it, and went further to develop a whole system of psychology that would account both for the illness and the effectiveness of his therapeutic methods. The technique was based on the three basic concepts of the unconscious, the libido theory, and transference-resistance as the core of the therapeutic progress. These are still the basis of all rational therapy, the development of which is a history of the development, criticism, and emendations of Freud's underlying concepts. The battles within psychoanalysis have also obscured the real development of psychological science, since so many practitioners seek mainly to discredit Freud and hoist their own ideas and their own claims to fame. Jones's *Life and Work of Sigmund Freud*, one of the great biographies of the twentieth century, has been ridiculed, condemned, or ignored because it is too "adulatory." Let us admit frankly that Freud deserves adulation, just as the other great thinkers of the recent past, Darwin and Einstein, deserve it.

With these remarks as preface, let us see what Freud actually did. Psychoanalysis began for all practical purposes in 1900, with the publication of *The Interpretation of Dreams*, although an earlier paper in 1894, on the defense neuropsychoses, contains the first statement of a fundamental idea of psychoanalysis, namely, that neurotics defend themselves against unbearable ideas. Later this notion had to be expanded from neurotics to all people. There is thus a drive and a defense. For practical reasons Freud developed his ideas about drives before he worked out his ideas about defense. As Sandler (1983) has pointed out, the history of psychoanalysis does not proceed in a straight line.

Eventually Freud came to the conclusion that love and work are the key to the psychoanalytic philosophy, although he rarely put it in those terms (the actual data have been presented earlier and elsewhere). I have tried to expand this into the analytic ideal.

Psychoanalysts by and large have been shy of philosophical explanations. There are good historical reasons for this, since philosophy has been such a confused and inadequate field of study, relying more on armchair speculation than on anything else. If their writings are carefully examined, it is seen that every analytic therapist is guided by Freud's value system. For example, Solnit (1989) defines psychoanalysis as a system that sets up a transference neurosis, traces it to its childhood roots, through dreams and other unconscious fantasies analyzes the transference neurosis, and eventually enables the individual to work and to love. Psychoanalysis stays clear of involvement in the patient's life (principle of neutrality) and discourages action that would allegedly resolve the patient's neurosis (principal of abstinence).

We can easily trace how this analytic ideal was gradually formulated in the course of analytic history. Early on Freud was preoccupied with the id, until he saw that the id is the same in all human beings. In fact, the decisive change came about when he realized through his own self-analysis (Anzieu, 1975) that, as Sullivan put it later, "we are all more simply human than otherwise." Since all people have the same impulses, the differences must lie in the ego and superego. These also derive from the early childhood experiences so that the family becomes the basic psychodynamic unit of all psychology.

Freud's theory of the ego was made explicit in 1923, but it has been amended in many ways since. This kind of change is one of the factors that makes psychoanalysis hard to grasp, since the steps needed to reach any given point of view are rarely spelled out in full detail.

Through the years the crucial question has always been to determine the difference between the normal and the neurotic (and a fortiori the psychotic). Psychoanalytic theory has been built up around the varying answers to this question.

In the 1880s Freud took the conventional position that the neurotic was a deviant, the origins of whose symptoms were unknown. Then he ascribed them to sexual conflicts, discovering that the average person has just as many sexual conflicts as the neurotic. With his self-analysis in the 1890s he realized that the matter went deeper than genital sex, to infantile sexuality. The average person had the same infantile sexuality conflict as the neurotic.

Then in the early 1900s he thought that the difference must lie in the ego, a formulation that was developed in the 1920s: where the id was the ego shall be. His daughter Anna crystallized this position in her book *The Ego and the Mechanisms of Defense* (1936). From that point on it is no longer Freud but the general psychoanalytic position that has to be traced.

People then are differentiated by their defenses, not by their impulses. The neurotic defenses of repression, reaction formation, and hysterical somatization had to be differentiated from the psychotic defenses of denial, projection, and isolation.

That seemed adequate for a while, until World War II. Then the staggering psychological problems of the average draftee became known and again the difference between the neurotic and the normal had to be raised all over again.

Subsequent to World War II anthropological research and the postwar experience established the universality of neurotic conflicts and the fact that their manifestations were dependent on the culture: in Roheim's phrase, every culture has its own neuroses. The culturalists came to the fore, with the evidence that whole cultures can become or are neurotic.

In the actual practice of psychotherapy, it became evident that certain aspects of living were mishandled by the average patient. Love was conspicuous by its absence, so that the whole culture looked more like a hate culture than a love culture. Sexuality was a universal source of discomfort, and the sexual revolution went forward. People had little pleasure in their lives; masochism, or the enjoyment of suffering, was the rule rather than the exception. Feelings were repressed, especially by men, but they were also distorted by women in many different ways. The dictatorship of reason that Freud longed for was rarely seen; people were more irrational than rational. The self-image was badly deformed, so that eventually a new school of self psychology came to the fore. This was not in itself new, but did offer a somewhat different slant on the human problem. The family was not the solid secure base that the story books described; it was rather a hotbed of intrigues, passions, and battles, on the surface and under the surface. Communication, which Ruesch called the matrix of psychiatry, was not at the adult level that had been longed for. Rather people were pushed around by unconscious forces, which psychotherapy had to make conscious. Creativity was inhibited in the average person, who thus, in Maslow's phrase, lacked self-actualization.

The social order was disturbed in the extreme; wars, depressions, and the fight of each against each were the order of the day, not the peace and harmony claimed by apologists for the social order. Dictatorships and brutal, ruthless massacres were common. The term "genocide" was coined for the murder of millions by the Nazis. And finally, in spite of all advances in neuroscience, the psychiatric problem seemed to be based largely on social-familial causes. While organic factors were discovered here and there, neurosis was viewed as a psychosocial problem.

All of this had been uncovered by the time that World War II ended and our civilization had been stamped as one of "normalneurotics." In his study of schizophrenics, neurotics, and normals Bellak et al. (1973) had great difficulty with the concept of "normality." Finally the criteria chosen were: no record of psychiatric hospitalization or outpatient psychotherapy, no admission of the presence of neurotic symptoms and manifestations in response to the screening inventory, evidence of satisfactory adjustment in personal relationships and professional activities, and no apparent significant disturbances during the interview. In the schizophrenic sample he comments on the unreliability of psychiatric diagnosis.

Bellak estimated in 1973 that the drain on the economy from care for schizophrenics was $1.25 billion in 1966 alone. He regards it as likely that schizophrenia is indeed the number one public health problem. It strikes early in life — much earlier than the mean age (thirty three years) as first hospitalization suggests. Despite recent discharge rates of encouraging proportions, the schizophrenic disability probably continues in most cases after discharge. It is true that during the last fourteen years there has been a 30 percent decrease in the number of hospitalized schizophrenics. During 1988, for example, resident patients in state and county mental hospitals declined from 210,000 to 195,000. Over the same fifteen years, however, admission rates continued to rise. and in 1968 alone there were more than 320,000 episodes of illness diagnosed as schizophrenic in the United States. The "revolving door" phenomenon refers to the fact that while patients are being hospitalized for shorter periods, they are more frequently being readmitted. Even more crucial is that only from 15 to 40 percent of schizophrenics living in the community can be considered to adjust to an average level. To add to the problem schizophrenia poses, it must also be remembered that such epidemiological figures as are available suggest that from two to ten times as many schizophrenics may be in the community as are hospitalized. The most reliable expectancy rates suggest that up to 6 percent of the population may be diagnosed schizophrenic some time in their lives. And so far no convincing single explanation of the etiology or pathogenesis of schizophrenia has been produced.

Besides schizophrenia, many other psychological problems beset our society. President Bush in a radio address on the "war on drugs" accepted the estimate of some eight million drug addicts in the country, a staggering figure. By the 1980s it was generally accepted that our society is highly neurotic (in the general sense). One estimate is that now one person out of three will have had some therapy in the course of his or her life.

Thus whatever definitions are used, the differences between normal and neurotic become blurred and confused. A new philosophical orientation to the whole problem is needed, and the concept of the analytic ideal offers such an orientation.

The components of the analytic ideal correlate with the problems that therapists work at with their patients. Thus the unreliable concept of diagnosis should be and defacto has been replaced by a more sophisticated evaluation of the personality, such as Bellak's ego functions assessment, or the more commonsense categories listed in the analytic ideal.

In our highly disturbed society, the procedures adopted in psychotherapy are often pitifully inadequate. Many professionals are still working in the Kraepelinian framework rather than the analytic. Many, poorly trained, still accept the old misconceptions about neurosis and psychosis. The analytic ideal offers a new philosophy of therapy, the main features of which can be outlined here.

The Selection of Patients

At the present time an antiquated, outmoded system is in use where the patient has to be assured that he or she is neurotic enough to "need" therapy.

Instead, if the analytic ideal is consistently taught and consistently pursued, both selection and treatment are put on a more rational basis. In the practices of many advanced therapists this is already done, but most professionals in my experience have a hard time giving up the secure framework in which they were trained, even though they have learned that that framework is highly confused and faulty.

Neurosis can best be defined as distance from the analytic ideal. In accordance with this definition, problems can be evaluated in the light of the total functioning of the individual. Even when the problem seems trivial, reassurance drugs and manipulation are all undesirable.

Many therapists make the mistake of offering the patient a diagnosis or making a conventional diagnosis themselves. Such a procedure is damaging to the therapeutic process and should be avoided.

> Linda, a twenty-two-year-old college senior, was in an experimental program at one of the hospitals. Much to her surprise she was suddenly dropped from therapy and sent off on her own. She found a book of mine in the library and applied to me for help. Shocked by her experience, however, she was extremely cautious. All that she wanted was a referral to a therapist near her home (suburban New York). When asked what was bothering her she said: I am a borderline patient. When urged to go to analysis she said that it would only do her harm.

Karl Menninger, who has been particularly critical of the diagnostic methods of psychiatry, writes:

If one looks back to the psychiatry of 1900, or for that matter of 1920, one is aware of this vast difference, that, whereas then the patient and his symptoms were treated as if unrelated to the physician as a symbol of society, today in the evaluation of the personality and its attempted adjustments with society, psychiatry gives primary attention to the nature of the interpersonal relationship, the extent to which it is susceptible to modification by interpretation, the way in which it is modified and formed by the prevailing social structure in which the patient lives and has lived. (*A Psychiatrist's World*, p. 583)

Here Menninger is talking in his own way of the analytic ideal.

Yet the reliance on diagnosis has established itself firmly in the psychiatric and psychological world. Many psychologists were trained to do diagnostic examinations by means of the Rorschach and other tests, and they do not want to give up this special skill. At one time it was a highly popular approach, based on the conviction that the tests could predict the treatability of the patient, but that notion has long since been abandoned, since we have no good way of determining the treatability of any patient except by treatment.

There has long been a tradition of categorizing patients as treatable and untreatable, based on the notion that schizophrenics are untreatable, and that a latent schizophrenia not obvious at first may come out in the course of treatment. These remnants of psychiatric thinking have likewise been abandoned by forward-looking analysts, yet they are still often found. More evidence, if any were needed, that a thorough overhaul is a vital necessity in the field.

The paradox has long been noted in psychoanalytic thought that the most treatable patients are those who have a good history, in our terms, a history of being closer to the analytic ideal. This has been put in various ways. The healthy part of the ego makes a pact with the analyst to help the sick part. Or the healthier the ego the more likely the person is to make further progress. Reformulation of all these observations in terms of the analytic ideal makes very good sense.

Neurosis, if it has to be defined, may now be defined as the distance from the analytic ideal. The greater the distance the sicker the person. The greatest distance is shown by the deteriorated schizophrenic: such an individual has hatred instead of love, does not have sex, has no pleasure, is irrational, is often devoid of feelings, has no self-awareness, etc. Again the analytic ideal translates directly into the clinical picture. How are we to evaluate a psychotherapy patient at the beginning of treatment? Once more by the degree to which he or she has come close to the analytic ideal.

These principles should also be extended to education. There is a movement now to teach psychoanalysis to high school students. Usually it is taught together with academic psychology. In my experience, however, students are thoroughly bewildered by what is offered.

The findings of psychoanalysis should be molded to fit the educational picture. For example, a student of mine, Dr. Steven Luel, tried to see what the effects would be on students if they were encouraged to present their fantasies freely, even without any interpretation. He had his students report their dreams, write down their fantasies, and release themselves in other ways. The results were striking, even if hard to evaluate. In a society that leans heavily on repression as a defense mechanism, any break from this defensive posture comes as a great relief. That is one reason why in the beginning of therapy, when patients, often for the first time in their lives, are given an opportunity to release their fantasies, they feel better and many therapeutic benefits ensue.

In a research project at Mt. Sinai Hospital in New York, an interesting experiment has been going on for a number of years. The experimenters asked themselves the question: what is the difference between actors and schizophrenics? Actors move off into another world and then come back to this one. Schizophrenics move off into another world, and do not come back. So the possibility suggests itself of getting the actors to teach the schizophrenics how to come back to the real world, back from their delusions and hallucinations. The technique seems to have merit, and has been an ongoing project.

Is there then no patient who is untreatable? I am not saying that at all. There are many patients, low in intelligence, with few inner resources, who derive little or no benefit from psychotherapy. Yet even these patients sometimes show surprising reactions. Here is one instance.

John was a veteran who had been discharged from the service with a one hundred percent disability because of a condition of bronchiectasis. Before the war he had been a milk delivery man; after the war he was no longer able to work. Most of his time he spent watching TV, on a set that he had won in a church lottery. When he came for therapy he had a recurrent delusion that a woman was shooting an arrow through his heart. Even though the therapy stayed at an unbelievably realistic level, after a couple of months of once-a-month therapy, the delusion disappeared.

This case illustrates once more that we are just beginning to become aware of the healing effects of psychotherapy on people. John was, of course, anything but an ideal therapeutic patient, yet he responded to the process in a minimal way. The process of releasing fantasies seems to be one that benefits a great many people, since they have no other outlet for their burdens.

Susan, a depressed woman in her forties, spent the first five years of her analysis crying each session. Then she stopped crying, and began free associating, but could find nothing to say. To the question What comes to mind? she invariably replied: Nothing. Upon analysis of this response it was found that she interpreted it in terms of her Catholic background — any thought, no matter how trivial, may harbor evil. Unconsciously to her the therapist was trying to ferret out her evil thoughts. Once this was brought to light, she could talk more freely.

This example also shows how the analytic ideal can become directly applicable in the therapeutic situation. The therapist focuses on whichever component of the ideal is most difficult for the patient, in this case, talking.

The Selection of Therapists

What kind of a person should the therapist be? There is reasonable agreement on this in the analytic field, and such agreement has carried over into other approaches. The therapist should be a mature, well-analyzed person who can empathize with others and provide them with the warmth and sustenance that they did not receive during their childhood.

Undoubtedly the most important research study in this field is the study done by Henry, Sims, and Spray (1971, 1973), who investigated four thousand therapists from the four main mental health fields: psychiatry, psychology, social work, and psychoanalysis. They discovered that the entrants into any of these fields who finally do become psychotherapists are very similar in social and cultural background. They come from a highly circumscribed sector of the social world, representing a social marginality in ethnic, religious, and political terms. As therapists choose among the offerings in their particular training systems, they do so in ways that appear to fit into the choices of these systems. In this process the members of these systems become again alike in emphasizing particular views and experiences, and each emerges at the end of training with a firm commitment to the psychotherapeutic stance. Members of each group triumph over the manifest goals of their particular training system and become, with time, increasingly like their colleague psychotherapists in other training systems. Because of these similarities Henry calls psychotherapy "the fifth profession."

In another volume they found that the life ways of psychotherapists constitute an increasingly homogeneous and integrated system of belief and behavior that most often begins in early family religiocultural experiences and progresses selectively toward a common concept of a psychodynamic paradigm for the explanation of all behaviors — a paradigm that guides their choices and behaviors as they emerge from the training years into the practice of psychotherapy.

In sum: on the basis of previous training and experience, psychotherapists have learned not to rely on common, everyday criteria for categorizing individuals but instead view persons as concrete manifestations of a general theoretical framework. For most of the therapists practicing in Los Angeles, New York, and Chicago, this theoretical framework is composed of psychodynamic, particularly psychoanalytic, concepts derived from the Freudian and neo-Freudian schools of thought. Such concepts delimit the psychotherapist's world. The specialized world of the psychotherapist is one in which the terminology of everyday conversation is avoided and psychodynamic language becomes the basic mode of communication. To a certain extent, therefore, the psychodynamic paradigm serves to refine the social behavior of individuals so that they come to be viewed as functions of specific personal dynamics.

Henry and his colleagues describe a remarkable homogeneity in the sociocultural origins of members of the four mental health professions. Specifically there is a pronounced tendency for practitioners to claim a Jewish cultural affinity, to have Eastern European ethnic ties and foreign-born fathers, to have rejected, in adolescence, religious beliefs and political views of their parents, to have experienced, during their own lifetime, upward social mobility. These biographical characteristics have been found to be associated with those personal qualities that experts believe applicants to therapeutic training programs should have: an introspective orientation, an intellectual predisposition, and a relativistic perspective. Placed in the context of the patterns of professional selection and recruitment, the development of a commitment to a psychodynamic paradigm can be viewed as the product of the individual's total biography.

In the 1970s Robert Wallerstein surveyed the fifty-seven institutes that were then members of the International Psychoanalytic Association, receiving replies from twenty-eight (Wallerstein, 1978). Some of these replies were extremely brief, some lengthy with careful discussion of all the issues raised. In any case they offered a good crosssection of psychoanalytic thought on the question of training, which is no doubt still applicable. Wallerstein distinguished six major issues on which a variety of opinions emerged from the institutes' responses.

(1) The extent to which a real problem of training in compatibility is posed by our simultaneous intent to encompass two not necessarily congruent educational goals for our candidates in training — that is, educating for a science and training for a profession. About half of the responding institutes saw no meaningful distinction between the two goals and therefore no problem; the other half saw a related and thorny problem.

(2) Proper training prerequisites for psychoanalytic education are stated variously as the issue of medical vs. nonmedical training or the issue of a proper mixture of the potential student pool from which psychoanalysis should seek its renewal. Here the debate has persisted unchecked during the more than fifty years since Freud's publication of his book on lay analysis, with extremes on both sides. (The lawsuit brought by some American psychologists against the American Psychoanalytic Association and the International Psychoanalytic Association may ultimately create a more cohesive point of view.)

(3) The kind of curriculum that is best suited to our training institutes. Traditional in professional school education has been the uniform or essentially lockstep curriculum, in which all students are held responsible for mastering a common body of professional knowledge, skills, and attitudes. In graduate academic education in the university, however, more traditional has been individualized or tailor-made sequences geared to the very specific, differentiated interests and career goals of each student.

(4) The selection for training and the place of selection criteria, both positive and negative. Here we also had polar extremes, between the effort on the one hand at a total abolition of preselection, leaving anybody who was qualified free to go into analysis with any practitioner (in some cases, even advanced students) and the effort, on the

other hand, at the most rigorous screening and preselection before admission to training analysis under member institute auspices.

(5) The expectable degree of personality alteration to be achieved in personal analysis and in the overall training sequence. This issue is inextricably linked, of course, to the stance on the selection issue. Here there seemed to be fairly reliable correlations with the position of the selection issue: the Kleinian-oriented institutes, which tend to take gambles on candidates who might be deemed too "disturbed" by other institutes, tend concomitantly to engage in much longer analyses and to count on achieving more far-reaching personality changes.

(6) Last in this listing, but probably first in heated and controversial discussion in our current literature, is the role of the training analyst in the assessment of his or her candidates and in the monitoring of the candidates' progression through the institute. Important here is the distinction between reporting and nonreporting training analyses. Here again there was an equal division of voices into camps, with various positions in between.

Wallerstein concludes that "we have in full view now a range of experiments in training" (p. 503).

The careful study of selection processes in the analytic world stands in sharp contrast to the casual, almost careless, way of selecting candidates in the worlds of psychiatry, psychology, and social work. Evidently psychoanalysis has succeeded in creating a world of its own, in fulfillment of Freud's wishes when he said in 1926: "I should like to hand it over to a profession which does not yet exist, a profession of lay curers of souls who need not be doctors and should not be priests."

In the beginning Rorschachs and other test materials were used to screen out those candidates who were too disturbed, but after awhile these procedures were dropped and replaced by personal interviews.

In spite of all these precautions, the selection of candidates for psychoanalytic training is still far from perfect. Usually, once admitted to the institute, the candidates will be able to finish, but many complaints are heard. In the 1970s the American Psychoanalytic Association started a certification process that was designed to eliminate those graduates of psychoanalytic institutes whose work was not up to par. In this process about one-third of the applicants, all graduates of member institutes of the American Psychoanalytic Association, were found unsatisfactory and refused full membership. After much hesitation and wrangling, in the course of which some members wished to drop the failed candidates, it was finally decided that they would be offered extended associate membership. The matter has since been left at that. So little publicity is given to the certification procedure that it is hard to find out what is happening. The figure of one-third of the candidates rejected came out only during the discovery process in the lawsuit of the American psychologists against the American Psychoanalytic and the International.

The Patient Population

The patient population in Freud's day was highly restricted. Since contemporary ideas of friendship are heavily influenced by the therapeutic attitude, it is worth remembering that the traditional idea of friendship had three essential components: friends must enjoy one another's company, they must be useful to one another, and they must share a common commitment to the good. Today we tend to define friendship mostly in terms of the first component: friends are those we take pleasure in being with. Traditionally, it was the virtues indelibly associated with friendship that were central to the "habits of the heart." The classical idea of friendship made sense more readily in the small face-to-face communities that characterized early American communities than it does to us. In such small communities, it was obvious that people not only helped one another and enjoyed one another's company but also participated mutually in enterprises that furthered the common good. Friendships were by no means confined to local communities in early American society. Perhaps the classic example is the friendship of Thomas Jefferson and John Adams chronicled in the extraordinary series of letters that they wrote to one another. Jefferson expressed it in 1820, when they were both old men: "We have, willingly, done injury to no man, and have done for our country the good which has fallen in our way, so far as commensurate with the faculties given us. In the meantime be our last as cordial as were our first affections."

In the latter part of the nineteenth century George Beard popularized the term "neurasthenia" a generalized malaise that seemed to be affecting large numbers of "civilized, refined and educated" Americans at that time. While Beard and others blamed the new national disease on such heterogeneous phenomena as railway travel and the telegraph, overwork and more specialized occupations, they tended to sum up its causes under the phrase "modern civilization"; the same thing seems to be happening today. Bellak has coined the term "overload" to characterize the many demands that people make on themselves on the current scene.

It is clear from Bellah (and from Douvan, Kulka, and Veroff) that the analytic ideal has already penetrated middle America and that we have become, as one critic has put it, the most therapized people in history. This criticism comes from two misunderstandings: (1) therapy is seen as a correction of defects — the old notion of neurosis as a psychiatric disorder lingers; and (2) the soul-searching going on is seen as a search to get away from disease, as in the traditional approach to psychiatry, rather than as a search for a new kind of health, as in psychoanalysis.

Here a new distinction has to be made. Traditionally those in psychotherapy are sick and need a doctor to help them. People then look for certain symptoms, generally of the traditional variety, that require help and that in their opinion can be corrected. We call this symptom analysis. This is what Freud started with, and this is still the formulation congenial to most of the profession. The discussions in Bellah and other works show that something is entirely different. In the newer psychotherapy, people have a vision of a better life, which is the analytic ideal, and want to get there through therapy. We call this a liberation analysis. It is much more akin to certain kinds of traditional philosophy, which deal with the happy life, such as the Stoic and Epicurean movements of ancient times, or the existentialism of today. But these consequences of the analytic ideal have not been adequately formulated. The profession is still bogged down in a series of meaningless diagnoses. Even the professional literature argues endlessly about the "borderline" patient, when the answer is deceptively simple: the borderline patient is not overtly psychotic and not simply neurotic. The patient should be treated by the ideology and methodology of psychoanalysis, with the emphasis on the analysis of transference-resistance (Fine, 1989). Instead, there are interminable discussions of exact diagnoses, which cannot be had and which change every few years (DSM III and subsequent formulations). Insurance companies, untrained executives in personnel positions, and the like find themselves more comfortable with diagnoses, so they insist that they be made in accordance with the DSM categorizations. Ideologically the whole procedure is a farce, but it is forced on the profession that complies because it has to make a living.

In one case a deeply troubled social worker was covered by insurance for many years. Suddenly a decree came down that for the insurance to continue she had to show that she was unable to work. This was the one area in which she had remained reasonably intact. It could not be shown that her work life was seriously affected. Her request for insurance was refused.

This case is typical of the confusion that exists about psychotherapy on the current scene. The insurance companies are acting on the basis of the old psychiatry, while the patients are acting in accordance with the newer ideology of psychoanalysis. The resulting clash is settled by the insurance companies, who disburse the money, which provides power. On the other hand, many of the components of the analytic ideal are commingled with various symptoms that can properly be related to the old psychiatry, so the focus centers on those symptoms. If a person complains that he or she is anxious, that is understandable, so insurance forms are filled with diagnoses of "anxiety reaction" and the like, which are irrelevant to the true facts and to the true needs of psychoanalytic psychotherapy.

The confusion is shared by the old-line professionals who are asked to do the therapy. Even in psychoanalysis this has remained the case to some extent. Whereas forward-looking psychoanalysts have recognized that they are effecting a social revolution, which sociologists like Bellah readily comprehend, the older more conservative analysts deny the revolution, confuse it with the "erroneous cultural point of view," and fight it vigorously.

In the United States the traditionalists succeeded in ostracizing "lay analysts" from the profession for many years, that is, only physicians were permitted to train in their institutes. The famous Resolution Concerning the Training of Laymen was passed in 1938 and continued in force until recently. Psychoanalysis was alleged to be a medical specialty, without the slightest shred of evidence and entirely contrary to Freud's wishes. Nevertheless the prestige of the medical profession is so great in our society that the issue remained officially dormant for a long time.

In the meantime psychologists, social workers, and other nonmedical personnel did not remain idle. They prepared themselves in standard psychoanalytic training in spite of the official ban. For psychoanalytic training consists of personal analysis, which can be obtained anywhere an analyst is willing, of course work in analytic theory, offered in many places, and of doing analysis under supervision, which is also dependent simply on finding the right person, many of whom were readily available for a fee.

In this way a considerable number of nonmedical analysts were trained, formed societies, increased their numbers, and offered their own training. In the meantime it was discovered by lawyers in the American Psychological Association that the resolution banning the training of "laymen" was illegal. Accordingly a lawsuit was initiated against the American Psychoanalytic Association and the International Psychoanalytical Association in 1985. After three years of legal wrangling the psychologists won out and an agreement was reached allowing the admission of a substantial number of psychologists and other nonmedical persons to the institutes of the American, and granting American institutes that did not belong to the American the right to join the International. Following these changes, by 1989 a substantial number of the students in the American Psychoanalytic Association institutes were psychologists and other nonmedical people, while several of the institutes started and run by nonmedical people were admitted to the International.

While some high-placed persons in the American persisted in denying reality by saying that nothing had changed, it was clear that a revolution had occurred in the training of analysts in this country. Where this will lead no one can say at the present time.

In 1988 the *Psychoanalytic Quarterly* initiated a series of papers on the future of psychoanalysis by leading persons in the field. Generally they were optimistic but anticipated great changes in the selection of therapists as a consequence of the psychologists' victory in the lawsuit. In the first article Arlow and Brenner wrote:

> These issues lead quite logically to the future organizational life of American psychoanalysis. As nonmedical training institutes under the aegis of the International Psychoanalytical Association come into being in the US, they will undoubtedly recruit for their faculty members of the American Psychoanalytic Association and other medically trained psychoanalysts. It seems plausible to expect that there will be continuing and increasing collaboration between such institutes and institutes currently affiliated with the American Psychoanalytic Association. What kind of collaboration may eventuate out of such rapprochement? Could this possibly lead to more uniform standards of psychoanalytic training and practice? This seems to be an open question. Given the essential conservatism of many analysts and the conflicting professional interest of the various groups involved, it seems that it will take a long time for effective cooperation to develop. If uniform standards for training and practice are ever promulgated, it is most likely, as we indicated earlier, that they will be the work of political and economic bodies rather than of psychoanalysts.
>
> Of some things about the future of psychoanalysis we can be certain. Fortunately, they are the most important issues as well. Psychoanalysis will continue to furnish the most comprehensive

and illuminating insight into the human psyche. It will continue to stimulate research and understanding in many areas of human endeavor. In addition to being the best kind of treatment for many cases, it will remain, as it has been, the fundamental base for almost all methods that try to alleviate human suffering by psychological means. And above all, it will continue to be a compelling and adventurous enterprise for all those fascinated by the complexity of the human mind. (p. 13)

In their paper Wallerstein and Weinshel (1989) pointed to the bewildering changes in the conditions of practice confronting the new generation of analysts. They include (p. 364): (1) a diminishing number of psychoanalytic patients; (2) increasing numbers of mental health practitioners with little or no psychoanalytic knowledge or training; (3) increasing numbers of nonpsychoanalytically based alternative therapies, some verging on the cultist, and of self-help groups; (4) a systematic retreat from adequate insurance coverage for long-term psychotherapeutic care (even in countries where national health insurance is advancing or has already been achieved); (5) the growing preoccupation everywhere with cost effectiveness and cost containment (with psychoanalysis losing out to psychodynamic approaches, not only in the psychoses but in some borderline and neurotic disorders as well) and; (6) the growing preoccupation everywhere for peer review and utilization review systems, with their inevitable impingements on the privacy and confidentiality of the two-party therapeutic transaction.

The Presenting Problem

In the old days the situation was relatively simple: the person felt a pressing problem, it was evaluated as psychological, and the patient called a neurotic with various subclassifications, none of which had any real meaning but which sounded good (the DSM). As knowledge of the analytic ideal grew and spread among the general population this procedure changed considerably (Bellah; Douvan, Kulka, and Veroff).

Today it is the more aware, more sophisticated, and often the more successful persons who come to therapy.

Psychologists studying the corporate world suddenly discovered that success can be as much a problem as failure. Those who are at the top often spend long hours at work, sacrificing personal pleasure and the simpler joys of living. They are driven by a need to make more and more money, and do not know how to spend it, even in conspicuous consumption, as in Thorstein Veblen's days.

This has led to a new breed of therapist, called "coaches." These people dispense with the long-term treatment of inner problems and concentrate instead on quick resolution of the person's conflicts. They are called "executive coaches" by analogy with sports (almost all world-class tennis players, for example, have a coach).

This kind of executive coaching has become particularly popular on Wall Street. Some years ago a number of therapists noticed their Wall Street patients spent as much time discussing business problems as personal ones. The therapists argued that if they could combine the sensitivity of a therapist, the business acumen of an accountant, and the enthusiasm of a trainer they would have something spectacular. So they started the process known as "executive coaching."

This is but one of many examples where psychoanalysis has had to meet new problems of the more affluent, more successful, and better integrated individuals who nevertheless feel the need for help from the outside. The professional confusion and the social situation combine to form a paradox. Patients are being evaluated according to the outmoded criteria of nineteenth-century psychiatry, but they are motivated by the revolutionary philosophy of twentieth-century psychoanalysis. Thus all the books describing modern therapy speak of love, marriage, work, the self-image, and other aspects of the analytic ideal. But the insurance companies and the orthodox psychiatrists, who still have the power (Robitscher, 1980) and still call the tune, force people to list diagnoses that no longer have much meaning in today's world. Even the diagnosis of "neurasthenia" (literally, nerve weakness) which is almost completely outmoded in the United States, is still used in half the world in many different senses.

Even the diagnosis of schizophrenia and the psychiatric move toward drugs to treat it is of a highly dubious nature. In point of fact, physical methods have always been used to treat schizophrenics, and always with poor results. The paradox again arises that organic psychiatry misunderstands schizophrenics, yet acquires more and more power on how to handle these patients. The situation remains seriously troubled because of the exclusion of psychoanalysis from the official training of the major mental health professions. Freud once speculated about whether the acceptance of psychoanalysis by psychiatry was oral-erotic (the first stage of life) or oral-sadistic (the next stage) and felt that it was most likely the latter, aiming to destroy psychoanalysis rather than learn it.

Assessment of Results

So far it has been impossible to achieve any assessment of the results of psychoanalysis and other therapies with any reliability. The most careful and exhaustive study in the literature is that by Wallerstein (1986), but even here the results are none too impressive, and 25 percent of the patients studied remained "lifers," i.e., persons with lifelong dependence on therapy. In itself this is not bad. By analogy with a disease such as diabetes, for example, the diabetic has a lifelong dependence on insulin in one form or another; before insulin was developed the diabetic was doomed to an early death.

Smith, Glass, and McGaw (1981), using the technique of meta-analysis, concluded that there was a small positive effect from psychotherapy. Waskow and Parloff in their NIMH study found that psychotherapy was more effective than drug therapy. But on the whole the research is poor and the results difficult to interpret and easy to pick apart. Freud once said that the only real way to test the effectiveness of psychoanalysis is to let patients live their lives over again without analysis, which is obviously impossible.

Case histories still remain our most important source of information. But case histories are fragments of a great confession, in Goethe's phrase that Reik once used for one of his books. Shortly before he died Alexander reportedly made extensive recordings of therapeutic sessions in Los Angeles, which were then evaluated by other therapists. But according to the psychologist involved, Hedda Bolgar (personal communication), the material is so voluminous and unwieldy that they are unable to do anything with it.

In this field at present clinical experience rules, even though each person's clinical experience is different. Perhaps, as the field becomes more unified, more objective data may become available.

Yet there is still a flaw in this kind of thinking. It still apes the medical model: the patient has an illness; does he or she get over it or not. It is not that patients have adopted a way of life that is detrimental to their health or welfare — that would be too difficult to measure. And again the insurance companies step in to play a decisive role. When I was president of Division 39 (Division of Psychoanalysis) in 1980–81, there was a good bit of correspondence with NIMH and other governmental agencies. There was concern that the extension of insurance benefits on the lines that I proposed would result in the need to treat the whole population, which was both a financial and logistical impossibility. Yet here we have for the first time a technical tool that could promote the welfare of humankind on a massive scale, less expensive than a few nuclear bombs. The governments do not have the wit to grasp the opportunity.

Age of Patients

Psychotherapy has now advanced from a circumscribed pool of adults between twenty and fifty to the entire population. Children are being routinely helped, as well as old people. Even newborns have been shown to be amenable to therapy, as the ingenious work of Selma Fraiberg showed.

Schools of Psychoanalysis and Psychotherapy

The public has been literally bombarded by the idea of different schools of psychoanalysis and psychotherapy, each of which is claimed as a panacea by its adherents and propagandized vigorously.

This literature is more propaganda than sober science. Many of these specific forms of therapy flourish for a few years, and then disappear, like Rogerian therapy in psychology, Rankian therapy in social work, and primal scream therapy in psychiatry. Because of transference every form of psychotherapy will have some effect on a certain group of patients; then the novelty and the effect both wear off.

By contrast psychoanalysis becomes steadily more solidified and more unified. In this connection the extraordinary work of Freud deserves special emphasis. The basic Freudian basis for all psychotherapy has never been seriously questioned on any intelligent basis. Almost all the criticisms of Freud and psychoanalysis fall wide of the mark and are distortions of psychoanalytic theory when looked at more carefully. This is readily understandable, since Freud has been taught almost exclusively in psychoanalytic institutes to which few have had access. Currently the offerings in Freud are being expanded, especially in the light of the victory of the American psychologists in the 1985 lawsuit, and the situation may change dramatically in the next few years. But for the time being the reaction of most students to Freudian thought remains negative, and the problem remains one of education more than anything else. Some cursory comments on the alternative schools and the alternative therapies may be appropriate here.

Freudian therapy relies on the libido theory, the developmental process, and the working through of transference-resistance. Psychoanalytic theory went through many changes at the hands of Freud and many others. But when new theories were proposed, a strange situation developed. Either Freud's writings had not kept up with his new ideas, or his opponents (the proponents of new theories) quoted outmoded concepts, such as "actual neurosis," or an oversimplified version of instinct theory, which simply befogged all the relevant issues.

As a result, psychoanalytic theory since Freud has been misquoted more than quoted. In one of the local colleges in New York, for example, a course is given in psychoanalytic theory that omits Freud entirely.

In order to make the point that they are novel, writers like Thompson, Fromm, Horney, Kohut, and many others have more or less deliberately misstated what they understood the Freudian position to be.

It is difficult to accuse well-known innovators of deliberate fraud, but that is what any impartial observer would judge to be the case. At the same time they write popular books, which are widely sold, acquire a reputation, and are seen as authorities. It is no wonder that the student coming to such a field is justifiably confused.

Implications for Medicine and the Social Sciences

The expansion of the influence of psychoanalytic thought to medicine and all the social sciences is one of the outstanding developments of the twentieth century. During World War II all organized psychoanalytic activity came to a standstill. Before the outbreak of hostilities, psychoanalysis had always had a pitifully small group of followers. In the Vienna Psychoanalytic Society the roll of members for 1911–12 was thirty-four, and no other country had a group of even near that size. Freud's fear that the science would disappear, especially after the defections of Jung and Adler, seemed to be well founded.

Once peace was restored, psychoanalytic work could resume, yet at first there seemed to be few signs that it would flourish. At the annual meeting of the American Psychoanalytic Society in 1920 only ten persons attended. The president said he had heard that some of the members thought it advisable to discontinue the society because it had outlived its usefulness. To replace the official organization it was suggested that yearly informal gatherings be instituted, at which those interested could present papers on psychoanalysis. The motion did not carry.

But the war set off a tremendous upsurge in interest in psychoanalysis. Unlike the academic psychologies, whose scientific ignorance and stultifying refusal to recognize human suffering turned psychology into a third-rate science, here was a psychology that did have something to say about the breakthrough of humankind's most primitive and irrational urges, which had just caused such havoc in the civilized world. The great public interest was reflected in organizational growth.

The first postwar meeting of the International Psychoanalytical Association was held in the Hague, in the Netherlands, in 1929, with Ferenczi as president. Opposition was still intense and the organization had to be tightened up in many ways. Oberndorf (1953) relates that during this period he mentioned in a lecture that the sight of the genitals of an exhibitionist was a factor in the development of a hysterical eye symptom in a young woman. Two women students immediately submitted a formal complaint to the dean's office, which agreed emphatically with their point of view and chastised Oberndorf for his "bizarre interpretation."

The training regulations of the International were not firmly established until the Bad Homburg Congress in 1925. They lasted until 1938, when the American group declared its independence of the International. In 1938 the American passed its famous Resolution against the Training of Laymen, as a result of which nonmedical persons were no longer admitted to the training program of the American. This lasted until 1987, when it had to be rescinded because of the 1985 lawsuit by the American psychologists, which claimed that it was in restraint of trade and a violation of various anti-monopoly statutes. The monopoly of the oil trade and the forced breakup of the Rockefeller Standard Oil Co. were cited as a precedent.

Another highly significant event between the two world wars was the move to America by many distinguished psychoanalysts, for whom Hitler and the constant threat of war made life impossible on the continent. In 1926 the International Psychoanalytic Association numbered 294 members, of whom 58 were Americans, 47 Viennese, 56 British, and 39 Swiss (including, surprisingly, Jean Piaget). By 1938 the total number had grown to 556, but the proportions had changed radically. There were then 184 members in the American Association and 92 in the British, including associate members. The Americans, although still few in absolute numbers, had already become the dominant group. The American Psychoanalytic Society at that time had six constituent societies, of which the one in New York, with 77 members, was the largest.

At the 1938 meeting in Paris, Ernest Jones, as president, read a communication from the president and secretary of the American Psychoanalytic Association, which altered the entire structure of the International. The Americans demanded that the International should cease to exist as an administrative body and should resolve itself into a congress for scientific purposes only. They described the International Training Committee as a "paper institution" and resolved that they would no longer cooperate with it in any way. They further specified that the status of membership-at-large should not apply to individuals residing and practicing in the United States. The International appointed a committee to deal with these proposals, but the advent of the war made cooperation impossible. After the war, when the American Psychoanalytic Association had become more numerous than members in associations throughout the rest of the world combined, the proposals were adopted in total.

From then on the Americans ruled the world of psychoanalysis until the late 1980s, when the lawsuit challenged their unethical practices and fraudulent advertising that claimed that psychoanalysis was a branch of medicine (a proposition that Freud had vehemently opposed).

The political battles between the end of World War II and the reorganization of the American and International in 1987–88 to admit American lay analysts centered around the monopoly of health insurance by the medical profession. Various ruses and legal subterfuges were tried in an attempt to limit health insurance to the medical profession, but after awhile the psychologists, social workers, and other nonmedical persons were able to block these attempts. The courts and legislatures almost unanimously rejected these ruses.

As far as nonmedical analysis is concerned, official training was offered to non-M.D.'s. But in practice anyone who wanted to become an analyst could acquire training in the manner prescribed by the International. Training consisted of personal analysis, course work, and analysis under supervision (controls). This training was obtained by a number of people, who then set up their own training centers and helped others to become psychoanalysts.

The training system that is virtually universal today throughout the world was developed in the period between 1920 and 1938, between the two world wars. It resulted from the efforts of one person in one situation. The person was Max Eitingon, and the situation was Berlin of the Weimar Republic.

That Eitingon should have been the one to set the standard for psychoanalytic training is surprising. Freud was still alive and active in 1920, surrounded by a host of brilliant students in Vienna. Yet he left it to Eitingon's initiative to set up the first institute in Berlin, even sending him one of his favorite disciples, Hanns Sachs, as the first training analyst.

Eitingon was born in Russia, the son of wealthy Jewish parents (Pomer, 1966). Afflicted with a stutter, he took his medical degree, but because of his emotional conflicts he never took the examination that would have allowed him to practice; thus technically he always remained a lay analyst. Furthermore, he worshiped Freud with such biblical devotion that he never wrote a single technical paper; everything, in his opinion, had already been said by Freud, and the only task left was to disseminate his teachings (Jones, 1943).

Eitingon is usually said to have had some personal analysis with Freud, but all that it amounted to was a few casual talks in the evening, so that essentially the man who founded the system of psychoanalytic training was himself untrained. What he lacked in training he made up in devotion and dedication. In 1920 he moved to Berlin, where he founded an analytic clinic and institute financed by his personal funds. He remained there until 1933, when the Hitlerian tyranny forced him out. He then emigrated to Palestine, where he founded the Palestine Psychoanalytic Society, which he led until his death in 1943.

The horror of the Hitler period had obliterated the extraordinary cultural achievements of Germany in the Weimar period. Einstein lived there at the time, as did Max Weber and numerous other intellectual luminaries. The roster of students and faculty at the Psychoanalytic Institute reads like a who's who of psychoanalytic history. It was easily the most distinguished institute of that period, even though Freud led the group in Vienna. The system of education and training devised in Berlin has persisted to this day with no essential change. It has since been called the tripartite system: personal analysis, didactic instruction, and control analysis.

First and foremost was the *training analysis*. It was universally agreed that the future analyst should be analyzed by a more experienced person. At first this was called a "didactic analysis," based on the illusion, soon to be dispelled, that the "normal" person had no particular problems. Later the term "didactic" was dropped, and it was recognized that all analysis is therapeutic in nature. The intensity, duration, and outcome of this training analysis, as it came to be called, all varied widely. It may be assumed that since about 1930 every practicing analyst has been through a training analysis. At first it was brief, again under the illusion that the "normal" person had fewer problems, but gradually it lengthened until as Balint (1954) said: "Nobody has any idea how long a training analysis should or

does last." It is generally recognized that the controversies about the
training analysis have been at the heart of all dissensions and splits
in the psychoanalytic societies (Weinshel, 1982).

The psychoanalytic training consisted of a training analysis, theoretical instruction, and doing analysis under supervision (controls).
In addition, and most originally, control of the whole procedure was
shifted from the individual to the society; in fact, it became forbidden for any individual analyst, no matter how prominent, to take
over the training function. Perhaps this is one of the major reasons
for the numerous splits and dissensions in psychoanalytic societies.

The Expansion of Psychoanalytic Thought

Janet Malcolm has written that psychoanalysis unexpectedly expanded into the most influential system of thought since Christianity,
and a few words can be said about this expansion. There have been
periods of expansion and periods of retrenchment since the beginning. After World War I, as the wounds of the war began to heal,
a new spirit of optimism became noticeable, especially in the years
from 1929 to 1933, when Hitler put an end to it. The term "psychoanalytic movement" was born in these years, referring to the hope
that psychoanalysis through its therapeutic and educational efforts
might make a significant contribution to the welfare of the world. A
journal with that name was started in 1929, only to be forced to close
down in 1933.

One historically significant feature of the analytic experience after
World War I was the development in Russia. A sizable Russian group
was formed before the war, and continued after the Revolution. No-
tices of their activities were published regularly in the *International
Journal of Psychoanalysis* until 1928; thereafter all news from them
ceased. Ever since then, the attitude of official communism toward
psychoanalysis has been completely condemnatory; for years psychoanalysis was spoken of as the "last stand of capitalism." Thus from
1930 onward, psychoanalysis and psychoanalytic psychology were
limited to the democratic countries, hated by both extremes of the
right and the left. This fact has been insufficiently appreciated in the
evaluation of the cultural role of psychoanalysis.

With the Gorbachev regime, there have been a few indications of
a change in this attitude; one prominent Russian psychiatrist even
wrote a favorable article about Freud. But to date the destructive
repressive measures of the Stalin period, while considerably loos-
ened, have not yet been completely eradicated. Psychoanalysts are

still not trained in the Soviet Union, and until psychoanalytic therapy is really taught and practiced, the expansion of the field will be severely limited.

Apart from training facilities, which now (1990) number some seven thousand members in the International Psychoanalytical Association worldwide, psychoanalysis has moved into many different fields with varying degrees of influence. Expansion to children is a natural enough broadening of therapy; it began with the Viennese Hermine von Hug-Hellmuth, who published her first child case, the analysis of a dream of a five-and-a-half-year-old boy. In the 1920s came the better-known Melanie Klein and Anna Freud, who expanded child analysis into a full-fledged branch of the analytic community. Both had clinics in London, Anna Freud at the Hampstead Clinic, Melanie Klein at Tavistock; both attracted numerous followers and moved forward in many ways. It is gratifying yet surprising that these two leaders, who had a cordial dislike for one another (Melanie Klein considered herself a better daughter to Sigmund Freud than Anna) were able to get along together in the same British Society, which, almost alone in the world, has never had a serious split.

In his 1914 paper on narcissism, Freud had divided the treatment population into those with transference neuroses and those with narcissistic neuroses, characterizing the latter as patients who were unable to form a transference and therefore untreatable. Freud was not a hospital psychiatrist, however, and had no experience with psychotics. When psychiatrists came along who were working with psychotics and applied the principles of psychoanalysis to them, it soon became apparent that Freud's stricture was too severe.

The first to present the results of the large-scale psychoanalysis of psychotics was the American Harry Stack Sullivan (1892–1949). Writing at a time when the attitude toward the therapeutic amelioration of psychotics, including that of all the leading analysts from Freud on down, was one of almost total hopelessness, Sullivan reported on the more or less elaborate investigation of 250 young male schizophrenics seen at Shepard and Enoch Pratt Hospital near Baltimore. Of these he chose 100 of the first 150 serial admissions for more careful study relating onset to outcome. In these 100, the onset was insidious in 22, acute in 178. He reported that 48, or somewhat over 61 percent of those with acute onset, showed marked improvement. In a considerable number, the change amounted to a recovery from the mental disorder. "These figures would be remarkable even today." It should be remembered that the period covered in Sullivan's paper was 1924–31.

In his later years Sullivan became the spokesman for a new "inter-personal" approach, which was erroneously differentiated from psychoanalysis. Furthermore, after his death many of his followers almost deified him, while the more orthodox analytic community excoriated him unmercifully (Jacobson, 1954). Both of these extremes are erroneous and overlook Sullivan's close identification with psychoanalysis and his significant contributions to theory. These contributions are primarily two: that schizophrenia is treatable, and that the self system is an important and hitherto overlooked aspect of the personality.

In treatment terms, psychoanalysis before World War I had been largely a luxury of those who could afford to take off considerable time from their work and devote themselves almost entirely to the experience of psychoanalysis. In 1919 Freud had already predicted that sooner or later the state would have to pay attention to the mental health needs of the indigent, just as it was already paying more attention to their physical needs.

Spurred by this statement, a number of prominent analysts sponsored the formation of low-cost clinics. Again first and in a sense foremost was Eitingon, with the Berlin Clinic and Institute. One of the striking features of this clinic was the intensive analytic work and training that were conducted. Various attempts to shorten the analytic hours or to shorten the time required proved abortive and were discontinued. In 1928 Eitingon also reported that of the approximately 400 members then in the International Psychoanalytic Association, 66 had been trained at the Berlin Institute. Shortly thereafter Jones followed with a clinic in London, Alexander with one in Chicago. Once these pioneers had shown that low-cost therapy in a clinic was feasible, similar clinics appeared elsewhere.

Although psychoanalysts began with a considerable group of patients who produced somatic symptoms, namely, hysterics, it took some time before the full applicability of psychoanalysis to medicine was realized. Hysterics simulate somatic illness but do not alter their body structure. An entirely different problem is posed by patients whose tissues are actually affected by their emotional disturbances. For these the term "organic neurosis" was adopted, later to change to "psychosomatic disorders." More recently, now that so much evidence has accumulated on the effects of the mind on the body, usually called "stress disorders," the field has been dubbed "behavioral medicine." Both concepts and their applicability to behavioral medicine are far-reaching.

One of the recurrent criticisms of psychoanalysis in the early days was that its doctrines applied only to Viennese (or at best Western) neurotics. Nevertheless Freud's book *Totem and Taboo* (1913) made it obvious to far-sighted anthropologists that here was a psychology that could be useful to them. When the war ended, a number of field workers emerged who made free use of psychoanalytic concepts. Most prominent among them were Margaret Mead and Bronislaw Malinowski. In 1924 Ernest Jones gave a notable address (Jones, 1924; Fortes, 1977) on psychoanalysis and anthropology to the Royal Anthropological Institute in London, which helped to open new vistas on the applicability of psychoanalysis to anthropology. Since then, as in so many of the social sciences, psychoanalysis has entered into every form of anthropology and been embraced in many ways, although as usual the leaders remain staunchly conservative, preferring behavioral or commonsense psychology.

The 1920s and 1930s also saw further pioneering applications of psychoanalysis in many directions. August Aichhorn (1878–1949) undertook the treatment of delinquents and criminals in Vienna. Wulf Sachs in 1937 published the analysis of a South African medicine man, John Chavafambira (Loveland, 1947). Ernst Simmel pioneered in the treatment of drug addicts and in the development of the hospital case of patients using psychoanalytical principles. Heinrich Meng devoted himself to the application of psychoanalysis to mental hygiene. Hans Zulliger applied psychoanalysis to education.

All these efforts, now viewed as routine, met with considerable opposition when they started. Thus Hitschmann (1937) related that when the Vienna group petitioned for permission to open a low-cost clinic, the petition was referred to Von Wagner-Jauregg, who after a long delay recommended rejection. Finally the clinic was opened in 1922. Six months later the municipal authorities suddenly ordered it closed. Laypersons and medical students were not permitted to do treatment; furthermore, the clinic was forbidden to make any charges for its services. Despite all these obstacles it went on.

Similarly Oberndorf recounts that in 1927 when the New York Psychoanalytic Society, represented by himself, Brill, and Jelliffe, petitioned the State Board of Charities to start a treatment center, they were turned down because they were not attached to an established hospital or medical school.

The history of the attempts of psychoanalysis to make progress within the confines of the established professions could go on indefinitely, and still goes on. Resistance remains universal. Yet all in all psychoanalysis has made enormous strides and is now a worldwide movement with considerable influence in all democratic countries. Totalitarian systems, which live on violence, still have no use for it.

The entrance of psychoanalytic thought into the social sciences has proceeded along similar lines: first outright rejection, then admission of some advanced hardy souls, then extensive forays into the problems of that science, finally some compromise in which some theoreticians embrace analysis, while others do not. This process is still going on.

Perhaps most to be deplored is the adamant opposition of the leaders of the social sciences to any kind of psychodynamic thinking, which is only beginning to change now. But the going remains rough for all those who wish to promote the new science. In spite of all this, the social sciences and the entire culture have, as many have noted, wrought immense changes in the entire cultural picture.

11

Implications for Psychiatry

*T*HE IMPLICATIONS OF THE ANALYTIC IDEAL FOR PSYCHIATRY are enormous, but their proper evaluation leads to many controversies and has difficulty reaching objectivity. My comments in this chapter are in the analytic tradition, however, so let the chips fall where they may.

Through the years psychiatrists have contended that the brain is the seat of insanity and have tried innumerable physiological measures to influence the brain. Most of these have disappeared, some, such as the cruel lobotomies that cut the brain to pieces, after much protest.

Since the 1950s most previous physical methods have been discontinued in favor of drug therapies, which have been hailed as the "drug revolution." A careful appraisal of the effectiveness of the drug therapies has appeared (Fisher and Greenberg, 1977; Erlbaum, 1989). Their main conclusion is that "biological psychiatry is swimming in uncertainty" (p. 323). Not surprisingly, this book has simply been ignored by the psychiatric literature.

It has become clear, however, that there is no effective physiological treatment for the more severe mental disorders (nor for the less severe for that matter). So far as we can see today, the psychosocial treatments are most effective for all classes of psychological illness.

Since psychiatrists today do little other than give drugs, which are now claimed to be ineffective, the validity of conventional psychiatry as a discipline can be challenged with some justification.

In the first place the term "psychiatry" is misleading on the current scene. Properly speaking, psychiatry is an outgrowth of the medical assumption, going back to Griesinger in the nineteenth century that mind disease is brain disease. Further, the prestige of the medical profession in our society is so great that it often precludes all sense of impartiality; the doctor has become, like mother, the person who "knows best." Yet psychiatry has moved into many different quarters where it has neither the real authority nor the adequate background to speak properly.

Jonas Robitscher, a psychiatrist and psychoanalyst, in his book *The Powers of Psychiatry* (1980) makes a plea for a more rational approach to psychiatry. He shows: (a) how psychiatry has grown — even psychiatrists do not realize the extent of their influence; (b) how courts increasingly rely on psychiatric opinions that are of dubious validity; (c) how psychiatrists hold all the cards when they define "mental illness" and "normality"; (d) how psychiatrists determine our values; (e) what we need to know about invasive psychiatric treatment methods: lobotomy and psychosurgery, castration, electroshock, depot tranquilizers; (f) how psychiatry is used as an agent of social control and as a political tool by governments abroad and at home; (g) how some psychiatrists victimize their patients financially or sexually; (h) what psychiatry may be like in the future and what we must do to limit its power.

Psychiatry today is a mixture of medicine and psychoanalytic and clinical psychology. In none of these fields do psychiatrists have adequate knowledge or training, yet they continue, as Robitscher shows, to increase their power. Ellenberger (1974) divides the history of modern scientific psychiatry into three periods, which largely overlap each other:

(1) From 1800 to 1860 the center of psychiatric activity was the mental hospital. Its main concern was the description and classification of mental diseases and the devising of a "moral therapy" together with the study of brain anatomy.

(2) From 1860 to 1920 the center of psychiatric activity was the university psychiatric clinic. The trend was toward the elaboration of great psychiatric systems. A striking development occurred in the study of neuroses and culminated in the creation of schools of dynamic psychiatry. (Ellenberger fails to mention here that progress in the understanding of neuroses was almost exclusively the result of psychoanalysis, which was opposed at every step by organic psychiatry.)

(3) After 1920 came a psychiatric explosion, with an almost boundless widening of the field of psychiatry and its divisions into a multitude of subspecialties.

In the authoritative *American Handbook of Psychiatry* (1974) the editors included a chapter entitled "A General Assessment of Psychiatry" by Alfred H. Rifkin. He stated:

We do not ordinarily consider assessing fields like cardiology, ophthalmology, or pediatrics in the sense of determining their worth, although we may inquire into the efficiency of a particular procedure or a medication. Yet it seems appropriate to seek a general assessment of psychiatry. Why? The question reflects a certain uneasiness, a need to clarify the scope of psychiatry, to fix the proper limits of its concern, to determine the nature of the problems to which it should address itself, and to study the conceptual and technical tools fashioned for the solution of problems....

A proper assessment of psychiatry requires that the subject be viewed in historical perspective.... The physical sciences were the first to emerge from speculative philosophy. Psychiatry lagged behind as the understanding of human behavior long remained the province of metaphysics and theology....

Psychiatry is said by some to be in the throes of an identity crisis epitomized as a challenge to the "medical model." The challenge comes from many quarters and ranges from mild criticism to outright rejection....(p. 117)

He then goes on to say:

The major criticisms of the medical model are directed against special features attributed to that model and may be summarized as follows:

1. The medical model assumes the existence of a disorders of the body. Brain pathology produces specific neurological disorders, but psychiatry deals with functional disorders in which no structural or chemical alteration has been demonstrated. It is usually asserted that the mind is not an organ and in principle cannot be reduced to chemical, electrical, or other physiological processes.

2. The locus of the disorder is within the affected person and the disorder is to be corrected or removed by the physician as in the case with known diseases of the body. This is misleading because the real locus of the disorder may be, and usually is, outside of the individual, in the social system or his interaction with the social system.

3. The medical model fosters a superior, authoritarian attitude in the physician and a dependent, subservient attitude in the patient. Both are antithetical to successful treatment, which requires that the patient achieve a greater degree of independence or autonomy.

4. Not only are there no demonstrable structural or physiological changes but also there are no objective criteria for disturbed behavior. Mental illness can only be inferred from behavior that the illness is then supposed to explain, an obvious circularity in reasoning. Furthermore, judgment of behavior is subjective, tied to the value systems of the culture and open to various kinds of bias.

5. Because it depends on deviations from some norm, the medical model fosters conformity and stifles originality and creativity.

No better argument could be made for the usefulness of the analytic ideal than this critique of the medical model. Most therapists today are nonmedical, not medical, a fact that the public neither knows nor appreciates. We are moving away from the medical model, which dominated thinking about the "insane" for centuries, to the biopsychosocial model, which is the rule today (Engel, 1977).

The situation today seems to be getting worse all the time. Right now in New York City we are faced with armies of the homeless using public places like Grand Central Station to sleep, eat, go to the toilet, and even fornicate in full view of outsiders. An impartial observer would readily note that our social controls seem to be breaking down. In this sense the psychiatric revolution, which allegedly started with the discovery of the new miracle drugs in the 1950s, has failed. That is not to say that the drugs do not have any effect; certainly they have a powerful effect on the individual, but that they will revolutionize the tragic social situation in which we find ourselves is a myth.

Wherever we turn in psychiatry we find endless controversy and little certainty. Psychiatry has always placed its greatest reliance on physical methods of treatment; only the method has changed, not the rationale. In the 1930s it was electric shock, then came insulin coma, then lobotomies, then in the 1950s the neuroleptic and other drugs. On the basis of these drugs, and their alleged effectiveness, innumerable patients were discharged from mental hospitals before they were ready, turning our major cities into swamps infested by homeless schizophrenics. Lack of treatment and of a rational approach to the mentally ill has only led to increasing numbers of homeless, a phenomenon never seen before in American life.

Psychiatry has sold itself to the authorities and the general public by virtue of a deliberate ambiguity. On the one hand psychiatrists offer medication that allegedly cures or at least helps everything from anxiety to outright psychosis. On the other hand psychiatrists are also analysts (and up to now the official propaganda line has been that only psychiatrists can become analysts), and so they can also offer help by talk therapy. Marmor (1975) in his study of psychiatrists found that some 15 percent claimed to be psychoanalysts but had no psychoanalytic training; he said that this posed no problem, since the number of psychiatrists who were misrepresenting themselves was so small.

The United States is the only country in the world where psychoanalysis became linked to psychiatry, rather than pursuing an independent course. Apart from the loss of the analytic ideal in psychiatry, the results have been disastrous in many ways. Psychiatrists played a double game until recently: to begin with, they say, I have a drug that will cure you, and then they say: If that doesn't work I also have a talking therapy that will cure you. At the same time the official psychiatric association has always fought the psychoanalytic approach. Then again it is argued that standard psychiatric treatment is not much different from psychoanalysis, and may even be better. In all this double talk the vision is lost and the patient remains bewildered.

Politically the battle has centered around "lay analysis" (in quotation marks because there is no such thing), which the medical profession has fought and still fights with fanatical vigor. The fanaticism reminds one of Santayana's definition of fanatics: persons who redouble their efforts after they have lost sight of their goal.

In this quest to save everything for medicine, even the analysts have compromised their fundamental principles. In 1972 in the preliminary discussions about coverage for national health insurance, the American Psychiatric Association issued a position paper in which it essentially recommended exclusion of psychoanalysis and long-term psychotherapy from national health insurance coverage. After some hesitation the American Psychoanalytic Association proposed the following compromise:

> As a result of that meeting (with the psychiatrists) the Committee on Health Insurance concluded that a position statement of the American Psychoanalytic Association should not emphasize the special and unique features of psychoanalytic treatment,

but rather the similarities and commonalties of psychoanalytic treatment with the mainstream of psychiatric and medical care. It was felt that such an approach would be much more effective in offering a strong case for its coverage under national health insurance.

Psychoanalysts have long felt that they are suffering from the diminishing number of psychoanalytic patients. In order to get patients they were willing here to sacrifice the basic principles of psychoanalysis. No wonder that they reject the analytic ideal, with its vision of a happier future for humankind.

The battle, of course, was against lay analysis. Now that the American nonmedical analysts have officially been admitted to the International Psychoanalytical Association, hypocritical "compromises" of the kind described above, will, we hope, no longer be possible.

To evaluate psychiatry today it is necessary to consider both sides of what it offers: the medical and the psychological. The social should also be considered, but that is a broader question that applies to all the fields dealing with humans.

The drug revolution that began in the middle of the 1950s with the introduction of thorazine (chlorpromazine) seems less impressive today, thus repeating the experience of psychiatry from the nineteenth century on with all the seemingly miraculous treatments of the past. Critical observers have noted the following:

(1) While the drugs provide relief to some patients, the kinds of patients who benefit are the same as those who benefit by other forms of treatment, namely, those with the best premorbid history.

(2) Long-term studies (e.g., by Manfred Bleuler and Achte and Niskanen) show a high relapse rate and no significant change in the percentage of patients who are permanently helped. In other words, the drugs, when they do work, are merely a temporary palliative.

(3) The use of the drugs has coincided with a change in hospital policy leading to the discharge of large numbers of mental patients into the community. While they are able to maintain themselves in the community, although frequently rehospitalized for brief periods, they are unable to function as full-fledged members of society. Tissot (1977) puts it in what is probably the most objective review of the situation: "their future as human beings still remains very gloomy."

(4) The percentage of admissions and readmissions to hospitals depends primarily on the attitude of the community toward hospitalization, not on how "disturbed" or "socially adapted" the patients are. For example, Zwerling points out that in 1979 California and

New York had approximately the same population. Yet California, which had developed an extensive network of outpatient facilities, had only 11,000 patients in hospitals while New York had 47,000. Nevertheless, the majority view is that the accelerated discharge of mental patients from hospitals "is perhaps the most convincing proof of the efficiency of these agents (drugs)."

(5) The side effects of the drugs are by no means as minor as many psychiatrists have claimed. Tissot states that two patients out of three develop extrapyramidal syndrome, or difficulties with the brain structures that control bodily movements. In his small-scale series he observed two cases of malignancy, of which one was fatal. A large percentage of patients who take the neuroleptics over a long period of time develop tardive dyskinesia, or loss of control of various muscle groups. No treatment is known for this effect. Further, a recent paper (Mehta et al., 1978) reported that there is a higher mortality rate for patients with tardive dyskinesia. "Our results, if confirmed by prospective studies, indicate that tardive dyskinesia is a more serious problem than has generally been acknowledged."

(6) Family care of the mentally ill has been practiced since the twelfth century. The Belgian city of Gheel became famous for its capacity to handle the mentally incompetent, at first ascribing its powers to divine Providence, later simply accepting the fact that it could care for these unfortunates in the homes of the inhabitants. In other countries family care has been tried with varying degrees of success; even Kraepelin spoke of it favorably.

(7) Thus the introduction of the mental hospital in the eighteenth century and its current dismantling represent the beginning and the end of a long experiment, in which the pessimistic theories of Kraepelin and organic psychiatry have actually been proved wrong. Nevertheless, the belief in biochemical causation is so powerful that it tends to overshadow all the objective evidence.

(8) At present it is widely recognized that in the long run the rehabilitation of the schizophrenic must be carried on in the community (Chiland, 1977), although the drugs offer more relief in some cases. Nevertheless, in practice the situation remains deplorable. Ahmed and Plog, summing up the dissolution of state mental hospitals in 1976, wrote that:

> ...the question that we have answered till now is not where to care for chronic patients, but where not to care for them. In order to take care of the chronically disabled, we need a total care system which would see to their housing, use of drugs, train-

ing for a job, opportunity to work, and ways to ease the burdens of the community. We are now nowhere close to achieving such a total service system.

(9) Finally, it should be stated that the alleged untreatability of schizophrenics is to a considerable extent a myth. A good deal depends on when patients enter treatment, but if they do so early enough the percentage of improvement is fully as satisfactory as with drugs (Sullivan, 1931). This fact has been known for forty years but its proper application would require a thoroughgoing reformation that the psychiatric profession is not prepared to undertake. In practice, however, it is being carried out by the introduction of other mental health professionals into the field, first psychologists and social workers, more recently counselors of all kinds.

Once more a curious historical paradox appears. In the eighteenth century the care of the mentally ill was entrusted to the medical profession because the clergy was so cruel. By the twentieth century the medical profession had become so cruel that the care of the mentally ill was increasingly being turned back to nonmedical practitioners. Freud's wish to turn his teachings over to a new profession of lay curers of souls seems to be coming closer to realization than many realize (Hughes and Brewin, 1979).

Insofar as the second leg of psychiatry is concerned, the problem of therapy, the situation is also complex. For the most part psychiatric residency programs do not offer much in the way of training for psychotherapy; the psychiatrist has to pick it up haphazardly because of the opposition to psychoanalysis. Some learn, many do not. In the meantime the other professions have grown rapidly and are also offering their services. As a result psychiatrists tend to offer less and less psychological treatment, relying more and more exclusively on drugs.

After World War I when psychoanalysis began to study schizophrenia dynamically, a new, entirely different formulation came to the fore. First, schizophrenia was seen as a psychological disorder, though physiological factors could enter in, as in any psychological disorder. Second, it was seen as a state of despair, a feeling that no meaningful human relationship could ever be established. Clearly this state of despair must be related to the early mothering process, since its roots extend far back into the infantile period. Third, once the despair was recognized, more effective new methods of psychotherapy could be devised.

Sullivan's innovations have already been mentioned. In his condemnation of the Kraepelinian approach, he was very caustic. In 1930 he wrote:

> As I am but one of many who no longer entertain (Kraepelin's) views, I shall be content with stating that his formulation — the dementia praecox concept — has been a great handicap to psychiatric progress, a death sentence to many schizophrenic individuals, and an important factor in justification of the continued anachrony of the Institutional Care.

Today the situation is very mixed. There is no good summary that presents what is happening in a straightforward manner, and each of us must make our own observations.

The evidence that has accumulated in favor of the analytic position that schizophrenia is a state of despair brought about by grossly inadequate mothering in the early part of life is now considerable. The theory that there is a continuum from normality to psychosis appears much more plausible than the disease theory, which holds that psychosis is an inherited biochemical disorder. Historically, the analytic image of the human being as irrational, unconscious, and subject to the control of powerful internal forces has received ample substantiation. The evidence for the analytic position derives from at least five sources: (1) the family background; (2) the cultural factor (including the historical); (3) the effects of psychotherapy; (4) more careful long-term studies; and (5) the diagnostic confusion.

Analysts from Sullivan on have repeatedly shown that schizophrenia arises from a malevolent family structure, particularly from bad mothering. Frieda Fromm-Reichmann coined the term "schizophrenogenic mother." By a gradual process of successive degrees of frustration, the schizophrenic symptomatology eventually evolves out of this deprived childhood environment. In 1948 Fromm-Reichmann put it as follows:

> The schizophrenic is painfully distrustful and resentful of other people, because of the severe early warp and rejection that he has encountered in important people of his infancy and childhood, as a rule mainly in a schizophrenogenic mother. During his early fight for emotional survival he begins to develop the great interpersonal sensitivity which remains for the rest of his life. His initial pathogenic experiences are actually, or by virtue of his interpretation, the pattern for a never-ending succession of subsequent similar ones. Finally he transgresses the threshold

of endurance. Because of his sensitivity and his never satisfied lonely need for benevolent contacts, this threshold is all
too easily reached. The schizophrenic's partial emotional regression and his withdrawal from the outside world into an autistic
private world, with its specific thought processes and modes of
feeling and expression, are motivated by his fear of repetitional
rejection, his distrust of others and equally so by his own re-
taliative hostility, which he abhors, as well as the deep anxiety
promoted by this hatred.

   The bad experience with the mother is repeated with the father
and later with other figures. In a very real sense this discovery of the
long prehistory of schizophrenia is similar to another great discovery
of psychoanalysis, the long prehistory of sexuality.
   Why does the mother engender such serious hostility and distrust
in her child? Because she herself is seriously disturbed. Indeed, as Arieti (1974) points out, although he does not fully agree with the theory
of the schizophrenogenic mother, there is one unanimous finding in
all careful studies of the families of schizophrenics. In every case serious family disturbance was found. M. Bleuler (1978) has stressed
that every schizophrenic patient has a horrible childhood, although
the horror of each person is different from that of the others.
   Again this observation of family disturbance is not new. More than
a hundred years ago Griesinger, in spite of his organic predilections,
noted the frequency of eccentric parental behavior and commented
that, aside from genetic influence, the influences of such parents upon
their children must be taken into account. But the preoccupation with
biochemistry swamped any concern with familial and social features.
Once more it has become clear that organic psychiatry has followed
a pure theory, regardless of much available evidence contradictory
to this theory. The situation is in some ways comparable to the al-
chemists of the Middle Ages, who also wrote tomes on the strange
background of individuals.
   I am well aware that psychiatrists today are talking of the "explosion" in neuroscience, which they try to apply to every diagnostic
entity. But this is not new. There was an explosion in neuroscience
in Freud's day. He was a professor of neurology at the University of
Vienna, then the most prestigious university in the world. It is of considerable interest that after his early work Freud never again wrote
a paper on neurology, convinced that it was of no relevance. The
neuroscience explosion is no more real today than it was in Freud's
time; what has to be done is to connect the newer findings in neuro-

science with the clinical picture of neurosis and psychosis, and that is not done (Robitscher, 1980). On the other hand, the psychological argument goes back a long way, is supported by evidence from many different sources, has led to much therapeutic advance makes sense all around. It should not be dismissed as easily as many wish to do.

There is also a strong body of evidence in favor of the role of cultural factors in schizophrenia. Ireland and Croatia have the highest rates of schizophrenia in the world. Ireland also has the most sexually repressed society in the world, where the taboos are so strong that men and women will not even share the same beach.

In 1939 Faris and Dunham published their study on the relationship between mental disorders and urban areas. They were able to show that the incidence of mental disorder is by far highest in the center of the city and decreases progressively as one moves toward the suburbs.

Stimulated by this and other work, Hollingshead and Redlich (1958) then undertook a more thorough examination of social cases and mental disorder in the New Haven area. They found among other things that age- and sex-adjusted rates for schizophrenia patients in psychiatric treatment were more than nine times greater in the lowest social class than in the highest.

The Hollingshead-Redlich study was the first of many that demonstrated the inverse ratio between poverty and mental disorder. Almost invariably, even in a country as different from ours as Japan, the inverse ratio has been shown to hold.

Looked at from the opposite point of view, that of cultures where schizophrenia is rare, it has been found that in integrated communities where alienation is uncommon, schizophrenia is likewise uncommon. Eaton and Weil (1955), in their examination of the Hutterite communities in North America, found schizophrenia to be almost nonexistent.

Thus a consistent picture emerges. An alienated culture produces individuals who are severely frustrated in their childhood, which in turn predisposes them to mental breakdown. If later events worsen the earlier instability, there will be a high incidence of schizophrenia. If the culture is integrated and subjects the individual to relatively few traumatic breaks, the incidence of schizophrenia will be comparatively low. All this fits in very well with the conceptualization that schizophrenia is essentially a state of despair about ever having meaningful relationships with other people.

Anthropologist Oscar Lewis coined the term "culture of poverty" for children brought up in severely deprived environments. In such a culture children are brought up with hatred rather than love, are beaten unmercifully (at times to death), are deprived of real affection, are denied much schooling, and are disadvantaged in many other ways. Small wonder, then, that the children soon reach a state of despair that is virtually irreversible by our present techniques. And small wonder that both as children and as adults they become filled with hatred and violence that easily spill over. And psychiatry is always dependent on the culture's value system. Where the culture of poverty prevails, individuals cannot recognize how sick they are

The most careful long-term study in the literature is that by Bleuler, based on a follow-up of 208 patients admitted to the Burgholzli Hospital after he become its head in 1942. He had personally treated all of them and followed each until death, or for at least twenty-two years, together with the destinies of their parents, siblings, marital partners, and children. He was also in touch with other investigators who had carefully studied the course of 965 more schizophrenics. Many of his conclusions were in marked contrast to those of Kraepelin and the drug therapists.

(1) On an average, after five years duration, the psychosis does not go any further but tends rather to improve. This tendency to improve becomes evident only if the conditions of these patients are considered in detail.

(2) At least 25 percent of all schizophrenics recover entirely and remain recovered permanently.

(3) On the other hand, about 10 percent of schizophrenics remain permanently hospitalized as severe psychotics.

(4) Of the twenty-five who had reached a long-term favorable condition, not one was under long-term neuroleptic or other pharmacologic treatment, nor were most of the recovered patients cared for by the welfare agencies.

(5) So-called catastrophic schizophrenia, which is characterized by an early acute onset with no improvement, resulting in lifelong deterioration (the typical patient as described by Kraepelin), has virtually disappeared.

(6) The most common type of patient is the phasic-benign.

(7) A careful analysis shows that the factor that contributes most to patient improvement is the advances made in social and environmental therapy. Bleuler emphasized what his father had always stressed, that no patient should ever be given up.

The confusion of organic psychiatry is nowhere more clearly demonstrated than in the area of diagnosis. Diagnosis is a concept taken over from organic medicine; its application to "mental" illness is of relatively recent origin. Patchwork and arbitrary groupings characterize the system. In 1952 schizophrenia was changed to schizophrenic reaction. In 1968 it was changed back to schizophrenia. In 1979 it became schizophrenia disorders. The dishonest reclassification of homosexuality is well known (Socarides, 1974).

In sum, reviewing the family studies, cultural background, therapeutic results, long-term studies, and the diagnostic confusion, the following conclusions seem justified:

(1) Schizophrenia is primarily a psychogenic disorder deriving from long-standing inner conflicts going back to earliest childhood.

(2) It is not a medical illness in any significant sense but a state of despair about ever having meaningful loving relationships with other human beings.

(3) It is much more apt to surface in alienated or poverty-stricken societies because these factors make for a state of despair in their own right.

(4) The diagnostic category of "schizophrenia" as such tells us little; it should be replaced by a full-scale description of the personality.

(5) Many patients diagnosed as schizophrenic do respond to analytically oriented psychotherapy. Some achieve a full recovery.

(6) The tranquilizing drugs in some cases do provide temporary relief from the symptoms, but in the long run they do little. They may do harm: the side effects are often serious and lasting, sometimes permanent and on rare occasions fatal.

(7) The average hospital-trained psychiatrist with little more than the three year residency does not have the competence to do psychotherapy with schizophrenics.

(8) Therapists with the capacity for warmth, empathy and understanding have a much better chance to help the schizophrenic than those without. The professional degree is of secondary importance.

(9) On the current scene, and for the past two thousand years, the care and treatment of the psychotic have been a disgrace.

In broad outline, these arguments indicate that while psychiatry has been entrusted with the care of the mentally ill for some two hundred years, it has generally been wrong in its theoretical position, in its diagnostic systems, and in its treatment approaches. Rosen comments that throughout the nineteenth century psychiatric theory was a "tangle of confusion," and the twentieth century has not really been much better. Officially and unofficially, psychiatry has turned to mental hygiene and relies principally on adequate humane care for all patients. But new drugs are reported in almost endless profusion, only to be followed by a period of disillusion and discouragement. For their role as experts in mental hygiene, which involves a profound knowledge of many social sciences, psychiatrists are as a rule very poorly prepared. The alternative nonmedical professions, clinical psychology and social work, have in fact grown more rapidly than psychiatry and have taken over much of the domain previously reserved to the medical profession, often against fierce opposition by organized medicine.

The term "sick," so widely used by psychiatry, and its ally "mental illness" are both misleading. The shift in the patient population since World War II has been to the "normal" person, the average citizen who is trying to find happiness. Farseeing observers were aware of the potentialities for the future at an early date. In 1929, Ernest Jones made the following statement:

> The most outstanding [change in American psychiatry] and one on which the U.S. [has every right to congratulate itself] is what might be called the social consolidation of psychiatry; so impressed is the outside observer by this that it does not seem unmerited to say that America has actually created a new profession. In a very real respect one can almost say that the profession of psychiatry does not exist in any other country in the world.

Jones attributed the growth of the new profession to America's social conscience, which he valued highly. In the ensuing sixty years many of his prophecies have been fulfilled, though much remains to be done.

In terms of our main topic, the analytic ideal, psychoanalysis remains primary, while psychiatry is secondary, representing an application of this new science to certain types of patients. The current situation remains thoroughly confused.

Jason Robitscher

There are many critics of psychiatry. I don't wish to add to the list, but rather to ferret out the social theory of psychiatry and to see how it interacts with the analytic ideal. That there are many psychiatrists who are well-meaning doctors and who help their patients with their problems is taken for granted. But there are many abuses that we hear of all the time. Jason Robitscher (1980), himself a psychiatrist and also a lawyer, has written a significant book listing the abuses of power by psychiatrists; his book, *The Powers of Psychiatry*, is well worth a summary.

Robitscher's main thesis is that "psychiatric authority is a recent addition to the scene, that it comes to us with the imprimatur of science, although it is not always scientific, that it carries the weight of medical authority although it is only occasionally truly medical and that its power and influence are constantly growing."

Under psychiatry Robitscher includes psychoanalysis, psychology, and many other related disciplines. His book therefore gives a valid critique of all the psychological approaches to human conflicts, but he focuses particularly on the psychiatrist's abuse of power, as he sees it. Since he was a lawyer before he became a psychiatrist, and lawyers are trained to fight abuses of power, his point of view becomes especially pertinent.

He begins with a chapter on the scope of psychiatric power. On p. 3 he writes:

Psychiatry is different things to different people. It is hard to define and it is controversial. Many of its claims that it is a cure for emotional illness are unproven. Yet in spite of the weakness of the arguments for the efficacy of psychiatry, psychiatry continues to prosper and it increasingly extends its authority to cover every aspect of life. Individuals rely on it to work out complicated intrapsychic and interpersonal problems. Society relies on psychiatry to handle people who are disturbing.

In chapter 3 he discusses how the psychiatrist has acquired many legal functions, affecting civil as well as criminal matters. English courts recognized the effect of mental disorder, but they were not kind to most of the insane. A very severe degree of derangement had to be evident before mental state became the reason for deferring a trial or for escaping punishment. In the eighteenth century insanity as a criminal defense was increasingly common (although still infrequent according to modern standards) and for the first time psychiatrists were called in to help the court as expert witnesses. But what has become obvious today, almost a mockery, is that because one psychiatric expert might have a very different attitude from another on the all-important questions of free will and the ability to control actions, psychiatrists could be found to testify persuasively for either the prosecution or the defense.

The situation creates many paradoxes. After a condemned man has been saved from death because of his insanity, he will be examined periodically to see if he is sufficiently recovered to be put to death.

The reliance of the law on psychiatry gave psychiatrists power and influence far greater than that of other doctors. Psychiatrists were accepted as experts on all disordered behavior. They not only filled medical functions such as running mental hospitals and prescribing for and treating patients, but their advice was sought in legal, and later in social, decision making. By the late nineteenth century the psychiatrists took responsibility for maintaining a well-ordered society as well as for care of patients. They possessed medical authority, including the extraordinary power to commit, and legal and social authority.

In the twentieth century the advent of Freudian thought and new and more effective methods of treatment would make psychiatry even more useful to the legal system. Freud's theory of unconscious determination would make the psychiatrist the expert who alone could explain inexplicable actions. The talking therapies and new somatic methods of treatment were also useful.

In the next chapter he deals with the effect of psychoanalysis. He says that psychoanalysis and psychoanalytically oriented psychiatry originated with Freud. "The contributions of Freud have been incorporated into modern thought and life, and they have served to give psychiatrists and psychologists and other behavioral scientists, even those who profess themselves anti-analytic, greatly enhanced authority" (p. 29).

On the incorporation of psychosomatic ideas into psychiatry he says:

Many of the complaints that patients brought to the early analysts had traditionally been treated medically — loss of appetite or libido, gastrointestinal symptoms, insomnia. The doctors had always had purgatives or tonics or sedatives to deal with such conditions. Other conditions treated by analysts had also been treated by doctors, not because they felt they had any competency to deal with them, but only because no one else had any therapy to offer for obsessions, compulsions, phobias, uncontrollable anxiety, and hysteria. Before analysis, doctors often dealt with such conditions, recommending an effort of will or prescribing a sea voyage or a stay at a spa.... Depression has always been considered a psychiatric disease, but now unhappiness, loneliness and alienation have become "diseases," and from now on a suicide attempt would be seen not as morally wrong but as a product of sickness. (p. 31)

Defining the scientific validity of psychoanalysis, Robert Waelder has said that "psychoanalytic interpretation of single events, or a

psychoanalytic chart of an individual person, or general psychoanalytic propositions can hardly be proved on the basis of external,
physical, measurable data alone." But he asserted that the combi-
nations of such data with the data of a patient's self-observations
(including the self-observations pursuant to the tentatively proposed
interpretation) and with the data of our observations of the patient's
behavior, including verbal behavior, form a kind of evidence that is
just as convincing as the evidence found in the study of a single vari-
able in such fields where single variables can be meaningfully studied
in isolation.

Robitscher goes on to argue that the incorporation of Freudian
thought into medical practice increased the scope of psychiatry in
a number of ways. It enlarged the definition of mental illness to
the point where almost every personality could be seen as having
at least some neurotic aspects. It had given status to all these conditions — they could henceforth be seen as worthy of treatment and
treatable.... Psychiatrists had received from Freud a new kind of
power, different from and greater than any they had wielded before.
Psychiatrists and psychologists could now claim to understand what
was going on in the unconscious.

The post-Freudian emphases on social factors in mental and
emotional malfunctioning gave psychiatry other kinds of influence.
Freudian thought also infiltrated the popular mind.

Next he considers the psychiatrist and the prisoner. As psychiatry developed in the twentieth century it extended control over new
groups of people for whom it functioned more to control behavior
than to provide therapy. The first application of this widened scope
was helping the military function in wartime. After that it turned to
prisoners. The number of civilly committed patients grew rapidly and
by 1955 had reached a total of 550,000. Without real justification psychiatrists outdid each other in making extravagant claims for the use
of psychiatric authority over criminals, relying on the medical model
to justify their interventions.

Next he turns to extreme psychiatric authority. When patients are
diverted from the criminal justice system to the mental health system,
they frequently do not see themselves as ill and often do not have the
symptoms that usually indicate mental illness. Critics of psychiatry
describe flagrant cases of patients who have suffered under the massive force of public psychiatric authority, but the public psychiatrists
who are in charge of these patients are satisfied that they are fulfilling
a useful social function, and private psychiatrists do not meddle.

Then he considers the somatic therapies. Whether these did any good or not no one knows, but they were popular for quite awhile. He quotes one British historian:

> Came the era of Metrazol, modified insulin therapy, deep insulin therapy, psychosurgery and electroconvulsive therapy. Each form of treatment was adopted with the same lack of discrimination with which it was abandoned. But while discrimination was lacking, enthusiasm was not. Thus the very impetus of the therapeutic movement opened doors, threw down railings, and gave enormous help and encouragement to both staff and patients — but particularly to staff. The most therapeutic element in this therapeutic program was enthusiasm harnessed to the possibility of change. (p. 89)

On drugs he makes the following comments. Thorazine turned out to be a tremendous financial bonanza for the drug company that introduced it to the United States.

> The modern drug era in psychiatry has produced a revolution. Hospital wards that were once noisy and disorganized are now quiet and orderly. The average length of hospital stay has decreased, and the censuses of mental hospitals have been cut enormously. Many of the effects of the drug revolution are positive.... But a large price has been paid. The model of drug intervention for emotional symptomatology has led to a widespread use of drugs and other chemical substances throughout the population to maintain optimistic and stable moods. The use of marijuana and of other drugs on a wholesale basis was facilitated by the reliance many Americans had developed on chemical sources of well-being. The concept of chemical maintenance of mood supplanted the psychoanalytic ideal of "working through" conflicts. Valium, a minor tranquilizer, was prescribed in particular for almost any complaint or symptom and become the most widely prescribed drug in the US. It too turned out to be habit-forming. (p. 90):

The injectable tranquilizer is one of the most powerful methods of control that psychiatrists employ, but the ethics and the legal safeguards surrounding its use have received almost no attention.

Psychiatrists have also invented new methods of verbal therapy; one even uses astrology. No matter how ridiculous the therapeutic method is, if it is performed by a doctor or under a doctor's direction, it is eligible for medical reimbursement under insurance policies. Those who enjoyed the authority of the medical model had almost no limit to what they could do.

Criticism of the new approaches soon arose, however. Since the early days of psychiatry, psychiatrists had been seen as authoritative figures who had acquired unprecedented control over people and could use this power unwisely and dishonestly.

Robitscher feels that two books on legal psychiatry appeared in 1961 were especially important. Thomas Szasz published *The Myth of Mental Illness*, which for the first time brought the question of the imprecision of diagnosis and the treatment of the mental illness into the national consciousness. "Psychiatry would never again be the same" (p. 109). And Erving Goffman published *Asylums*, in which for the first time the interaction between hospitalized patients and staff was described to reveal the ritualization, the stigmatization, the old definitions and the other dehumanizing aspects of inpatient treatment. In chapter 9 Goffman takes up the issue of the politicization of psychiatry. In the 1950s and 1960s there began to be a greater demand for more psychiatric services. Criticism of the mental hospital was widespread. Harry Solomon, president of the American Psychiatric Association in 1958, called attention to the terrible condition of the state hospital system. He said:

> I do not see how any reasonably objective view of our mental hospitals today can fail to conclude that they are bankrupt beyond remedy.... In many of our hospitals about the best that can be done is to give a physical examination and make a mental note once a year, and often there is not enough staff to do this much. (p. 119)

The first thoroughgoing attack on psychiatric authority came in 1958 when Michael Hakeem, a sociologist at the University of Wisconsin, published a law review article titled "A Critique of the Psychiatric Approach to Crime and Correction." He described psychiatry as a "propagandistic discipline clamoring for power."

The community mental health movement started in the 1960s as a result of criticism of the state hospitals, which were acknowledged to be notoriously bad. Without meaning to do so, this movement has led to increased ability of the state to control behavior.

In part 2 Robitscher considers the dilemmas of psychiatric power. The first dilemma he takes up is the problem of defining mental illness. The most devastating attack on psychiatry is the claim that there is no such thing as mental illness, that we label as mentally ill those in our society who make us feel anxious or uncomfortable, social deviants, those who are out of step. Diagnosis is a stumbling block; psychoanalytic psychiatrists are willing to refrain from diagnosing. Even the term "psychiatrist" has remained undefined, although the APA in 1973 appointed a task force to define officially the terms "mental illness" and "psychiatrist." There is no agreement on how much medical psychiatry there should be. The medical identification is disputed by anthropologists who assert that much of mental illness is defined culturally. He finally concludes:

> Psychiatrists are forced to exert authority because some people in society run out of control and demand that authority be imposed upon them, that psychiatrists should keep in mind that they are not truly medical, at most they are medico-social. Since psychiatry has never been able to define mental disease, the medical basis for psychiatric authority must always be scrutinized.

It has been argued, with some justification, that psychiatric classification corresponds not to real disease but only to psychiatrists' subjective perceptions, largely culturally determined. Of the APA's new DSM he says:

> Like a number of other observers, I feel that the APA's new diagnostic system does not represent an improvement and that it does demonstrate publicly the inconsistencies of psychiatric thought and the increasingly unscientific and pragmatic nature of diagnostic classification. (p. 182)

The next topic considered is problems of prediction. He points out that when psychiatrists label someone as mentally ill, they gain power over that person, but when they are able to label that person not only mentally ill but dangerous and in particular likely to continue to be dangerous, they gain the ultimate in power: the power to take away liberty, the power to keep confined, possibly for a lifetime, and, under new laws that have not received enough attention, even the power to determine that a person convicted of a capital crime can never cease to be dangerous and must be executed as a protection for society. No one except psychiatrists and juvenile court judges has the right to lock up people who have not been charged with any crime.

In the next chapter he discusses stigmatization and discrimination. He speaks of the power of psychiatrists to make diagnoses, to predict future behavior, and to put people into difficult situations where they are forced to cope with stigma and discrimination in addition to battling with mental symptoms; his main thesis is that these powers are too great.

The third section takes up how psychiatrists exercise their power. He begins by saying that "psychiatry differs from all other fields of medicine in a deplorable lack of facts on which all psychiatrists can agree." Much of the power of psychiatry relates not to prescriptions and pills and treatment of patients, but to evaluation and determination. Psychiatrists are entrusted to make evaluations that determine committability, employability, responsibility, the capability to raise children, the ability to drive a car, and many others. Commitment, employment decisions, control of military personnel and prisoners, adoption decisions — these are ordinary powers commonly exercised by psychiatrists. There are also extraordinary exercises of psychiatric power that literally cut deeper and receive even less attention. Many psychiatrists use intrusive methods without the consent of the patient, arousing considerable debate and questioning.

Psychiatrists tend to usurp authority. Many believe that the widening definition of psychiatric illness will lead inexorably to "psychiatric fascism" where psychiatrists, justified by the reliance on the medical model, would be given control over almost every phase of human life.

Psychiatry has its ideological uses. Nazi Germany and contemporary Russia show two different ways it can serve the state. By 1941 a Czech war crime commission estimated the number of persons killed in the "euthanasia" program of the Nazis at 270,000. There has been more awareness of the Russian use of psychiatry to enforce ideological conformity. Psychiatry has been used not to exterminate people but to exterminate their ideas. The ultimate political power a psychiatrist can possess is to determine who is qualified to rule and to lead. Psychiatrists possibly came close to exercising this ultimate power during the last days of the Nixon administration. Gradually psychiatry has also developed the ambition of dealing with people in the aggregate — social engineering. Psychiatrists may disagree on which of their colleagues are qualified to screen candidates for public office but few doubt that they themselves are.

Psychiatrists have also had a tremendous effect on our values (for example, the analytic ideal). Changes resulting from psychiatric teaching and practice have occurred gradually over a period of two hundred years. Often they have met with great opposition and reaction.

Part 4 is on the limits of psychiatric authority, and is by far the most critical section of the book. It is no doubt because of the damning indictment in this section that the book has been largely disregarded by the psychiatric profession; as has always been true of psychiatry, and of others as well, the best way to avoid valid and realistic criticism is to ignore it.

Chapter 22 is entitled "The Psychiatrist Oversteps His Bounds." He says that even when psychiatric practice is grossly improper patients who are victims of bad treatment do not recognize it as such. Malpractice, he claims, is common but is hard to prove. In fact, he maintains, the ordinary practice of nonsomatic, nonorganic therapy involves a good deal of malpractice. He fails to state that one reason for this is that the average psychiatrist, who has not been through an analytic institute, is actually largely untrained in the nuances and difficulties of verbal psychotherapy.

Many psychiatrists and therapists are scrupulous in not revealing confidential information, but others are notoriously indiscreet. Robitscher does not consider sufficiently here how the pathology of patients may enter into their feeling about the revelation of some inconsequential aspect of their treatment. In one case in which the childhood therapy of an adult was presented some thirty years later, the patient was shown the case history. He approved of everything, except for one item. Before he was born, the family had moved from New York to Philadelphia; he insisted that this should be changed to a move from New York to Boston.

Robitscher claims that the exploitation of patients occurs most easily in private practice when the patient has developed an erotic or positive transference. Here a technical problem arises: whether to gratify the patient or not. When therapists talk of gratification it is often hard to know what level they mean. Also he discounts the fact that many patients will sometimes fabricate accounts of gratification because it makes them superior to others who did not get such gratification. One patient, for example, went around saying that his analyst found him so interesting that he habitually extended his hour, when that was simply not the case.

The most sensational and most common accusations of malpractice involve sexual activities with the patient. In 1978 the *Miami Herald* published a story by Gene Miller, "Sex and the Psychiatrists" (June 4–7, 1978). The series documented the ineffectiveness of the state licensing board in enforcing professional standards. Here the prudery of the community must be taken into consideration. In one case a woman accused her psychiatrist of making sexual advances to her because during their session (a consultation) he had crossed and uncrossed his legs several times. Most damaging, however, is not

the occasional psychiatrist who oversteps the bounds, but that today
there is little indication that psychiatry is concerned enough with psychiatric practice to devote time and energy to such a housecleaning
effort.

In chapter 23 Robitscher turns to the commercialization of psychiatry. In part this derives from believing that the psychiatrist is
performing a medical service rather than a humanistic one. The early
analysts were highly idealistic; this did not carry over to the next
generation. In his presidential address in 1952 Robert Knight said:

> They [the candidates] are not so introspective, are inclined to
> read only the literature that is assigned in institute courses, and
> wish to get through with the training requirements as rapidly
> as possible. Their interests are primarily clinical rather than
> research and theoretical. Their motivation for being analyzed
> is more to get through this requirement of training rather to
> overcome neurotic suffering in themselves or to explore intro-
> spectively and with curiosity their own inner selves. (p. 122)

In other words, Knight was saying that many candidates for analytic training tend to lose sight of the analytic ideal and so turn
therapy into a business, like any other, the prime goal of which is to
make money. Unfortunately there is much truth to this accusation.
In the lawsuit against the American and International Psychoanalytic
Associations it was brought out that a major reason for banning nonmedical analysts from training was economic: to have lay analysts
practicing would lower the income of the medical analysts. The most
evil financial practice of psychiatry results from insurance coverage
that pays for inpatient, but not outpatient therapy. In such cases the
psychiatrist may prefer to hospitalize the patient, even though that
is not called for on therapeutic grounds. But, after all, we live in a
materialistic society and psychiatrists can hardly be faulted for doing
what everybody else does (or at least so the argument goes). He particularly damns for-profit hospitals, stating that "there are no figures
available on how much the mental health dollar accrues to for-profit
hospitals, but the diversion is occurring at an accelerating rate." With
the pressure to maximize material gain in medicine and psychiatry
a number of fraudulent practices arose. Health care has become so
profitable that more and more fraud is inevitable. Organized crime is
known to have invested in the nursing-home industry, and it is readily
conceivable that it can spread into the fast-growing field of for-profit
mental health care. He concludes:

> When it becomes commercial, psychiatry dwindles down to a treatment of symptoms and exploitation of techniques, a pretense of interpersonality that achieves only impersonality, a pretense of helping another that helps only the self. Many psychiatrists do not approve the commercialization of psychiatry. They follow a code that prohibits fraud and personal publicity and the other concomitants of the new materialistic psychiatry. But almost no psychiatrist speaks out against it. They turn their eyes away from the sight of the money tree being shaken and if they become aware of it, they hold their tongues. In the absence of a protest from the psychiatrists who do not exploit psychiatry, those who do, flourish. (p. 456)

While certain aspects of Robitscher's book seem exaggerated, such as his treatment of the breach of confidentiality, on the whole his points are well taken and stand as a serious indictment of the everyday practices of the profession. Psychiatry has gone too far.

Actually the argument is about the two sides of psychiatry — the organic and the psychological. The combination of these two in one person or one ideology is not based on any scientific data and should be abolished. To call mental illness an "illness" is misleading and harmful; Szasz's argument on this point is well taken. If there is any demonstrable illness, it should be handled, but if there is not it should be labeled unhappiness.

Another psychiatrist who has been very critical of psychiatry's claims is Lee Coleman (1984). Coleman states: "If society is ever to deal effectively with the problems of deviant behavior, violence and criminal responsibility it now places on psychiatrists' shoulders, this power must be completely abolished" (p. ix).

Robitscher's claim that psychiatry is constantly seeking to acquire more power over people finds ample confirmation in the statements of many professionals. James, for example, McConnell, a psychologist, expressed the wish for power in particularly stark form (1977):

> The day has come when we can combine sensory deprivation with drugs, hypnosis and astute manipulation of reward and punishment to gain almost absolute control over an individual's behavior. It should be possible then to achieve a very rapid and highly effective type of positive brainwashing that would allow us to make dramatic changes in a person's behavior and personality. I foresee the day when we could convert the worst criminal

in a matter of a few months — or perhaps even less time than that.

McConnell's claim about criminals is particularly pernicious because all evidence suggests that psychiatry is almost totally helpless with criminals.

With regard to drugs, everyone who has examined the question, except for the psychiatrists who benefit directly from their use, finds the newer classes of drugs are extremely dangerous and frequently misused. In 1977 the California State Assembly Office of Research found that:

> Drugs are being prescribed in excessive dosages; some evidence exists that high dosages are for the convenience of the staff. The possibility of neurological impairment, tardive dyskinesia, is greatly increased by high dosages and poor monitoring. Prescribing patterns are frequently irrational. (p. 141)

This study also concluded that (p. 142):

> On both inpatient acute care and care for chronic patients, the dangers of the drugs are underestimated and the effectiveness of the drugs inflated. In acute care, medications are often used more often than necessary and sometimes too soon after admission. Some patients are receiving very high dosages early in their treatment, increasing the risk of sudden death and other adverse reactions.

The very real dangers of these drugs have been further documented by California's Department of Health. Responding to public outcry over many unexplained deaths in the state's mental institutions, the department conducted an investigation of all state mental hospital deaths between October 1973 and October 1976. The study found that of all the deaths, "ten percent continued to pose questions of professional practice or procedural deficiencies." The major cause of these questionable deaths was excessive medication. Listed as "major problem areas" were excessive dosages of psychoactive drugs; failure to recognize symptoms of overdose; use of medication to which the patient was allergic; inappropriate choice of medication; inappropriate polypharmacy (giving several drugs at once); and failure to monitor blood drug levels. At Napa State Hospital, the hospital with more suspicious deaths than any other, it was found that most of them were caused by "excessive prescribing."

When the question of overprescribing drugs has been brought to court, similar conclusions have been reached by the courts. In a number of cases mental patients have filed suit against the hospitals and doctors holding them, asking the court to call a halt to the indiscriminate use of forced drugging. In each case, the judge decided that while the doctors claimed they used drugs for treatment and treatment alone, the patients were right when they alleged that drugs were being used excessively. In Ohio, United States District Judge Nicholas Walinski decided in favor of the patients at Lima State Hospital. He noted:

> Widespread use of psychotropic drugs, both in terms of the numbers of patients receiving drugs and the dosages they receive is not, however, necessarily supported by any sound medical course of treatment. Put simply, the testimony at trial established that the prevalent use of psychotropic drugs is countertherapeutic and can be justified only for reasons other than treatment — namely, for the convenience of the staff and for punishment. (Coleman, 1984, p. 143)

Even when the drugs work, they merely create a zombie-like personality. In one hospital where this writer was recently called in for consultation about a patient, it was stated that the majority of the patients slept seventeen hours a day, and that no therapy of any kind was being given. The fundamental questions regarding forced drug treatment are ethical rather than medical.

Furthermore, as Coleman points out, diagnoses have been changed to conform to a belief, frequently unfounded, that certain drugs will help that condition:

> Today psychiatrists all too often put their primary emphasis on arriving at the "right combination" of mind-altering drugs. This is nothing new for psychiatry. Over and over psychiatry has developed new ways to alter the bodies of mental patients, and therefore change behavior and feelings, claiming that these alterations proved that a medical disease was being treated. Two hundred years ago, bleeding worked because madness resulted from too much blood in the brain. Only forty years ago lobotomy worked because it corrected disordered circuits in the frontal

lobes of the brain. Now drugs supposedly treat as yet undefined
brain diseases that cause mental breakdown. (p. 151)

There is, on the other hand, the well-established fact that many
mental illnesses will respond to simple care and custodial treatment.
Bleuler's study of the 208 patients at Burgholzli is still the most careful study of schizophrenics ever conducted on such a large scale And
he found that 25 percent get better without any medication at all,
which is the same figure that was always cited before modern physical methods were introduced. The moral treatment with which the
nineteenth-century asylum started was also highly effective; sometimes 90 percent improvement was reported.

Arguments pro and con on the use of drugs are exceedingly complicated, sometimes involving a detailed knowledge of many branches
of medicine as well as biochemistry. It is not fair to impose such a
burden on one person. The function of evaluating the drugs should be
entrusted to one person specially trained in that area, and that person
should have no other duties. Then some greater clarity will ensue.

But the myth of medical and biochemical competence persists.
Even now psychologists, enticed and intrigued by the huge profits
in drug therapy, far greater than in any kind of psychotherapy and
much easier to manipulate, are clamoring to the state legislatures for
the right to prescribe mild tranquilizers and anxiolytic drugs. As psychologists, their materialistic urges are not different from those of
psychiatrists, and it would be unfortunate if the right to give drugs
were indiscriminately given. Instead, continued research on drugs is
essential in view of all the well-established reports of side effects and
adverse reactions.

As for the other side of psychiatric competence, that of psychotherapy, another error comes to the fore. It is assumed that there
is nothing much to the practice of psychotherapy: just talk to patients and they will eventually get better if they are amenable to
treatment (neurotic) or worse if they are not (psychotic). Even the
little training that is given to the average psychiatrist in a residency
program is being challenged by more organically minded psychiatrists
as superfluous, so that many psychiatrists today come out of their
residency experience with literally little or no training in psychotherapy.

This is parallel to the commonsense image of a neurosis. If a man
insists on walking on cracks in the sidewalk or if a woman has hysterical screaming fits, just tell them to calm down and their behavior will
change. Freud had already commented on this error, which prevailed

in his day. For that matter, look at Freud's own background and you will see that he had no training whatsoever in psychotherapy. He had to invent it, at which he did an extraordinary job. But average psychiatrists or psychologists are unable to do such a job, and even with all the knowledge in the world, without real analytic training they are inadequately prepared.

The need to train psychiatrists in psychoanalysis was recognized by the first generation of psychoanalysts after World War I. But it was fought on two grounds. First most psychiatrists did not want training; they "knew" what they were doing (the myth of commonsense psychiatry). Second there were many nonmedical people who were trained as well; their training did not differ in any respect from that of the physician. So why limit psychotherapy to the physician? No reason, but the myth of medical competence took over, in much the same way as with drugs.

Psychotherapeutic Technique and the Analytical Ideal

Usually the opposition to psychoanalysis and analytic training has taken the form of creating other "schools." Many different forms of psychotherapy are on the market; all are inadequate. In all of them the analytic ideal is missing. The following comments are appropriate:

(1) All of these techniques were developed after World War I when there were a number of persons with degrees but no training in psychotherapy who did not know what to do with the hordes of patients society had thrust upon them.

(2) All of the founders and their followers avoided the long and difficult but spiritually rewarding path of psychoanalytic training. A common feature of all of these methods is that no training is required to learn them or to practice them (e.g., right after the war Rogers offered a six-week training program to teach psychologists how to cure everybody in eight easy lessons).

(3) As a rule no theory of personality is offered. In practice bits and pieces of analytic theory are incorporated here and there, commonly with insufficient understanding of analysis.

(4) All began with an attack on psychoanalysis as "ineffective." Misrepresentations, often of the grossest kind, are usual. All were started by persons who had refused to go into analytic training.

(5) For the most part the emphasis is on whatever works. This is most explicit in Glasser's reality therapy, which explicitly adopts

the American success ethic without reflecting on the consequences. Insofar as this is so, they represent technique without vision.

(6) Some, like Rogers and the Gestaltists, do have a vision, usually expressed as self-actualization. Rogers stressed the therapist's need to care for the patient, ignorant of the fact that this has always been one of the cardinal tenets of psychoanalysis. Rogers's system is reminiscent of Christian faith healing. The Gestalt vision of self-actualization is a partial reformulation of the analytic ideal.

(7) Most have adopted names that carry propagandistic messages directed against psychoanalysis. Thus Rogers is client-centered (now person-centered), implying that analysis is analyst-centered. Behavior therapists deal with behavior, allegedly because analyst do not. Reality therapists deal with reality, analysts do not. RET therapists are rational, implying that analysts are irrational. These names serve to obscure one all-important commonalty: none of these therapies ever pays real attention to the patient. They are all directives for how the therapist should behave and largely ignore the clinical and theoretical realities of the patient's responses. These clinical realities immediately lead to the observations of transference and resistance, which are at the root of all therapy. Whatever they call themselves, they are all thus essentially intellectual approaches without feelings, or the unreflective release of feeling without thought.

(8) For the most part these techniques go back to the Freud of the 1890s, when the main formula was: Make the unconscious conscious.

(9) Most of them make vague claims about results; others claim to be supported by a variety of "confirmatory" studies. The usual statement is that all therapists do some good and no one can be shown to do better than any of the others.

(10) Thus all of them represent the cultural reaction to the discovery of psychotherapy and the need for therapy after World War II. Their appearances, programs, and claims can only be understood in the light of the cultural conditions of the past thirty-five years.

Reviewing the psychotherapy training of the average psychiatrist, it is clear that it is highly inadequate. The psychiatrist is primarily trained in medicine, does not study analysis, and does not practice it, although many propound the misrepresentation that there is no difference between a psychiatrist and a psychoanalyst. In all cases, the analytic ideal, the basic ingredient of all psychoanalytic therapy, is conspicuous by its absence. At least it can be said that psychiatric treatment with psychotherapy does not maim or kill anybody, as the somatic treatments occasionally do.

No doubt many will react to this section by saying that I am an analytic enthusiast who is pushing analysis too far. I plead guilty to being an enthusiast but not to pushing it too far. It is high time that analysts, who have studied the subject far more intensively than any other school of thought, should stand up for what they have learned and not bow to the untutored and insolent attacks of persons like Fritz Perls or Albert Ellis.

12

Implications for Psychology

*I*N HIS INFLUENTIAL BOOK, *A History of Experimental Psychology*, Boring quotes Ebbinghaus's remark that "psychology has a long past, but only a short history." Academically trained psychologists have been taught to emphasize behaviorism, learning theory, and their own version of scientific method, allegedly but not really copying the methods of the older physical sciences.

Experimental psychology, clinical psychiatry, and psychoanalysis all began at about the same time, toward the latter part of the nineteenth century. They have all developed at the same time, largely independent of one another. Any person who tries to combine the three faces formidable obstacles, yet the need for unity is great.

In the atmosphere of the 1890s, when Freud's serious work began, it would have been quite possible for psychology to take up the study of psychoanalysis and to pursue it to its logical conclusions. Instead it bogged down in what Nagel has called a "parochial" view of science and became strongly behavioristic until about 1950, and still is, to some extent, today. Like all other sciences, academic psychology comes to psychoanalysis with some preconceptions that it is unable to shake. The natural result is that those who wished to study psychoanalysis went elsewhere. The new discipline of clinical psychology began to be pursued seriously after World War II, in the 1950s, and was essentially independent of the older academic psychology, which viewed itself as experimental and called psychoanalysis simply "bad science." Just as the organic hypothesis confuses psychiatrists, the experimental hypothesis, that truth can be reached only via objective experimentation, confuses psychologists. The result is understandably a hodge-podge. Yet Wundt insisted that the higher mental faculties cannot be studied by experimentation, while Boring (1913) in his history stated:

> The experimental psychologist, so it has always seemed to me, needs historical sophistication within his own sphere of expertness. Without such knowledge he sees the present in distorted perspective; he mistakes old facts and views for new, and he remains unable to evaluate the significance of new movements and methods. In this matter I can hardly state my faith too strongly. A psychological sophistication that contains no component of historical orientation seems to me to be no sophistication at all....
>
> At the other temporal extreme, it is plain that there is as yet no historical perspective found. I have thought it unsafe to say very much about psychology since 1910....(p. ix)

Later Boring adds:

> Perhaps I should also say why there is so much biographical material in this book, why I have centered the exposition on the personalities of men more than upon the genesis of the traditional chapters of psychology....
>
> Behaviorism seems to have been a movement in the Zeitgeist, not a simple revolution. Instead of giving it a chapter to itself, I have turned [the chapter] to behavioristics, have picked up the threads of animal psychology and of objective psychology from the earlier chapters, and have then passed on through behaviorism proper to the newer positivism and what has sometimes been called operationism. (p. x)

As Boring indicates here, the theoretical conflict within academic psychology has long been posed as the conflict between "scientific" psychology, which is based on behaviorism and learning theory, and psychoanalysis, which is based on clinical psychology and clinical experience. This is a clash of personalities, not resolvable by simple objective means. Over and over we find that persons who have been through a personal analysis are more favorable to its concepts and assumptions, while those who have not are simply blind to what the psychoanalysts are saying and have been saying. Thus scientific dispute has become a personal fight.

From a scientific point of view the fundamental point at issue is the concept of consciousness. Behaviorists tend to view consciousness as a given that cannot be further analyzed, while psychoanalysis views consciousness as the key to the unconscious, stressing instead the overwhelming role that the unconscious plays in the functioning of the human being. It is the unconscious that gives rise to the description of psychoanalysis as a "depth psychology"; without a concept of the unconscious, psychoanalysis argues, no significant statements can be made in most areas of psychology.

The Growth of Clinical Psychology after World War II

Although psychology as such goes back a long way, its present flourishing state really goes back to the period after World War II, when the need for psychological services of all kinds was recognized. In 1940 the membership of the APA (American Psychological Association) was less than a thousand; it was an organization of fuddy-duddies who did little for themselves or other people — a true "academic" discipline in the worst sense of the word. In many leading universities there was not even an independent department of psychology. Today there are well over 70,000 members in the APA, and the clinical divisions are by far the largest; before the war they did not exist at all. In 1969 the Division of Psychotherapy was founded; in 1979 the Division of Psychoanalysis. When the Division of Psychoanalysis was founded, one eminent psychologist got up to insist that psychoanalysis was not part of psychology, but he was voted down. It is generally estimated that only 10 percent of the membership is in theoretical work that has nothing to do with clinical.

There has already been a reaction to this clinical emphasis. In 1945, when clinical departments were being founded all over, Columbia University started one but dropped it after two years because it was not "scientific" enough. More recently a group of learning theorists has attempted to withdraw and start an APA of their own that would be purely theoretical, but they have found few followers. The clinical emphasis in psychology is by now well established and unlikely to change.

The establishment of the Division of Psychoanalysis in 1979 (Division 39) was an event of the utmost importance and has had far-reaching consequences. Beginning with about one thousand persons, it quickly grew to some twenty-five thousand. Once the division had become consolidated, a lawsuit was started against the American Psychoanalytic Association and International Psychoanalytic Association to force those bodies to admit nonmedical persons on a par with medical, and to force the International to admit the nonmedical institutes that had developed.

Since the scientific status of psychoanalysis is under such constant attack, especially by psychologists, a few words are in order here about the problem. "Philosophers of science" such as Hook, Popper, Ricoeur, and most recently Gruenbaum have repeatedly proclaimed that psychoanalysis does not meet the requirements of science. This claim has repeatedly been refuted (Fine, 1983), most effectively perhaps by Waelder's paper (1962) in which the Hook symposium of 1962 was reviewed. Waelder distinguished five levels of theory that have varying degrees of relevance. (1) observation, (2) clinical interpretation, (3) clinical generalization, (4) clinical theory, and (5) metapsychology. Then he adds: "The degree to which these various layers in psychoanalytic writings are known to the outside world is in inverse ratio to their relevance for psychoanalysis."

As Freud had repeatedly pointed out, science begins with observations, and the significance of the observations of psychoanalysis remains largely lost on the academic world of psychology. That human beings have dreams, which appear to have meaning, that they have sexual conflicts, that each possesses an unconscious, that much of the personality is layered in a structure of anxiety and defenses against the anxiety, all this and much more is simply never taught, even though much of it is in accord with experimental data (Fisher and Greenberg, 1977).

Philosophers of science who have written about psychoanalysis almost always refer to the therapeutic situation rather than to the scientific structure of theory. Therapy per se cannot prove anything in particular, since it has to be geared to the immediate needs of the patient. While psychoanalysis as a therapy is of vital importance, even more vital is psychoanalysis as a system of psychology.

In point of fact, much that is taught in psychology courses today comes from psychoanalysis, without acknowledgment. As long ago as 1943 Kris, Herma, and Shor (1943) showed that when a theory is considered dubious it is labeled "psychoanalysis" by psychologists; when it is accepted into psychological theory, its psychoanalytic origin is disowned. The basis of psychological functioning in the family, the role of the parents and the internalized parents of the superego, the fact that "the intellect is a speck afloat on a sea of feeling," the widespread incidence of neurotic and psychotic disorders (hitherto unsuspected), the availability of techniques for ameliorating neurotic and psychotic difficulties, the effect of emotions on learning capacities and intellectual functioning and numerous other propositions are incorporated into psychology (clinical for the most part) without recognizing their origin.

The dominance of the physical sciences in the formulation of scientific theory has long been noted. Less attention has been paid to the fact that other sciences have progressed in different ways, e.g., biology. The eminent biologist Ernst Mayr (1982), who is highly critical of a scientific methodology based exclusively on the physical sciences, makes the following comment, which is also pertinent to psychoanalysis:

> ... it seems to me that progress in the biological sciences is characterized not so much by individual discoveries, no matter how important, or by the proposal of new theories, but rather by the gradual but decisive development of new concepts and the abandonment of those that had previously been dominant. (p. 856)

Further confusion results from the attitude of many psychoanalysts who arrogate to themselves the right to proclaim what they believe to be the truth without giving their opponents a chance to argue the case. This pontifical attitude stems in part from the difficulties of psychoanalytic doctrine (Hartmann, 1964) but even more strongly from the political organization of psychoanalysis, in which dissension from the opinion of the group leaders carries with it the serious consequences of expulsion from the school, with consequent loss of income and prestige.

Consider, for example, the concept of the "self." We are told that Kohut has formulated a new "psychology of the self" that may (in his opinion should) replace classical psychoanalysis. Few psychologists have taken this claim seriously, for the simple reason that the concept of the self has been common currency in psychology for 150 years (Fine, 1985). Freud referred to the "self" at numerous points in his writings; Roheim in 1921 wrote a seminal article on the self, which was published in one of the central organs of psychoanalysis, *Imago*, and which so far as I have been able to determine has been completely disregarded in spite of its profundity and relevance. Nor is it true that the word "ich" should be translated as "self"; the two terms are distinct in German and distinct in English. German has a perfectly good word for self, *Das Selbst* (the title of Roheim's paper). Linguistic usage gives a slightly different turn to "self" in English than to *Selbst* in German, but after all both are Germanic languages and the differences are exaggerated.

Many other examples could be cited in which analysts are fighting political battles rather than real theoretical arguments that would really contribute to the advancement of psychoanalytic theory. If the political climate of psychoanalysis could somehow be removed (perhaps as a result of moving it to university departments, perhaps otherwise) this needless disputation might be avoided (Kernberg, 1986). At the same time the basic elements of psychoanalysis could be elucidated more clearly to the average student of psychology.

Within the official structure of psychology, the most notable rapprochement between psychology and psychoanalysis came in 1979 with the formation of Division 39, the Division of Psychoanalysis. The considerable accomplishments of this division since then may be noted here.

Review of Psychoanalysis

It is now about ten years since Division 39 was first proposed, and some eight years since it was officially admitted as a division of the APA. In this brief period, there have been some notable accomplishments by the division. The membership has increased to about three thousand or almost 5 percent of the APA membership. A journal has been founded and published quarterly, which compares favorably with other journals in the field. An annual program has been instituted, alternating between the east and the west coasts. An ABPPP diplomate is in the process of formation. Although it remains an interest group, various sections have been set up, some of which are limited to trained analysts.

Particularly noteworthy is the lawsuit against the American Psychoanalytic Association and the International charging these bodies with violations of the antitrust statutes. Although it was called a settlement in 1989, it was really a total victory for the psychologists. One more momentous change has already occurred: the decision by the International to admit as members societies that do not belong to the American. Since these new societies will, in the beginning at least, be composed largely of psychologists, this amounts to the first official recognition by medical analysts that psychologists can be competent psychoanalysts. Thus psychoanalysis is no longer linked exclusively to the medical profession and the term "lay analyst" will disappear.

In order to effect the change in the International, the American Psychoanalytic Association has decided to change the nature of its tie to the International and no longer be an exclusive regional association with full authority. But it is striking that in making this change the International will be carrying out one of Freud's wishes, which it was never willing to do while he was still alive. In 1929 when the International was experiencing a conflict about the free admission of nonphysician candidates, Freud empowered Eitingon and Ferenczi, who were going to the Oxford Congress, to suggest that a friendly separation be arranged between the American and the European societies, and he added that in his opinion the opposition to lay analysis was "the last mask of the resistance against psychoanalysis and the most dangerous of all" (Jones, *Life and Work of Freud*, vol. 3, p. 298).

Thus the formation of Division 39 has brought us one step closer to a cherished wish of Freud's, that analysis should be the basis of a new profession, of lay curers of souls who need not be doctors and should not be priests. Some of the profound implications of this view of Freud's will be explored in the present chapter.

In her book *The Impossible Profession* Janet Malcolm has commented that psychoanalysis has resounded through the intellectual, social, artistic, and ordinary life of our century as no cultural force has since Christianity. Most psychoanalysts have been rather narrowly concerned with the refinements of technique and have failed to see the enormous relevance of psychoanalysis for a constructive change in our society. Again the formation of Division 39 will necessarily force psychoanalysts to focus more on the role of psychoanalysis in the broader cultural sphere. In this broader cultural sphere psychoanalysis has laid claims to being of relevance in all the sciences that deal with psychological matters. In some it is of more relevance, in others less; but it is always relevant. What I should like to do is reexamine some of the controversies that have arisen and present, from a positive point of view, the psychoanalytic position.

Psychology

From Freud's earliest days he viewed psychoanalysis as a systematic approach to psychology, even though he functioned in his daily life as a physician. But he recognized quite soon that the key to mental and emotional disturbance lay in psychology, not in the organic disorders that his contemporaries were researching (and that others still are). Shortly thereafter he discovered that neurosis is by no means confined to a few odd eccentrics, but that in one way or another it exists in everybody. He had, as he put it, all humankind as his patient, which was why psychoanalysis has become so important.

Looking back at the historical picture, there was actually no reason in 1900 why psychology could not go along with him. William James in particular was not far from his position, and the first public lectures on psychoanalysis were given at Clark University in 1909 under the auspices of G. Stanley Hall, a psychologist.

Psychology, however, was not ready to embrace psychoanalysis; soon a reaction set in. From Watson on, in the second decade of this century, behaviorism became the dominant creed of psychology and, with some changes, has remained that ever since. Though behaviorism has changed in many ways, its emphasis on rigorous experimentation has never wavered. Psychology could become a science, it was argued, only if it adopted the methods of the exact sciences, which had produced such far-reaching results.

From then on psychoanalysis led a checkered existence among academic psychologists (clinical psychology did not really exist as yet). Psychoanalysis was branded unscientific and ruled out of the schools.

It is paradoxical that in spite of this wholesale condemnation, one of the early publications of the APA, *Psychoanalysis as Seen by Analyzed Psychologists* (1940) was very favorable to psychoanalysis. Edwin Boring, who could be expected to be most antagonistic to psychoanalysis, wrote (Boring, 1913):

> Apparently psychology is not yet in a position to validate or invalidate psychoanalysis experimentally — with selected groups and carefully chosen controls. Hence we are reduced to the collection of case histories, and critical autobiographical histories by sophisticated scientifically minded persons ought to be worth more than the enthusiasm of naive persons about an event which has helped them.

In the same symposium Franz Alexander commented that the feud between experimental psychology and psychoanalysis has no rational foundation, only an emotional one.

In spite of this favorable reaction by a host of leading psychologists, the official antipsychoanalytic line was soon laid down by Robert Sears in his *Survey of Objective Studies of Psychoanalytic Concepts* (1943). Sears argued that while many hypotheses may emanate from psychoanalysis, the further analysis of psychoanalytic concepts by nonpsychoanalytic techniques will be relatively fruitless so long as these concepts rest in the theoretical framework of psychoanalysis (p. 145). From Sears through the present (the latest version is Gruenbaum, *The Foundations of Psychoanalysis*, 1984) this argument has remained unaltered and been swallowed whole by one generation of psychologists after another.

There are two fundamental flaws in all these criticisms of psycho-analysis: first of all, they fail to understand what psychoanalysis is. Perhaps the best rejoinder is that by Robert Waelder (who started as a professor of physics) in his review of the Hook symposium of 1959 (*JAPA*, 1962).

Let us consider for the moment only the first of Waelder's levels: that of observation. Freud always emphasized that observation was the basis of his work and that if the observations change, his con-clusions would have to change. It is easy enough to show that the observations of psychoanalysts were for a long time totally ignored (e.g., dreams) or misunderstood; indeed they are still largely ignored or misunderstood.

In spite of one hundred years of unremitting investigation the no-tion persists in many quarters that psychoanalytic observations apply only to certain persons called "neurotics" and do not apply to "nor-mals." The problem here is first that the difference between neurotic and normal, even in our own culture, is one of degree, not of kind, and second that the "normal" or average in any culture may be, and of-ten is from a more objective standpoint, disturbed, sometimes highly disturbed (see chapter 11).

Most significant is that the observations made by psychoanalysis, on which the entire theory rests, apply to all persons in the culture and to all human beings in general; the differences lie only in the variations created by local circumstances (both cultural and familial). For example, the observation that human beings are overattached to their mothers and require a long period to break or outgrow the attachment is a universal finding.

A further commentary is necessary here. Almost all critics of psychoanalysis, from Sears to Gruenbaum, assume that psycho-analysis is only a form of therapy; they overlook the large body of thought that has gone into the construction of a systematic psycho-logical approach. The efforts of many theoreticians have been directed toward clarifying the essential bases of such a psychoanalytic theory of psychology (Fine, 1975). As Freud had emphasized, this large view of psychology is a more essential contribution of psychoanalysis than its therapeutic applications, which depend so much on circumstances peculiar to each individual and each culture.

The second major flaw in the argument that psychoanalysis is un-scientific because it does not adhere to the methods of the more exact sciences is that it fails to understand what the methods of the exact sciences were and are. Specifically the role of the unifying concept has been virtually ignored.

In their book *The Evolution of Physics* (1938) Einstein and Infeld write: "Fundamental ideas play the essential role in forming a physical theory. Books on physics are full of complicated mathematical formulae. But thought and ideas, not formulae, are the beginning of every physical theory" (p. 277).

They further emphasize that physics really began with certain concepts: "The great results of classical mechanics suggest that the mechanical view can be consistently applied to all branches of physics, that all phenomena can be explained by the action of forces representing either attraction or repulsion, depending only upon distance and acting between unchangeable particles" (p. 65). Einstein saw his great contribution as clarifying concepts such as space, time, and gravitation through what he called "the most important invention since Newton's time: the field" (p. 244).

Such a view of the development of physics is not found in the oversimplified philosophies of science that attempt to explain science to the uninitiated (as in academic psychology).

By a happy coincidence in physics there is a combination of the ability to observe natural phenomena and the existence of new mathematical tools that can explain these phenomena. No such coincidence exists in psychology (Nagel, 1961).

Physics began with observations and concepts: psychoanalysis does the same thing. The difference lies in the nature of the material under investigation; the methods (observation-concept-explanation) are really essentially the same.

Ernst Mayr (1982) has stressed that a similar situation exists in biology. He writes:

> ... it seems to me that progress in the biological sciences is characterized not so much by individual discoveries, no matter how important, or by the proposal of new theories, but rather by the gradual but decisive development of new concepts and the abandonment of those that had previously been dominant. (p. 856)

Another similarity between psychoanalysis and biology lies in the theory of evolution. Charles Singer, the historian of science (1941), once commented that the appeal for the acceptance of evolution is not that there is any evidence for it, but that any other proposed interpretation of the data is wholly incredible. This remark applies to much of psychoanalytic theory as well.

The multiplicity of new concepts has led to another error on the part of the experimentalists: they have tried to verify or validate the concepts experimentally. This is a logical fallacy. Concepts are either useful or not; hypotheses deriving from them can be validated, but the concepts themselves cannot. The remark above concerning evolution is a case in point. Similarly the unconscious, one of the basic psychoanalytic concepts, permits no validation as such. But a proposition such as the relationship of a man (or woman) to the opposite sex is strongly influenced by the unconscious memories of the relationship with that person's mother (or father) lends itself to confirmation or disproof.

It is high time for psychology to discard these hoary chestnuts and recognize psychoanalysis for what it is — a highly developed systematic approach to the human being, which defines its terms as well as it can, seeks confirmation or disproof in appropriate ways, and makes a meaningful contribution to the whole body of psychological science.

Generally speaking, psychoanalytic propositions cut across conscious and unconscious determinants, so that they can readily be verified in some instances, or only with difficulty, if at all, in others. This collaboration between investigation along conscious and unconscious lines has been going on ever since Freud launched the discipline in 1900 (it is best to date psychoanalysis from *The Interpretation of Dreams;* what preceded was general neurological theorizing, similar to what other neurologists of that day had done).

By now a substantial body of information has accumulated as Freud had hoped (Freud, 1923), and methods are available to expand and systematize this information. The problem is more a practical one: there is no one source that contains everything that has been discovered. To find out what the claims of psychoanalysis are the student must go through not only Freud but the entire body of literature that has developed since. Still, this is only a practical problem, not a theoretical objection to psychoanalysis. One understandable reaction to the absence of the kind of handbook that Hartmann once called for has led to numerous misstatements about what psychoanalysis asserts. These have to be corrected, again a practical problem, not a theoretical objection.

Freud touched upon almost every science that deals with human beings; others have expanded his leads. Thus we have not only a psychoanalytic psychology and psychiatry but also a psychoanalytic history, psychoanalytic anthropology, psychoanalytic economics (to the extent that psychology is applicable), and so on. Academic psychology has been too narrowly concerned with the validation of every proposition offered, rather than participating fully in the enterprise of extending psychoanalytic theory to all aspects of human experience.

Wundt himself, generally regarded as the father of experimental psychology, did not feel that the higher mental functions could be approached in an experimental manner; he spoke of experimental and "ethnic" psychology, which is called clinical psychology today.

The Expansion of Psychological Inquiry

Technically, the shift to a broader view of the field was embodied in the development of clinical psychology, which began to offer Ph.D.'s in this area from 1945 on. As usual, the older generation fought the intrusion of the newer ideas. One prominent university, for example, offered clinical psychology for two years, then dropped it because it was not "pure" psychology. Psychoanalysis and psychoanalytically oriented research were of course the core of the new clinical psychology. By now the clinical field represents the majority of the APA membership, though as a hangover from the past it still generally fails to recognize the scientific validity of psychoanalytic methods, which seem so irrational to many. But, as has been noted, it is not the method that is irrational, but the human being.

Yet with all this, it has to be recognized that the rationality of the human being is in one sense always present. Only it is present in the unconscious rather than the conscious. Thus with enough effort such seemingly bizarre material as dreams and schizophrenic productions can be shown to have a rational structure.

The expansion of psychological inquiry has proceeded and will proceed further in two different directions. First of all, in spite of its promises, the limits of experimental investigation will have to be recognized. Ruth Wylie, for example, in her exhaustive summary of 4500 experiments on the self (1974) concludes that there is a "paucity of definite findings" (p. 685) and indeed "numerous resounding failures to obtain support for some... strongly held hypotheses." In spite of this pessimistic view, she does not consider that the experimental method is not the most appropriate for a study of such a complex concept as the self. It is clear to many that the study of such vital but complex topics as the self, love, happiness, and the like cannot be conducted along classic experimental lines, and that when it is done a large amount of wasted motion results. Thus the first expansion leads to a more realistic acceptance of the importance of observation and allied analytic methods.

The second expansion is that, like Freud and psychoanalysts in general, the domain of psychological inquiry will be considerably enlarged by extending it to the allied sciences, history, anthropology, economics, sociology, philosophy, and the like. Whatever is human is a legitimate subject of psychological inquiry (Fine, 1981).

Of necessity such an extension will lead to a breaking down of the barriers among the various disciplines. While all the social sciences started with breaking away from philosophy toward the end of the nineteenth century, they have gradually begun to coalesce as they have recognized that they deal with the same people in a different light. I would propose that the unifying force behind this unification, both now and in the future, will be a psychoanalytic view of humankind. By admitting openly that the psychologist can pursue psychoanalysis as well as the medical practitioner, a wide door is opened, which can only become wider in the future.

Psychiatry

Closest to psychoanalysis is psychiatry, the study of the "mentally ill." Quotation marks are used here because the very definition of mentally ill has led to so many disparate points of view. Besides being a theoretical discipline, viewed by its practitioners as a branch of medicine, psychiatry is also a profession, subject to the vagaries of economic forces that afflict both the medical and all other professions. These economic forces may be of considerable weight; Sabshin, for example, stated frankly that economic issues are paramount and would be paramount through the 1980s, if not beyond. The accusation that physicians misstate their theoretical findings and misuse them for economic gain is by no means uncommon; the multiplicity of malpractice suits in the past few years attests to that with great eloquence. The same considerations apply to psychology as a profession, and similar caution is needed in interpreting its findings. At least there is the dubious caveat, however, that psychologists who practice and psychologists who teach are separated by a wide gulf.

Even the term "psychiatry" did not exist in Freud's early years; everything developed at the same time. Gradually, however, psychiatry has evolved and taken over virtually all administrative control of the management of the mentally ill as well as practical domination of the profession of psychotherapy.

Crudely but accurately put, psychiatry is based on the assumption that brain damage of one kind or another is at the root of mental and emotional illness, while psychology is based on the alternative assumption that neurosis and psychosis are psychosocial disorders. Prior to World War II the only viable alternative to organic psychiatry of the Kraepelinian variety was psychoanalysis. Since then, however, two new professions have arisen, clinical psychology and psychiatric social work. In spite of the fiercest opposition, these two professions have persisted until today there are probably more nonmedical therapists practicing than medical.

Theoretically, psychiatrists should be trained in psychotherapy as well as in the organic approach. It would appear, however, that there is less and less training in psychotherapy going on, and that the organic approach has become routine.

The enthusiasm of contemporary psychiatry for its current drug procedures should be viewed with caution, in the light of the historical record. Kolb and Brodie (1982), proponents of the organic approach, state that "the history of the therapy of schizophrenia has been characterized by the use of various methods that temporarily had enthusiastic proponents but failed to stand the test of time" (p. 401).

Furthermore, according to these authorities, roughly one-third of schizophrenics who are hospitalized during the first year of their illness make a fairly complete recovery; one-third improve and become able to return to outside life but remain damaged personalities; the remaining third require indefinite care. These figures do not differ markedly from those in existence one hundred years ago. Overall, then with some exceptions, the organic approach has scarcely changed the outcome of the treatment of schizophrenia in the past hundred years. In addition, however, psychiatry constantly tends to seek greater power for itself (Robitscher, 1980). On occasion it has resorted to somatic "cures" that have had the most dire consequences for the patients involved, such as psychosurgery (Valenstein, 1986).

Today, the neuroleptics have become the treatment of choice for schizophrenics. Yet many have argued that the claims for their efficacy are seriously exaggerated. In the most recent review of the data Warner (1985) concludes that (1) the neuroleptics have not improved the long-term outcome of schizophrenia; (2) the neuroleptics are not the principal reason the large mental hospitals have emptied; (3) the outcome of schizophrenia is not similar in all cultures; and finally (4) "schizophrenia is an illness that is shaped, to a large extent, by political economy" (Mosher, p. 956).

The case that first attracted most attention to the neglect that schizophrenics suffer in mental hospitals was *Wyatt vs. Stickney* in Alabama in 1971. The presiding judge in that case found the conditions to be highly deplorable and ordered large-scale reforms. The reforms would have brought into mental hospitals considerably extended staffs of psychologists and social workers. Rather than admit these other professions to help the patients, the psychiatric profession (as a whole, not individuals) preferred to close the mental hospitals and throw the patients out on the street. The homelessness problem that is now so acute was one consequence of this professional protectionism; together with homelessness goes an increase in crime on the part of mentally disturbed patients with poor control (Kolb and Brodie, pp. 856–957).

These remarks should not be interpreted as casting any aspersions on the many competent and conscientious psychiatrists who have devoted their lives to the care of the mentally ill. But it is important to see the other side. Critics of psychiatry such as Szasz, Robitscher, Breggin, and others have simply been ignored.

The close connection between psychoanalysis and psychiatry came about through the neglect of psychoanalysis by the other disciplines, especially psychology. Freud himself was of course the great proponent of lay analysis, even proposing in 1929 that American and European psychoanalysis should have a peaceful separation, since the American psychoanalysts were so adamantly opposed to lay analysis (Jones, 1957).

In any case, psychiatry is not the only branch of medicine that is relevant to psychoanalysis: internal medicine, endocrinology, nutrition, and many others play a role as well. The point is that factual data should be forthcoming, not opinions that merely buttress the status of the profession in the eyes of the public.

Psychoanalysis

Since our main concern is with psychoanalysis, most attention will be paid to the controversies and developments in our field. Many, like Gedo (1981), speak of a sense of crisis in contemporary psychoanalysis. Recently Kernberg (1986), one of the leaders in psychoanalytic education, published a remarkable paper in which he stated, "I believe that psychoanalytic education is suffering from various disturbances, which, by analogy, might be examined as an illness affecting the educational structures of psychoanalytic institutes and societies" (p. 799).

He claims that psychoanalytic education today is all too often conducted in an atmosphere of indoctrination rather than of open scientific exploration. He then speaks of the paranoid (not even in quotation marks) atmosphere that often pervades psychoanalytic institutes. Creative thinking and scientific productivity have diminished, according to Kernberg. Institutes have been structured so that they correspond most closely to a combination of the technical school and the theological seminary. "Idealization processes and an ambience of persecution are practically universal in psychoanalytic institutes" (p. 815). He recommends as optimal a model of analytic training based predominantly on the university college and art school.

While we can welcome Kernberg's suggestion that psychoanalysis should be taught in universities, this suggestion has been made many times before — and rejected almost unanimously. Recently the Hebrew University and the London College have appointed a professor of psychoanalysis, a post ably filled by Dr. Joseph Sandler for several years, and now being rotated. But this is still far from a systematic course of study led by a group of competent scholars; it is still only a one-person job.

The analytic institute, which Kernberg excoriates, was the product of the refusal of the universities to teach psychoanalytic psychology. Some historical comments are in order here. Freud himself, though a full professor of neurology at the University of Vienna, in his day (before World War I) was permitted only to give occasional series of lectures on psychoanalysis, most of them poorly attended.

When World War I ended, there was a small group of psychoanalysts who were eager to pass their knowledge on to students. As is well known, the first institute was set up in Berlin in 1920, thanks to the generosity of Max Eitingon, one of Freud's special "circle." In his statistical summary of the work of the Institute, written in 1930, Otto Fenichel reported that from its inception until 1930, that is, ten years, there were a total of 1955 consultations, which led to 721 psychoanalyses. Of these he classified 116 as improved, 89 quite improved (*wesentlich gebessert*), and 111 cured, while 117 analyses were still in progress. The age range went from under five to over sixty. Particularly striking is the list of occupations of the patients: 69 working men, 157 hand workers, 46 household servants, 28 physicians, 124 artists, 160 students, 249 without occupations. These (with the exception of physicians, artists, and students) would largely today be considered unsuitable for psychoanalysis. The analyses were not supported by Sickness Insurance. The analyses were for the most part classical analyses with sessions four or five times a week. The analysts were either members of the German Psychoanalytic Association or students, all of whom worked without fee (Maetze, 1970).

Very soon a course of training was introduced, which included (1) introduction to psychoanalysis; (2) dreams, libido theory, infantile sexuality; (3) technique; (4) special theory and characteristics of neuroses, perversions, character disturbances; (5) theoretical problems; (6) seminar on the psychoanalytic literature, especially the "Freud seminar"; (7) colloquium on novelties in psychoanalysis and its allied fields; (8) psychoanalysis and the practicing physician; (9) course for practical-theoretical development; (10) special themes; (11) reading and seminars on the extra-therapeutic application of psychoanalysis. This last included (a) general; (b) literature and art; (c) psychoanalysis and sociology; (d) law and criminality; (e) philosophy; (f) religion; (g) education. Lectures for the public were also offered.

The list of persons who participated in this institute reads like a who's who of psychoanalytic history: Fenichel, Rado, Horney, Hanns Sachs, Simmel, Anna Freud, Alexander Bernfeld, Eitingon, and others.

The average analysis at that time lasted "at least" two hundred hours. Yet even with this abbreviated period, the analysts involved took a heavy burden on themselves, in which they participated gladly. It was an experiment that has never been repeated in psychoanalytic history, yet it laid the foundation for all future analytic training.

An innovation of far-reaching and decisive importance was the requirement that every therapist should have a "training analysis." Hanns Sachs, the first training analyst, wrote of this training (1930):

> What is involved is that the future analyst must learn something which other persons easily, gladly and permanently overlook, and that they are in a position to maintain this observational capacity even when the results are in sharp contradiction to their own wishes and feelings....As one sees, analysis needs something which corresponds to the novitiate of the church. With the accumulation of theoretical knowledge, or book knowledge, no matter how complete, this demand cannot be fulfilled. Analysis requires of those who practice it, a continual focus on things which are generally overlooked or contrary to cultural demands, such as infantile sexuality, the Oedipus complex and ambivalence in human relationships. The only somewhat certain method to reach this goal is the training analysis, which must therefore be seen as an essential part of analytic training, impossible to replace by any other means. (p. 53)

No barrier was set up against nonmedical analysts. In Abraham's course of 1923 (p. 30) there were 75 students, of whom 54 were physicians, 9 teachers, 7 members of the philosophical faculty, and a few others. In 1929 only 47 of the 117 students were physicians. Karen

Horney, who was in charge of the organization of teaching, wrote that "there was neither clarity nor unity about the criteria for admission and about particular questions of the curriculum (*Lehrganges*)" (p. 48). She placed particular emphasis on the presence of "personal aptitude." She saw that unreliability of the person or a lack of psychological talent could not be compensated for by personal analysis. Horney stated (p. 51) that the training analysis would have to last "at least one year" (an admonition that makes one smile today).

Two other innovations of the Berlin Institute have been significant: the system of control analysis, in which the candidates present their cases to more experienced analysts, and the concept that the institute should take charge of all training, making it impossible for individual practitioners to train others on their own. Control analysis has presented various problems, along the same lines as the position of training analysts. The "control" exercises great power, as does the training analyst; in fact, the power of the institute lies mainly in these two figures. Wherever power enters, conflicts enter, so it is not surprising that they have given rise to numerous problems.

But the greatest difficulties have arisen because of institute control of education. Undoubtedly the numerous splits that have been such a marked feature of the psychoanalytic movement have been due largely to this policy of institute control. In fact, of the original group in Berlin, Horney, Rado, and Alexander all later went on to form institutes of their own, all under their own personal control in the beginning; they were unable or unwilling to tolerate the demands made by the authorities. After Horney, Silverberg, and Thompson broke off from the New York Psychoanalytic Institute in 1941; each formed another institute within one year, based on different principles. Rado broke off a few years later to ally himself with a medical school (Fine, 1979).

The mainstream psychoanalytic tradition, represented by the training practices of the Berlin Institute, nevertheless persisted to become the model for institutes all over the world.

Based on this model, the International Psychoanalytical Association went on to become a powerful international body of currently some seven thousand practitioners, spread all over the world. While personal analysis, controls, and course work are at the heart of this training system, numerous individual differences persist, some of a fundamental nature, such as what types of persons to admit to training. In the Jerusalem congress of 1977, a precongress conference on training was held (Wallerstein, 1978) in which every facet of training (including training analysis) was questioned as to its purpose and necessity. Prior to the congress Wallerstein had queried all the member institutes of the International about their views. Such widely divergent views surfaced that Wallerstein could only conclude that "we have in full view now a range of experiments in training" (p. 503). Thus psychoanalysis is by no means to be regarded as a finished science, but as a body of theory in constant process of reformulation (Sandler, 1983).

The institute system under which psychoanalysis is presently taught has led to innumerable battles. Chief among them has been the appearance of widely divergent schools of thought, led by charismatic figures who seek to impose their own point of view on a group of devoted followers. This unfortunate consequence might have been avoided had the universities done their job of teaching psychoanalysis to their students, but then as now they have consistently refused to do so.

In their turn the charismatic figures have led rather checkered careers, characterized by changes in their own points of view. One inevitable consequence has been confusion among the students, which is not dispelled until they become full-fledged practitioners in their own right. Mercano (1986), the head of the Venezuelan society, describes how in his institute the students dutifully give the instructors back what they are taught, never daring to disagree in public. They read the material given to them and their own material. Then once they are free of the institute, each goes his or her own way. It is this need to agree with the leaders in public and disagree with them in private that plays such a strong role in the paranoid structure of the institutes that Kernberg (1986) describes.

Another unfortunate outcome of the institute system is that the leaders misrepresent the positions of their opponents, sometimes almost deliberately. At times, this is unavoidable, since so many analysts have reached positions in their thought that can only be called bizarre; I have in mind such persons as Wilhelm Reich in Norway and the United States (incidentally his ex-wife's biography of him clearly shows that he was distinctly paranoid toward the end of his life), Jacques Lacan in France, and Hyman Spotnitz in New York, as well as many others.

No doubt the most important system of misrepresentation relates to Freud himself. Working over a period of some fifty years, Freud allowed his thought to change, grow, and be reformulated in many ways. Oberndorf, in his history of psychoanalysis in the United States, relates how in the 1920s every time a new paper of Freud's appeared the members would be traumatized, unsure of what the master meant and how his new ideas were to be handled. The result has been either indiscriminate idealization or indiscriminate condemnation. For example, to question Freud in many institutes the student runs the risk of being expelled. In others institutes (such as the culturalist groups of the American Academy) to agree with Freud is tantamount to expulsion from the group. The result, not unexpected, is an atmosphere of intimidation in all psychoanalytic groups and a wholesale misrepresentation of what psychoanalytic theory is all about. The myth that there are different "schools" of psychoanalysis is perhaps the most blatant example of such misrepresentation.

In order to gain a secure foothold, it is wisest to pass in review how Freud's thought actually did develop and what happened to it before and after his death (Fine, 1990).

It was not, however, inevitable that the opposition to Freud should have taken the extreme turn it did; this can be ascribed to the hate culture that dominated Western civilization at the time (and still does). Jones gives some trenchant examples. Ziehen, a German psychiatrist, announced that everything Freud wrote was simply nonsense. In 1910 Collins, a New York neurologist, objected to a paper by Putnam, a leading American neurologist who was in full sympathy with Freud, that Putnam's paper was made up of "pornographic stories about pure virgins." And so on. Jones is quite correct when he says, "I would issue a formal warning against believing everything that may appear in print about Freud, even if it purports to be a memory of Freud's conversation, since much of it is so untrue as to convey a quite mistaken impression of his personality" (*Life*, vol. 2, p. 128). And of his theories, we should add.

Today, although knowledge of Freud is much more widespread, Jones's admonition is still relevant. The recent "revisionist" literature, denying that there was any real opposition to Freud (Sulloway, Decker, etc.), is grossly misinformed (Fine, *The Anti-Freudian Crusade*, 1985, 1986).

The first psychoanalytic system based on psychosexual development, transference-resistance, and the unconscious formed the conceptual basis for a new psychology, which Freud and his students then proceeded to develop. There were other areas of psychology that could be explored in different ways: learning skills, the cognitive functions, development, intelligence, and the like. But the Freudian system carried one closer to the heart of the human experience.

Freud's ideas caught on slowly. At the first international conference, at Weimar in 1911, fifty-five people attended, including some visitors (Jones, p. 85). In contrast, it may be mentioned that the total membership of the International Psychoanalytic Association, as reported at the latest congress, is about seven thousand, with an estimated five hundred new members every year. There are also thousands of analysts who are not members of the International. Thus from small beginnings a truly international movement has grown.

Yet despite all growth, the universities have, almost without expectation, refused to recognize the existence of psychoanalysis as a serious body of work, with an enormous literature that has to be studied carefully, like any other body of literature. The program of the Berlin Institute, described above, could easily at any time have become the basis for a doctorate in psychoanalysis or psychoanalytic psychology, but such a possibility has always been rejected by the academic community. Recently a bequest of $1 million to set up a chair of psychoanalytic anthropology was turned down by a major university because "psychoanalysis is not a science" (personal communication). As Freud often reminded us, it would be a serious mistake to underestimate the resistances to psychoanalysis.

Little of this analysis could be presented in a dispassionate way to an audience of college students; hence the universities continue their traditional resistance, relegating psychoanalysis to an "alternative form of psychotherapy" or classifying it as a system that has a "general speculative background that can only be called romantic and fantastic in the extreme, made to serve an astonishingly successful therapeutic method" (Randall, 1976 [first edition 1926], p. 516).

One of the theses of this chapter is that Division 39 should move toward independent departments of psychoanalysis in the universities, teaching much the same material that institutes now teach but without all the political involvements in institutes. Thus the resistance of the universities must be fully explored.

To clarify the basis on which psychoanalysis can be taught (as it is now being taught, but outside the universities) we can go back to Freud again, since whether one agrees with him or not, he remains the towering figure in this field, and his views cannot be ignored.

The first psychoanalytic system, while it was viewed almost exclusively as psychotherapy, was really a system of psychology. If we consider the primitive state of psychology in 1900, Freud's approach represents a major step forward.

Why was it not adopted more generally? Largely because of the disturbed world situation. Ours, as I have tried to show elsewhere, is a hate culture, in which the most common feeling people express toward their fellow human beings is one of hostility, or in the extreme (and it has been extreme for millions) hatred. Psychoanalysis is essentially a philosophy of love, as Freud insisted many times. The first system, that of the id, in fact, provided a fairly reasonable and simple philosophy of normality and neurosis. Normality involves going through the various psychosexual stages, culminating in a union of tender and sexual feelings toward a person of the opposite sex, which we call love. Neurosis is due to a fixation or regression to one of the earlier stages of development. Psychotherapy involves helping individuals move from their fixation of an earlier state to a stage of genital love. Instinctual desires, of which they are many, have to be sublimated. Transference and resistance interfere with the therapeutic process, but they are also universal human characteristics. Such was the fairly simple philosophy of psychoanalysis up to World War I. That it requires a restatement now is a sign of the almost limitless confusions into which psychoanalysis has been thrown.

It is clear here that the material that Freud uncovered could easily have become the basis for a doctorate in a university. The curriculum of the Berlin institute merely carried out Freud's essential ideas; it could easily have been converted into an academic Ph.D. program and center for further research.

After World War I Freud moved on to elaborate his ideas. In 1923 the concept of the superego heralded the beginning of ego psychology, thus a more complete psychology, which, after Hartmann, included both the conflictual and nonconflictual areas of the personality. The book on group behavior (1921) was a magnificent beginning, embodying still more profound insights. His daughter Anna's work on *The Ego and the Mechanisms of Defense* (1936) consolidated much information about the defensive process, and when reexamined fifty years later, still requires almost no alteration (Sandler, 1983). Although Freud spoke of the self in a commonsense way (Fine, 1986), he did not elaborate on the concept; that remained for others (though Kohut's elaboration is seriously inadequate). Identity, the contribution of Erik Erikson (1950), is also a post-Freudian development.

Paradoxically, in spite of his emphasis on childhood, even maintaining that the entire personality was fixed in the first five years of life, Freud paid little attention to the mother-child relationship. That is a field that has developed enormously since about 1949 (cf. Bowlby, 1981), though the central notions of separation anxiety and object loss both came from Freud.

At this point we have to consider the other side of psychoanalytic history — the splitting into various "schools," the rigidity, the cries of heresy reminiscent of the Inquisition (though not as violent, thank God).

If one examines the alternative schools more closely, several pertinent facts stand out. First of all, they one and all begin with a misinterpretation of Freud; thus he is supposed to have said that everything was sexual, or that therapeutic progress could only come from biochemistry, etc. This misinterpretation began with Jung, whose envy and hatred of Freud were only too obvious, even leading him to an ill-concealed flirtation with the Nazis in the 1930s. The history of psychoanalysis is full of fratricide and growth. Jung had some good ideas, but the harm that he did to the movement was immense. Adler, though he also misunderstood Freud, was a milder individual who simply wished to go his own way. His defects are largely those of superficiality, which ignores the depths of psychological misery. In part this was due to his Marxist approach, in which he thought that the problems caused by the economic system were much greater than those created intrapsychically, as most Marxists believed before World War I, and still believe today. (They have yet to explain the wholesale violence, almost unprecedented in history, released by so many of the Marxist revolutions of the twentieth century.)

Jung and Adler were Freud's immediate associates. If they could not really understand what Freud was talking about, it is not surprising that others could fail as well. Jones's admonition to be wary of *any* statement made about Freud is still pertinent; consider, for example, the brief storm caused by the absurd claims made by Masson in his book *The Assault on Truth*, which nevertheless gained him a one-day notoriety.

Nonanalysts have rarely, if ever, been able to grasp the psychoanalytic approach. As Jones (1957) pointed out, when historians, educators, and others do acquire training in analysis, they usually prefer to give up their original field and become analysts. Hence the application of analysis to the special areas in which they operate suffers.

But why all the splits within psychoanalysis? Since we are approaching a new state in psychoanalytic history, the divisions should not be met with denial, but with an attempt at understanding.

The culturalist group (who are now frequently referred to as object-relations theorists) began to come forward in the 1920s. Their major thesis is that neurosis is culturally determined. An examination of the historical record shows that before World War II there was no disagreement on this score. Roheim (1932), for example, said that each culture has its special neurosis. Fenichel, in his treatise on *The Psychoanalytic Theory of Neurosis* (1945), discusses specifically the culturalist claims. He writes: "Our comments make it plain that the insight into the formative power of social forces upon individual minds does not require any change in Freud's concepts of instincts" (p. 588).

It was only after the war that the lines hardened between the culturalists and the "pure" Freudians. Culturalists would not hear of instincts; Freudians would not hear of social forces. At the same time the American Psychoanalytic Association was undergoing a radical reorganization (Fine, 1990), with approved institutes, limitation to the medical profession (with the exception of occasional "waivers"), a more standard curriculum, and the like. The result was the longest and largest split in the history of psychoanalysis, with the formation of the American Academy of Psychoanalysis in 1956.

Many causes could be adduced for this split, the foremost undoubtedly being personal rivalry. But in terms of the system it has to be attributed to the split into institutes, with only certain persons permitted to do training analyses, with a certain doctrine or set of doctrines that had to be adhered to, on pain of expulsion from the institute.

Anyone who is familiar with the inner workings of an institute will grasp how this worked, and still works today. Since the institute controls training and doctrine, disagreement almost immediately leads to expulsion. While the analytic institute has no legal standing as such, expulsion is seriously feared by many analysts (witness the lawsuit). It affects their affiliations, their teaching positions, and ultimately even their practices, since students will not go to a "dissident" and the institute referral system will not refer. Kernberg's recent critique of the institute system, referred to before, is very much to the point.

Even though analysts are fully familiar with the harmful effects of repression, they ignore the effects of repression within their own societies. Somehow the British have managed to hold together the adherents of Anna Freud and Melanie Klein in spite of their wide divergences; we can certainly learn from them (Rayner, 1986).

Another factor that has played a great role is simply narcissism. Everybody wants to do something new, to be important, to be a leader. In Italian universities the chief professor in any department had absolute power; he was known as *il barone*. Analysts too like to be barons.

Among the many innovations that came out of the Berlin institute, two in particular need further discussion. One is the requirement of personal analysis; the other is the system of institute control. Personal analysis is surely the sine qua non of competent analysts, yet it is carried out, as Anna Freud once pointed out, in violation of many of the rules that govern ordinary analysis: social contacts persist, the analyst has too much power over the analysand, excessive hostility toward the analyst has serious consequences for the student, rumors about the training analyst's private life are rife, etc. Some institutes want the personal analysis to be finished before the student is permitted to take courses; but for economic and personal reasons this is rarely feasible.

Since we know now that the entire population is in need of analytic help, it would make more sense to have students go into analysis, say at the end of their junior year in college (as many of them actually do). From this group of students who have had some analysis, a better idea can be obtained about who will or will not make a competent analyst. That is, the evaluation of the success or failure of the personal analysis should be removed entirely from the training society. There are too many students, as Knight once pointed out (1953), who simply sit through an analysis, read only what is required, and are in a rush to get into a lucrative practice.

As for institute control of training, that too has led to many abuses. In a recent article in the magazine *New York* Dimitia Schwartz (1986), a journalist, describes the deep underlying resentments present in the New York Psychoanalytic Society, where the directors appoint the faculty and the faculty appoints the directors; newcomers have little chance to get ahead.

Apart from the rifts within institutes, certain points of view from time to time become prominent, attract many adherents, then virtually disappear. This can be ascribed to the difficulties in understanding psychoanalysis. Freud himself changed his mind in many ways throughout his career, yet usually neglected to say so when he did. The result is that it is hard today to understand Freud, especially in the milieu from which he came, and even harder to understand all the other charismatic figures who appear from time to time on the psychoanalytic stage.

What is needed in this situation is primarily education. Yet psychoanalytic education is hard to come by. Those who attend a given institute have to accept what is taught, even if it is blatantly wrong. The result is that analysts are all too often very poorly informed about their own field. As an example one can take the infiltration of Melanie Klein's ideas into more traditional analysis. At first spurned because of the outer nature of her doctrines, analysts gradually came to see that she had a good point about the mental life of the infant in the first year of life. Yet Kleinians also insisted on accepting all of her doctrines, including such absurdities as the death instinct.

What can Division 39 do in this situation? Here a new philosophy of education and training can come into play. The great majority in the division went through traditional programs in psychology, then special programs in psychoanalysis. Since education is one of the prime needs in our field, the division should undertake this task.

Academic psychology, as currently taught, and psychoanalysis are still poles apart. This situation can be recognized and utilized for constructive purposes. What is needed are departments of psychoanalytic psychology, attached to yet in a real sense fully independent of the main psychology departments. These departments will be based on what we know about psychoanalytic psychology today. No one will be left out, but likewise no one will be accepted uncritically, including Freud.

The students accepted for this department will already have had substantial analytic experience in their undergraduate years and will be able to demonstrate a maturity of character, stability of relationships, and a degree of happiness beyond that ordinarily expected. With such students considerable progress can be made.

The department will have the right to issue Ph.D.'s. The thesis will not be an experimental study, almost always a waste of effort, but a careful case study. There is still too little case material in the literature. Our science is based primarily on our case material. It is essential to put this together in teachable form, and to teach it.

Research will continue as it has gone on in psychoanalysis from Freud's day on. This research can extend to many other fields; it is still true that all sciences that deal with human beings touch upon psychoanalysis at some point, some very closely, some at a distance. Again experimentation may be useful at times, a waste of effort at other times.

Following Freud's lead, the research efforts can be extended to all the social sciences, which likewise do little more than dissipate valuable talent. The social sciences broke away from philosophy at the end of the nineteenth century; this was a step forward because the philosophy in existence then was little more than a sterile repetition of irrelevant formulas, far from human concerns. Today we do have an analytic philosophy, which is vitally close to human concerns, and proper use should be made of it.

Psychoanalytic theory can be combined with knowledge from all other sources to create a complete science of humankind. Actually this is what has happened; it remains only to give it more formal recognition.

The sophisticated reader will have noticed that what I am proposing here, in the form of a new university curriculum, was suggested by

Freud years ago ("The Question of Lay Analysis," SE, XX, p. 252).
His remarkable prescience in this area can only be admired. In the
same book (1926) he wrote:

> If it is impossible to prevent the lay analysts from pursuing
> their activities and if the public does not support the campaign
> against them, would it not be more expedient to recognize the
> fact of their existence by offering them opportunities for train-
> ing?...And, if they were offered as an inducement to the possi-
> bility of receiving the approval of the medical profession and of
> being invited to cooperate, might they not have some interest in
> raising their own ethical and intellectual level? (SE, XX, p. 258)

Again, the question must be raised: What, after all, is psychoanalytic theory? Students ordinarily study a variety of texts, in accordance with the orientation of their institute, but fail to see the whole
picture. Division 39 should therefore also undertake the preparation
of a series of texts that will present the essence of psychoanalytic
psychology in an up-to-date and meaningful way.

Finally, two further points can be made. I believe that it was
Max Planck, who was in his day bitterly attacked for his seemingly
paradoxical quantum theory, who said that new ideas never win out
directly; they win out only when the old guard dies out. Similarly in
psychology and psychoanalysis. Enough of the old guard has disappeared to allow psychoanalysis to exist in the American Psychological
Association, an eventuality that would have been unthinkable thirty
years ago (it was actually proposed in 1960 and refused on the usual
grounds that "psychoanalysis is unscientific"). The proposal to have
an independent department of psychoanalytic psychology established
in all universities will of course be rejected by the present generation,
just as the idea of a division of psychoanalysis was rejected when
it was first suggested around 1960. It prevailed only because enough
psychologists were trained in psychoanalysis to see its value. In the
same way only when more psychologists are trained in all aspects
of psychoanalysis, the need for independent departments of psychoanalytic psychology in the universities will be seen as a worthwhile
idea and put into effect. Perhaps in one generation, perhaps two. But
time is on our side.

Although here I speak with no authority, this also suggests a fruitful
way in which to make the lawsuit constructive. Let the medical analysts and the psychological analysts join together to set up and finance
these independent departments. For a while the universities will ob-

ject strenuously. As more people in the social sciences are properly trained in scientific methodology, based on direct study of the human being, rather than the large-scale waste of motion that results from the present experimental approach, such proposals will occur more often and, we hope, be accepted.

The mental health professions have been built up in an arbitrary, ad hoc manner, even though they show so many similarities (cf. Henry, *The Fifth Profession*, 1971). As a result the training programs in psychiatry, psychology, and social work are all seriously inadequate. As understanding of the basic truths of psychoanalysis penetrates more and more (cf. Bellah et al., *The Therapeutic Revolution*), the structures of the existing degree programs will necessarily change to conform more closely to human realities. When that happens, we will truly have one mental health profession that can move humankind ahead. A dream perhaps, but no one knows better than psychoanalysts how vitally important dreams are in human existence.

13

Implications for the Social Order: The Age of Awareness

*W*HILE PSYCHOANALYSTS FOR THE MOST PART have stuck to their traditional technical problems, many others have seen the potential implications of the analytic ideal for the social order.

In a recent paper Joseph Montville tries to apply the analytic ideal to the political sphere. He is a diplomat with the U.S. Department of State. He writes (1989):

> Fine (1977), expanding on Freud's dictum that a normal person is one who can work and love, describes an analytic ideal.... This analytic ideal can be described as the goal of a full psychoanalysis. But it is also a goal of a global society whose members, in the nuclear age, must strive to such a level of balance and integration which would finally inhibit the surges toward group violence and war making which have characterized human history.

Montville quotes Freud to the same general effect, although this aspect of Freud has often been overlooked by many of his followers. In *The Question of Lay Analysis* in 1926 Freud wrote:

> As a depth psychology, a theory of the mental unconscious, [psychoanalysis]...can become indispensable to all the sciences which are concerned with the evolution of human civilization and the major institutions such as art, religion, and the social

302

order. It has already, in my opinion, afforded those sciences remarkable considerable help in solving their problems. But these are only small contributions compared with what might be achieved if historians of civilization, psychologists of religion, philologists and so on would agree themselves to handle the new instrument of research which is at their service.

Later Montville says:

What I call the greening of diplomacy concerns how I discovered a theoretical explanation in psychoanalytic literature for political phenomena I had encountered as a reporting officer at American embassies and consulates in the Middle East and North Africa, and as a political analyst in Washington. In fact, the theory I discuss is what has made sense to me in light of practical experience. I think it is safe to say that the views which follow have been reality tested. A number of these ideas are receiving respectful attention in the Department of State and in the intelligence community.

He goes on to make the following comments: Volkan and Mack together and separately have elucidated the process by which the individual in adolescence acquires consciousness of membership in a broader, politically self-conscious identity group. As Mack has written in a richly informative essay, the historical experience of common hurts or wounds, usually inflicted by another group, appears to be of central importance in creating a sense of national identity for a people. Victimization destroys the defensive structure. It exposes the victim (or victim group) to unrelieved conscious anxiety about real threats to its existence. This state of anxiety is extremely difficult to endure, and it produces a toleration of and need for constant defensive action — whether cynicism, militancy, violence, or even terrorism — to assure survival in what is seen as a relentlessly hostile environment. Many examples of victimization of groups and the attendant fears are given.

Montville offer the proposition that the scientific study of human behavior — that is, psychology — suggests that tribes and nations can ease or resolve long-enduring political conflicts, characterized by narcissistic rage and victimhood, by working to reaffirm that innate value of their adversaries through acts of respect, vigorous self-analysis, self-criticism, and contrition. There are some examples in the last forty years where victims and oppressors were able to establish relationships based on the mourning process. The actual initiatives in accepting responsibility and asking forgiveness were not necessarily taken by high-level leaders, but rather by persons who had or came to have the confidence and respect of their leaders.

He goes on to make a plea for the conscious renunciation of hostility and aggression. In one case Canon Baker (1981) wrote a paper on Ireland and Northern Ireland. He writes:

> Politicians in England tend to talk as though we had nothing to do with the situation until we were brought in to sort out feuding Northern Irelanders.... Because our methods were largely compounded by injustice, atrocities and callous neglect, we rendered the enterprise ultimately hopeless. It had no moral foundations and so, in the end, we were inevitably forced to abandon it.

And finally he says:

> If there is a "greening of diplomacy" it means that strategies of conflict intervention and resolution are being developed and discussed by responsible diplomatic officials and unofficial but enlightened citizens in many countries of the world. Sometimes unofficial diplomatic — or peace-making — intervention... seems appropriate. But at key points, national and international authorities have to take responsibility for the formal protection of the basic right to life and developmental potential of all human beings on the face of the earth.
>
> There is no excuse for not going forward with this vision. Thanks to psychoanalysis we now know too much about the dark side of humankind to avoid actively confronting it and defending against it. This knowledge must become part of the world's conventional wisdom. Psychoanalysts and psychologists must work vigorously to teach this knowledge widely. (p. 317)

A skeptic might say that Montville's plea to turn the other cheek has been tried before and found wanting; the persons who preached it most vigorously often turned out to be more savage than wild beasts, as Pfister once put it. But still Montville's plea is a humane and farsighted one. If followed wisely, it could certainly lead to an amelioration of humankind's lot on earth.

Montville's paper is in line with the thinking of many forward-looking people who try to apply the findings of depth psychology to the terrible problems that we face. In this sense our times can be called the *age of awareness*, much more so than previous ages when evil was ascribed to the devil or inner demons. Evil and hostility, though to some extent inherent in the human being, still result primarily from poor upbringing (Brenner, 1972) and are correctable through better education and psychotherapy.

In this sense psychotherapy is particularly significant as the psychoanalytic contribution to a better world. If they make an effort to do so, human beings can get over their powerful hatreds of other people. It is by no stretch of the imagination an easy task; the numerous splits and arguments among psychoanalysts are proof of that. The arguments presented in previous chapters are clear evidence that some psychotherapy is essential for almost all humankind. While such a universal program may seem like an impossible task, it is still worth trying.

One plea can be made to all psychotherapists, which is within their reach: Stop trying to undermine Freud and try to learn what he really had to offer. The division into different "schools of psychoanalysis," as we have seen before, is merely a narcissistic reaffirmation of the individuals who propose them, not a serious effort to discover new facts or new points of view. It is perhaps unfortunate that Freud did as much as he did, but that he did so is a fact.

In order to produce a real change in the state of the world, what is needed most at this juncture and what is most readily available is to teach psychoanalytic psychology correctly. This would embrace not only psychology but also all the social sciences. History, for example, has been badly mauled by the historians, who have generally played it safe by avoiding all embarrassing but crucial questions. According to our analytic theories, based on the evidence presented to us by chroniclers, the mass of humankind has generally fallen more into the borderline range than anything else; the notion of "normality" has to be seriously reevaluated, and its relevance for all the wars, massacres, and murders that make up the history of the world brought to light.

As various books cited in the text show, many enlightened people are well aware of how disturbed the average human being is, but do not quite know what to do about it. Where Freud lived in an age of discovery, in which many new facts had to be discovered or uncovered, we are living in an age of awareness.

In this age of awareness, for the first time we see how sick humankind is and always has been. As a result we can formulate a rational approach, based upon adequate scientific evidence, by which a new creative kind of living can be substituted for the old neurotic ways in which humankind has always been immersed.

The contrary position is that what is new in our age is the anxiety, not the awareness. It is true enough that each new day brings more evidence of the enormous burden of anxiety that modern human beings carry with them. Rennie and his co-workers (1962) have estimated that some 80 percent of the ordinary New Yorkers they studied were disturbed, a considerable proportion seriously incapacitated. Hendin, Haylin, and Carr, in a routine investigation of average nurses (the purpose was methodological, not substantive), discovered that they all had problems, some quite severe. They could only call their sample a "nonpatient" population, to get away from the meaningless cliché of "normal." Leighton has documented the ills that befall Americans, Canadians, and Africans. In a fascinating compilation, Ari Kiev has brought together many varieties of counterphobic magic employed by contemporary "primitive" societies to counteract the ubiquitous fears of their peoples. While the psychiatric situation in the Soviet Union is obscured by the political need to appear happy and the Pavlovian form of magic, what goes on there appears to be reasonably similar to what goes on in our own country (see Winn's recent collection of papers).

If we search for the promised land of Nirvana in the past, the results are just as devastating. As the year A.D. 1000 approached, a large percentage of the population of Europe was convinced that the world was coming to an end. The great French historian Jules Michelet described the spiritual atmosphere of the Middle Ages as one of despair. The witchcraft persecution that finally led people to substitute physicians for clergy as "healers" of the mentally ill sounds far more pathological than the usual delusions of a hospitalized schizophrenic in our own day. Consider, for example, how an attractive woman was to defend herself against the charge of kissing the devil's behind on a lonely street corner while looking the other way. In such proceedings the judges (members of the clergy) were considered to be "sane," while the accused was "possessed," and usually doomed whatever she did.

And lest it be thought that merely turning the clock back a hundred years would lead us to an era of sanity, we need only be reminded that that was the period that gave birth to Freud. Historians have all too naively assumed that the average person in times past was sane; there is no objective evidence to corroborate this assumption, and a wealth of data to contradict it.

Nor have anthropologists fared any better with the obscure preliterate (to avoid the insidious comparison of "primitive") societies that they have studied. The ubiquity of magic covers up feelings of overwhelming fear, as Charles Odier has shown in his classic work.

Cannon has even postulated a physiological mechanism to account for the phenomenon of "voodoo death," or literally dying of fright, occasionally reported by field-workers. It is true that on rare occasions some societies have been found that exhibit some reasonable degree of mental health, but they are so few and far between that anthropologists shudder when they have to discuss the problem seriously. Fortunately they have developed a mystique of scientific detachment that allows them to sidestep the entire question.

The list of sociological, historical, and anthropological data could be extended indefinitely. Enough has been presented to document the thesis that with isolated exceptions human beings are and always have been frightened, unhappy, neurotic creatures who at best have controlled their anxieties by an elaborate, magical, ritualistic mumbo-jumbo. And the number of millions who have been sacrificed to prove that one form of magic is superior to another staggers the imagination.

It is this view of the human condition that must be used as a backdrop to place psychotherapy in proper perspective. That very few people are receiving psychotherapy need be of little concern; penicillin is a powerful drug even though there are millions who do not have access to it. Correctly seen, *psychotherapy is the first scientific attempt to make people happy.*

This thesis must be elaborated in two directions. First of all, scientific psychotherapy must be compared with nonscientific. And second, psychotherapy must be related to the social structure.

Psychotherapy, like medicine, is as old as humankind. But it has never before been based on an adequate knowledge of the exact sciences. In fact, the statement is often made that before the advent of modern science, medicine was more likely to do harm than good, and the same is true for psychotherapy.

The science that psychotherapy is based on is modern psychology, particularly psychoanalysis and its development (rather than deviations, a misleading concept). As "true" scientists, we like to repeat with Newton that we are like children playing with pebbles on the beach, with a vast unknown universe lying before us. Yet in all justice we must also aver that the understanding of the human being acquired since 1900 is enormous. It is by no means final. Quite the contrary; it continues to grow and change at a rapid rate. But that does not alter the fact that there is now for the first time a solid and substantial body of information that illuminates the psychotherapeutic enterprise.

There can be no doubt that prescientific psychotherapy, like prescientific medicine, at times obtained results. But it is hard enough, as many keep reminding us, to clarify the results that we get today. What happened in other eras can only be conjectured.

The relationship between psychotherapy and the social structure is a complex one. Freud's thesis in *Civilization and Its Discontents* — that culture necessarily leads to neurosis — is a one-sided oversimplification. Actually, in the same work, Freud also said that while whole civilizations could be and have become neurotic, psychoanalysis is in a position to provide the corrective measures for this condition. Fromm in his book *The Sane Society* has tried to elaborate on some of the implications of Freud's work.

In order to depict in sufficient detail the connections between psychotherapy and society, it is necessary to have clearly in mind the kind of ideal that modern psychology can now propose. This ideal differs in a number of significant respects from the "normal adjustment" that the unanalyzed individual at best achieves.

These differences between the analytic ideal and the social ideal can serve as a measure of the maturity or mental health of any given society. Inasmuch as it is the goal of psychotherapy to help individuals, so far as possible, remold themselves in the light of the analytic ideal, this process thereby serves to transform society. *In the larger scheme of things, societal therapy is the ultimate goal of the psychotherapist.*

The Analytic Ideal and the Social Order

It is time to spell out those details of the analytic ideal that are particularly pertinent to the social order. As this is done, the real agreements and disagreements in the field can fruitfully be brought to the fore.

(1) *The pursuit of pleasure is a positive good.* Human beings are biological organisms, with built-in physiological mechanisms that lead to pleasure or pain.

It is surprising how many religions and philosophies have contradicted this simple principle. The Ten Commandments say nothing about the pursuit of pleasure. Buddhism begins with the proposition that all life involves suffering; that it also involves pleasure is ignored.

Specialists in ethics have generally held a hedonistic philosophy in poor repute. Insofar as there is any valid argument against the hedonistic position, it is that excesses of pleasure will inevitably lead to suffering. This is undoubtedly correct. But it does not alter the fact that with proper foresight the judicious pursuit of pleasure leads to a happy life, while the pursuit of suffering leads to an unhappy one.

The principle involved here is a simple generalization of a common psychotherapeutic procedure. People in our society tend to suffer far too much. Frequently, as a reaction, they indulge in pleasure bouts — drinking, sex, drugs — only to wake up with a hangover after it is all over. Apart from the unconscious meaning of the outlet chosen, the trouble lies with lack of foresight, not with the pleasure as such. In psychotherapy the goal is to help persons acquire more control over their capacity to secure pleasure. Sometimes, because of the weak ego of the patient, it is necessary to forbid certain types of pleasure temporarily, not because they are bad but because the patient cannot handle them. As the ego becomes stronger, the taboo is lifted. Whatever the technical therapeutic means are, the ultimate goal is to allow individuals to enjoy life more.

(1) *Pleasure is age-specific.* A great deal is now known about the developmental process, both physiologically and psychologically. One age's doing is another age's undoing. Fixation and regression could be viewed as processes that deny the age-specific character of pleasure. Life should be looked upon as a journey from one form of pleasure to another; the one who lingers too long becomes neurotic. Generally speaking, the overaccentuation of some form of pleasure that is not suitable to the chronological state of the individual has its roots in some interpersonal disturbance.

Furthermore, the refusal of any age-specific pleasure has lasting effects on the further history of the person. Oral deprivation may lead to death (marasmus). When the infant remains alive, it frequently suffers from a feeling of severe deprivation that remains for the rest of the person's life.

This developmental interconnectedness, in which the outcome at any one state depends very heavily on what happened earlier, makes it extraordinarily difficult to generalize about normal behavior at any point in the person's life. It also provides an important theoretical foundation for a basic thesis of this chapter that psychotherapy is an essential feature of the human enterprise.

(2) *Sexual gratification should be encouraged.* Of the numerous pleasures available to human beings, none has led to more bizarre repressive measures and more needless controversy than sex. It is still necessary for the psychotherapist to reaffirm that sexual pleasure is one of the most important sources of happiness available to the human being.

Although sex, like any other id gratification, is now seen as a complex result of ego factors rather than a simple instinctual release, this does not alter the proposition that, other things being equal, sexual pleasure is a life-affirmative value. In view of the tendency of many recent writers to lump sexuality with addiction, alcoholism, and other acting-out disorders, it is desirable to be as specific as possible about our position in this respect.

We have long taken it for granted that masturbation in childhood and sexual intercourse in adolescence are perfectly normal activities. They are harmful only when pursued to excess, or when they have undesirable consequences.

Sexual intercourse in adolescence, however, while privately encouraged by the great majority of psychotherapists, meets with formidable social obstacles. Restrictive laws, pregnancy, abortion, and venereal disease are among the many problems that must be handled. Here the analytic ideal is squarely at odds with the social. It appears that in spite of all the difficulties, the analytic ideal is gradually winning out.

While it is winning out behaviorally, however, it has by no means won out psychologically. Time and again we see adolescents and young adults who are consumed with guilt, both conscious and unconscious, about their sexual activities. For the fullest enjoyment of sexuality this guilt must be overcome. That can be done only psychotherapeutically.

For large groups in society, sexual pleasure in marriage has become a socially sanctioned ideal. Numerous books are freely available that give detailed instruction on how to secure such pleasure. Yet for all that it must be remembered that there are large classes in society, for example, the devoutly religious, who are still as antisexual as their ancestors were five hundred years ago. There is still a long way to go before society fully accepts sexual gratification even in marriage.

When it comes to extramarital intercourse, we find opinions rather sharply divided. But a dispassionate evaluation of human experience should convince us that for most men monogamy is neither an attainable nor a desirable ideal.

No doubt there are wide individual differences here. Some people seem to be content with a single relationship, either because it is inherently so satisfying or because they find so much happiness in other activities. For many others this is by no means the case.

It is of course true that many patients arrive at the analyst's office burdened by the guilt of an extramarital affair. Often this guilt is conscious. Yet it is equally true that many others arrive burdened by the dead weight of marital fidelity. Usually guilt here is unconscious. Yet the pattern of marital fidelity is as destructive to one kind of person as that of marital infidelity is to another.

Anthropologists have shown that ours is among the most restrictive of all societies with regard to extramarital sexuality. Of the various sexual taboos this restriction has probably been affected least by the progress of psychotherapy. There is no theoretical or clinical evidence that the restriction should be maintained with all possible force. Nor it is to be supposed that the spread of extramarital intercourse would materially affect happiness in marriage. What we are witnessing today is a transformation of all values, including those pertaining to marriage. It can only be said that the attempt to make marriage satisfy all the emotional and sexual needs of both partners fails more often than it succeeds.

(3) *Human beings should release their positive emotions.* Human beings are feeling animals. In order to be happy, they must experience a wide range of positive emotions, such as joy, excitement, love, enthusiasm, and the like. The acceptance of pleasure and sexuality lays an adequate basis for these emotions; their denial blocks them.

There is little room for argument here, except that the image of a feeling person is contrary to the social ideal of our society and many others. Here again, psychotherapy steps in to change the social structure.

(4) *Love should predominate in human relationships.* The development of human relationships proceeds from the helpless dependency of the infant to the full-bodied love of the mature individual.

Because of the numerous neurotic meanings attached to the word "love," numerous misunderstandings arise here. I have elsewhere suggested that love goes through five stages: attachment, admiration, physical (sexual) enjoyment, total enjoyment, devotion. For the adult the most appropriate definition of love is mutual enjoyment.

Such a definition conflicts with the social ideal and has numerous corollaries that conflict with it as well. Primarily, psychological insight is sharply contradictory to the notion that it is possible to love one person and one person alone for an entire lifetime. Love should be viewed as a force within the individual, an active power rather than a passive reaction. To "love" is healthy; to "fall in love" is neurotic. If this were recognized, the whole fabric of interpersonal relations would undergo an extraordinary transformation.

(5) *Hatred and other negative emotions are harmful to the human spirit.* Hatred, resentment, envy, jealousy, and other negative emotions are mainly reactions to frustration, not instinctual drives in the same sense as sexuality. The goal of psychotherapy is to eradicate these emotions, or at least to reduce them to a minimum. While it is true that our efforts in this respect are often far from successful, in a

good percentage of cases the patients do manage to free themselves to lead more constructive lives.

At this point a theoretical issue of considerable importance arises. If hatred is an instinctual reaction, it can be reduced or neutralized, but not eliminated. The task of the psychotherapist then is to help patients release their hostilities.

Many therapists do work within such a framework. The net result is that they produce hostile people, which is both socially and individually undesirable. If, however, hatred is the result of frustrations, a consistent lessening of these frustrations will lessen the hatred. Since hatred and its concomitant violence are central to all social problems, this issue becomes a vital aspect of the interaction between psychotherapy and society.

(6) *The individual should have a meaningful role in the family.* The nuclear family, derived from the biological fact that it takes a man and a woman to produce a child, is a universal phenomenon. Perhaps for that reason a meaningful role in the family becomes a psychological desideratum.

While the family itself is as old as history, its contribution to human happiness has only recently been recognized. Many revolutionary movements, such as Christianity, communism, and Nazism, at some point deliberately tried to destroy the traditional family structure. Even psychoanalysis in the early days emphasized the harm that family conflicts did to the child, particularly those surrounding sexual repression. It took a long time to redress the balance.

Every person in the family derives benefit from the particular role that he or she plays in it. Two dangers arise here, which psychotherapy routinely handles. One is the unstable family, where the normal roles are disrupted for one reason or another. The other is the excessively stable family, where there is no real expression of feeling or spontaneity. More recent research has shown that these families operate on the basis of scapegoating one member. Typical are the parents who "sacrifice" themselves for the children, who then feel terribly guilty because of the awful burden placed upon them.

(7) *The individual should have some sense of identity in the larger society.* Once a sense of identity in the family is achieved, it should be extended to the larger society. Human beings must have some sense of community. Perhaps the major polarity that people in our society face is that between the individualist and the organization man. Each has advantages, each disadvantages. Psychologically, what seems to count more than anything else is consistency in the choice of role.

(8) *Human beings should be engaged in some satisfying form of*

work. Traditionally work has been regarded as a necessary evil. The English "gentleman" (a gentle man — one who is not cruel), the Spanish "caballero" (man on horse), the French "seigneur" (lord), the German "Herr" (master) were all social ideals, still operative, that were opposed to work. Their image has been assimilated by the average person who seeks to retire at an early age.

In an otherwise worthless book, La Piere has coined the term "the Freudian Ethic" for the philosophy of contemporary psychotherapy. It is contrasted with Max Weber's classic formulation of the Protestant ethic.

The Freudian ethic, like the Protestant, sees work as a positive good. Work is a way in which human beings use their abilities and relate constructively to others.

Modern psychology has stressed the active character of human nature, as opposed to the earlier image of a *tabula rasa* on which anything can be written. Work gratifies this need for activity.

Many sociologists, following Marx, have maintained that people today are alienated from their work. While this is often true, there is little reason to believe that it is much more typical of people today than of people in previous ages. It is a sociological parallel to the psychological myth that ours is the age of anxiety.

It could rather be maintained that for the first time human beings have sufficient command over the forces of nature to choose the areas in which they will exert their greatest efforts. Thus it becomes the task of a well-ordered society to regulate the work activities of its members in a manner that will optimize mental health. It is at this point that the insights of psychotherapy can make a meaningful contribution.

(9) *Some form of creative activity is desirable for everybody.* Here it is first necessary to distinguish between inner and outer creativity. Inner creativity is a novel experience for the individual who experiences it, although it may be routine hat to everybody else. Most typically, it is seen in the growth of a normal child, which proceeds by a series of creative experiences.

Outer creativity is an achievement that offers something new to the outside world. Psychotherapy indicates that everybody has the capacity for inner creativity; the capacity for outer creativity is relatively limited. In this discussion we are interested mainly in the inner form.

The psychological need for creativity arises essentially from the unmanageability of the id. There are simply too many instinctual impulses; many simply cannot be expressed in a socially acceptable manner. A creative outlet provides the most desirable vehicle for channeling these impulses.

(10) *Psychotherapy is a lifetime process.* In one form or another psychotherapy should be continued throughout the person's life. The reason for this is that psychotherapy provides a growing self-awareness, and this growth process need never stop. At each new stage in life new problems arise, new conflicts emerge, new decisions about life have to be made. In all these situations self-understanding is the most important tool at the individual's disposal.

By psychotherapy here we do not mean only the formal face-to-face process. Self-analysis, group contacts, meaningful individual relationships with mature people — these are all part of the psychotherapeutic undertaking. From time to time, however, a return to some form of brief formal psychotherapy is indicated for many people.

Ideally the proposals made by Freud in his paper "Analysis Terminable and Interminable" could be applied to every analysis. There Freud suggested that every analyst should go back to analysis every five years, while in the interim periods self-analysis would be of great value. In view of the ways in which analysis has changed since then, the time period can certainly be altered, but the spirit of Freud's paper is one with which we can still be in essential agreement.

Societal Therapy

Having sketched, in a regrettably brief fashion, the main features of the psychotherapeutic ideal, it is now time to examine the relationship of this schema to the contemporary social structure. The consistent application of this ideal to alter society is what I call societal therapy.

In the early days of psychotherapy the emphasis was mainly on the id. Much vital information was uncovered. But it was realized later that id material can be fully understood only in relationship to the ego.

Since the advent of ego psychology in 1923, much knowledge has been accumulated about the genesis of the ego in the family structure and about the relationship of the ego to the larger order of society. In fact, it can be said that the relationship between the individual ego and society is similar to that between the id and the ego. Neither can be understood without the other.

Sociologists have long been critical of psychotherapists on the grounds that they ignore the social milieu. Conversely, psychotherapists have been critical of sociologists because they tend to leave out the individual. No full science is achievable without an integration of the two fields. Fortunately both the conceptual framework and sufficient factual information are at hand to effect such an integration.

This book is an excursus in Utopiology, if we may be permitted to speak for the science of Utopias. It seeks to determine how society can be altered to make human beings happier. Its thesis is that society can be so altered by a consistent application of psychotherapeutic principles. Unlike other utopian approaches, however, it frankly admits that to many of the questions raised we have no final answer. Without devaluing in any way the answers that have been found, it concentrates rather on the directions in which these answers can be found.

It needs no special argument to show that in terms of the ten desiderata of the good life listed above, our society turns in a very poor performance. Much serious thought must therefore be given to how psychotherapy can help to effect a change in this deplorable state of affairs.

In the *New York Times* of July 18, 1965, Professor Ivan Morris has described the postwar Japanese movement of "Soka Gakkai," which means absolute happiness. The Soka Gakkai is an evangelical movement that preaches nonviolent tactics, a neosocialist political philosophy, a free sexual attitude, and a strong sense of interpersonal solidarity. So far it is not very different from many other evangelical movements in the history of humankind.

What is most intriguing in Professor Morris's description of the Soka Gakkai is the widespread use of group therapy. There are frequent group meetings in which members unburden their problems to each other's sympathetic ears. Morris calls these "therapeutic discussions." Whether this novel feature is the result of the contemporary Western emphasis on psychotherapy he does not say. It would be most useful to get more details of how this group therapy works out.

No doubt the most novel point made above is that psychotherapy should be a lifetime process. This needs fuller elaboration.

Scientific psychotherapy was introduced into Western civilization by Freud. While some psychoanalysts eventually recognized that psychotherapy is closer to philosophy and education than to medicine, the acceptance of psychotherapy has been mainly on the basis that it is needed for "sick" people.

This point of view must undergo considerable alteration. The sickness of people resides primarily in their inability to lead a meaningful life; the symptoms are a consequence. It is therefore necessary to assert in a forthright manner that psychotherapy seeks to teach people to live happily. Its antecedents, its philosophy, and its methods all differ radically from the orthodox medical treatment of illness.

The effectiveness of psychotherapy is a most difficult question. Three assertions can be made. First of all it is an extraordinarily powerful tool, undoubtedly the most powerful ever devised to change the human mind. Second, in spite of its power, its results are all too frequently disappointing. And third, most psychotherapists from Freud on have been convinced that prevention is far easier than cure.

Psychotherapy is an education in self-understanding. At the present time nobody completes this education once and for all. Whether that will be possible when children are brought up in a more sensible manner remains to be seen.

Personality is formed in interaction with other people. It can only be changed to any significant extent by new interactions with new people. Self-analysis, except as part of a broader psychotherapeutic process, is extremely limited; without formal psychotherapy, that is, systematic communication with a trained person, it is almost always useless.

Society must therefore make provisions for the training of a large number of psychotherapists. If there were a hundred times as many therapists as there are now, the number would still be insufficient.

Yet it is remarkable that there is no standardized training for psychotherapy, that in fact candidates must go through a large amount of material, whether in psychiatry, psychology, or social work, which is irrelevant or positively harmful to the ultimate goal of doing psychotherapy. A prime requirement must therefore be the clarification of what makes a psychotherapist, to set up programs that provide the necessary training.

There is enough broad agreement by now as to how the therapist should be prepared for his task. This can easily be put together into a formal program leading to a recognized doctor's degree. The Kubie plan is one way; many similar ones have been suggested.

It has been argued, and rightly so, that our resources are inadequate to produce the number of psychotherapists needed. While this is certainly true for the foreseeable future, it should not be looked upon as an argument against therapy, as has been done in some quarters, but rather as a challenge to make the best use of the available resources.

Here there are two possibilities. First, group therapy can be developed on a broader scale to reach larger numbers of people, even though it is doubtful whether the group experience is as deep as the individual experience; and second, nonprofessional leaders can be trained to handle social groups of various kinds.

Something of this sort seems to be going on in the Soka Gakkai movement. It can be done here on a more rational basis. The prime needs are to produce more meaningful experience within the individual and to get away from stultifying and boring experiences in the group. For both of these purposes the psychotherapist is best fitted to serve as the main agent by which our society can effect major changes in its inner life.

The desirability of replacing feelings of hate by feelings of love is recognized by all therapists. As a beginning, then, a Society of Love could be created. This society would make use of individual psychotherapists, group therapists, and lay group leaders to engage in regular discussions of the personal lives of the members. Theoretically only such regular discussions extended over long periods of time can have a permanent effect.

In other words, psychotherapy should become part of an organized movement to reorganize the social structure. Psychotherapeutic social reform can be contrasted with the various other approaches that have been offered.

First of all, every society tells its members, explicitly or implicitly, that if they observe the ethos of the community they will be happy. Any unhappiness, the general assumption holds, must come from extrasocial sources — magic, sorcery, agitators, brain pathology, and the like. The trouble with this assumption is that it is simply untrue. For the most part unhappiness that does not conflict with social custom very sharply has simply been ignored.

Modern psychosocial research has solidly established the fact that each society creates certain kinds of unhappiness that it considers perfectly normal. We can speak in every case of an adjustment neurosis and of a maladjustment neurosis. Only the latter has been given much consideration historically; for an understanding of the former we must turn to the insights of psychotherapy. What we are talking about here is the adjustment neurosis of our own society.

Second, social reformers have generally been interested in institutions rather than people. Get rid of private property, the Marxists argued, and you will have done away with hostility. History has not borne them out. Unionize the workers, give them good living conditions, the liberal labor movement held, and they will be happy. The facts are otherwise.

This should not be construed as any argument against social reform. Quite the contrary. The institutions of society should be altered in many ways, but it is important to realize what will be accomplished by such institutional change and what will not. The inner discontent of human beings is not materially affected by such outer changes; it can only be attacked internally.

Third, religious thinkers have generally urged people to forget the world and find the kingdom of heaven within: "Give unto Caesar that which is Caesar's, and give unto God that which is God's" was the solution in the early days of Christianity. There are two difficulties with this approach. First, it is impossible. Religious freedom can exist only within a certain social order, and religion cannot forget the social order. The Romans tolerated Christianity, but the Christians themselves, when they became the Caesars, did not tolerate any form other than their own, often narrowly defined. And second, the inner happiness that religion offers is either illusory or not the kind that appeals to sophisticated people of today (or of other days, for that matter). It is too opposed to indestructible human needs, such as sexuality or the need for communication. It rests upon guilt imposed by authority, rather than self-actualization.

If there is a real external problem, the patient in psychotherapy must learn how to handle it. On a larger scale, if there are oppressive social conditions, people must feel strong enough to change them, sometimes, if necessary, by force. Not turning the other cheek, but the normal use of aggression is required.

But again, following the analogy of individual psychotherapy, social change alone does not bring happiness; it merely paves the way for it. It must be followed up by inner change if happiness is the goal.

As an example, take the case of nationalism. Freedom from external oppression has always been a cry that could rally people to the flag. Yet once freedom is achieved, as it has been over and over again, the same problems recur.

On the other hand, psychotherapy differs from religion in that its philosophy of living is closer to essential human nature. A further difference lies in the recognition of the human need for communication and the provision of adequate means for satisfying this need (group therapy, group discussions under trained leaders).

Paradoxically, psychotherapeutic social reform thus steers a middle road between traditional external change of the social institutions and traditional religious inner transformation. Based on a scientific understanding of human nature, it seeks to build a better world by a persistent gradual change of the present one. Its major contribution lies in the recognition that there are many inner conflicts that can be changed only psychotherapeutically.

The other parts of the psychotherapeutic philosophy have already been discussed at sufficient length — pleasure, sex, feelings, promotion of love, restriction of hatred, family role, identity, work, and creativity. None of these is novel in human history; what is novel is their unification into a cohesive way of living.

Other philosophies, both past and present, have overemphasized one aspect of living at the cost of others. This pure hedonism often leads to excesses that are harmful; for example, it has frequently led to violence. The advocacy of feeling by the Romantics was all too frequently coupled with intense suffering, since that is a feeling tool. On the other hand, the bourgeois image of the family has created people who look like characters in Grant Wood's pictures — lifeless, without zest, spontaneity, or feeling.

What the psychotherapeutic philosophy stresses is balance. To some extent a person must participate in each aspect of the ideal to have a happy life. No doubt the different ingredients will vary for different individuals, but it is well to remember our clinical experience that extremes in any direction produce much misery.

It may be objected that a psychotherapeutic vision of human happiness is completely unrealistic at the present juncture. And yet a vision, even if it cannot be realized in the immediate future, serves a constructive purpose. It is better to light a candle than to curse the darkness. History has played a curious trick on humankind in that physics and psychology both have reached a stage of world-shaking maturity at the same time. Just when humankind discovered the means by which it could effect its own destruction, it was also in the process of perfecting techniques for securing its salvation.

The physicists have responded to the challenge by forming political action committees. Although as scientists we are always humble about the vastness of our ignorance, we should also be cognizant of the magnitude of our achievements. Psychology, in spite of all its limitations, has come far enough along to offer a positive program for happiness. It is time for psychology to organize for political and social action. The psychotherapeutic philosophy described here could serve as a basis for such action.

It is not fashionable for an intellectual to talk in positive terms of America. Yet it is well to remember that it is in this climate and this alone — the United States and Western Europe — that psychotherapy has been able to flourish. Psychotherapy is a positive plan for happiness, an outgrowth of the humanistic philosophy that for centuries has represented the finest ethical ideals of Western civilization. In the cold war, we have ignored this important psychological weapon, exporting as a rule the worst that America has to offer rather than the best.

Select Bibliography

Abbreviations

CP	*Collected Papers*
IJP	*International Journal of Psychoanalysis*
JAPA	*Journal of the American Psychoanalytic Association*
PQ	*Psychoanalytic Quarterly*
PSC	*Psychoanalytic Study of the Child*
SE	*Standard Edition of Freud's Works*

Ahmed, F. I., and S. S. Plog, eds. 1976. *State Mental Hospitals: What Happens When They Close.* New York: Plenum.

American Psychiatric Association. 1980. *Diagnostic and Statistical Manual, III.* Washington, D.C.

Anzieu, D. 1975. *L'auto-analyse de Freud et la decouverte de psychanalyse,* second edition. Paris: Presses Universitaires de France.

Arieti, S. 1976. *Creativity: The Magic Synthesis.* New York: Basic Books.

Ayer, M. 1954. *Philosophical Essays* London: Macmillan.

Axelrad, S., and S. Brody. 1978. *Mothers, Fathers, and Children.* New York: International Universities Press.

Bakan, D. 1967. *On Method.* San Francisco: Jossey-Bass.

Barkey, S. 1972. *The Future of Work and Leisure.* Paladin: London.

Baron, F. 1972. *Artists in the Making.* New York: Seminar Press.

Basaglia, F. 1977. *Psychiatry Inside Out.* New York: Basic Books.

Bellak, L., M. Hurvich, and H. Gediman. 1973. *Ego Functions in Schizophrenics, Neurotics and Normals.* New York: Wiley.

————, and L. Goldsmith, eds. *The Broad Scope of Ego Function Assessment.* New York: Wiley.

Bergmann, G. 1943. "Psychoanalysis and Experimental Psychology, A Review from the Standpoint of Empiricism," *Mind* 512, 122–40.

Bertaux, D., ed. 1981. *Biography and Society: The Life History Approach in the Social Sciences.* Beverly Hills, Calif.: Sage.

Bieber, I. et al. 1961. *Homosexuality.* New York: Basic Books.

Blos, P. 1979. *The Adolescent Passage.* New York: International Universities Press.

Bleuler, M. 1978. *The Schizophrenic Disorders*. New Haven: Yale University Press.

Blumstein, P., and P. Schwartz. *American Couples*. New York: William Morrow and Co.

Boring, E. 1913. *A History of Experimental Psychology*. New York: Harper's.

Brazelton, T. B. 1973. *Neonatal Behavioral Assessment Scale*. London: Heinemann.

Brenner, C. *The Mind in Conflict*. New York: International Universities Press.

Cannon, W. B. 1957. "Voodoo Death." *Psychosomatic Medicine* 19, 311–15.

Capellanus, A. 1941 (original 1180). *The Art of Courtly Love*. New York: Columbia University Press.

Chiland, C., ed. 1977. *Long-Term Treatment of Psychotic States*. New York: Human Sciences Press.

Coleman, L. 1984. *The Reign of Error*. Boston: Beacon Press.

Cuber, J., and P. Harroff. 1965. *The Significant Americans*. New York: Appleton.

De Mause, L. 1974. *The History of Childhood*. New York: Psychohistory Press.

Douvan, F., A. A. Kulka, and J. Veroff. 1981. *The Inner American*. New York: Basic Books.

———. 1981. *Mental Health in America*. New York: Basic Books.

Einstein, A., and L. Infeld. 1938. *The Evolution of Physics*. New York: Simon and Schuster, 1942.

Ellenberger, H. 1970. *The Discovery of the Unconscious*. New York: Basic Books.

Engel, G. L. 1977 "The Need for a New Biomedical Model: A Challenge for Biomedical Science." *Science* 196, no. 426, 129–36.

Esman, A. 1977. "Changing Values: Their Implications for Adolescent Development and Psychoanalytic Ideas." In S. Feinstein et al., eds. *Adolescent Psychiatry,* vol. 5, 18–24.

Evans, N. J. 1949. "The Passing of the Gentlemen." *Psychoanalytic Quarterly* 17, 19–43.

Faris, F. S. L., and H. W. Dunham. 1939. *Mental Disorders in Urban Areas*. Chicago: University of Chicago Press.

Fenichel, O. 1945. *The Psychoanalytic Theory of Neurosis*. New York: Norton.

Fine, R. 1975. *Psychoanalytic Psychology*. New York: Jason Aronson.

———. 1979. *The Intimate Hour*. New York: Avery.

———. 1981. *The Psychoanalytic Vision*. New York: Norton.

———. 1982. *The Healing of the Mind*. New York: Macmillan.

———. 1983. *The Logic of Psychology*. Latham, Md.: University Press of America.

———. *The Logic of Psychology and Other Essays*. Washington, D.C.: University Press of America.

———. 1984. "The Protestant Ethic and the Analytic Ideal." *Journal of Professional Psychology*.

———. 1985. *The Meaning of Love in Human Experience.* New York: Wiley.

———. 1986. *The Forgotten Man.* New York: Haworth Press.

———. 1986. *Narcissism, the Self and Society.* New York: Columbia University Press.

———. 1989. *Troubled Men.* San Francisco: Jossey-Bass.

———. 1990 *The History of Psychoanalysis.* New Expanded Edition. New York: Continuum.

Firestein, S. 1978. *Termination in Psychoanalysis.* New York: International Universities Press.

Fisher, S., and R. D. Greenberg. 1977. *The Scientific Credibility of Freud's Theories and Therapy.* New York: Basic Books.

———. 1989. *The Limits of Biological Treatments for Psychological Distress.* Hillsdale, N.J.: Erlbaum.

Fortes, M. 1977. "Custom and Conscience in Anthropological Perspective." *International Review of Psychoanalysis* 4, 127–54.

Freud, A. *Collected Works.* 8 vols. New York: International Universities Press.

Freud, S. 1953–74. *The Standard Edition of the Complete Psychological Works of Sigmund Freud.* Edited by J. Strachey. London: Hogarth Press and Institute for Psychoanalysis. 24 vols. All references, unless otherwise noted are to the *Standard Edition*, abbreviated SE.

Friedan, B. 1963. *The Feminine Mystique.* New York: Norton.

Friedemann, G. 1960. "Leisure and Technological Civilization. *International Social Science Journal* 12, 509–21.

Fromm, E. 1955. *The Sane Society.* New York: Rinehart.

Fromm-Reichmann, F. 1948. "Notes on the Development of the Treatment of Schizophrenics by Psychoanalytic Therapy." *Psychiatry* 11, 263–73.

Frosch, J. 1983. *The Psychotic Process.* New York: International Universities Press.

Galenson, E., and H. Roiphe. 1981. *The Infantile Origins of Sexual Identity.* New York: International Universities Press.

Gardell, B., and G. Johansson, eds. 1981. *Working Life.* New York: Wiley.

Gay, P. 1986. *The Tender Passion.* New York: Oxford University Press.

Gebhard, P. S. 1963. *Sex Offenders.* New York: Harper and Row.

Gedo, J. 1981. *Beyond Interpretation.* Chicago: University of Chicago Press.

Gelles, R. J. 1972. *The Violent Home.* Beverly Hills, Calif.: Sage.

———, and M. Straus. 1980. *Behind Closed Doors.* New York: Anchor/Doubleday.

Guilford, J. P. 1967. *The Nature of Human Intelligence.* New York: McGraw-Hill.

Hamburg, D., et al. 1967. "Report of Ad Hoc Committee on Central Fact-gathering Data of the American Psychoanalytic Association." *JAPA* 14, 841–61.

Harlow, H. 1974. *Learning to Love.* New York: Jason Aronson.

Harris, M. 1968. *The Rise of Anthropological Theory*. New York: Thomas Y. Crowell.

Hartmann, H. 1939. *Ego Psychology and the Problem of Adaptation*. New York: International Universities Press.

———, E. Kris, and R. M. Loewenstein. 1946. "Comments on the Formation of Psychic Structure." *PSC* 2, 11–38.

Hazo, H. 1957. *The Idea of Love*. New York: Praeger.

Hendin, H., W. Haylin, and A. C. Carr. 1965. *Psychoanalysis and Social Science Research*. New York: Doubleday.

Henry, J., and B. Henry. 1944. *Doll Play of the Pilaga Indian Children*. New York: American Othopsychiatric Association.

Henry, W., et al. 1971. *The Fifth Profession*. San Francisco: Jossey-Bass.

Herzberg, F. 1959. *The Motivation to Work*. New York: Wiley.

———. 1959. *Work and the Nature of Man*. New York: Wiley.

———. 1974. "Work Satisfaction and Motivation-Hygiene Theory," *Book Forum* 1, 213–21.

———. 1976. *Work and the Nature of Man*. New York: World.

Hewlett, S. 1986. *A Lesser Life: The Myth of Women's Liberation*. New York: William Morrow and Co.

Hitschmann, E. 1937. "A Ten-Year Report of the Vienna Psychoanalytical Clinic." *IJP* 13, 245–55.

Hoyt, E. P. 1983. *The Kamikazs*. New York: Arbor House.

Hughes, R., and R. Brewein. 1979. *The Tranquilizing of America*. New York: Harcourt Brace Jovanovich.

———. 1980. *The Tranquilizing of America*. New York: Warner Books.

Hunt, M. 1959. *The Natural History of Love*. New York: Knopf.

Huxley, A. 1932. *Brave New World*. Garden City, N.Y.: Doubleday, Doran.

Jacobson, E. 1954. "Contribution to the Mechanism of Psychotic Identification." *JAPA* 2, 239–62.

Jones, E. 1929. "Psychoanalysis and Psychiatry." *CP*, 365–78.

———. 1943. "Obituary of Max Eitingon." *IJP* 24, 190–92.

———. 1957. *The Life and Work of Sigmund Freud*. New York: Basic Books.

Kernberg, O. 1984. *Severe Personality Disorders*. New Haven: Yale University Press.

———. 1986. "The Institutionalization of Psychoanalytic Education." *JAPA* 14, 243–72.

———. 1986. "Institutional Problems of Psychoanalytic Education." *JAPA* 24, 801–34.

———. 1969. "A Contribution to the Ego-Psychological Critique of the Kleinian School." *IJP* 50, 317–33.

Kiell, N. S. 1988. *Varieties of Sexual Experience*. New York: Basic Books.

Kievo, A. 1964. *Magic, Faith and Healing*. New York: Free Press.

Kinsey, A. C. et al. 1948. *Sexual Behavior in the Human Male*. Philadelphia: W. B. Saunders Co.

———. 1953. *Sexual Behavior in the Human Female.* Philadelphia: W. B. Saunders Co.

Klein, M. 1960. "Some Theoretical Conclusions Regarding the Emotional Life of the Infant." *Psyche* 14, 284–316.

———, et al. 1960. *Contributions to Psychoanalysis.* London: Hogarth Press.

Knight, R. P. 1953. "The Present Status of Organized Psychoanalysis in the U.S." *JAPA* 1, 197–221.

Kohut, H. 1979. "The Two Analyses of Mr. Z." *IJP* 60, 3–28.

Kolb, L. C., and H. K. H. Brodie. 1982. *Modern Clinical Psychiatry.* Philadelphia: W. D. Saunders.

Kris, E., J. Herma, and J. Shor. 1943. "Freud's Theory of the Dream in American Textbooks." *Journal of Abnormal and Social Psychology* 38, 319–34.

Kubie, S. S. 1954. "The Pros and Cons of a New Profession." A doctorate in medical psychology. *Texas Reports on Biology and Medicine*, vol. 12, 125–70.

Lambert, M. J., E. R. Christensen, and S. S. De Julio, eds. 1963. *The Assessment of Psychotherapy Outcome.* New York: Wiley.

La Piere, R. T. 1949. *The Freudian Ethic.* Des Moines: Duell Sloan and Pierce.

Lapidus, G. 1978. *Women in Soviet Society*, Berkeley: University of California Press.

Laplanche, J., and Pontalis, J.-B. 1973. *The Language of Psychoanalysis.* New York: Norton.

Lea, H. C. 1866. *A History of Sacerdotal Celibacy.* N.p.

Leighton, A. H. 1963. *The Character of Danger.* New York: Basic Books.

Levi, A. 1978. Article on philosophy, in *Encyclopaedia Britannica*, fourteenth edition, 201–25.

Loveland, R. 1947. "Review of W. Sachs: *Black Anger.*" *PQ* 16, 574–77.

Lowie, R. S. 1920. *Primitive Society.* New York: Boni and Liveright.

Lynch, J. J. 1985. *The Language of the Heart.* New York: Basic Books.

McClelland, D. C., and J. W. Atkinson. 1957. *The Achievement Motive.* New York: Appleton-Century-Crofts.

McGrath, J. 1986. *Freud's Discovery of Psychoanalysis: The Politics of Hysteria.* Ithaca: Cornell University Press.

Maetze, G. 1970. *Psychoanalyse in Berlin: Meisenheim am Glan.* Verlag Anton Hain.

Malcolm, J. 1981. *Psychoanalysis: The Impossible Profession.* New York: Knopf.

Marmor, J. 1975. *Psychiatrists and Their Patients.* Washington, D.C.: American Psychiatric Association.

Mayr, E. 1982. *The Growth of Biological Thought.* Cambridge, Mass.: Harvard University Press.

Mehta, B. 1978. "The Mortality of Patients with Tardive Dyskinesia." *American Journal of Psychiatry*, vol. 135, 371–72.

—— et al. 1978. *American Journal of Psychiatry.*

Menninger, K. 1959. *A Psychiatrist's World.* New York: Viking.

——. 1963. *The Vital Balance.* New York: Viking.

Mercano, S., ed. 1986. "Dominant Trends in Latin American Thought." In R. Fine, ed. 1987. *Psychoanalysis around the World,* vol. 3, no. 1. New York: Haworth Press.

Michelet, J. 1939. *Satanism and Witchcraft.* New York: Citadel Press.

Montagu, A. 1963. *Anthropology and Human Nature.* New York: McGraw-Hill.

——. 1978. *Learning Non-aggression.* New York: Oxford University Press.

Montville, J. V. 1989. "Psychoanalytic Enlightenment and the Greening of Diplomacy." *JAPA* 37, 297–318.

Murdoch, G. 1949. *Social Structure.* New York: Free Press.

Murphy, G. 1972. *Historical Introduction to Modern Psychology.* New York: Harcourt.

Nagel, E. 1961. *The Structure of Science.* New York: Harcourt, Brace and World.

New York Times, August 1989: articles on feminism.

Oberndorf, C. 1953. *A History of Psychoanalysis in America.* New York: Grune and Stratton.

Obholzer, K. 1982. *The Wolf Man Sixty Years Later.* New York: Continuum Press.

Odier, C. 1948. *Anxiety and Magical Thinking.* New York: International Universities Press.

Otto, H. 1972. *Love Today: A New Exploration.* New York: Association Press.

Parin, F., F. Mergenthaler, and M. P. Parin. 1980. *Fear Thy Neighbor as Thyself.* Chicago: University of Chicago Press.

Patmore, C. 1849. *The Angel in the House.* London: Oxford University Press, 1949.

Person, E. 1989. *Romantic Love.* New York: Norton.

Pfister, O. 1944. *Christianity and Fear.* London: Allen and Unwin.

——, and S. Freud. 1926. *Letters.* New York: Basic Books.

Pleck, E. 1987. *Domestic Tyranny.* New York: Oxford University Press.

Pomer, S. 1966. "Biography of M. Eitingon." In F. Alexander et al., *Psychoanalysis Pioneers,* 51–62.

Post, S. ed. 1972. *Moral Values and the Superego Concept in Psychoanalysis.* New York: International Universities Press.

Proceedings of Lawsuit GAPP vs. American Psychoanalytic Association and International Psychoanalytical Association. Summary 1988.

Putnam, J. J. 1971. *James Jackson Putnam and Psychoanalysis: Letters.* Cambridge, Mass.: Harvard University Press.

Rangell, L. 1954. "Psychoanalysis and Dynamic Psychotherapy." *JAPA* 2.

——. 1982. "The Self in Psychoanalytic Theory." *JAPA* 20, 883–91.

Rayner, E. 1987. "Psychoanalysis in Britain." In R. Fine, ed. *Psychoanalysis around the World,* pp. 45–60. New York: Haworth Press.

Rennie, T., et al. 1962. *Mental Health in the Metropolis*. New York: McGraw-Hill.

Rifkin, A. H. 1974. "A General Assessment of Psychiatry." I. S. Arieti, ed. *American Handbook of Psychiatry*, vol. I, 117–30.

Robitscher, J. 1980. *The Powers of Psychiatry*. Boston: Houghton Mifflin.

Roheim, G. 1921. "Das Selbst." *Imago* 7: 1–39, 142–79, 310–48, 453–504.

———. 1932. "Psychoanalysis of Primitive Cultural Types." *IJP* 13, 1–224.

Rohner, R. P. 1975. *They Love Me, They Love Me Not*. New Haven: HRAF Press.

———. 1981. *The Warmth Dimension*. New Haven: HRAF Press.

Russell, B. 1958. *A History of Western Philosophy*. New York: Simon and Schuster.

Sachs, H. 1930. "Die Lehranalyse (The Training Analysis)." In *Zehn Jahre Berliner Psychoanalystisches Institut*, 53–59.

Sandler, J. 1959. "The Body as Phallus: A Patient's Fear of Erection." *IJP* 40, 191–98.

———. 1983. "Reflections on Some Relations Between Psychoanalytic Concepts and Psychoanalytic Practice." *IJP* 64, 35–50.

Schwartz, P., and P. Blumstein. 1983. *American Couples*. New York: Morrow.

Searles, H. F. 1965. *Collected Papers on Schizophrenia and Related Subjects*. New York: International Universities Press.

Sears, R. R. 1943. *Survey of Objective Studies of Psychoanalytic Concepts*. New York: Social Science Research Council.

Smith, M. L., G. V. Glass, and A. B. McGaw. 1981. *Meta-analysis and Social Research*. Beverly Hills: Sage.

Solnit, A. 1989. Unpublished communication on definition of psychoanalysis.

Spitz, R. 1965. *The First Year of Life*. New York: International Universities Press.

Spruiell, V. 1989. "The Future of Psychoanalysis." *PQ* 58, 1–28.

Stolorow, R., D. Stolorow, and Socarides. 1989. "A Case of Delusional Merger." *IJP* 70, 315–25.

Sullivan, H. S. 1940. *Conceptions of Modern Psychiatry*. New York: Norton.

Szasz, T. 1961. *The Myth of Mental Illness*. New York: Harper.

Tissot, R. 1977. "Long-term Drug Therapy in Psychoses." In C. Chiland, ed. *Long-Term Treatment of Psychotic States*, 89–171.

Valenstein, E. 1973. *Brain Control*. New York: Wiley.

Veblen, T. 1899. *The Theory of the Leisure Class*. N.p.

Waelder, R. 1962. "Review of S. Hook, ed., *Psychoanalysis, Scientific Method and Philosophy*." *JAPA* 10, 617–37.

Wallerstein, R. S. 1978. "Perspective on Psychoanalytic Training around the World." *IJP* 59, 477–575.

———. 1986. *Forty-two Lives in Treatment*. New York: Guilford Press.

———, and E. M. Weinshel, 1989. "The Future of Psychoanalysis." *PQ* 58, 341–73.

Warner, R. 1985. *Recovery from Schizophrenia*. London: Routledge and Kegan Paul.

Weber, M. 1904. *The Protestant Ethic and the Spirit of Capitalism*. New York: Scribner's, 1958.

Weinshel, E. 1982. "Training Analysis." *International Review of Psychoanalysis*.

————. 1982. "Functions of the Training Analysis and Selection of the Training Analyst." *International Review of Psychoanalysis*, vol. 9, part 4, 434–44.

Wif, A. 1949, 1950. "The Psychoanalysis of Groups." *American Journal of Psychotherapy* 3, 16–50; 4, 576–68.

Wilhelm, R. ed. 1974. *Philosophers on Freud*. New York: Jason Aronson.

Winn, R. B. 1961. *Psychotherapy in the Soviet Union*. New York: Grove Press.

Winnicott, D. 1975. *Through Pediatrics to Psychoanalysis*. New York: Basic Books.

————. 1989. *Fragment of an Analysis*.

Withey, Lynne. 1981. *Dearest Friend: A Life of Abigail Adams*. London: Free Press.

Wolf Man. 1971. *The Wolf Man*. New York: Basic Books.

Wylie, R. 1974. *The Self-Concept*, second edition. Lincoln: University of Nebraska Press.

Index

329